FOUNDATION PRESS

LEGAL ETHICS STORIES

By

Deborah L. Rhode
Professor of Law
Stanford Law School

David Luban
Professor of Law
Georgetown University Law Center

FOUNDATION PRESS
New York, New York
2006

© 2006 By FOUNDATION PRESS

       395 Hudson Street

       New York, NY 10014

       Phone Toll Free 1–877–888–1330

       Fax (212) 367–6799

       fdpress.com

Printed in the United States of America

ISBN–13: 978–1–58778–935–9
ISBN–10: 1–58778–935–3

 TEXT IS PRINTED ON 10% POST CONSUMER RECYCLED PAPER

This book is dedicated to our legal ethics students—our own best teachers

*

ACKNOWLEDGMENTS

Some of the legal ethics stories contained in this book have been adapted from earlier publications.

Alex Beam, *Greed on Trial*, was originally published in The Atlantic Monthly, vol. 293, no. 5, June 2004, pp. 96, 98-102, 104-06 and 108. Reprinted with permission of the author.

Roger C. Cramton, Spaulding v. Zimmerman: *Confidentiality and its Exceptions*, is adapted from Roger C. Cramton and Lori P. Knowles, *Professional Secrecy and Its Exceptions*: Spaulding v. Zimmerman *Revisited*, Minnesota Law Review, vol. 8, November 1998, pp. 63-127. Used with permission of the Minnesota Law Review.

Michael Mello, United States v. Kaczynski: *Representing the Unabomber*, includes material adapted from Michael Mello, *The Non-Trial of the Century: Representation of the Unabomber*, Vermont Law Review, vol. 24, Winter 2000, pp. 417-535, and Mello's book The United States Versus Theodore John Kaczynski: Ethics, Power and the Invention of the Unabomber, Context Publications, 1999.

Milton C. Regan, Jr., *Bankrupt in Milwaukee*, is adapted from Regan's book Eat What You Kill: The Fall of a Wall Street Lawyer, © University of Michigan Press, 2004. Reprinted with permission.

David B. Wilkins, *Race, Ethics, and the First Amendment: Should a Black Lawyer Represent the Ku Klux Klan?*, is adapted from an article of the same name, which appeared originally in The George Washington Law Review, vol. 63, no. 6, August 1995, pp. 1030-70.

The editors wish to express their gratitude to Mary Tye, of Stanford Law School, for her assistance and efforts at every stage of editing this book.

*

LEGAL ETHICS STORIES

*

FOUNDATION PRESS

LEGAL ETHICS STORIES

*

INTRODUCTION

David Luban

From their first day in law school, students learn that law consists of something called "doctrine" (torts doctrine, contract doctrine, First Amendment doctrine) and that the way to learn doctrine is by studying judicial opinions. Judicial opinions give a brief statement of "the facts," and then analyze the law by abstracting from facts to rules and principles—the doctrine.

Legal Ethics Stories, like the other volumes of *Law Stories*, aims to remind us that ultimately, law is about human beings, not about "doctrines" or even "cases." Oliver Wendell Holmes, Jr., inspecting the bound volumes of case reports, once remarked that "[i]t is strange to think of that monotonous series as a record of human lives...."[1] *Law Stories* insists that the series is anything but "monotonous," because the human lives it contains are real and vivid. If the reports seem monotonous, it is only because judicial opinions have other purposes than telling us the stories behind the cases. The volumes of *Law Stories* aim to fill that gap, by telling those stories, with their colorful characters, their complex motivations, and their all-too-frequent ambiguity. Stories come naturally to us, because human beings are born story-tellers and story-hearers. We experience our own lives as stories unfolding through time, stories radiating out from ourselves and encompassing the people around us. We make sense of human events as complex narratives weaving together the separate stories of all their actors. Judicial recitations of "the facts," though certainly an improvement over mere manipulation of legal rules, cannot substitute for properly-told stories.

Going beneath the cases to the stories is especially important in legal ethics. Legal ethics, unlike subjects such as constitutional law, is not organized around landmark decisions. There are practical reasons why this is so. The rules of legal ethics have always been underenforced by the courts, and as a result the jurisprudence is sparse compared with other areas of law. Underenforcement arises from structural facts about law practice and professional discipline. A great deal of what goes on between lawyers and clients is shielded by the attorney-client privilege and the ethical duty of confidentiality, and never sees the light of day. Clients and adversaries often have no idea when a lawyer has misbe-

---

1. Oliver Wendell Holmes, Jr., The Occasional Speeches of Justice Oliver Wendell Holmes 57 (Mark DeWolfe Howe, ed., Harvard University Press, 1962).

haved, and, realistically, misbehavior will generally come out only if another lawyer is willing to blow the whistle. Chapter 2 of this book tells the story of one such whistle-blower, Colette Bohatch Mele, and paints a vivid picture of the daunting obstacles a conscientious lawyer can face. Even when the facts of lawyer misbehavior come to light, victims seldom have incentives to pursue grievances against attorneys, and the bar disciplinary process has lacked capacity to address the vast majority of misconduct. All too often, the volunteer lawyers who hear disciplinary cases see matters from the lawyer's point of view, and perhaps think "there but for the grace of God go I." Even when ethics cases do get adjudicated by appellate courts, these are almost always state rather than federal courts, and their rulings often have little influence on other jurisdictions. For all these reasons, the law governing lawyers derives far more from the bar's interpretations of rules than from court decisions. Fundamentally, legal ethics has more to do with moral thought that never leaves the privacy of the lawyer's office than with any form of official jurisprudence.

The stories in this book mostly do come from reported cases, but the authors and editors did not choose them because these are "landmark" cases in a doctrinal sense. Rather, in most instances we chose them because they dramatize, often in a striking way, the pressures lawyers face, the ethical decisions they confront, the institutions they work in, and the choices they make. Extraordinary though some of these cases are, they typify issues that most lawyers confront in one form or other at some time in their careers.

The Four Subjects of Legal Ethics

Legal ethics is not a single subject. In fact, the term "legal ethics" refers to at least four distinct, though overlapping, topics.

1.   As countless lawyer jokes testify, for most people legal ethics has to do with untruthfulness and greed. Unethical lawyers are those who lie to clients and courts, or cheat their clients and adversaries. Two chapters in *Legal Ethics Stories* center on conduct that is unethical in this basic sense. Stephen Gillers, in Chapter 4, tells the story of a prosecutor's office hid exculpatory evidence—repeatedly—resulting in at least one innocent man serving seven years in prison for child abuse. And Milton Regan, in Chapter 7, describes the downfall of a partner in a prestigious Wall Street law firm who went to jail for concealing a conflict of interest from a court. Dishonesty figures in other stories as well. The whistle-blowing story Leslie Griffin relates in Chapter 2 concerned Colette Bohatch's suspicion that her partner was overbilling a corporate client; and Michael Mello's tale of the Unabomber's case in Chapter 5 involves the unusual circumstance of defense lawyers who manupulated, and may have deceived, their own client to spare him the death penalty.

2.   Among the leadership of the profession, a different issue lies at the forefront of professional ethics. This is what is often described as *professionalism*—or rather, the supposed loss of professionalism and the rise of commercialism. In the professionalism debate, the basic moral issue concerns the erosion of time-honored norms and ideals by market forces and vulgarly market-oriented practitioners. In the eyes of many bar leaders, commercialism debases the profession. It goes hand-in-hand with competition—and competition drives down not only price but quality, leading to impersonal, assembly-line service. Until the mid–1980s, the ethical codes of the professions focused to a remarkable extent on limiting market competition by fixing prices and banning advertising. (Price-fixing, in the form of mandatory minimum fee schedules, ended only when the Supreme Court held that it violates antitrust law; and the ban on advertising collapsed under a First Amendment challenge.[2]) The organized bar has also been remarkably energetic in prosecuting unauthorized practitioners—ostensibly to protect vulnerable clients, but also to limit competition. In Chapter 9, David Vladeck tells the story of the Delaware bar's efforts to shut down a lay advocate on behalf of disabled children. The bar's campaign against less expensive alternatives to lawyers arguably represents the seamy side of "professionalism"—professionalism as an enemy of access to justice for people who cannot afford lawyers. But it would be unfair to think of the professionalism campaign as nothing more than masked self-interest on the part of lawyers. Professionalism advocates generally support pro bono service as part of the professional ideal. When lawyers reject pro bono cases because they don't want to antagonize wealthy clients who disapprove, many lament that market values have vanquished the core values of the professions—service, craft, and altruism.

In recent years, the bar has engaged in vigorous debates over "multi-disciplinary practice" (MDP), in which lawyers partner with other professionals such as accountants in a single firm in order to provide clients (particularly corporate clients) with "one-stop shopping" for legal and financial services. In most jurisdictions, MDP violates ethics rules that prohibit lawyers from forming partnerships with non-lawyers for the practice of law, on the theory that such partnerships undermine the lawyers' independent judgment.[3] The MDP debate has been at the forefront of arguments about professionalism, particularly as large accounting firms hire enormous numbers of salaried lawyers and begin to compete with traditional law firms. The law firms complain that the accounting firms have a different ethos, more oriented toward the bottom line and less toward the traditional ideals of the service profes-

---

2.   Goldfarb v. Virginia State Bar, 421 U.S. 773 (1975)(minimum fee schedules); Bates v. State Bar of Arizona, 433 U.S. 350 (1977)(advertising).

3.   ABA Model Rules of Professional Conduct, Rule 5.4(b).

sions. Chapter 4, describing a case of abusive tax shelters aggressively hawked by an accounting giant, lends credence to these accusations. It also tells the story of one brave lawyer, Mike Hamersely, who—like Colette Bohatch—was willing to draw an ethical line in the sand in the face of fierce pressure from his employer. Yet the bar, too, can become astonishingly fixated on the bottom line. Alex Beam, in Chapter 10, tells the remarkable story of the Massachusetts tobacco lawyers who went to court to win $1.3 billion in fees over and above the $7,700 per hour they had already been paid.

   3. In addition to problems of honesty and professionalism, legal ethics includes moral dilemmas that arise because lawyers operate under a distinctive "role morality" that on occasion requires actions that seem wrong from the standpoint of commonsense morality. Within the court-room setting, the adversary system requires lawyers to act as one-sided partisans for their clients, regardless of whether their clients are right or wrong. The classic statement of the zealous advocate's role morality comes from the nineteenth-century jurist Lord Brougham:

> An advocate, in the discharge of his duty, knows but one person in all the world, and that person is his client. To save that client by all means and expedients, and at all hazards and costs to other persons, and, amongst them, to himself, is his first and only duty; and in performing this duty he must not regard the alarm, the torments, the destruction which he may bring upon others. Separating the duty of a patriot from that of an advocate, he must go on reckless of consequences, though it should be his unhappy fate to involve his country in confusion.[4]

Brougham's rhetoric may sound overblown, but many lawyers have taken it as the ultimate expression of the ideal of zealous advocacy. What is striking about Brougham's dictum, of course, is that commonsense morality condemns rather than praises someone who pays no regard to "the alarm, the torments, the destruction which he may bring upon others." If Brougham is right, being an advocate cancels ordinary moral obligations, or perhaps even turns them upside-down.

   Some moralists object that no such role morality could possibly be legitimate. After all, merely joining the bar cannot magically abolish ordinary moral obligations to be mindful of the interests of others.[5] The British historian Macaulay sardonically described a lawyer as someone

   4. 2 The Trial of Queen Caroline 8 (J. Nightingale ed., 1821). For discussion of Brougham's famous dictum, see Deborah L. Rhode, An Adversarial Exchange on Adversarial Ethics, 41 J. Legal Ed. 29 (1991).

   5. See, e.g., Richard Wasserstrom, Lawyers as Professionals: Some Moral Issues, 5 Human Rights 1 (1975); Wasserstrom, Roles and Morality, in The Good Lawyer: Lawyers' Roles and Lawyers' Ethics 25 (David Luban ed., Rowman & Allanheld, 1983).

who would, "with a wig on his head, and a band round his neck, do for a guinea what, without those appendages, he would think it wicked and infamous to do for an empire."[6] The obvious implication is that wicked and infamous deeds remain wicked and infamous regardless of whether the doer wears the barrister's wig and band. Other critics have argued that the adversary system provides far weaker justification for the advocate's role morality than most lawyers suppose.[7] However well-taken those criticisms may be (and the matter is far from settled), no one denies that the adversary system requires partisanship from lawyers on behalf of causes and clients that may not be to their liking. If Brougham is right, then the basic ethical problem underlying law practice is not that lawyers lie and cheat, in violation of their ethical obligations. The problem is rather that lawyers fulfilling their ethical obligations may be compelled to do things on behalf of clients whose activities are morally objectionable.

The paradigm of such zealous advocacy is criminal defense of the guilty. Many people resent the criminal defender whose skill allows a guilty criminal to go free; yet few deny that criminal defendants ought to have lawyers, and so in this case the lawyer's role morality may seem to be at least a necessary evil. But the lawyer's role morality is not limited to criminal defense. It underpins duties that all lawyers recognize. Notably, the bar justifies the ethical duty of confidentiality by arguing that unless clients can trust their lawyers with all their secrets, they will not tell their lawyers the information needed to represent them, and the adversary system will fail. Similarly, conflict-of-interest regulations are supposed to preserve lawyers' independent judgment, so that they can better fulfill their partisan roles. Even lawyers who will never see a courtroom insist on the ideal of zealous advocacy, with its companion duties of confidentiality and disinterest.

Several of our stories deal with issues that arise from the lawyer's role morality and from the nature of the adversary system. Chapter 6 tells the story of *Spaulding v. Zimmerman*, one of the most poignant cases in the jurisprudence of confidentiality, which pits the lawyers' role morality against the possibility of saving someone's life. And Chapters 4 and 5 ("In the Pink Room" and "Representing the Unabomber") describe situations where advocates' desire to win cases led them to take steps that arguably crossed ethical lines—in one case, by withholding exculpatory information from the adversary, and in the other, by riding

---

6. Thomas Babington Macaulay, Macaulay's Essay on Bacon, in 6 The Works of Lord Macaulay 163 (G. Trevelyan ed., 1900).

7. See, e.g., David Luban, The Adversary System Excuse, in The Good Lawyer, supra note 5, at 83; Deborah L. Rhode, In the Interests of Justice 49–115 (Oxford University Press, 2000).

roughshod over the client's own desires in order to save him from being executed.

    4. Finally, "legal ethics" often denotes the formal ethics rules of the bar. The American Bar Association began to codify ethics rules in 1908, and produced three generations of rules, the Canons of Professional Ethics (1908), the Code of Professional Responsibility (1969), and the Rules of Professional Conduct (1983). The names themselves indicate a gradual shift in regulatory philosophy, from the hortatory and moralistic to the black-letter regulation of conduct. With the addition of the *Restatement of the Law Governing Lawyers* (2000), the legal subject of legal ethics completed a century-long process of turning a subject with moral overtones into a technical field of law. This transformation has two obvious advantages. First, it no longer assumes a consensus on ethical norms, and therefore better accommodates a legal profession far more diverse than the overwhelmingly white, male, Protestant, east-coast bar of a century ago, which often mistook its own biases for first principles of ethics.[8] Second, turning legal ethics into legislation made the subject less spooky, and easier to analyze using the traditional tools of the lawyer's trade. Today almost all states have adopted some variant of the ABA's Model Rules, and contemporary lawyers have grown used to thinking of "ethics" as a bar-review subject testable through the multiple choice questions on the MPRE (about which the conventional witticism holds that if you have to guess, always go for the second most ethical of the four choices).

    At the same time, however, the legalization of ethics carries costs. De-moralizing the subject can be, quite simply, demoralizing, as stirring statements of ideals turn into persnickety rules with exceptions crying out to be loopholed. The distinguished legal theorist Martti Koskenniemi warns that "once you define a right, you delimit it. And once you delimit it, you offer a formally valid argument for someone to deny that right."[9] What Koskenniemi fears about rights applies equally to the legalization of lawyers' ethical duties: once you define the duty through a rule, you delimit it; and once you delimit it, you offer a formally valid argument for someone to deny that he or she actually has the duty. To take a simple example: Model Rule 1.6(b)(1) permits lawyers to reveal client confidences "to prevent reasonably certain death or substantial bodily harm"—which leaves open the argument that the lawyer was not "reasonably certain" that the client would carry out his threats or that

---

    8. See Jerold S. Auerbach, Unequal Justice: Lawyers and Social Change in Modern America (Oxford University Press, 1976); Geoffrey C. Hazard, Jr., The Future of Legal Ethics, 100 Yale L.J. 1239 (1991).

    9. Martti Koskenniemi, The Pull of the Mainstream, 88 Mich. L. Rev. 1946, 1962 (1990).

the bodily harm the client was threatening to commit would not be "substantial."

None of the legal ethics stories told here takes the legalization of ethics as its explicit theme—but the underpinning of enforceable legal obligations that structure legal ethics is present in each of them. Furthermore, once legal ethics gets recognized as a branch of law, it inevitably interacts with other branches of law: with contract and partnership law in Chapter 2; with tax law in Chapter 3; with constitutional law in Chapter 4; with anti-discrimination law in Chapter 8; with bankruptcy law in Chapter 7; and with disability-rights law in Chapter 9.

These, then, are the four principal strands of legal ethics: one might call them the Ethics of Honesty, the Ethics of Professionalism, the Ethics of Role, and Ethics as Hard Law. But of course, lawyers are not simply disembodied occupants of professional roles. The legal profession is a cross-section of society. It consists of people with identities of their own, quite apart from whatever professional identity they have. In Chapter 1, David Wilkins examines a famous case that pitted an African–American lawyer's professional convictions against his racial identity, when, as an ACLU volunteer, he was asked to represent a Grand Dragon of the Ku Klux Klan. So too, the legal profession faces the same issues of gender and racial diversity, of glass ceilings and real or imagined discrimination, as the society at large. In Chapter 8, Deborah L. Rhode examines the first sex discrimination case against any law firm or professional organization, Nancy Ezold's suit against Wolf, Block, Schorr and Solis–Cohen.

The Stories

The stories are arranged as follows. We begin with the most basic fact about lawyers: that lawyers are people with consciences and identities of their own. In many respects, this idea underlies most of the stories, but it figures prominently in the first three.

As mentioned above, Chapter 1, "Race, Ethics, and the First Amendment," concerns an African–American lawyer, Anthony Griffin, who was both a civil libertarian and a champion of civil rights. Griffin volunteered for the ACLU as well as being General Counsel of the Port Arthur, Texas branch of the NAACP. As ACLU lawyer, he was asked to represent Michael Lowe, the Grand Dragon of the local Klan, who had run into legal troubles by harassing African-Americans attempting to move into an all-white housing project. The State of Texas attempted to obtain the Klan's membership lists—ironically, a tactic that southern states had employed against the NAACP during the civil rights movement, and that the Supreme Court had found unconstitutional in *NAACP v. Alabama*. So Griffin found himself in the odd position of defending an important

civil-rights-era precedent by defending a Klansman. David Wilkins explores the delicate question of racial loyalties, and raises important
issues of whether Griffin, swept up by zealous representation of his
client, went even farther than legal ethics requires. One prominent item
of faith among many lawyers is that everyone "deserves a lawyer" (a
principle that, regrettably, lawyers often forget when a client has insufficient money to retain a lawyer). Thus, the Griffin case has to do not only
with issues of identity and conscience, but also with the distribution of
legal services in American society. Here, however, the primary question
is not whether Lowe "deserved a lawyer," but whether he deserved
Griffin. Many people criticized Griffin for his decision to represent Lowe,
and—as Wilkins explains—Griffin paid a price for the courage of his
convictions.

So did Colette Bohatch. The background of her case is a Catch–22
facing lawyers in firms. Bar discipline depends on lawyers being willing
to report misconduct by other lawyers, because usually no-one other
than another lawyer is in a position to recognize it. Rule 8.3 of the ABA's
Model Rules of Professional Conduct requires that "[a] lawyer who
knows that another lawyer has committed a violation of the Rules of
Professional Conduct that raises a substantial question as to that lawyer's honesty, trustworthiness or fitness as a lawyer in other respects,
shall inform the appropriate professional authority." But law firms, like
other American businesses, operate on an employment-at-will system in
which a lawyer fired in retaliation for blowing the whistle generally has
no recourse. The law therefore fails to protect lawyers who are fulfilling
their legal obligation. Hence, it represents an act of considerable personal courage for a lawyer to report misconduct by a partner. As Leslie
Griffin relates, Colette Bohatch did so in a discreet way, reporting the
misconduct she perceived (wrongly, her firm insisted) to higher-ups in
the firm rather than "reporting out," but the firm nevertheless terminated her partnership. Her lawsuit against the firm is one of the two
leading cases on whether the law will protect a lawyer who blows the
whistle. In the other, *Wieder v. Skala*, 609 N.E.2d 752 (N.Y. 1992), the
New York Court of Appeals allowed the lawyer to sue for wrongful
discharge, finding that the permission to practice law ethically is an
implied term in the employment contract. Bohatch was not as fortunate,
as the Texas Supreme Court found that her law firm had the right to
terminate her partnership.

Richard Posner has quipped that "[s]ocial welfare might increase if
the IQs of all tax lawyers could be reduced by 10 percent."[10] Chapter 3
tells the story of a large accounting firm whose legal department made
millions by selling intricate but abusive tax shelters to wealthy custom-

---

10. Richard A. Posner, Overcoming Law 54 (Harvard University Press, 1995).

ers. Tax is an interesting subject from a moral point of view, simply because for most of recorded history people have regarded tax avoidance as an amoral cat-and-mouse game between the taxpayer and the tax collector. Yet one basic rule in American tax law is that a business loss absorbed in genuine entrepreneurial activity yields a legitimate tax break—but the same loss accrued solely to get the tax break amounts to fraud. Even in tax avoidance, right and wrong intentions matter, and the art of devising tax shelters consists in walking the delicate line between the two. As Tanina Rostain tells the story, KPMG's overwhelming ethos of "sell, sell, sell"—sell the "product" (the tax shelter) as quickly as possible—drove it over the line. It is a cautionary tale of commercialism gone wrong, but it is also a morality story about a lawyer in KPMG's tax department who refused to go along.

The next two stories focus on the two sides of criminal law. In Chapter 4, Stephen Gillers tells a wrenching story of a young teacher whose life was shattered by accusations of sexually abusing a child in his classroom. Eventually, he was vindicated, when an investigator in a lawsuit discovered that the prosecution had withheld exculpatory facts from the defense, violating its *Brady* obligations as well as the professional ethics of prosecutors. Unlike defense lawyers, prosecutors are expected "to seek justice, not merely to convict"—even in an adversary system.[11] But, faced with the mission of crime control, institutional pressure to score victories, and adversarial advocacy on the other side, some prosecutors wrongly develop a sense of entitlement to cut corners in order to win the fight. They become the equivalent of police officers engaged in "testilying"—lying in their testimony to ensure that the "guilty" do not escape on a technicality.

Good defense lawyers often feel the same need to win at all costs, because they see themselves as the lone champion standing between their client and the penitentiary. Nowhere is this pressure greater than in capital cases—at least for conscientious lawyers who take their job seriously. (Regrettably, not all death penalty lawyers do.) Consider the case of Theodore Kaczynski, the "Unabomber," the eccentric and reclusive mathematician who spent years as a terrorist, mailing home-made bombs to scientists and business executives because of his opposition to technological society. In Chapter 5, Michael Mello describes the struggle between Kaczynski and his defense lawyers, who believed that the only way to save their client's life was to put on a psychiatric defense that he found humiliating and objectionable. Mello, who represented Kaczynski on appeal, criticizes Kaczynski's defense counsel, all of them strong

---

11. The quoted language is from the ABA Model Code of Professional Responsibility, EC 7–13; the Model Rules likewise comment that "[a] prosecutor has the responsibility of a minister of justice and not simply that of an advocate." MR 3.8, cmt. 1

death-penalty opponents, for manipulating and deceiving Kaczynski to
save his life.

Ordinarily, criminal defenders and their clients share the goal of
acquittal or at least the reduction of the penalty. But sometimes clients
have goals that are not in their own self-interest (at least as their
lawyers perceive that interest), and lawyers may wish to override the
client's choices for the client's own good.[12] The Supreme Court has
approved such lawyer paternalism in *Jones v. Barnes*, 436 U.S. 745
(1983), a case in which an appellate lawyer refused to include non-
frivolous arguments that the client wanted in his brief, presumably
because they were losers that would detract from the brief as a whole.
The Model Rules give scant guidance in cases where the client's instructions seem self-destructive. Rule 1.2(a) states that "a lawyer shall abide
by a client's decisions concerning the objectives of representation and
. . . shall consult with the client as to the means by which they are to be
pursued." The client chooses the ends, the lawyer chooses the means
(consulting with the client but not necessarily obeying the client)—but
how do you tell whether Kaczynski's desire not to be portrayed as (in his
words) "a grotesque and repellent lunatic" is an end or a means?[13] Rule
1.14 instructs lawyers whose clients have diminished capacity to, "as far
as reasonably possible, maintain a normal client-lawyer relationship with
the client." The rule also permits lawyers to "take reasonably necessary
protective action"—but it provides scant guidance to flesh out either of
these vague directives. After Kaczynski accepted a plea bargain giving
him life without parole—his only alternative to the psychiatric defense—
he wrote:

> Perhaps I ought to hate my attorneys for what they have done to
> me, but I do not. Their motives were in no way malicious. They are
> essentially conventional people who are blind to some of the implica-
> tions of this case, and they acted as they did because they subscribe
> to certain professional principles that they believe left them no
> alternative. These principles may seem rigid and even ruthless to a
> non-lawyer, but there is no doubt my attorneys believe in them
> sincerely.[14]

Chapter 6 turns to the ethics of confidentiality, which along with
zealous advocacy and avoiding conflicts of interest stands as a central
pillar of the lawyer's role morality. What happens when maintaining
confidentiality will lead to severe harm to another person? *Spaulding v.*

---

12. See David Luban, Paternalism and the Legal Profession, 1981 Wisc. L. Rev. 454.

13. Quoted in U.S. v. Kaczynski, 239 F.3d 1108, 1121 (9th Cir. 2001)(Reinhardt, J.
dissenting).

14. Quoted in Michael Mello, The Non–Trial of the Century: Representations of the
Unabomber, 24 Vt. L. Rev. 417, 502 (2000).

Zimmerman is one of the most often-cited cases to raise this question. Here, the lawyers learned that their adversary had a potentially-fatal heart injury that he himself did not know about. To warn him would cost their client money, because the injury probably resulted from the automobile accident their client caused. Until recently, bar ethical rules forbade lawyers from revealing confidences under these circumstances. Both the ABA Code and the Model Rules permitted disclosure of confidences only to prevent the client from committing a crime—and standing pat without revealing Spaulding's medical condition was no crime. In August 2003, after decades of controversy over the contours of confidentiality exceptions, the ABA finally enacted a rule permitting lawyers to reveal information "to prevent reasonably certain death or substantial bodily injury." As observed above, however, the rule can be argued in either direction on the *Spaulding* facts. How probable must Spaulding's death or injury be to count as "reasonably certain"? Better than 50–50? Better than 30–70? The rule does not specify, and so a lawyer reluctant to reveal client confidences can readily argue that even today's rule does not permit disclosure. When *Spaulding v. Zimmerman* was decided, revealing the injury was not a lawful option unless the defendants' lawyers got their client to consent, which they might have attempted to do on grounds of morality or simple decency. Remarkably, Roger Cramton's interviews with the surviving participants show that defense counsel never even broached the subject with their client.

Part of the problem, as Cramton notes, arose because defense counsel, although nominally representing the driver of the automobile, were really retained by the driver's insurance carrier, and regarded themselves as insurance-company lawyers. Why ask their client for permission to reveal information when the *de facto* co-client was the insurer, and only the insurer's money was on the line? Bar rules insist that in such cases the driver is the "real" client, but the institutional structure in which insurance company defenders work undermines that doctrine.[15] This fact highlights an important fact about legal ethics: institutions and their structures matter. The first three chapters of this book placed emphasis on the lawyer's conscience; but conscience never works in a vacuum, and for every lawyer willing to buck institutional pressures there are many more whose moral judgment sways under the influence of the firm or setting where they practice.

---

15. The bar rules are Model Rule 1.8(f)(forbidding lawyers from accepting compensation by a third party unless there is no interference with their independent judgment) and 5.4(c)(forbidding a lawyer from permitting a third party who pays the lawyer's fees to "direct or regulate the lawyer's professional judgment"). There is a large literature on the conflict between bar rules and institutional realities in insurance practice. See, e.g., Charles Silver, Does Insurance Defense Counsel Represent the Company or the Insured?, 72 Tex. L. Rev. 1583 (1994); Stephen L. Pepper, Applying the Fundamentals of Lawyers' Ethics to Insurance Defense Practice, 4 Conn. Ins. L.J. 27 (1997).

Milton Regan focuses on these issues of institutional influence on moral decision-making in Chapter 7. His story (which he tells more fully in his book *Eat What You Kill: The Fall of a Wall Street Lawyer*[16]) examines closely what drove John Gellene, a respected bankruptcy partner in a prestigious Wall Street firm, to commit bankruptcy fraud by failing to disclose his own conflict of interest. Regan rejects the two most common explanations in this high-profile case: that Gellene was a bad apple, or alternatively that he was the "fall guy" for the firm. Instead, Regan explores the intersection of personal traits—such as Gellene's competitive, overachieving personality—with the structure of modern law firms, which place an enormous premium on rainmaking (client acquisition). In the "eat what you kill" system of many large law firms, partnership shares are a function of revenue-generation. That makes partners very reluctant to turn down business, and puts their financial interests on a collision course with the conflict-of-interest rules, which require lawyers to decline representations whenever their firm repre- sents an adverse party. Gellene is not the only law-firm partner who has gone to jail for fraudulently concealing a conflict of interest because he did not want to say no to a potentially lucrative client.[17] Equally importantly, decades of research in social psychology have demonstrated that people's moral judgment is affected, often unconsciously, by the actions and attitudes of colleagues and co-workers. Gellene may not have consciously realized that he was doing anything wrong.

The dynamics of unconscious wrongdoing are especially prevalent in contexts of race and gender discrimination. In Chapter 9, Deborah L. Rhode tells the story of *Ezold v. Wolf, Block, Schorr, and Solis Cohen*, the first-ever gender discrimination case against a law firm. Nancy Ezold was passed over for partner at Wolf, Block, even though (some evidence suggested) less qualified men had made partner. Her sex-discrimination lawsuit against the firm was particularly painful to the firm because Wolf, Block is a firm that originally came into existence because of discrimination against Jewish lawyers; the firm's partners regard it as a beacon against discrimination, and argued that Ezold was passed over based on the merits. As Rhode's interviews reveal, both sides of the suit remain convinced that they were right—and the litigation did not settle the matter, because Ezold won at the district court level but lost on appeal as the Third Circuit Court of Appeals re-assessed the evidence. Here, as much as anywhere, it seems impossible to transcend the competing perspectives and stories of the participants. There is simply no Archimedean point from which to settle the matter conclusively.

---

16. University of Michigan Press, 2004.

17. For another well-known example, see United States v. Bronston, 658 F.2d 920 (2nd Cir. 1981).

Yet national data indicate that substantial gender disparities persist in law firm partnerships. In the legal profession as a whole, men outnumber women approximately three to one; but among partners in law firms, men outnumber women more than six to one.[18] In years past, this disparity was often explained by pointing to the fact that substantial numbers of women entered the legal profession recently, and are therefore a younger cohort. According to this theory, women are underrepresented at the partnership level because of age, not gender. But this explanation no longer holds water, if it ever did. Today, significant numbers of women have been in the legal profession for decades, and law partners are not an especially elderly group. Undoubtedly, many women leave the partnership track to have families rather than because of discrimination. But the Ezold case, with its starkly different perspectives on the same work history, highlights the intensely subjective nature of performance assessment in law firms—and where there is subjectivity, the possibility of conscious or unconscious bias is never far away.

As many of these stories indicate, the practice of law is, among other things (some would say above all) a business. By and large, legal services are delivered through the market system, where the rule is pay to play. Criminal defense, which guarantees legal representation to all defendants regardless of finances, represents one large exception, although even there, the best lawyers are ferociously expensive, and reasonable doubt may carry an unreasonable price-tag. But in the civil arena, money rules. Although law is a $100 billion per year industry, less than $1 billion is dedicated to delivering legal services to low-income Americans, and experts estimate that at least 95% of the legal needs of America's 45 million low-income residents remain unmet.[19] Middle-class Americans, too, are priced out of many legal services.

David Vladeck begins Chapter 9 with a brief discussion of the problem of access to justice. One possible response to the high cost of legal services lies in opening the market to non-lawyer providers, who might deliver some legal services at lower cost. However, unauthorized practice of law (UPL) statutes forbid non-lawyers from offering legal services, and bar ethics rules forbid lawyers from assisting UPL.[20] Vladeck, at the time a litigator for Public Citizen Litigation Group, became involved in the case of Marilyn Arons, a non-lawyer who has spent more than thirty years helping parents obtain educational services for their disabled children, and who was prosecuted for UPL by the State

---

18. See generally Deborah L. Rhode & David Luban, Legal Ethics 80 (Foundation Press, 4th ed. 2004).

19. For a comprehensive recent study of the problem, see Deborah L. Rhode, Access to Justice (Oxford University Press 2004).

20. Model Rule 5.5.

of Delaware. Vladeck describes the complex litigation of *In re Arons* step-by-step, not only exploring the underlying issues of access to justice, but also providing a window into the way that public interest lawyers make their strategic choices and plan their cases. Here, the state's anti-UPL laws were in tension with the Individuals with Disabilities Education Act (IDEA), a federal statute that permits parents at school board hearings to be advised "by individuals with special knowledge and training with respect to children with disabilities." *In re Arons* thus raised delicate questions of whether the IDEA pre-empts inconsistent state laws, and whether in fact the anti-UPL statutes are indeed inconsistent with the IDEA.

One time-honored device to provide counsel for otherwise-unrepresented individuals is the contingency fee, where the lawyer gets nothing if the case loses, but takes an agreed-on percentage of the award if the case prevails. Typically, the contingency fee will be much higher than a corresponding hourly fee—a practice that lawyers justify by pointing out that the surplus helps subsidize the cases that lose. In effect, the surplus counts as a kind of "insurance premium," and the contingency-fee system pools and spreads the risk of all the lawyer's cases, just like an insurance policy.[21] Sometimes, however, the contingency arrangement can result in enormous fees going to lawyers for relatively little work, and often for very little risk. In such cases, the contingency fee system appears to provide windfall profits for lawyers.[22]

In Chapter 10, journalist Alex Beam tells the story of one such case. It is, if not the most egregious, then certainly among the most startling. The case involves private lawyers who represented the State of Massachusetts in litigation against the tobacco industry. When the case settled, the lawyers received what most people would consider an enormous paycheck: $775 million in legal fees out of an $8.3 billion settlement. The lead law firm got $178 million on $10 million invested in time and expenses.

However, $775 million represented only 9.3% of the total tobacco settlement, and the law firms' agreement with the state promised them 25%. For that reason, the tobacco lawyers went back to court to ask for

---

21. For an analysis of the contingency fee as "litigation insurance," see David Luban, Speculating on Justice: The Ethics and Jurisprudence of Contingency Fees, in Legal Ethics and Legal Practice: Contemporary Issues 109–112 (Stephen Parker & Charles Sampford eds., Oxford University Press, 1995).

22. The leading critic of contingency fees on such grounds is Lester Brickman. See, e.g., Brickman, Effective Hourly Rates of Contingency-fee Lawyers: Competing Data and Non-competitive Fees, 81 Wash. U. L. Q. 653 (2003); Brickman, Contingency Fee Abuses, Ethical Mandates, and the Disciplinary System: The Case Against Case-by-Case Enforcement, 53 Wash & Lee L. Rev. 1339 (1996); Brickman, Contingent Fees Without Contingencies: Hamlet Without the Prince of Denmark?, 37 UCLA L. Rev. 29 (1989).

another $1.3 billion. Bar ethical standards require that lawyers' fees be "reasonable." But it is anyone's guess as to what counts as a reasonable fee when the absolute magnitude of the numbers staggers the imagination. In the end, the jury awarded the lawyers an additional 1.3%—close to $100 million, but far less than they had asked. The result, as Beam notes, permitted both sides to claim victory.

In all these stories, we see a three-sided interaction between individual conscience, institutional setting, and legal rules. Each of these is important; none can be understood apart from the other two. We hope that these stories help illuminate the issues lawyers face and the choices they make—for better or for worse.

*

1

Race, Ethics, and the First Amendment: Should a Black Lawyer Represent the Ku Klux Klan?

David B. Wilkins[1]

Introduction

The headline in *The New York Times* read: "A Klansman's Black Lawyer, and a Principle."[2] The black lawyer in question is Anthony Griffin, a cooperating attorney in the Texas Chapter of the American Civil Liberties Union ("ACLU") and, until the events described in the *Times* article, the General Counsel for the Port Arthur Branch of the National Association for the Advancement of Colored People ("NAACP"). In his former capacity, Griffin agreed to represent Michael Lowe, the grand dragon of the Texas Knights of the Ku Klux Klan ("KKK" or "Klan"), against efforts by the Texas Commission on Human Rights ("Commission") to compel Lowe to turn over the Klan's membership list. This action eventually cost Griffin his position with the NAACP.[3]

The *Times* headline succinctly sums up the issues presented in this controversial case. As the first clause suggests, Griffin's decision to represent the Klan raises important questions about the relationship between personal identity and professional role. Why would a lawyer (particularly one with such a demonstrated commitment to civil rights)

---

1. Kirkland & Ellis Professor of Law and Director of the Program on the Legal Profession and the Center on Lawyers and the Professional Services Industry, Harvard Law School. This essay is adapted from an article of the same name appearing in 63 George Washington Law Review 1030 (1995). In addition to deleting many footnotes and making some minor editorial and stylistic changes, the postscript has been enlarged to discuss events that occurred after the article's initial publication.

2. Sam H. Verhovek, A Klansman's Black Lawyer, and a Principle, N.Y. Times, Sept. 10, 1993, at B9.

3. Nat Hentoff, A Free–Speech Lawyer Fired by the NAACP, Wash. Post, June 25, 1994, at A21.

agree to represent an organization that has brutalized and intimidated African–Americans for more than a century? The underlying facts of this case make this concern particularly salient.

The Klan had been engaged in a systematic campaign to terrorize the handful of blacks who were moved into an all-white housing project in all-white Vidor, Texas.[4] This attempt to desegregate Vidor was in turn based on a federal court's explicit finding of blatant and widespread discrimination by state and federal officials responsible for the distribution of public housing in Texas.[5] The Texas Commission on Human Rights argued that it needed the Klan's membership list to prosecute those Klansmen who sought to shield their illegal activities by wearing hooded sheets and by enforcing a code of silence through threats and intimidation.[6] By opposing the state's request, isn't Griffin helping to perpetuate the very racist practices that, in his capacity as General Counsel to the NAACP, he fought so long to eradicate?

As the *Times* headline's second clause implies, the solution proposed by Griffin and his supporters for this seeming paradox is a legal principle: the First Amendment. The conventional wisdom is that the Constitution's guarantee of free expression, and the corollary right to associate freely with like-minded individuals, entitles the Klan to keep its membership list confidential. It is this constitutional principle, the argument goes, and not the Klan's atrocities, that Griffin is defending. According to this line of thinking, the true irony is the NAACP's failure to appreciate the importance of these First Amendment concerns—

---

4. For a thorough account of the Klan's terror tactics, see Bruce Tomaso, Defending His Defense: Black NAACP Attorney Draws Fire for Representing Klan Leader, Dallas Morning News, Aug. 31, 1993, at 1A (reporting that hooded men knocked on the doors of black residents telling them to "get your nigger babies out of Vidor" and walked through the halls threatening to burn down the housing project). See also Only the Killers Were Colorblind, Sacramento Bee, Sept. 5, 1993, at A31 (quoting one of the blacks who attempted to integrate the Vidor project as claiming that, "I've had people who drive by and tell me they're going home to get a rope and come back and hang me"); Klansmen Sued for Harassment, Boston Globe, Oct. 22, 1994, at 10 (quoting the Texas Attorney General's statement that "[t]he Klan went as far as offering to pay white children money to beat up black children who moved into the housing project" in Vidor).

5. *See* Young v. Pierce, 628 F. Supp. 1037, 1057 (E.D. Tex. 1985) .

6. See Movant's Motion to Compel Compliance with Subpoena Duces Tecum, Written Interrogatories, Requests for Production, and Requests for Admissions, and Motion for limited Protective Order and Brief in Support Thereof, at 9–10, Hale v. Texas KKK, No. 93–07414 (Tex. D. Ct. Oct. 15, 1993) (order compelling the KKK to produce its membership list) ("Without the identities of those individuals known to or by Lowe to have been involved in KKK activities in or about Vidor or Orange County, Texas during the time period when acts of intimidation and coercion were being perpetrated against citizens and public officials because of their efforts to integrate publicly funded housing, the TCHR will not be able to identify witnesses or potential parties to the acts of intimidation and threats of violence."), rev'd, Ex parte Lowe, 887 S. W. 2d 1 (Tex. 1994).

particularly in light of the Supreme Court's 1958 decision in *NAACP v. Alabama,* which upheld the NAACP's right to keep its membership list private on First Amendment grounds.[7]

These competing characterizations of Griffin as either an apologist for the Klan or the defender of First Amendment freedoms—are part of a long standing debate over how the public should regard a lawyer who represents a client whose views the lawyer opposes (or ought to oppose). Advocates of the first view, which I will refer to as the "effects thesis," emphasize the lawyer's connection to the wrongs allegedly committed by his client. In the 1950s, for instance, lawyers for the Communist Party were accused of being complicit in their client's stated desire to overthrow the United States government.[8] Similarly, in the 1970s, Jewish lawyers in the ACLU were condemned by members of the Jewish community for defending the Nazis' right to march in Skokie, Illinois.[9] In the 1990s defense lawyers for accused Nazi John Demjanjuk and the perpetrators of the World Trade Center bombing have been criticized for lending their efforts to the causes of these notorious individuals.[10] The charge of complicity is particularly stinging in cases such as Griffin's and the Skokie incident, where it is joined with allegations of disloyalty. It is bad enough, the argument goes, that anyone is prepared to represent these vile interests; but it is outright betrayal for a black lawyer to defend the Klan or for a Jewish lawyer to defend Nazis.

The other side of the debate, which I will call the "rights thesis," highlights the importance of preserving the underlying constitutional principles at stake in these cases. Unless lawyers are prepared to defend the rights of communists, Nazis, and the Klan, no one's right to free expression and association will be safe. Lawyers who defend this important principle are not complicit in their clients' wrongs for the same reason that criminal defense lawyers are not culpable when they successfully defend the guilty: lawyers are morally accountable for process, not outcomes. The charge of disloyalty therefore misses the point. Whatever personal scruples a lawyer might have against defending a particular client on the basis of the lawyer's own identity or affiliations are irrelevant to his or her professional obligation to uphold the rights of all Americans.

---

7. 357 U.S. 449 (1958).

8. See Jerold S. Auerbach, Unequal Justice 234–35 (1976).

9. See Aryeh Neier, Defending My Enemy 7 (1979).

10. See, e.g., Adam Freedman, Book Review, Nat'l Rev., Dec. 31, 1994, at 65 (reviewing William Kunstler's *My Life as a Radical Lawyer,* and criticizing him for representing a defendant in the World Trade Center bombing case as well as many other unpopular clients); Monroe Freedman, Must You Be the Devil's Advocate?, Legal Times, Aug. 23, 1993, at 19 (criticizing Mike Tigar for representing John Demjanjuk).

Rights theorists appear to have the upper hand in both the courts and the court of public opinion. In June 1994, the Supreme Court of Texas concluded unanimously and without argument that the order to compel the Klan to reveal its membership list violated the Klan's First Amendment rights under *NAACP v. Alabama*.[11] Moreover, Griffin, like his ACLU colleagues fifteen years before, has generally been lauded in the press for his professionalism and courage.[12] Nevertheless, a significant minority—and arguably an even greater percentage among blacks—continue to regard Griffin as a "Judas" who sold out the real and concrete interests of black Americans in the name of an ethereal "principle" that has little relevance to blacks in Vidor or elsewhere.[13]

In this essay, I challenge this standard dichotomy. My purpose in doing so is not so much to question the prevailing consensus that Griffin is an honorable man who acted with the best of intentions. For reasons specified below, I believe that Griffin made a reasonable determination (although not one that I would have made myself) that representing the Klan was consistent with his life-long commitment to the cause of racial justice. Instead, I believe that framing the debate over Griffin's actions in terms of an up or down vote on either the Klan or the First Amendment obscures important questions about the scope and content of the professional norms and legal principles that ought to apply in these circumstances and how these "public" values ought to respond to the legitimate pull exerted by a lawyer's personal commitments and group-based affiliations.

To get at these neglected issues, we must disaggregate the global dispute between effects and rights theorists into a series of more focused inquiries. Specifically, six different questions merit separate attention, each of which I will address in turn: (1) is the Klan entitled to a lawyer?; (2) does any lawyer have an ethical obligation to represent the Klan, or, to put the point somewhat differently, may a lawyer refuse to represent the Klan, and if so for what reasons?; (3) are there reasons why a black lawyer should decline to represent the Klan in circumstances where a white lawyer would be permitted (or required) to do so?; (4) should this

---

11. See Ex parte Lowe, 887 S.W.2d 1, 3 (Tex. 1994).

12. See, e.g., Taking a Tough Stand for Free Speech, Chi. Trib., Sept. 3, 1993, at 26 (The Tribune's editors praised Griffin and noted that if "such devotion [as Griffin's] to principle had been more common in our history[,] [t] he burden of the NAACP, among others, would have been lighter."). In 1994, Griffin received the William Brennan Award from the Thomas Jefferson Center for Free Expression. See Hentoff, supra note 3, at A21 (noting that Justice Brennan declared that what he knew about Griffin's actions made him "proud to have my name on this award").

13. See All Things Considered: African American ACLU Attorney Represents Klan in Texas (NPR radio broadcast, Sept. 19, 1993) (noting that many blacks have called Griffin a "Judas" for representing the Klan).

black lawyer, in light of his unique history and experience, have agreed to represent the Klan in this case?; (5) is there a "conflict of interest" between Griffin's representation of the Klan and his work for the NAACP, or are there other grounds that justify that organization's decision to terminate Griffin?; and (6) should Griffin be praised for his conduct, and, equally important, does the attention that generally accompanies such public glorification create any additional obligations either for Griffin or those who honor him? After examining each of these troublesome issues, I will conclude with a postscript describing subsequent events and offering some tentative conclusions about the general relationship among professionalism, personal morality, and group identity.

I. The Right to Counsel

Much of the rhetorical punch of the rights thesis comes from the widely shared view that in our system of justice everyone—no matter how reprehensible—is entitled to a lawyer. This consensus rests on a broad array of empirical and moral arguments that need not be restated here. Suffice it to say that most Americans believe that in our highly legalized society, it is fundamentally unfair to deprive people of their liberty or property without giving them an opportunity to present their side of the story in its best light.

Two important limitations on the right to counsel restrict its explanatory power in the category of cases we are now considering. First, in civil cases, such as the Texas Commission's suit against the Klan, the "right to counsel" is not a guarantee that a litigant will actually be represented by counsel. Unlike criminal cases, where the Sixth Amendment compels the government to appoint counsel for indigent defendants, civil litigants are "guaranteed" the assistance of counsel only when they can afford to pay for the services they receive or are able to convince an attorney to handle the matter for free. Thus, as a practical matter, our adversary system contemplates that many civil litigants will proceed without the benefit of counsel, even in cases where the government is seeking to terminate important rights or benefits. Thousands do so every day.[14] As a result, it is not accurate to say that our judicial system has determined that it is fundamentally unfair to deprive someone of their rights—even constitutional rights—unless they have a lawyer. Second, even someone who can afford the high cost of legal services may not be "entitled" to be represented by a lawyer if what she wants her attorney to do falls outside the bounds of permissible advocacy. Thus, a lawyer may not knowingly present frivolous claims or defenses, counsel or assist her client in illegal or fraudulent conduct, or

---

14. See Deborah L. Rhode, Access to Justice, 81–86 (2004); William W. Shwarzer, Teaching Judges How to Cope, Legal Times, Dec. 19, 1994, at 20.

take any action designed merely to harass or maliciously injure another.[15]

Given these two caveats, the standard claim by rights theorists that any limitation on the right to counsel borders on totalitarianism rings hollow. Nevertheless, one would have to push quite hard to stretch these limitations far enough to encompass a general ban on representing the Klan or other similar organizations. The strongest argument that effects theorists can mobilize in favor of such a ban is the claim that the Klan is nothing more than a terrorist organization that the state should attempt to destroy by any legal means at its disposal. Assuming this to be true, however, the Klan still should have the right to ensure that the state's means are in fact legal. Even the Mafia, admittedly a criminal organization with no redeeming social value, ought to be entitled to challenge the legality of government conduct. It is one thing to say that the state has no duty to subsidize access to the civil justice system. It is quite another to say that the government is free to ignore the civil rights of those whose views society rightly rejects.

Of course, the result might be different if we could be certain that the claims or defenses that the Klan might seek to raise would always be legally frivolous or in furtherance of an ongoing crime or fraud. Some of the Klan's legal maneuvers in this case appear to fall into this category and therefore, I argue below, should not be pursued by any lawyer. Moreover, at some level, anything that one does to promote the Klan's interests (even its legitimate legal interests) makes it easier for that organization to engage in the kind of terror tactics that have been going on in Vidor. The same indictment, however, can be leveled against every criminal defense lawyer who can predict with reasonable certainty that if his or her client is acquitted (regardless of the client's guilt), the client will commit future crimes. The constitutional questions raised by the Klan are not frivolous under any plausible definition. To say that they ought not have a lawyer to present these arguments simply because it is likely that the Klan is and will continue to be engaged in criminal conduct is to advocate a significant and unjustified restriction on the right to counsel.

II.   Conscientious Objection

Rights theorists often seem to presume that simply because the Klan has a right to be represented by counsel, every lawyer has an ethical obligation to represent the Klan. This overstates the extent of any individual lawyer's professional obligation.

---

15. See Model Code of Professional Responsibility DR 7–102 (A)(1),(2), (7) (1980) [hereinafter Model Code]. The ABA's Model Rules of Professional Conduct contain similar prohibitions. See Model Rules of Professional Conduct Rule 3.3 (1983) [hereinafter Model Rules] (barring frivolous claims and defenses).

Bar ethical codes have long instructed lawyers to "assist the legal profession in fulfilling its duty to make legal counsel available."[16] This mandate however, has never been interpreted to require a lawyer to accept any particular case that might come to her attention.[17] To the contrary, a lawyer is free to turn down a given case for any reason, including the most banal (and undoubtedly the most common) reason of all: the client can't afford to pay the freight. From the perspective of the individual practitioner, therefore, the ethical commitment to make legal counsel available is a background norm that does not compel a specific decision in any particular case. In other words, no individual lawyer has an ethical obligation to represent the Klan.[18]

The issue becomes more complicated, however, when a lawyer refuses to take on a client because he disagrees with the client's views. The rules of professional conduct urge lawyers not to turn away unpopular clients or causes.[19] In order to facilitate this objective, the Model Rules of Professional Conduct ("Model Rules") specifically state that a "lawyer's representation of a client ... does not constitute an endorsement of the client's political, economic, social or moral views or activities."[20] Nor, in an implicit rebuke of the effects thesis, do the rules hold lawyers legally or morally accountable for wrongful actions that a client might take as a result of their legal advice, so long as they do not actively assist in the wrongdoing or otherwise transgress the bounds of the law.[21] Instead, lawyers who represent unpopular clients are celebrated in professional lore for providing a vital service to society.[22] Ironically, one of the most commonly cited examples in this lore is the fictional lawyer Atticus Finch who, in the 1950s book and film *To Kill a*

---

16. Model Code, supra note 15, Canon 2.

17. See *id*. EC 2–26 ("A lawyer is under no obligation to act as adviser or advocate for every person who may wish to become his client.... ").

18. As famed criminal defense attorney William Kunstler succinctly put the matter when explaining why he would not represent the Klan even though he represented the accused World Trade Center bombers: "[E]veryone has a right to a lawyer, that's true. But they don't have a right to me." Sonya Live (CNN television broadcast, Nov. 5, 1993), available in LEXIS, Nexis Library, CNN File.

19. See, e.g., Model Code, supra note 15, EC 2–27 (urging lawyers not to "decline representation because a client or cause is unpopular").

20. Model Rules, supra note 15, Rule 1.2(b).

21. See, e.g., id. Rule 1.2 cmt. para. 9 (cautioning that just because "a client uses [a lawyer's] advice in a course of action that is criminal or fraudulent [does not], of itself, make a lawyer party to the course of action").

22. In the words of one influential report, "[o]ne of the highest services the lawyer can render to society is to appear in court on behalf of clients whose causes are in disfavor with the general public." Professional Responsibility: Report of the Joint Conference, 44 A.B.A. J. 1159, 1216 (1958).

Mockingbird, braved the bigoted fury of his small town neighbors to defend a black defendant falsely accused of rape.

The profession has good reasons for being worried about unpopular clients gaining access to legal services. Standing up to public pressure invariably is difficult, and if history is any guide, few lawyers will be willing to jeopardize the community goodwill necessary for their economic survival.[23] The real question, therefore, is why the obligation to take on such unpopular cases is not mandatory. To be sure, not every despised client is like the black defendant in *To Kill a Mockingbird*, that is, both factually innocent and a victim of racial prejudice. Nevertheless, once we concede that even factually guilty people who advocate views that society ought to reject are entitled to a lawyer, the question remains why the profession should count on the aspirational pull of professional honor to ensure that these services are provided rather than directly ordering lawyers to do so.

It is possible to offer two quite different justifications for the bar's decision to treat the representation of unpopular clients as a professional honor rather than a mandatory duty. The most commonly articulated ground rests on the client's interest. Thus, the Model Rules specifically allow lawyers to refuse to accept a court appointment in circumstances where "the client or the cause is so repugnant to the lawyer as to be likely to impair the client-lawyer relationship or the lawyer's ability to represent the client."[24] The second ground, offered primarily by commentators, focuses on the lawyer's moral right to control his or her own labor.

Important consequences flow from the choice between these two rationales. The first ground implies that clients ought to be given the final word. If the possibility of poor service is the only reason why a lawyer should refuse to take a controversial case, then a fully informed client ought to have the right to consent to that risk. Although we might believe that few clients will take advantage of this right, there will certainly be circumstances where it would be prudent for a particular client to do so. Michael Lowe's delight in being represented by a black lawyer nicely illustrates the point. As Lowe told the reporter from *The New York Times*: "The way I look at it, he has to do a good job for me.... If he doesn't win, people are going to say, 'Yup, that's what you get for taking an African–American lawyer.' Everybody will know I got sold down the river by the A.C.L.U."[25] In effect, Lowe seems happy with the arrangement because of Griffin's opposition to the Klan. At the same time, Griffin (assuming that he was forced to take the case against his

---

23.   See Deborah L. Rhode, In the Interests of Justice, 58–59 (2000).

24.   Model Rules, supra note 15, Rule 6.2(c).

25.   See Verhovek, supra note 2, at B9.

wishes) could be disbarred or sued for malpractice if he were to fail to pursue zealously the Klan's objectives to the full extent permitted by law. Under these circumstances, it might be perfectly rational for the Klan to consent to be represented by a black lawyer even though the Klan is, in the lawyer's view, so "repugnant" as to "impair representation."[26]

Although courts have occasionally compelled lawyers to accept a case against their will, it is highly unlikely that any court or bar association would give clients ultimate power to demand representation. The second justification for making the duty to represent unpopular clients honorific as opposed to mandatory—that a lawyer has a right to control his or her own labor—helps to explain why. Given our society's commitment to both individual autonomy and moral pluralism, it would be fundamentally wrong for the state (or the profession) to compel individuals to commit what they consider immoral acts for the sake of the greater good. A lawyer who believes that it would be morally wrong to lend her professional skill to a particular cause ought not to be forced to do so just because the client can see some strategic advantage in the arrangement.

Once we accept this justification, however, it is impossible to contend that lawyers bear no moral responsibility for their decision to represent particular clients. To this extent, effects theorists are right. If a lawyer has the moral right to refuse to accept a case, then the decision not to exercise this option—in other words, to agree to take the case— also carries moral significance. Even if one accepts that there is a morally significant distinction between committing a harmful act and failing to do something that would be morally praiseworthy, the decision to undertake a representation in the face of strong moral arguments that one ought not to do so is to *act*, and therefore to be subject to moral critique. Moreover, one cannot justify this action solely by referring to the demands of the role itself because, as we have seen, that role specifically allows for conscientious objection. Nor does the "right to counsel" provide a sufficient independent ground unless (perhaps) the lawyer is the last lawyer in town. The claim that "this person deserves legal representation" is fundamentally different from the argument that "I should provide that service." In order to arrive at the latter conclusion, a lawyer must examine the specific legal and moral considerations at issue in the particular case.

III. Race and Role

One would be hard-pressed to deny that Anthony Griffin's race is the primary reason why this case has attracted so much media attention. Griffin's race is featured prominently in virtually every media account.

---

26.   Model Rules, supra note 15, Rule 6.2(c).

And why not? Who could resist the delicious irony of Lowe and his girlfriend peeking around Griffin's office before their first meeting only to discover such tell-tale clues to their new lawyer's identity as his NAACP pin and several books on black history?[27] Aside from its obvious titillation value, however, there is a serious question whether the fact that Griffin is black should make any difference in our evaluation of his conduct.

Griffin sometimes talks as if he believes the answer to this question is no. For example, in an interview after the Texas Supreme Court's decision, Griffin asserted that during the last year he has routinely challenged "the racism of those black folks who told me I should have let a white lawyer take that case" as well as "the racism of Anglos, who regarded me as some kind of oddity because I was a black man who represented the Klan."[28] Such sentiments are surely understandable given this country's long history of using racial rhetoric as a means of denying that blacks are entitled to—or even capable of—individual agency and self-determination. Moreover, given that we are ultimately asking a moral question—i.e., should Griffin have agreed to represent the Klan under these circumstances?—we cannot avoid confronting the strong presumption in favor of universalism in general and colorblindness in particular in both our moral and legal culture.

It is a mistake, however, to move from the indisputable claim that all men and women are created as moral equals to the conclusion that racial identity plays no role in moral decision-making. I have previously defended this complex and controversial proposition at some length.[29] For reasons that will become clear below, I present only the broad outlines of this defense here.

No one can seriously deny that for black Americans race continues to exert a major influence over every significant facet of our lives. It literally colors the way that we are perceived by the world at the same time that it shapes our self-perception. As a result, blacks are inextricably linked to each other in a manner that makes it predictable that the actions of individual blacks will affect the fate of the black community as a whole, and that ties the opportunities available to any individual black to the progress of the group. These race based ties have moral as well as social significance. For many blacks, group membership is an important

---

27. Verhovek, supra note 2, at B9 (describing this discovery and reporting that Lowe turned to his girlfriend and exclaimed, "'Holy Moly, I think this guy's black!.'").

28. Hentoff, supra note 3, at A21; see also Kevin Moran, Black Lawyer Giving his Best to the Klan: Galveston Man Calls his ACLU Work a Way to Safeguard First Amendment, Houston Chron., July 27, 1993, at 1A (paraphrasing Griffin as stating that the case "has nothing to do with race").

29. See David B. Wilkins, Two Paths to the Mountaintop? The Role of Legal Education in Shaping the Values of Black Corporate Lawyers, 45 Stan. L. Rev. 1981 (1993).

source of pride and strength, and therefore an important part of human flourishing. But even those who view racial identity only as an unjust burden that must constantly be challenged should also recognize that the race consciousness of others affects their moral decision-making, both in terms of their own actions (for example, the arguably wrongful but nevertheless predictable manner in which the actions of an individual black person affect the interests of the group) and the actions of others (for example, in the way that they have benefited by the struggles of other blacks). The essential point is that in today's America, race matters in ways that go beyond individual choice.[30] This reality must be taken into consideration by any moral theory that purports to tell us how to live in the world as it is.

The facts of this case highlight the danger of ignoring both the social and the moral significance of race. Residential segregation is one of the most pressing problems facing black Americans today. When blacks are denied the opportunity to move into white communities, they lose a whole constellation of related advantages in education, municipal services, job opportunities, and social connections. From the black community's perspective, therefore, issues relating to the First Amendment rights of the Klan must be viewed in the wider context of its right to obtain unfettered access to the sources of upward mobility in American society.

Moreover, the argument that blacks would face the same danger if the Klan were represented by a white lawyer is not fully persuasive in this context. Both Griffin and Lowe recognize that in all likelihood, Griffin's presence at counsel table has improved the Klan's chances of successfully resisting the State's disclosure order.[31] For better or worse, many white Americans are likely to interpret Griffin's willingness to take on this matter as an indication that even the Klan's most bitter enemies believe that its arguments merit careful consideration. Similarly, it is at least conceivable that a substantial number of whites will also take the fact that the Klan was able to secure the services of a black lawyer as some confirmation of the growing sentiment that the Klan is merely a "fringe" organization whose "speech" causes no real harm.[32]

---

30. I borrow the phrase from Cornel West. See Cornel West, Race Matters (1993).

31. As Lowe gleefully exclaimed to a reporter: "It couldn't get any better than this.... I need a minority in my corner." Elizabeth Gleick, The Odd Couple: A Black Attorney Defends a Texas Klansman in a Racially Heated Case, People, Sept. 20, 1993, at 71. For his part, Griffin acknowledges that by appearing on Lowe's behalf, he "dramatically underscores their sincerity over their position." Gary Taylor, Klan, Texas Embroiled in Legal Tug of War, Nat'l L.J., Aug. 16, 1993, at 10 (paraphrasing Griffin).

32. See Martin Berg, Lawyers Find Cross–Burning Case is Something Different, L.A. Daily J., Sept. 12, 1991, at 1, 12 (quoting a lawyer representing the Klan in a cross-burning case as saying that white supremacists were far less dangerous than crack dealers and that

Finally, given the undeniable fact of racial identification, it is likely that blacks will feel a special sense of harm when those who terrorize them are represented by a black lawyer.

Notwithstanding his above quoted remarks, I do not believe that Griffin fundamentally disagrees with the claim that, as a black lawyer, he must take account of the consequences of his actions for other blacks. As even his detractors concede, Griffin has dedicated a substantial part of his professional energies to highlighting and combating the racist oppression of blacks. Moreover, in virtually all of his interviews, Griffin repeatedly states that he "understand[s] the anger" of blacks from within the NAACP and elsewhere, that he feels an obligation to respond to their concerns and that he believes his representation of the Klan will ultimately benefit the black community.[33]

Griffin is right to reject the essentialist assumption that his identity as a black American totally defines who he is or what he is entitled to believe. As a free and equal moral actor, he demands the right to entertain beliefs and undertake commitments that may or may not be shared by other blacks. He is also cognizant, however, that he cannot and should not make these choices in a vacuum. Although his racial identity does not define him, his moral, economic, and spiritual connection to the black community does have an important claim on his decisions, at least when those decisions are likely to have predictable consequences for other blacks. He has an obligation to weigh these race-based considerations against both legitimate professional duties (acquired by virtue of his status as a lawyer) and his unique commitments as an autonomous member of society.

IV. Civil Liberties and Civil Rights

The structure of Griffin's arguments clearly demonstrates his desire to justify his actions by pointing to some positive connection between defending the Klan and advancing the black community's struggle for equality. Thus, although he begins from the classic rights theory perspective that protecting the Klan's associational rights is a necessary precondition to safeguarding the rights of all Americans, he invariably also emphasizes that blacks have a special interest in this constitutional doctrine.[34] Similarly, when Griffin invokes his professional obligation as

---

these groups were not "'dangerous or a threat to the community [because] [t]hey're completely ignored by mainstream America'").

33. All Things Considered, supra note 13.

34. See, e.g., Verhovek, supra note 2, at B9 (quoting Griffin as saying, "[i]f you take away [the Klan's] rights, you take away my rights also" and that "'[p]eople forget'" that the same arguments used against the Klan were also "used against the NAACP . . . and the Black Panther Party"); Nat Hentoff, Lawyer for the NAACP—and the Klan, Wash. Post, Sept. 4, 1993, at A27 (reporting that Griffin told his critics at the NAACP that any decision

a lawyer to "defend the Bill of Rights ... [even] for people I despise," the name he invokes to personify this commitment is Thurgood Marshall.[35]

The limitations that Griffin places on his willingness to be the Klan's lawyer also underscore the delicate balance he is attempting to strike. For example, Griffin states that he would not feel obligated to defend Lowe or any other Klan member against criminal charges involving threats to blacks living in Vidor.[36] Nor is Griffin willing to become friends with Lowe or refrain from strongly criticizing the Klan's objectives or actions.[37] Finally, Griffin has neither asked for, nor in all probability would he accept, any money for representing the Klan.[38] As he has repeatedly stated, his sole interest is in defending the constitutional principle that the government cannot interfere with associational rights by obtaining membership lists that might be used to harass or intimidate those with unpopular beliefs. Upholding this principle, Griffin fervently contends, is in the best interest of the black community.

Given this constellation of arguments and commitments, it is fair to ask whether Griffin's actions are likely to advance his self-professed goal of safeguarding the interests of the black community. When we do so, we see that neither Griffin's assessment of the benefits of representing the Klan, nor the distinctions he offers between what he is and is not willing to do for the Klan are fully persuasive.

A. Protection Versus Absolutism

It is not difficult to marshal persuasive arguments in support of Griffin's claim that blacks benefit from a strong, universal interpretation of the First Amendment. Notwithstanding recent scholarship emphasizing the limited success of the civil rights movement, it is nevertheless clear that black leaders from Thurgood Marshall to Martin Luther King relied heavily on arguments about the universal applicability of constitu-

---

allowing the State access to the Klan's membership list could "one day haunt them", and quoting the following from an editorial in the *Galveston County Observer News: An African American Monthly Newspaper*: "For those who do not want the Ku Klux Klan to have their rights protected, you should consider which of your rights you are willing to give up because the Klan has to give up theirs. It may be you giving up yours tomorrow.").

35. See Tomaso, supra note 4, at 8A (quoting Griffin as citing Marshall).

36. See Verhovek, supra note 2, at B9 (reporting that Griffin "would feel no obligation to defend Mr. Lowe on criminal charges").

37. See id. (quoting Griffin as saying: "'I told Mr. Lowe this was not about me liking him or him liking me.'"); All Things Considered, supra note 13 (quoting Griffin as describing the Klan as a "terrorist organization" with a "history against our community, and they're a trip-mine of everything wrong about this country ... for black folks").

38. See Verhovek, supra note 2, at B9 (noting that "[t]he case is not about money" and that Mr. Griffin is a pro bono, unpaid lawyer for the Klan).

tional rights. Moreover, Griffin is also surely correct when he emphasizes that the Bill of Rights in general, and the First Amendment in
particular, has been an important source of support for black efforts
challenging government supported racism. *NAACP v. Alabama* is only
one of a long line of cases where blacks have successfully challenged
efforts by hostile state governments to diffuse protests by silencing or
intimidating participants. Griffin and his ACLU compatriots also can
make a strong case that blacks ought to be skeptical of content-based
restrictions on first amendment rights. History is replete with examples
of such restrictions being invoked to punish blacks whose views are often
portrayed as radical or dangerous.[39]

This impressive history, however, does not support the claim that
advocates of racial justice should be in favor of *every* argument that
conduct which might conceivably fall within the First Amendment's
ambit actually deserves constitutional protection. Griffin cites *NAACP v.
Alabama* in support of his classic slippery slope argument that blacks
have an important stake in protecting the Klan's associational rights. In
NAACP v. Alabama, however, the Court expressly recognized that the
Klan might not be entitled to the same constitutional protection as the
NAACP.[40] The Court held that, by demonstrating a "controlling justification," a state could compel the production of an organization's membership list even in circumstances where that action is likely to have a
deterrent effect on associational activity. The Court relied on its earlier
decision in *Bryant v. Zimmerman*, in which it upheld a New York
statute, requiring any organization that demands an oath as a condition
of membership to file its membership list with the state against a First
Amendment challenge by Klan members. In distinguishing *Bryant*, the
Court in *NAACP v. Alabama* took note of the "particular character of
the Klan's activities, involving acts of unlawful intimidation and violence, which the Court [in *Bryant*] assumed was before the state legislature when it enacted the statute, and of which the Court itself took
judicial notice."[41]

Embedded in the very precedent Griffin cites, therefore, is a principled argument for distinguishing the Klan and the NAACP: the former
has a demonstrated history of violence and intimidation and the latter
does not. The facts underlying the state's efforts to obtain the Klan's
membership list in this case underscores this distinction. This is not a

---

39. For a critique of content-based restrictions on speech from the vantage point of
the struggle for racial justice, see Henry L. Gates, Jr., Let Them Talk, New Republic, Sep.
20 & 27, 1993, at 42 (discussing how the First Amendment was repeatedly invoked to
protect civil rights protesters in the 1960s and 1970s).

40. See NAACP v. Alabama, 357 U.S. 449, 465–66 (1958).

41. See NAACP v. Alabama, 357 U.S. at 465. See Bryant v. Zimmerman, 278 U.S. 63
(1928).

"pure speech" case like *Brandenburg v. Ohio* in which the Supreme Court unanimously held that the First Amendment protected a Klan leader from prosecution for burning a cross on an open field as a symbol of the group's hatred of blacks.[42] Nor is it analogous to protecting the Nazis' right to march peacefully in Skokie. Instead, the state in this case is seeking to prosecute acts of criminal violence perpetrated by individuals who, by dressing in sheets, have simultaneously announced their identity as Klan members while attempting to shield their identity as individuals from the police. This conduct is consistent with the Klan's long history of "unlawful intimidation and violence," of which the Court, in *NAACP v. Alabama*, conceded it was appropriate to take judicial notice. As a result, just as the Mafia would not be able to invoke the First Amendment to prevent government investigators from seeking access to its "membership list," the Klan should not be able to use the constitution as a means of shielding its unlawful conduct by claiming that disclosing the identity of its members might discourage them from participating in what is essentially an equivalent criminal enterprise.

In light of the distinction between, on the one hand, upholding the Klan's right to engage in peaceful (albeit hateful) speech and, on the other, helping hooded criminals conceal their identities from the police, one might plausibly distinguish Griffin's conduct from that of other black attorneys who have represented the Klan in prior cases. Thus, even an effects theorist might concede that Eleanor Holmes Norton, a distinguished black civil rights lawyer and long-standing delegate to Congress from the District of Columbia, made a reasonable judgment when she agreed to file an amicus brief on behalf of the ACLU in *Brandenburg v. Ohio* on the ground that protecting pure speech, no matter how repugnant, was ultimately in the black community's best interest. That same person, however, could reasonably reject Griffin's argument that he made a similarly reasonable judgment in agreeing to argue that the First Amendment should be interpreted to shield the Klan's membership list when the state has made a credible showing that this intrusion is necessary to stop Klan members from engaging in the kind of violence and intimidation expressly recognized in *Bryant v. Zimmerman.*

Or so the argument might go. My point here is not that there are no legitimate objections to this line of reasoning. For example, one might believe that creating a "Klan exception" is inherently unstable, or that distinguishing between the Klan and the NAACP on the basis of the former's history of violence might deny constitutional protection to groups like the Black Panther Party or the Nation of Islam that have been, at least in the eyes of white America, more closely linked to

---

42. Brandenburg v. Ohio, 395 U.S. 444 (1969).

violence. Those who put forward these or other similar arguments, however, must specifically confront the question of whether the dangers they envision might not be preferable to allowing the Klan to continue brutalizing defenseless blacks by wrapping itself in a constitutional principle that was never intended to condone such terror tactics.

This challenge cannot be met, as the Texas Supreme Court asserted in dismissing the Klan exception, by noting that the United States Supreme Court's "decisions in the First Amendment area make ... plain that its protection would apply as fully to those who would arouse our society against the [NAACP's] objectives."[43] The Klan does more than simply "arouse our society" against the black community's demands for justice; for more than a century, it has actively engaged in a widespread, systematic, and deadly campaign to terrorize and intimidate black Americans. By acknowledging this crucial distinction, the Klan exception suggested in *NAACP v. Alabama* offers at least the potential for enlisting state resources in the fight against Klan terror without endangering legitimate associational rights.[44] Following this lead, courts could conclude that an organization with a history of unlawful conduct, combined with evidence of continuing violence, forfeits its right to keep its membership lists absolutely confidential.

At least two courts have adopted this approach in civil actions against the Klan.[45] In both cases, the court took judicial notice of the Klan's history of violence against blacks to support limited discovery by civil plaintiffs of Klan membership lists.[46] Neither decision is exactly on point; indeed both courts specifically denied state officials access to the lists. Nevertheless, in light of these precedents, the challenge for Griffin is to explain why advocating as he did that the Klan's history of, and current participation in, violence is irrelevant to the constitutional inquiry is in the best interest of the black community, as opposed to refusing to take the case on the ground that a court should hold that the Klan forfeits its right to keep its membership lists private in circum-

---

43. Ex parte Lowe, 887 S.W.2d 1, 3 (Tex. 1994) (quoting NAACP v. Button, 371 U.S. 415, 444 (1963)).

44. Lowe testified that "the survival of the Texas Knights of the Ku Klux Klan will be effectively undermined if he is forced to disclose the identities of the members of the organization." Application for Writ of Habeas Corpus at 26, Lowe (No. D–4506). Unless we think that there is some independent reason for wanting the Klan to survive, we should only mourn this result if we have legitimate grounds for believing that the Klan's passing will endanger some other speech or activity that we believe to be valuable.

45. See Marshall v. Bramer, 828 F.2d 355 (6th Cir. 1987); United States v. Handley, 591 F. Supp. 1257 (N.D. Ala. 1984), *rev'd*, 763 F.2d 1401 (11th Cir.), *cert. denied*, 474 U.S. 951 (1985).

46. See Marshall, 828 F.2d at 357; Handley, 591 F. Supp. at 1271.

stances where the state can demonstrated that it is engaged in violent conduct consistent with the history recognized in *Bryant v. Zimmerman*.

B. Clean Rights and Dirty Hands

Griffin might contend that his unwillingness to represent Lowe in any subsequent criminal prosecution provides a partial response to this challenge. Gaining access to the Klan's membership list, he asserts, is not the only way for the state to stop Klan terror. Increasing police protection, planting informants in the Klan, and enlisting the cooperation of white residents all provide additional avenues for cracking down on threats and intimidation against blacks in Vidor. To the extent that these efforts bear fruit, Griffin states that he would feel no obligation to assist the Klan in avoiding its just deserts.[47]

It is important to note that by taking this position, Griffin implicitly acknowledges that it is not necessarily in the black community's interest to ensure that every conceivable constitutional argument is raised on the Klan's behalf. Criminal proceedings present constitutional issues no less than civil enforcement actions, starting with the basic right of every criminal defendant to be represented by counsel. Moreover, the risk that the state will trammel the Klan's rights under the Fourth, Fifth, or Sixth Amendment during the course of a straightforward criminal prosecution is at least as salient as the danger to the Klan's First Amendment rights posed by the state's enforcement efforts to date. Indeed, many commentators assert that the obligation to represent unpopular clients is most strongly justified in the criminal context.[48]

Undoubtedly, Griffin believes that the Klan is entitled to a criminal defense lawyer who will raise these constitutional objections. He simply asserts that he feels no obligation to be that lawyer. Griffin has not clearly spelled out why he would refuse to take such a case. His vehement assertion that he is currently representing "the First Amendment" and not Klan terror suggests that he may believe that helping the Klan to avoid criminal liability—even by constitutionally sanctioned means—would implicate him more directly than his present work in the Klan's violence against blacks.

As a general proposition, this argument is problematic. In this case, Griffin could make a strong claim that the state did not exhaust all of its available avenues for putting an end to Klan violence in Vidor before seeking disclosure of the Klan's membership list.[49] There is, however, no guarantee that these alternative avenues will be successful.

---

47. See Verhovek, supra note 2, at B9.

48. See e.g., David Luban, Are Criminal Defenders Different?, 91 Mich. L. Rev. 1729 (1993).

49. For example, despite its defeat in the Supreme Court of Texas, the State has apparently learned enough about the identities of suspected Klan terrorists to file a civil

Moreover, the line between "representing The First Amendment" and "defending racist criminals" will often be a fine one indeed. Griffin's comical yet revealing response to the state's efforts to prevent the Klan from "adopting a highway" in Vidor underscores the fallacy of categorically separating constitutional rights from criminal wrongs. In December 1993, the Klan applied to "adopt" the stretch of highway abutting the Vidor project.[50] The Commission moved to block the Klan's request on the ground that it would allow the Klan to circumvent a restraining order issued by the United States District Court for the Eastern District of Texas preventing Klan members from engaging in threatening or intimidating conduct within a specified distance of the housing project.[51] The Commission argued that by sending hooded Klansmen to "clean up" the highway and posting signs declaring the road a ward of the Klan, the Klan would be able to continue its terror tactics in direct violation of the injunction.[52] The federal court agreed with the Commission, ruling that the Klan's request was a "subterfuge to intimidate those minority residents already living" in the development.[53]

Griffin appealed the trial judge's order. According to Griffin, the State's denial of the Klan's application is "pretty asinine," given the fact that other "controversial" organizations—including pit bull owners, nudists, prison inmates, a smokers rights organization, and the Austin Gay-Lesbian Political Caucus—have all been allowed to adopt a stretch of road.[54] Indeed, Griffin asserts, only partly in jest, that the state is in no position to deny the Klan's application, because it allowed a tall Texan's club to adopt a road, "without considering the reaction from people who are short." Instead of fighting the Klan's request, Griffin asserts, the Klan's opponents should "go out and dump a whole bunch of trash" on the Klan's stretch of road; "if they don't pick it up," he concludes, "then you can take it away."[55]

---

suit seeking hundreds of thousands of dollars in actual and punitive damages as well as broad equitable relief. See Determination of Reasonable Cause, Charge of Discrimination, and Notice of Opportunity for Hearing, Hale v. Lowe, No. 1930041–HU (Tex. Comm'n on Human Rights filed Oct. 19, 1994) [hereinafter Charge of Discrimination]; Klansmen Sued for Harassment, supra note 4, at 10.

50. See Texas v. KKK, 853 F. Supp. 958, 959 (E.D. Tex. 1994), aff'd, 58 F.3d 1075 (5th Cir. 1995).

51. See id.; Hale v. Texas KKK, No. 93–07414 (Texas D. Ct. Feb. 3, 1994) (order granting temporary injunction).

52. See Scott Pendleton, Texas Officials Step Up Crackdown on Ku Klux Klan Intimidation Acts, Christian Sci. Monitor, Mar. 1, 1994, at 2.

53. Texas v. KKK, 853 F. Supp. at 960; see also, Gary Taylor, Highway Robbery, Claim Knights of a Clean Klan, Nat'l L.J., July 4, 1994, at A23.

54. Taylor, supra note 53, at A23.

55. Id.

Griffin's equal protection argument is specious. As he is well aware, the Klan is not being denied its own stretch of highway because it is more "controversial" than nudists or pit bull terrier owners. It is being denied the right to adopt this particular stretch of road because, as the Court of Appeals unanimously concluded, unlike any other group on Griffin's list, the Klan obviously intends to use this privilege as a means of continuing its terror campaign against black residents in Vidor.[56] For any lawyer to advance the contention that granting tall Texans a stretch of road without consulting short Texans somehow precludes the state's action in this case would be a sad testament to the profession's failure to police the boundary between zealous advocacy and frivolous chicanery. For a black lawyer to assert that representing this "principle" somehow makes him less complicit in the Klan's violence against blacks in Vidor than if he had agreed to defend the Klan on criminal charges borders on hypocrisy.

The last part of Griffin's flippant statement is equally troubling. Exactly who does Griffin expect to dump this trash? The black residents who are currently living in fear of leaving their apartments lest some hooded goon tell them that he is "going home to get a rope and come back and hang" them?[57] Even if black residents could dump trash when the Klan wasn't watching, is it really plausible to suggest that they could expect even their most supportive neighbors to look kindly on someone who despoils the street that runs in front of their building? It is one thing for Griffin to suggest from the comfort of his Galveston office that black residents in Vidor need to understand that "life is intimidating" and "we can't protect against that."[58] It is quite another for him to seek to minimize his own participation in perpetuating these intimidating conditions by using an attempt at farce to gloss over the real dangers inherent in the situation.

Moreover, on what grounds is Griffin—who is the Klan's lawyer, despite the fact that the phrase sometimes "sticks in [his] throat"[59]— encouraging people to literally dump garbage on his client's interests? Isn't it a violation of ethical rules for a lawyer to "[p]rejudice or damage

---

56. See Texas v. KKK, 58 F.3d 1075, 1080 (5th Cir. 1995) ("The State's desire to prevent the participation of the Klan in the program is not due to the opinions of the Klan, but rather results from the foreseeable impact of program participation by the Klan, given the past conduct of the Klan, upon the peace and privacy of the project residents and use of the state's highways.").

57. Only the Killers Were Colorblind, supra note 4, at A31 (quoting one of the black residents of Vidor's account of the kind of harassment he was subjected to on a daily basis).

58. Wendy Benjaminson, Klan Hits a Dead End in Effort to Adopt Road, Houston Chron., May 8, 1994, at 1.

59. Tomaso, supra note 4, at 1A.

his client during the course of the professional relationship'"?[60]

At this point, one might be tempted to shrug Griffin's "dumping trash" comments off as an innocuous attempt to inject some humor into an otherwise tense situation. Even if this was all there was, one should still ask whether a lawyer who professes to owe his primary allegiance to the victims of Klan terror ought to make jokes of this kind. There may, however, be more to Griffin's comments than this explanation suggests. To understand what else may be motivating Griffin, one has to view his civil/criminal distinction in the context of his broader attempt to distance himself from his client.

C. Separating the Personal from the Political

From the outset of this case, Griffin has insisted on being both the Klan's staunchest advocate and its toughest critic. His initial warning to Lowe that the two "need not talk about politics [or] race" because "we'd end up on the floor in a fight" has not stopped Griffin from sharing his views about these issues—and about his client—with the public.[61] Griffin repeatedly emphasizes that he believes that the Klan is a terrorist organization whose message of hatred and intolerance should be condemned at every turn.[62] By constantly reiterating his views about the Klan, Griffin hopes to keep the public's (and the black community's) attention focused on the constitutional issue at stake.

Griffin's attacks on his client raise important ethical questions. Certainly, the rules of professional conduct do not envision lawyers publicly ridiculing their clients' conduct or goals, let alone urging citizens to act adversely to their clients' interests, as Griffin did in the adopt-a-highway matter. Even the rules that allow lawyers and clients to mutually agree to limit the scope of a lawyer's representation do not seem to contemplate the kind of directly adverse actions taken by Griffin in this case.[63] Moreover, Griffin's conduct clearly runs counter to the vision of the lawyer as a full-service public relations firm currently espoused by many prominent attorneys. This view posits that a lawyer who represents an unpopular client must personally commit herself

---

60. See Model Code, supra note 15, DR 101(A)(3).

61. Verhovek, supra note 2, at B9.

62. See Talerico, Michael Lowe: Texas Grand Dragon a Classic Study in Paradox, Times–Rev., Aug. 23, 1994, at 1, quoted in Charge of Discrimination, supra note 49, at 29 (quoting Griffin as saying "'the Klan is the Klan. . . . The Klan are terrorist as far as I'm concerned.'").

63. See Model Rules, supra note 15, Rule 1.2(c) (stating that a "lawyer may limit the scope of the representation if the limitation is reasonable under the circumstances and the client gives informed consent."). See also Rule 1.8(b) ("A lawyer shall not use information relating to representation of a client to the disadvantage of the client unless the client gives informed consent.").

wholeheartedly to the task of winning public support for her client's cause. In this view, a lawyer who keeps her distance from an unpopular client, acts to reinforce the prevailing perception that the client does not deserve legal protection.

Griffin is nevertheless justified in bucking this trend. Effects theorists correctly worry that people will view Griffin's willingness to represent the Klan as a sign that this organization is no longer a real threat to blacks. Griffin's comments help to dispel this falsehood. Equally as important, by continually speaking out against his client's atrocities, Griffin reaffirms his fundamental right to maintain his own moral dignity even while representing an organization that he rightly abhors. So long as Lowe is aware that Griffin intends to speak out on these issues, one can view any resulting harm to the Klan as part of the implicit price that organization is paying for the benefit of obtaining Griffin's services. The fact that Lowe continues to express confidence in Griffin's representation, even in the face of the latter's criticism of the Klan's activities and objectives, suggests that Lowe finds the trade-off acceptable.

Unfortunately, other statements by both Griffin and Lowe demonstrate how difficult it is to separate the message from the messenger. Lowe clearly understands the unique opportunity created by Griffin's presence in the case. He has skillfully used this opportunity to gain a wider audience for his message. For example, because of Griffin, Lowe has been interviewed by local and national media. In these interviews, he has had the opportunity to portray himself, à la David Duke, as a populist opposed to government "intervention and interference,"[64] as opposed to a racist intent on putting "Negroes back in the cotton fields," as he once said before he'd entered the national spotlight.[65]

Moreover, Griffin and Lowe's strange alliance has given Lowe many opportunities to humiliate Griffin, and, more insidiously, for Griffin to humiliate himself. Thus, Griffin told a national radio audience that one example of Lowe's "cryptic" sense of humor was his statement that Griffin's decision to represent him made him feel so good that it just made him want to "go out and do a cross-burning."[66] Even more painfully, Lowe reports that at their first meeting, Griffin told Lowe that he hoped Lowe didn't mind if they shook hands.[67] To be sure, lawyers

---

64. See, e.g., Kevin Moran, KKK Chief Likes His Black Lawyer, Houston Chron., July 29, 1993, at 25A; Verhovek, supra note 2, at B9.

65. See Verhovek, supra note 2, at B9.

66. See All Things Considered, supra note 13. Griffin claimed that upon hearing this remark he said a "nice profanity, . . . laughed, and hung the phone up." Id. Griffin added, "Whether [Lowe was] telling a joke, I don't know." Id. To which the NPR reporter answered: "Yeah, that's the question." Id.

67. See Moran, supra note 64, at 25A.

frequently have to put up with their client's "cryptic" jokes and embarrassing idiosyncrasies. When these foibles perpetuate racial subordina-
tion, however, the pettifogger's ritualistic genuflections to his paymaster
(in spirit if not in fact) take on a much more ominous tone.

Finally, it is virtually impossible for someone in an adversarial role
to keep their clients, and more importantly their client's view of the
world, at arm's length. It is a familiar truth in social science that those
who are called upon to support positions that they initially find morally
abhorrent will search for ways to reduce the distance between their
beliefs and their practices. Notwithstanding all of his valiant efforts to
the contrary, there is substantial evidence that Griffin has fallen prey to
this pervasive social phenomenon. His defense of the Klan's "right" to
adopt the stretch of highway in front of the Vidor project is a perfect
example. More generally, according to press reports, Griffin often refers
to the state's efforts to investigate the Klan as a "witch hunt."[68] In the
light of the undisputed record of Klan violence in this case, only an
advocate in the truest sense of the word could take this position.

None of this should detract from Griffin's genuinely praiseworthy
efforts to keep the Klan's terror tactics in the public eye. His statements
underscore his commitment to the First Amendment principles he claims
to be protecting. The fact that he is litigating the case pro bono only
serves to substantiate his bona fides.

D.   Freedom Fighter or Mercenary?

As a purely conceptual matter, rights theorists ought to treat the
fact that Griffin is representing the Klan pro bono as irrelevant to their
evaluation of his conduct. In their view, Griffin is justified in pressing
the constitutional issue regardless of whether he is being paid for his
services. The assumption in our system is that legal services are distrib-
uted through the marketplace. Although a willingness to donate a
portion of one's professional energies to those who cannot afford legal
services is an acknowledged professional virtue, that virtue stands logi-
cally independent from the underlying merits of the cause. In other
words, the lawyer who vindicates an important constitutional principle
for a fee is no less virtuous than the one who does so for free, just as the
fact that the lawyer is donating his services is no excuse for presenting
frivolous claims or defenses.

Although the issue is more complex for effects theorists, the conceptual conclusion ought to be the same. Most of the material consequences
for the victims of Klan violence are unlikely to be affected by whether
Griffin is receiving a fee for his efforts on behalf of the Klan. Similarly,
the psychic injury to blacks in Vidor of seeing a black lawyer standing up
for their persecutors will also be unchanged, although one might contend

---

68.   See, e.g., Tomaso, supra note 4, at 1A (paraphrasing Griffin to this effect).

that these residents may feel an even greater sense of betrayal because Griffin is donating his services to (from their perspective) such an unjust cause.

This is not, however, the way that either Griffin's supporters or detractors have treated the pro bono issue. In virtually every press account, the fact that Griffin is not being paid by the Klan is considered an important factor in his favor; even among those who fundamentally disagree with his decision.[69] It is possible to interpret this nearly universal response as an implicit rejection of the classic assumption that underlies both of the conceptual arguments outlined above: that pro bono clients receive the same services as paying ones. For example, one might take the view that when lawyers are not being paid, they have more control over their clients' actions and goals. Does anyone really believe that a paying client would allow her lawyer to encourage her opponent to "dump trash" on her goals without quickly terminating the relationship? Perhaps from their very different vantage points, both rights and effects theorists hope that the leverage created by Griffin's pro bono status will give him more room, on the one hand, to present the constitutional issue more effectively, or, on the other, to moderate the Klan's violence against blacks.

Not surprisingly, neither side is quite prepared to own up to these hopes. Unfortunately, it is not hard to find examples of lawyers in non-fee-for-service settings who appear to impose their own goals and interests on their clients. But the specter of lawyers manipulating their non-paying clients in ways that they would not (or could not) accomplish in a paying context is sufficiently troubling that it is unlikely to form the basis for the uniformly favorable reaction to Griffin's decision to represent the Klan pro bono.

Instead, that reaction is most plausibly explained by factors that move us out of the consequentialist realm of rights and effects theory. Quite simply, both Griffin's supporters and detractors take his willingness to represent the Klan pro bono as strong evidence of the sincerity of his commitment to the First Amendment considerations presented by this case. Regardless of whether it will make him a more vigilant defender of the Constitution or a more effective voice of conscience for his nefarious client, Griffin's willingness to take on this controversial case without pay demonstrates that he is a man of integrity who has the courage of his convictions.[70] And integrity, even for Griffin's detractors,

---

69. See, e.g., Kevin Moran, Black Lawyer in Hot Water with NAACP, Houston Chron., Aug. 23, 1993, at 11A, 13A (reporting that some NAACP members were particularly upset at Griffin because they "erroneously believed [he] was getting paid to represent the Klan").

70. Indeed, there is evidence that Griffin paid a steep financial price for his decision. See Clay Robinson, Revise Law Protecting Jurors, Media Representatives Urge: 3 Receive

is a positive moral good that must be taken into consideration in reaching a meaningful all-things-considered judgment about the propriety of his conduct.

E. Integrity and Autonomy

Griffin is passionately committed to a strong civil libertarian point of view. He believes that the First Amendment entitles the Klan or any other group to "meet and organize" and "to say as many abhorrent, horrible, nasty, violent, vicious things as they want to say."[71] In addition, he believes that the best way to ensure freedom of expression for all Americans is to keep the government completely out of the business of regulating speech or any other expressive conduct.

Griffin clearly believes that this approach to the First Amendment is in the best interest of the black community. Even if one disagrees with this assessment for the reasons outlined above, however, one must nevertheless acknowledge that Griffin has the right to incorporate these deeply held personal beliefs into his decision making calculus. To do otherwise, as I argued earlier, is to raise race-based considerations to the point where they suffocate black individuality.

It is in this respect that the concept of integrity is relevant to our assessment of Griffin's conduct. By integrity, I mean an individual's efforts to harmonize his or her diverse commitments into a meaningful life plan and to act, so far as possible, in accordance with the actual requirements of that plan. Griffin's membership in the ACLU exemplifies his commitment to a particular vision of the government's role in regulating expression. His willingness to defend this vision—at great cost and without any expectation of personal gain—for those whose views he detests is commendable precisely because it underlines his moral commitment to his chosen values.

Of course, simply because Griffin is entitled to consider his deeply held views about the Constitution (and his corollary commitment to his colleagues at the ACLU) in deciding whether and how to represent the Klan does not render his judgment on these issues immune from public review and criticism. If Griffin's personal commitments were to lead him to join the Klan, our condemnation should be unaffected by whether the convictions that led him to take these actions were deeply held. As I have indicated above, some of Griffin's decisions—most notably, his actions in

---

Freedom of Information Awards, Houston Chron., Sept. 17, 1994, at 31A (quoting Griffin as stating that his firm lost $1.5 million in profits). The psychic cost to Griffin was undoubtedly at least as great as the financial loss. As I discuss in Part VI, however, Griffin may also have received compensating benefits from the publicity associated with the case.

71. Moran, supra note 28, at 1A.

the adopt-a-highway matter—ought to be critiqued on precisely these grounds.

Nevertheless, it would be wrong to cast Griffin's central claims about the First Amendment and the importance of standing up for those with unpopular views in this light. His argument that government attempts to regulate expression almost always unfairly stigmatize the powerless—a category in which blacks are likely to be represented disproportionately—rests on sound historical data and is consistent with contemporary experience. Although Griffin exaggerates when he suggests that professional obligations compel his decision to press this point on the Klan's behalf, it is nevertheless reasonable for him to believe that taking this action is not ruled out-of-bounds by his countervailing obligation to advance the cause of racial justice.

Moreover, the charge of "Judas" is particularly inapt in this case once one places Griffin's decision to represent the Klan in the larger context of his life. Griffin has dedicated a substantial part of his personal and professional energy to serving the ends of racial justice. This history bears directly on our moral evaluation of any particular action that Griffin might take that has consequences for the black community. Given that group-based obligations must coexist with legitimate professional duties and important personal commitments, it will often be impossible for all of the legitimate claims of any one of these spheres to be recognized at any given moment. As a result, the moral life of black lawyers inevitably involves a series of tradeoffs, in which legitimate demands from each of these competing spheres are negotiated and resolved in order to reach concrete judgments in particular cases.

Given this reality, integrity does not imply a unitary, hierarchically ordered set of values that structures one's entire life plan, but instead resides in giving each competing commitment its moral due. Today's compromise must therefore be seen in the context of what was done yesterday and what will be done tomorrow. Griffin has earned the black community's trust and appreciation. Even if one believes, as I do, that strictly from a racial justice perspective it was a mistake for Griffin to undertake this representation, it is ludicrous to conclude that in reaching this judgment, Griffin has somehow betrayed his people.

Just because Griffin is a man of integrity, however, does not mean that he should be shielded from any adverse consequences stemming from his decision. Although some members of the Port Arthur Branch of the NAACP have wrongly impugned Griffin's integrity, it does not necessarily follow that they were also wrong to vote to remove him from his position as General Counsel.

V.   Positional Conflicts and the Public Interest

NAACP officials might offer two distinct justifications for their decision to terminate Griffin from his post as General Counsel. The first is purely substantive: it was morally wrong for Griffin to represent the Klan and therefore he is not fit to be a member of the NAACP. The second sounds in process and professional ethics: it was wrong for Griffin to represent the Klan *at the same time* that he was representing the NAACP, and because he was unwilling to resign from the former representation, the latter engagement had to be terminated. These two positions are interconnected. Both implicitly reject Griffin's claim that defending the Klan in this case is fully consistent with the NAACP's efforts to promote the cause of racial justice. The choice between them nevertheless has important consequences.

The first position implies a different answer than the one I have proposed to one or more of the first four questions discussed in this essay. According to this view, representing the Klan is like joining the Klan, that is, it is an action that no person (and certainly no black person) should take even if we are unprepared to ban Klan activity altogether. The logic of this position (if true) not only supports the NAACP's decision to fire Griffin from his position as General Counsel, but would compel his expulsion as well. Someone who is the equivalent of a Klan member should be shunned by people of good will everywhere and certainly has no place in an organization devoted to championing black rights.

Such total condemnation is not justified. Griffin's argument that it is in the NAACP's interest to protect the Klan's First Amendment rights is plausible even if it is not fully persuasive. It is therefore false to equate it with an argument in support of joining the Klan. More importantly, given *NAACP v. Alabama* and other cases in which the NAACP benefited from a robust interpretation of the First Amendment, it would be irresponsible for this organization not to consider arguments of the kind Griffin raises. It is unlikely, however, that NAACP leaders would pay much attention to these issues if everyone with Griffin's views were summarily expelled from the organization. In today's overheated rhetorical climate, there is a very real danger that blacks who challenge the prevailing orthodoxy will be excluded from the political debate. When this happens, we both disserve black individuality and stifle ideas that might help us better achieve our goals. Given the important role that it still plays in shaping the nation's understanding of racial injustice, the NAACP should not bar anyone whose views about how best to serve the interests of the black community fall within a broad zone of reasonableness.

Just because Griffin should not be expelled from the NAACP, however, does not mean that the organization was wrong to dismiss him as their General Counsel. Even conceding that Griffin's First Amendment arguments are reasonable and important, the board of directors could nevertheless justifiably conclude that someone with Griffin's erroneous (albeit reasonable) views should not occupy a leadership position in the organization. Indeed, as General Counsel, Griffin was more than just a "leader" in the Port Arthur branch; he was its chief legal advocate. Under these circumstances, it was not unreasonable for the head of that office to conclude: "You can't represent the NAACP and the Klan at the same time."[72]

One can make a strong argument that Griffin's simultaneous representation of both the NAACP and the Klan is prohibited by the formal rules of professional responsibility. Those rules generally require some showing that the two clients' interests are "directly adverse" before labeling the situation as a conflict of interest.[73] In this case, Griffin's dual representation may very well meet this standard. The NAACP was not a party to the state's efforts to obtain the Klan's membership list at the time Griffin agreed to represent Lowe, nor does it appear that the NAACP was formally a party in the underlying litigation to desegregate Texas public housing.[74] Nevertheless, there may still be a formal conflict. The conflict rules protect a lawyer's independent judgment as well as prevent lawyers from advocating directly adverse interests. Thus, the comment to Rule 1.7 cautions lawyers that a conflict of interest exists if there is a significant risk that a lawyer's ability to "consider, recommend or carry out an appropriate course of action for the client will be materially limited as a result of the lawyer's other responsibilities or interests."[75] In this case, once Griffin began representing the Klan it would have been extremely difficult for him to recommend that the NAACP (his other client) assist one of the black victims of Klan terror in bringing a civil lawsuit seeking, inter alia, the Klan's membership list as a tool for identifying the specific individuals responsible for his or her

---

72. Moran, supra note 69, at 11A (quoting Raymond Scott, the chair of the Port Arthur branch).

73. See Model Rules, Rule 1.7(a) ("a lawyer shall not represent a client if the representation involves a concurrent conflict of interest. A concurrent conflict of interest exists if (1) the representation of one client would be directly adverse to another client . . . " unless certain conditions are met).

74. In his deposition, however, the Commissioner suggested that "representatives of the NAACP" sat on an advisory board relating to integrating the Vidor project. See Deposition of William Hale at 27, Hale v. Texas KKK, No. 93–07414 (Tex. D. Ct. Oct. 15, 1993) (order compelling the KKK to produce its membership list), rev'd, 887 S.W.2d 1 (Tex. 1994). This fact underscores the potential conflict discussed in the text.

75. Model Rules, Rule 1.7, cmt. para. 8.

injuries. Yet such a lawsuit might very well have promoted the NAACP's interest in stamping out Klan activity.

Even if there is no formal conflict of interest, it is perfectly clear that the fundamental interests of the two organizations are directly in conflict. As the president of the Port Arthur branch succinctly stated, "The goal of the NAACP is to end discrimination. The goal of the Klan is to promote discrimination."[76] Regardless of whether the two organizations are directly involved in the same controversy or otherwise fit the formal conflicts requirements, their missions are always and irrevocably opposed.

The ethical status of "positional conflicts" of this sort is currently a hot topic among both lawyers and legal scholars. Advocates of increased regulation argue that positional conflicts undermine both loyalty and confidentiality. For example, a lawyer's effectiveness in one case might create a precedent that would weaken a client in another matter.[77] Moreover, even in circumstances where the matters at stake are unrelated, there is still a danger that the lawyer will learn confidential information from the first client that might be relevant to the position he is arguing for the second client (or vice versa).

Those who oppose increased regulation of positional conflicts emphasize that giving clients broad veto power in this area is likely to have an adverse effect on the availability of legal services in general and pro bono services in particular. Thus, many large law firms actively discourage (and sometimes even prohibit) their lawyers from engaging in pro bono or law reform activity that might create precedents that could one day be used against the firm's clients. In recognition of this danger, the Model Rules expressly provide that a lawyer may engage in certain legal services or law reform activity notwithstanding her client's adverse interests in the matter so long as there is no direct conflict.[78]

If the NAACP were an ordinary client, or Griffin was an ordinary lawyer, the balance between these two points of view would tilt against the NAACP's decision. Neither loyalty nor confidentiality concerns seem very compelling in this case. In terms of the central conflict between the NAACP and the Klan—in the words of the Port Arthur president, "ending discrimination" versus "promoting discrimination"—there is no question where Griffin's loyalties lie. Even at a more concrete level, the two clients' immediate legal interests are adverse only to the extent that the Klan seeks to rely on a legal precedent set by the NAACP that the latter organization would like to distinguish. Nor is there much danger,

---

76.   Tomaso, supra note 4, at 8B.

77.   See Model Rules, supra note 15, Rule 1.7 cmt. para. 24.

78.   See Model Rules, Rule 6.3 (legal services work); id. Rule 6.4 (law reform work).

given the legal focus of the dispute between the state and the Klan, that Griffin will betray the NAACP's confidences in the course of his work for the Klan. Finally, Griffin's work for the Klan is precisely the kind of pro bono representation that an expansive reading of the conflict rules might put in danger. Given these circumstances, the fact that a private client in the NAACP's position might not want to see an adverse precedent created in an area central to its interests is not a sufficient harm to justify denying a pro bono client the lawyer of his choice.

The NAACP, however, is no ordinary client. Instead it is an advocacy organization whose sole purpose is to advance the "positions" of its members. When one of its lawyers subverts one of these positions, it suffers an injury every bit as severe as when its economic interests are attacked. It therefore is entitled to be represented by lawyers who are passionately committed to its positions.

The result might be different if Griffin were simply a lawyer who sometimes did work for the NAACP. But his status as General Counsel placed him in a materially different position. NAACP members have a right to expect that whoever occupies this role will constantly be looking for ways to advance the group's interests as they have defined them. The NAACP might have wanted its General Counsel to help black residents in Vidor file civil suits against the Klan. Or they may have wanted their counsel to investigate the possibility of intervening in the state's enforcement suit to ensure that the views of the victims of Klan terror were not forgotten in that proceeding. Indeed, after Griffin was dismissed, the NAACP's national office filed a brief in the Texas Supreme Court in support of the Klan exception to *NAACP v. Alabama*. As General Counsel, it was his duty to fully and fairly evaluate each of these options from the vantage point of the NAACP's understanding of its interests. Once Griffin began representing the Klan, he was no longer able to perform this function effectively.

These have been trying times for the NAACP and its constituents. After years of decline, Klan activity has begun to rise. Vidor is a perfect case in point. Lowe and other Klan members used the federal court's desegregation efforts as a rallying point for increasing Klan visibility and membership. At the same time, many white Americans are skeptical about the continuing existence of pervasive, overt racism and are unsympathetic to what they perceive to be unwarranted demands for racial justice. To meet these challenges, the NAACP needs to mobilize all of the resources at its disposal. It therefore has a right to expect that its General Counsel would, in the words of a board member, "defer to another lawyer to handle matters involving the Klan."[79] When Griffin

---

79. See Moran, supra note 67, at 13A.

refused to do so, the organization was justified in looking for a General Counsel who would.

VI.   Remembering the Real Heroes

Griffin deserves to be commended for his courage and devotion to principle. Whether or not one agrees with his decision, the fact remains that he defended, at great personal risk and expense, one of our most cherished constitutional liberties in precisely the kind of situation where these freedoms are placed in greatest jeopardy. It is not surprising, therefore, that many have chosen to honor Griffin and many more have sought to publicize his cause.

Griffin's new found notoriety has clearly been something of a mixed blessing. Undoubtedly, in some respects he has profited from all of the attention. From another vantage point, the publicity (some of it quite hostile) must have felt like a burden and a distraction. Regardless of which consequence predominates, however, the resulting flood of attention and awards raises important questions about why Griffin is being honored, and what additional responsibilities ought to accompany his new celebrity status.

Those who praise Griffin have many different agendas. Civil libertarians like the ACLU seek to reward his service to their cause, encourage similar actions by other lawyers, and educate ordinary citizens about the importance of preserving constitutional rights even for society's outcasts. In other settings, however, there are likely to be more troubling motivations at work.

Consider, for example, the organized bar. As I argued earlier, the image of the lonely lawyer defending an unpopular client's constitutional rights is an important professional trope. By constantly invoking this example, the profession conveys the impression that ordinary citizens can count on lawyers to defend their most important rights. In return, the profession seeks freedom from both public scrutiny and state control. Thus, when bar leaders honor Anthony Griffin they also send the reassuring message that the profession is delivering on its stated promise to make legal counsel widely available.

The problem is that this implicit message is false. Legal counsel is not widely available except to corporations in the Fortune 500 and individuals in the top income brackets. Most lawyers do little or no pro bono work and, as I have indicated, the bar's record with respect to representing unpopular clients is spotty at best.[80] The plight of poor blacks in the legal system is even bleaker. Blacks have less access to legal

---

80.   Deborah L. Rhode, Pro Bono in Principle and in Practice 123 (2005).

services than whites at the same time that they are disproportionately more likely to encounter threatening legal problems.[81]

These sad truths do not mean that the ABA should not honor lawyers like Griffin who do fulfill their obligation to public service. At the same time, the public should not be lulled into thinking that these celebrations indicate that the bar is generally holding up its end of the social bargain. Certainly, those who are truly interested in meeting the legal needs of poor blacks should not allow Griffin's example to dissuade them from pressing for mandatory pro bono programs, liberalized unauthorized practice rules, or any other state-intervention that might actually improve this traditionally underserved population's access to justice.

Moreover, it is ironic, to say the least, that out of all of Griffin's many acts of courage and devotion to principle, the one for which he is the most celebrated involves representing an organization opposed to everything he has dedicated his life to preserving. Many factors underlie this paradoxical turn of events. The one that I want to emphasize, however, highlights the way in which even praiseworthy conduct can be harnessed in the service of an invidious cause.

As history repeatedly shows, nothing will make a black person more famous—and, in many circles, more popular—than criticizing what is perceived to be the prevailing orthodoxy among black leaders. For the NAACP's opponents, honoring Griffin presents a welcome opportunity to ridicule the civil rights organization. Not surprisingly, the NAACP has always had its share of detractors. The organization's effort to reach out to more radical elements in the black community, however, has prompted an outpouring of criticism by both conservatives and many of the group's longtime allies.[82] By celebrating Griffin's courage, these critics can chastise the NAACP for moving too far from its integrationist roots. The fact that Griffin's case also allows certain conservative critics to portray the Klan as a victim of both an overzealous government and an anti-libertarian civil rights community only adds to their anti-"p.c." glee.

Griffin cannot be held responsible for all of the many uses to which others will seek to put his story. Nor is the fact that others may misuse one's criticisms a sufficient ground for silencing dissent. Griffin can, however, try to avoid being used as a pawn for causes that ultimately disserve his broader commitment to the struggle for racial justice. Thus, even if he believes that the legal profession should be self-regulating, he should still remind his audience that honoring one man's efforts is no substitute for developing a comprehensive program designed to meet the

---

81. Rhode, supra note 14, at 111–12.

82. See Ellis Cose, The Fall of Benjamin Chaviz, Newsweek, Aug. 29, 1994, at 27; Steven A. Holmes, In Debt: After Ouster of Chaviz, Uncertainty for NAACP, N.Y. Times, Aug. 28, 1994, s 4, at 2.

black community's chronic legal needs. Similarly, even if he agrees that the NAACP has strayed too far from its roots, he should be careful not to convey the additional impression that the venerable organization is no longer an important voice that deserves attention and respect.

With few exceptions, Griffin has done everything in his power to prevent others from misstating or misusing his position.[83] Yet in all of his published interviews, he has never once mentioned the actual victims of the Klan's terror campaign in Vidor. This handful of courageous black men and women braved almost unimaginable abuse in their attempt to end segregation in Vidor once and for all. They are the real heroes in this story. Griffin's financial and psychic losses are little more than a drop in the deep bucket of their daily pain and sacrifice. It is unfortunate that neither he nor his supporters have found the time to honor their courage and commitment to principle.

VII. *Postscript*: Lawyering in a Multicultural World

In the wake of the Texas Supreme Court's decision, the media frenzy surrounding the alliance between Griffin and Lowe died down. The Commission abandoned its efforts to get the Klan's membership list in favor of pursuing civil actions against several known Klan members, including Lowe in both his individual and official capacities.[84] State officials also persuaded a handful of courageous blacks to replace those who were driven out of Vidor by the Klan's terror tactics. True to his word, Griffin did not represent the Klan in these subsequent proceedings. True to his values, Lowe continued to lead demonstrations against the government's efforts to desegregate Vidor.[85] Two years later, Lowe and the various Klan sects settled the litigation with the Commission by agreeing to stay away from the housing complex and stop harassing its black residents. Violations of the agreement are subject to a $10,000 fine.

---

83. Griffin was wrong to refer to his critics at the NAACP as racists, thereby raising the bugaboo of political correctness. See Hentoff, supra note 3, at A21 (quoting Griffin as saying, "I challenged the racism of those black folks who told me I should have let a white lawyer take that case.").

84. The Commission's Charge of Discrimination underscores the actual danger posed by Lowe and his fellow hate mongers. See Charge of Discrimination, supra note 49. According to the Charge, Lowe bragged to several Klan members that during the 1970s he bombed or vandalized a black church, a synagogue, and a radio station, (id. at 25); threatened to kill a black resident of the Vidor project, (id. at 28); organized activities designed to intimidate black residents into leaving Vidor, (id. at 28–29); threatened the health and safety of any Klan member who cooperated with the Commission's investigation, (id. at 31); and recruited and associated with others who threatened to blow up the Vidor project if it were integrated, (id. at 38–39).

85. See Cindy Horswell, No Gathering of the Klans, Houston Chron., July 8, 1995, at 37A; Mark Horvit, The Texas Klan as Divergent as its 2 Dominant Personalities, Houston Post, Dec. 4, 1994, at A1.

Although the Klan appears to have abided by the formal terms of the settlement, Klan-inspired violence against blacks in the Vidor area continued. In June 1998, just a few months after the Vidor settlement, three white residents of Jasper, Texas—a town less than sixty miles from Vidor—chained a black man named James Byrd to the back of their pickup truck by his ankles and dragged him along a rural road for more than two miles. Byrd's body, minus his head and an arm, was discovered the next day across from a local cemetery.

The incident sparked a national outcry against hate crimes. In nearby Vidor, however, it provided yet another occasion for the Klan to mobilize. Led by Darrell Flinn, a Vidor native and the Imperial Wizard (not to be confused with the Grand Dragon) of a Klan organization closely affiliated with Lowe's, the Klan sponsored a "Homekoming of Klan Rally" in Jasper to show support for the three men arrested and charged with Byrd's murder.[86] Taking a page from Lowe's playbook, Flinn was careful to style himself and his organization "as simply one more victimized group demanding its rights."[87] "We do not advocate violence anymore," he told a reporter covering the rally, unless, that is, "we are met with violence."[88]

In time, the furor surrounding the Byrd case also died down. The government secured convictions against the three men charged with Byrd's murder, two of whom were sentenced to death. In response to the public outcry over the heinous nature of the crime, the Texas House of Representatives passed the James Byrd Jr. Memorial Hate Crimes Bill. The bill, however, never became law; then governor George W. Bush failed to push the legislation, and it never reached the Senate Floor.[89] The issue of Mr. Bush's failure to support the Byrd legislation briefly resurfaced during both the 2000 and 2004 presidential campaigns, but like other race issues in both contests, it failed to garner significant public attention.

For his part, Anthony Griffin has returned to his normal routine as well. Griffin continues to practice in Galveston, Texas where he handles a variety of civil rights and civil liberties matters—although apparently none for Lowe or the Klan. Notwithstanding his dismissal by the Port Arthur Branch of the NAACP, Griffin has remained active in civil rights issues. He filed, an amicus brief on behalf of the Thurgood Marshall

---

86. Terri Langford, Klan members return to Jasper for rally on courthouse square, Oct. 11, 1998.

87. David Grann, Firestarters: My Journey to Jasper, 219 NEW REPUBLIC 16 (1998).

88. Id.

89. Michael Gillispie, Crusade: Racial and Religious Exclusivism in George Bush's America, Media Monitors Network, *available at* http://www.mediamonitors.net/gillespie12.html.

Legal Society urging the Fifth Circuit to reconsider its decision in
Hopwood v. State of Texas outlawing affirmative action, and he wrote a
law review article critical of Justices Thomas and Scalia's "colorblind"
jurisprudence.[90]

Griffin has been even more active in civil liberties matters. In his
most celebrated case since representing Lowe, Griffin represented parents and children who opposed a school practice of allowing a student to
lead a prayer over the public address system at high school football
games.[91] Griffin reported taking the case after the American Civil Liberties Union experienced difficulty finding another lawyer.[92] In a 6–3
ruling, the Court ruled in favor of Griffin's clients.[93]

Subsequent cases have also vindicated many of the positions Griffin
advocated during his representation of Michael Lowe, although, as in
Lowe's case, not without controversy.[94] In *In re Bay Area Citizens
Against Lawsuit Abuse*, the Texas Supreme Court, in striking down a
lower court order compelling a non-profit organization to disclose its
membership list, quoted extensively from its opinion in *Ex Parte Lowe*.[95]
In *Virginia v. Black*, the United States Supreme Court handed the Klan
another First Amendment victory when it struck down a jury instruction
implying that cross-burning in public is prima facie evidence of an intent
to intimidate under a state hate-crime statute.[96] In a passionately worded
dissent, Justice Clarence Thomas complained that the Court's reasoning

---

90. *See* Hopwood v. State of Texas, 84 F.3d 720 (5th Cir. 1996); Anthony P. Griffin,
Is the Diminution of Civil Rights the Road to a Color–Blind Society? The Law of Mea Culpa
Notwithstanding, 21 Thurgood Marshall L. Rev. 1 (1995–6).

91. *See* http://archive.aclu.org/court/prayer.html.

92. See Bill Jeffreys, Impact Players, Anthony Griffin: Law Firm of Anthony Griffin,
Galveston Rookie Victory, Texas Lawyer, December 18, 2000, at 70.

93. Santa Fe Independent School v. Doe, 530 U.S. 290 (2000). Not all of Griffin's
cases have been so successful. In May 2004, Griffin was sanctioned $18,000 for filing a
frivolous suit alleging employment discrimination. The judge issuing the decision called the
case "one of the most abusive of the system that this court has seen in its entire thirteen
year tenure" and noted that "even a minimal investigation into the facts and law of this
case would have revealed the abject frivolity of all of the Plaintiff's claims." News, 20
Texas Lawyer 3, May 17, 2004. In one of the many ironies that seem to spring up in this
case at every turn, the article reporting Griffin's sanction appeared fifty years to the day
after the Supreme Court issued its historic ruling in *Brown v. Board of Education*, which
paved the way for the kinds of discrimination cases that Griffin was attempting to bring.

94. This vindication does not extend to Griffin's handling of the "adopt-a-highway"
case. The Fifth Circuit refused Griffin's motion for a rehearing *en banc* of its decision
barring the Klan from adopting the stretch of highway in front of the Vidor housing
project. *See* State of Tex. v. Knights of Ku Klux Klan, 58 F.3d 1075 (5th Cir. 1995).

95. *In* re Bay Area Citizens Against Lawsuit Abuse, 982 S.W.2d 371, 379 n.6, 382
n.10 (Tex. 1998).

96. Virginia v. Black, 538 U.S. 343 (2003).

ignored the "common understanding of the Klan as a terrorist organization, which, in its endeavor to intimidate, or even eliminate those it
dislikes, uses the most brutal methods,"[97] and that as a result of the
decision, "physical safety will be valued less than the right to be free
from unwanted communications."[98] Similarly, in a recent opinion, the
Second Circuit relied on both *NAACP v. Alabama* and *Bryant v. Zimmerman* in holding that the although the First Amendment protects the
Klan's membership list, it does not invalidate an anti-masking statute of
the kind at issue in *Bryant* on the ground that prohibiting mask wearing
does not impede association.[99]

Although the arguments Griffin put forward in defending Lowe
against the state's attempt to obtain the Klan's membership lists are
now generally regarded as expressing settled law, the issues raised by
the representation itself will not be so easily put to rest. To be sure, it is
not every day that a black lawyer represents the Klan, or a Jewish
lawyer defends the rights of Nazis. Nevertheless, questions about the
relationship among professional role, group affiliation, and personal
morality arise in many more mundane areas of legal practice. Consider,
for example, a black lawyer defending a company accused of race
discrimination, or a woman defending an accused rapist, or a Korean–
American lawyer negotiating a joint venture with a Korean company. In
each of these settings, one can at least ask the question whether the
lawyer's status as a member of a given racial, gender, or national group
will or should affect the manner in which she performs her professional
role. Indeed, in the wake of the O.J. Simpson case, even black prosecutors find themselves being accused of being "Uncle Tom[s]" when they
prosecute black defendants.[100]

These kinds of questions are likely to become even more prevalent
in the future. As blacks, for example, move into the legal mainstream,
some black lawyers will inevitably find themselves representing clients
who, either directly or indirectly, participate in the subjugation of other
blacks. Similarly, as more Americans both claim and reject various

---

97. Id., at 390 (Thomas, J., dissenting)

98. Id., at 400 (Thomas, J., dissenting)

99. Church of American Knights of the Ku Klux Klan v. Kerik, 356 F.3d 197 (2d Cir. 2004).

100. See Benjamin A. Holden, A Black Prosecutor is Judged as He Seeks Conviction of Rap Star, Wall St. J., Feb. 5, 1996, at 1 (describing this phenomena as the "Darden Dilemma" after the black prosecutor in the Simpson case). For an excellent analysis of the complex issues at the intersection of identity and professional role raised by the conduct of the lawyers in the Simpson prosecution, *see* Margaret M. Russell, Beyond "Sellouts" and "Race Cards": Black Attorneys and the Straightjacketing of Legal Practice, 95 Mich. L. Rev. 766 (1997). For my own take on Russell's thoughtful analysis, *see* David B. Wilkins, Straightjacketing Professionalism: A Comment on Russell, 95 Mich. L. Rev. 795 (1997).

aspects of their racial, gender, religious, and national identity, questions about the relationship between these issues and the traditional understandings of the lawyer's role are bound to increase.

It will undoubtedly be difficult to make progress on these issues and I offer only the briefest outline here.[101] Discussions about race must circumvent a number of treacherous land mines. Chief among these is the danger that any attempt to equate status with conduct will quickly slip into either essentialism or political correctness. In addition, any discussion about the significance of black identity must confront thorny questions about who is black and whether "white" identity (or white ethnic identity) carries similar moral weight. Nevertheless, as Griffin's story illustrates, when we refuse to look at race, we miss much of what is important about these cases to both the participants and to the public.

Standing alone, neither rights theory nor effects theory provide a satisfactory mechanism for resolving these cases. Rights theorists ignore the discretionary space that every lawyer is given to choose her clients and causes. The choice that "I" should represent this client is inherently a moral one that must take account of predictable consequences in the real world. In today's America, race will often play an important role in what these consequences will be. Effects theorists, on the other hand, undervalue the weight that lawyers ought to assign to the preservation of the legal framework. The moral calculus that a lawyer should use in deciding whether to devote her professional energies to a particular client is not the same as the one she would employ if she were an ordinary citizen being asked to render non-legal assistance to this same person. Lawyers have a special responsibility to ensure that the promise of "equal justice under law" emblazoned above the entrance to the Supreme Court amounts to more than just empty rhetoric. Finally, neither of these theories tells lawyers how to balance whatever instrumental effects their actions are likely to have on others against their personal interest in moral integrity.

Once we reject these simplistic understandings, however, we are in uncharted waters. Neither professional codes nor traditional moral theory supply a convincing account of how a lawyer should balance the legitimate competing demands created by her profession, her group-affiliation, and her unique goals and aspirations. By carefully examining cases like Anthony Griffin's, we can begin to discover how these theoretical issues relate to the concrete actions that a lawyer might take on behalf of a particular client.

---

101. For my extended attempt to grapple with these complex questions, *see* David B. Wilkins, Identities and Roles: Race, Recognition, and Professional Responsibility, 57 Maryland L. Rev. 1502 (1998).

For example, Griffin's case demonstrates that notwithstanding their familiar shortcomings, carefully crafted professional rules could provide limited, but nevertheless important, guidance. Thus, even if First Amendment considerations counsel against preventing lawyers from talking to the press, the rules of professional conduct ought to make clear that a lawyer is under no obligation to follow the full-service public relations model of legal practice. Similarly, the ethics rules could distinguish between positional conflicts involving advocacy organizations and those relating to private clients, in much the same way as the solicitation rules distinguish between public interest lawyers and private practitioners in paid cases.[102]

Of course, the structure of rules, and their inevitable connection to disciplinary enforcement, places a limit on their usefulness in this context. More generally, the profession could make clear in its ethos and values that identity can play a legitimate role in defining what constitutes responsible advocacy. And, even more importantly, that ethical decisions are not simply a discrete set of on/off, yes/no choices to be made and then forgotten. A morally satisfying professional life is just that—a life long project involving a continual effort to define, balance, and account for the diverse moral commitments that legitimately call upon our efforts and beliefs.

Once one puts it in these terms, however, it is clear that difficult ethical questions are ultimately addressed to the character of individual practitioners. Studying how lawyers have attempted to negotiate the complex relationship between identity and professional role offers at least one method for the profession to reflect on which virtues will be appropriate for the multicultural legal world of the twenty-first century.

---

102. See Model Rules, Rule 7.3(a)(prohibiting in-person solicitation "when a significant motive for the lawyer's doing so is the lawyer's pecuniary gain"). See also Esther F. Lardent, Positional Conflicts in the Pro Bono Context: Ethical Considerations and Market Forces, 67 Ford. L. Rev. 2279, 2294 (1999) (arguing that "Current ethical standards and writings offer far too little guidance to enable lawyers to comfortably address the complexities of positional conflicts"); Norman W. Spaulding, The Prophet and the Bureaucrat: Positional Conflicts in Service Pro Bono Publico, 50 Stan. L. Rev. 1395 (1998) (same).

*

2

Bohatch v. Butler & Binion: The Ethics of Partners

Leslie C. Griffin[1]

For Colette Bohatch, her case was always about ethics, namely her ethical obligation to report the senior partner at Butler & Binion who was overbilling their client Pennzoil. Her belief that she was doing the right thing sustained her for eight years, from the time she reported John McDonald to her law firm's managing partner in July 1990 until the Texas Supreme Court decided her case in January 1998. Dissenting Justice Rose Spector agreed that Bohatch's case concerned ethics. Her dissent held that partners violate their fiduciary duty when they punish compliance with the ethics rules and that Butler was liable to Bohatch for damages. The case's moral lesson was summarized in the quotation from Huckleberry Finn that Spector placed in her dissent's opening lines: " 'What's the use you learning to do right when it's troublesome to do right and ain't no trouble to do wrong, and the wages is just the same?' "[2]

Butler & Binion saw the issue differently. For Butler's managing partners and their lawyers, the case was simply about coexistence in a partnership. They did not understand how a lawyer who accused her partner of misconduct could continue working with him. They believed they were justified in asking Bohatch to leave the firm. Justice Craig Enoch expressed their perspective in the opening sentence of his opinion for the Texas majority: "Partnerships exist by the agreement of the partners; partners have no duty to remain partners."[3]

Each side sought a clear solution, one upholding ethics and the other protecting partners. The court favored partnership over ethics when it ruled that the partners of Butler & Binion owed Bohatch no fiduciary

---

1. Larry & Joanne Doherty Chair in Legal Ethics, University of Houston Law Center, lgriffin@uh.edu.

2. Bohatch v. Butler & Binion, 977 S.W.2d 543, 558 (Tex. 1998).

3. Id. at 544.

duty. Although he agreed with that result, concurring Justice Nathan Hecht criticized the simple solutions of both majority and dissent. He believed that mistaken whistleblowers (like Bohatch) may not recover tort damages, even if they report misconduct in good faith, but that partners may be liable for the breach of fiduciary duty in other cases.[4]

Throughout the Bohatch case, the attempts to balance the demands of ethics against the duties of partners provoked conflicting and some-times confusing arguments about ethics, partnerships, wrongful dis-charge, breach of fiduciary duty, and breach of contract. Although the ethical issues present in Bohatch—overbilling and the attorney's obli-gation to report misconduct—are significant and recurring problems in the legal profession, in the final decision they were trumped by partner-ship law. The specific lesson of Bohatch—that whistleblowers may pay a personal or professional price for their decisions to report misconduct—illustrates a broader question that plagues the law of lawyering, i.e., to what extent can the practice of law accommodate the individual lawyer's morality?

This essay explores how the ethical issues in Bohatch were trans-formed into questions of partnership law, in the process leaving ethical questions about reporting misconduct and overbilling unresolved.

I. Ethics: Bohatch Decides to Blow the Whistle

Colette Bohatch joined the Washington, D.C. office of the Houston law firm Butler & Binion as an associate in September 1986. Immediate-ly before that she was Deputy Assistant General Counsel for Oil and Gas Litigation at the Federal Energy Regulatory Commission [FERC]. At Butler she continued her regulatory work, primarily by representing the oil company Pennzoil on FERC matters.[5] Pennzoil was the primary client of the D.C. office; indeed, the oil company was the reason why Butler & Binion had a D.C. office. Pennzoil persuaded Butler & Binion to open a Washington office in 1985 with a request that John McDonald do their regulatory work. McDonald had been Pennzoil's lawyer at Baker & Botts, another Texas law firm, until he moved to Butler and became the senior partner in Butler's D.C. office.[6] McDonald then hired Bohatch to use her FERC expertise to benefit Pennzoil.

From the time of her arrival in 1986, Bohatch worked with Mc-Donald on Pennzoil's regulatory needs. She became a partner in January 1989 based upon McDonald's recommendation; the Houston partners did not independently review the Washington office's partnership decisions.[7]

4. Id. at 554–56.

5. Id. at 544.

6. Author's Interview of Robert Hayden Burns, Houston, Texas, May 7, 2004.

7. Id.; see also December 17, 1992 Deposition of Louis Paine, p. 79, lines 15–18.

Pennzoil also wrote a letter of recommendation in support of her partnership.[8] There were then three partners in the D.C. office who worked on Pennzoil matters: Bohatch, McDonald, and Richard Powers. McDonald prepared Pennzoil's bills.

Once she became a partner, Bohatch saw the firm's written reports of attorneys' billable hours, but not the bills to Pennzoil. She worried that McDonald, whose office was next to hers, could not be working the number of hours that he billed. She saw and heard him, for example, watching the show "Exercising With Jake" on the television in his office, going out for long lunches, spending hours shopping for clothes (which he would display when he returned to the office), buying artwork for the office, taking photography lessons and taking pictures around the office. She estimated that he worked only 3–4 hours a day, but his posted hours reflected double that amount.[9]

Bohatch discussed her concerns with Richard Powers, who agreed that he occasionally had questions about McDonald's billing.[10] While McDonald was out of the office in March 1990, Bohatch and Powers took his daily diary, i.e., the desk calendar on which McDonald handwrote his billable hours, from the secretary's desk and photocopied it. From these diaries the secretaries entered the numbers that Bohatch saw in the billing reports. According to Bohatch, Powers helped her to photocopy the diaries, but Powers stated that Bohatch initiated the photocopying and then handed him a copy.[11]

The record of the daily diaries was troubling because of McDonald's notation of the words "same as" on many calendar dates. The diary for March 1990 is representative. On March 12, McDonald recorded a total of eight hours, broken down into three two-hour units and two one-hour units. All the hours were billable to Pennzoil ("PZL"), but for different matters. Then six more days—March 13, 16, 19, 20, 21, and 22—were marked "same as 12th."[12] Some days were marked "same as" even though the copied date included phone calls of specific lengths to named clients, suggesting that McDonald and the client had had conversations

---

8. Author's Interview of Colette Bohatch Mehle, Washington, D.C., May 18, 2004.

9. Colette Bohatch's Application for Writ of Error in the Supreme Court of Texas, December 15, 1995, at 10–12.

10. August 1, 1990 Letter from Colette Bohatch to Louis Paine, Plaintiff's Exhibit 3, Civil Case 91–53813; see also Deposition of Robert Bruce Reynolds, February 4, 1993, at 45 (discussing his handwritten notes of a conversation with Richard Powers indicating "R. Powers. Not comfortable with John charging time on the file."); December 1, 1992 Deposition of Richard Powers, p. 26, lines 3–22 (hours that were charged seemed high).

11. Testimony of Richard Powers, Trial Transcript, Volume V, March 17, 1993, at 609.

12. Appendix to Colette Bohatch's Application for Writ of Error in the Supreme Court of Texas, December 15, 1995, at 10–12.

of the same length, and at the same time, on different days.[13] In testimony prepared for Bohatch, Yale law professor and professional responsibility expert Geoffrey Hazard concluded, "It seems very unlikely that the hours on the subsequent day or days broke down exactly as those on the initial day, and clients would ordinarily regard such documentation as inadequate. Hence, the entry 'same' does not correspond to recognized practice."[14] Hazard observed other deficiencies in McDonald's diaries:

> For many days, the only entry is a gross number of hours (for example, "8.0") without any subdivision of time or specification of the tasks or matters involved. For many other days, the only entry is a gross number of hours and an indication of the client as "PZL," indicating Pennzoil. Under recognized standards there would be identification for each day not only of the client but of the specific matters or tasks, to facilitate review of work within the firm and to justify billings to the clients.[15]

According to Bohatch, keeping such an incomplete diary violated the law firm's billing policies; her own diaries were much more meticulous and specific in their entries.

Bohatch debated what she should do about her suspicions of misconduct. She consulted two friends who were lawyers, namely Ray Becker and Roger Mehle.[16] Although he did not work for Butler, Mehle's law firm (Royer, Mehle & Babyak) rented space within the Butler offices. Mehle had observed McDonald's work hours. Bohatch also conferred with fellow partner Richard Powers, using him as a "sounding board" to help her analyze her options. Moreover, because Bohatch was a member of the District of Columbia Bar, she consulted the D.C. Bar rules for guidance on identifying her obligations about the overbilling.[17]

In 1990, D.C. lawyers were governed by a version of the Model Code of Professional Responsibility, which did not require lawyers to report the misconduct of other attorneys to a disciplinary authority unless they

---

13. Colette Bohatch's Application for Writ of Error in the Supreme Court of Texas, December 15, 1995, at 18. The April 2, 1990 diary shows a telephone call of 1 1/2 hours with Richard Edmonson, a Pennzoil lawyer. The entries on April 3, 4, 5, and 6 simply say "same as 2nd." There were similar recordings of phone calls on April 23, with "same as" for April 24, 25, and 26.

14. Report of Geoffrey C. Hazard, Jr. to Eliot P. Tucker, Bohach [sic] v. Butler & Binion, October 1, 1992, filed in 14th Court of Appeals, Houston, Texas, October 8, 1993, No. C14-93-903.

15. Id.

16. Bohatch married Mehle in 1998.

17. Bohatch Mehle Interview, supra note 8.

were requested to do so by a "tribunal or other authority."[18] Hence Bohatch had no obligation under the bar's rules to inform the bar of allegations of McDonald's overbilling. The D.C. Bar, however, was then considering the adoption of the ABA Model Rules, which included a proposed Rule 8.3 that required attorneys "to inform the appropriate professional authority" of another attorney's violation of the Rules.[19] Bohatch recalls that a draft of the new rules crossed her desk and forced her to seriously consider reporting McDonald.[20] Although the D.C. Bar eventually adopted Model Rule 8.3, it did not apply to conduct that occurred before January 1, 1991 or to Bohatch's choice.[21] Bohatch decided that the best thing to do was to report McDonald to Butler's managing partner, Louis Paine, when she attended the firm's annual meeting.

Bohatch attended the firm's Houston meeting in July 1990 and asked Paine to meet with her. Over breakfast on Sunday, July 15, Bohatch told Paine about her suspicions of overbilling. Paine promised Bohatch that he would investigate her allegations. Although fellow Washington partner Richard Powers was also in Houston for the weekend, and observed the meeting between Bohatch and Paine, he did not join Bohatch's complaint. Bohatch informed Powers that she had reported McDonald.[22] He did not support her criticisms of McDonald from that point on. Back in Washington the next day, Monday, July 16, Powers apparently told McDonald about Bohatch's report to Paine.[23] Later that day, McDonald angrily told Bohatch that Pennzoil was dissatisfied with the quality of her work and that she could not continue to work for Pennzoil without his direct supervision. Bohatch was stunned because she had never heard any complaints about her work until she reported McDonald to the managing partner.[24]

---

18. DR 1–103(A) was in effect until January 1, 1991, and provided: "A lawyer possessing unprivileged knowledge or evidence concerning another lawyer or a judge shall reveal such knowledge or evidence upon proper request of a tribunal or other authority empowered to investigate or act upon the conduct of lawyers or judges."

19. Proposed Model Rule 8.3 provided: "A lawyer having knowledge that another lawyer has committed a violation of the Rules of Professional Conduct that raises a substantial question as to that lawyer's honesty, trustworthiness, or fitness as a lawyer in other respects, shall inform the appropriate professional authority."

20. Bohatch Mehle Interview, supra note 8.

21. Preliminary Report of Mark W. Foster to Eliot P. Tucker, September 30, 1992.

22. Bohatch, 977 S.W.2d at 544.

23. August 1, 1990 Letter from Colette Bohatch to Louis Paine, supra note 10. Powers denied that he told McDonald, see December 1, 1992 Deposition of Richard Powers, pp. 51, 54. Powers says that McDonald told him that Paine had seen Powers in the lobby in Houston. Id. at 58.

24. Bohatch, 977 S.W.2d at 558–559 (Spector, J., dissenting); December 27, 1990 Letter from Colette Bohatch to Louis Paine, Plaintiff's Exhibit 10, Civil Case 91–53813.

Bohatch complained to Paine about the retaliation and loss of work. On July 31, McDonald reassigned her Pennzoil work to a new associate. From that day, until she left the firm in September 1991, she billed no more time to Pennzoil.[25]

II.   Partnership Law: The Partners Investigate the Allegations[26]

After he spoke with Bohatch on July 15, Paine assigned the investigation of McDonald's billing to another Butler partner, Robert Hayden Burns, who had been with the firm since 1972. Burns and Paine spoke with McDonald immediately after the allegations were made. McDonald told them that Pennzoil's John Chapman, the primary contact between Pennzoil and Butler, had been unhappy with Bohatch's work for some time and had asked McDonald to supervise it.[27] McDonald told them that he had never informed Bohatch of Chapman's complaints because he "was trying to avoid controversy."[28] Now he was upset that he had not told her and others about the complaints because it would look like "he was taking punitive action because she had raised these allegations."[29] Of course, Bohatch believed that McDonald's actions were retaliatory because she had never heard any criticism of her work before she reported his overbilling.

Burns interviewed Chapman, who worked constantly with John McDonald. Burns already knew Chapman because he had represented him and Pennzoil on another matter.[30] Burns says that to call what he did an "investigation" is an "overstatement," but he did talk to Chapman and review the bills.[31] The bills did not include either the daily diaries or the firm's internal billing reports. Instead, they listed one total amount due based on services rendered. Chapman told Burns that he was satisfied with the amount of Butler's bills, but that he was concerned about the quality of Bohatch's work.[32] Chapman's supervisor at Pennzoil, Richard Edmonson, and Pennzoil General Counsel James Shaddix later agreed with Chapman that they had no problem with the bills, and both Chapman and Shaddix testified to that point at the trial.[33]

---

25. Id.

26. Author's Interview of Louis Paine, Houston, Texas, April 23, 2004.

27. Robert Hayden Burns Deposition, p. 64, lines 1–18.

28. Id. at 65, lines 4–5.

29. Id. at 65, lines 10–17.

30. Id. at. 61–62.

31. Burns Interview, supra note 6.

32. Burns Interview, supra note 6; Testimony of Robert Hayden Burns, Trial Transcript, March 17, 1993, at 567.

33. Burns Interview, supra note 6; Testimony of John Chapman, Trial Transcript Volume V, March 17, 1993, at 637–644; Testimony of James Shaddix, Trial Transcript Volume VI, March 18, 1993, at 743.

Bohatch argued that Butler and Binion had conducted a sham investigation, and that Butler had turned the Pennzoil executives against her. She believed that Butler led Chapman to think that she had retaliated against McDonald <u>after</u> McDonald criticized her work. Hence Chapman and the others thought they were protecting McDonald against Bohatch's unfair allegations, instead of the reverse.[34]

Another possible explanation for Pennzoil's support of McDonald was that the executives would look incompetent if they acknowledged that they had approved inflated bills.[35] Hayden Burns refused to believe that a "man like John Chapman, who was a very serious guy and straight shooter" would testify falsely on such a matter. Kathleen Magruder, who did FERC work at Pennzoil under Chapman's supervision, offered another explanation for Pennzoil's rejection of Bohatch's complaint. After McDonald took Pennzoil's work from Baker & Botts to Butler & Binion, Magruder explained, there was a "gentlemen's agreement" that a "certain billing level would be, if not guaranteed, at least expected every month, probably to compensate them for having taken on McDonald as a partner."[36] Chapman once told Magruder that he "always knew within a couple of thousand dollars what the bill is going to be every month."[37] With such an agreement in place, the Pennzoil executives might have been less concerned with the daily timekeeping issues that had caused Bohatch to initiate her complaint

Evidence of such a "gentlemen's agreement" might have settled the matter. If Pennzoil and Butler did not have an hourly billing agreement, then perhaps McDonald's daily diaries were irrelevant, he did not violate any billing standards, and Bohatch's complaint was unfounded. Magruder, however, never testified at the trial, and Butler did not produce evidence of a non-hourly arrangement. Moreover, Bohatch's attorney, Jamie Gorelick, expressed skepticism about this explanation of the billing. If Butler had a non-hourly agreement with Pennzoil, Gorelick explained,

> one would think that someone could have said that to Colette Bohatch at the outset. If I'd been the managing partner and another partner came to me and said I'm unhappy about the billing records and I had an agreement with the client that settled that, I would have told her about it. That would have been a very normal,

---

34. Testimony of Colette Bohatch, Trial Transcript Volume II, March 16, 1993, at 213; Colette Bohatch's Application for Writ of Error in the Supreme Court of Texas, December 15, 1995, at 21.

35. Bohatch Mehle Interview, supra note 8.

36. Author's Telephone Interview of Kathleen Magruder, July 15, 2004. Magruder was deposed by Butler & Binion but did not testify at the trial.

37. Id.

straightforward thing for them to say. They could have avoided years of litigation, I would think. If there were an explanation, it seems to me that the partners would provide the explanation [when she made the complaint].[38]

Pennzoil's support of McDonald's billing was a crucial factor to the outcome of the case. For Paine, that ended the matter. If the client was satisfied, then "what alternatives do you have? What are you going to do, fire McDonald? Take McDonald off Pennzoil?" Paine did not understand how Bohatch could continue to work in that office "for someone she called a fraud and cheat."[39] "I was faced with the prospect of her having called her boss a criminal and Pennzoil not wanting her to work for them, he said."[40] Paine flew to Washington, and, on August 23, 1990, told Bohatch that she would either have to accept a job in the Houston office or leave the firm.[41] Bohatch disputes the claim that she was offered a job in Houston.[42] She was permitted to stay at Butler while she looked for a new job; she continued to draw her partnership salary of $7,500 a month, to keep her office, secretary and benefits, and to use the firm's resources to help her find new employment.[43]

The partners considered this to be a generous arrangement, and from that point on focused on Bohatch's obligation to find a new job rather than her allegations about McDonald. Several partners also suspected that Bohatch had ulterior motives for her conduct. Burns, for example, came to believe that Bohatch's "motivation was to get McDonald out of the picture in Washington with the hope that she and Dick Powers could play a bigger role with Pennzoil."[44] Louis Paine perceived a "trumped-up deal" between Powers and Bohatch to oust McDonald. "They would love to have gotten rid of him, but they had zero chance to

---

38. Author's Telephone Interview of Jamie Gorelick, August 24, 2004.

39. Paine Interview, supra note 26.

40. Quoted in Amy Boardman, Texas Supreme Court Gives Whistleblower a Second Chance, Texas Lawyer, November 4, 1996.

41. Paine Interview, supra note 26.

42. Bohatch Mehle Interview, supra note 8; Bohatch recalls that "Paine offered her a position in the Houston office if the Pennzoil FERC work ever went away. This offer to work in the Houston office was made to Ms. Bohatch before Paine told her that she was going to have to leave the firm and the [sic] is no evidence that the offer was ever renewed after Paine allegedly determined that Ms. Bohatch's report was false. The jury could properly conclude that she did not have the opportunity to work in the Houston office and that even if she did, Respondents were not justified in requiring her to leave her home and her FERC law practice in Washington, D.C." Petitioner's [Bohatch's] Post–Submission Brief in the Supreme Court of Texas, No. 95–0934, no date stamp.

43. Bohatch, 977 S.W.2d at 558.

44. Burns Deposition, supra note 27, at p. 77, lines 19–25 and p. 78, lines 1–6.

get that business because of McDonald's relationship with the client."[45]

Bohatch carried out her search for new employment in a tight job market. In January 1991 the management committee decided not to give her a yearly bonus for 1990. A week later, the committee reduced her tentative partnership share for 1991 to nothing. Then they ended her monthly payment of $7,500 as of June 1, 1991. Those three actions formed the basis of Bohatch's breach of contract claim.[46] On August 6, 1991 she was told that she must leave the firm by November 1, 1991. Bohatch started a new job as a contract partner at the law firm of Duncan & Allen on September 4, 1991; she filed a lawsuit against Butler & Binion on October 18; she was officially expelled from the firm on October 21, 1991.[47]

III. Ethics v. Partnership Law

A. Summary of the Cases. Bohatch sued Butler & Binion for wrongful discharge, breach of fiduciary duty, and breach of contract. The case was tried to a Harris County, Texas jury on March 15–18, 1993. The wrongful discharge claim was dismissed on summary judgment. The jury found for Bohatch on both the fiduciary duty and contract claims. They awarded her $57,000 for lost wages, $250,000 for mental anguish, $4 million in punitive damages against Paine, Burns and McDonald, and attorneys' fees of $246,000.[48] Judge Scott A. Brister of the 234th District Court reduced the punitive damages against the partners to $237,141 because Bohatch had not introduced evidence of the individual partners' net worth and because he did not think partnerships could be held vicariously liable for the partners' breach of fiduciary duty.[49] Judge Brister then asked Bohatch to elect one theory—either tort or contract—for the damages award. She chose the tort (breach of fiduciary duty) claim with its punitive damages, thereby forfeiting the attorney's fees that were awarded on the contract.[50]

---

45.   Paine Interview, supra note 26.

46.   Bohatch v. Butler & Binion, 905 S.W.2d 597, 604–606 (Tex. App.—Houston [14th Dist.] 1995).

47.   Id. at 599–600.

48.   Id. The $57,000 award for lost wages included $22,000 for the lost bonus of 1990 plus $35,000 for the lost monthly pay and partnership share of 1991. The $246,000 of attorney's fees included $175,000 for trial fees and $71,000 for a conditional appeal (i.e., 50,000 for Court of Appeals, $20,000 for making an application for writ of error to the Supreme Court and $1,000 if writ of error was granted.).

49.   Brister set the following amounts for the partners: John McDonald, $74,287; Hayden Burns, $64,287; and Louis Paine $98,567. Id. at 599, 601; see also September 24, 1993 letter from Hon. Scott Brister to Eliot P. Tucker & Larry D. Knippa, filed September 24, 1993 in 234th District Court, Case No. 91–053813, Colette Bohatch v. Butler & Binion, et al.

50.   905 S.W.2d at 601.

The 14th District Court of Appeals in Houston dismissed the breach of fiduciary duty claim, but ruled that Butler & Binion had violated the partnership contract by not notifying Bohatch properly of the loss of the monthly draw and the termination of her 1991 partnership interest. The appeals court found that the firm had acted properly in denying her the 1990 bonus, however, so Bohatch was left with damages of $35,000 for lost wages plus her attorneys' fees.[51]

The Texas Supreme Court agreed there was no breach of fiduciary duty and upheld the contract award of $35,000 plus interest and attorneys' fees. By that time, the amount of fees plus interest totaled about a half million dollars, which was not covered by Butler's insurance.[52]

Although the Supreme Court's conclusion appears simple, the opinion, which included a majority, concurrence, and dissent, was not so straightforward. Indeed, from beginning to end, there was always some confusion about how to characterize the case, whether as a matter of ethics, partnerships, corporate law, breach of fiduciary duty, contract, overbilling, or the duty to report misconduct. In attempting to sway the court, Bohatch's lawyers emphasized ethics; Butler's lawyers focused on partnerships. The following sections explain the strategies the lawyers developed to persuade the courts to see things their way.

B. Trial Strategy

1. Bohatch's Pre–Trial Lawyer, Jamie Gorelick. After Paine asked Bohatch to leave the firm in September 1990, she hired Jamie Gorelick to represent her interests. Gorelick, later Deputy Attorney General of the United States and a member of the Commission Investigating the Terrorist Attacks of September 11, 2001, was then an attorney at Miller, Cassidy, Larroca & Lewin in Washington, D.C., working "as a general litigator doing all kinds of cases."[53] Bohatch hired Gorelick not only because of her prominent reputation as an officer of the D.C. Bar (she served as its president in 1992) but also because Bohatch's sister and Gorelick's husband had trained together in medicine.[54] Gorelick had been chair of the D.C. Bar Ethics Committee for many years, and was often retained on legal ethics matters including intra-firm disputes.[55]

---

51. Id. at 604–606.

52. Butler & Binion v. Hartford Lloyd's Insurance Co., 957 S.W.2d 566 (Tex. App.— Houston [14th Dist.] 1995) (ruling that the policy did not cover intentional and willful acts, and that the insurance company had no duty to indemnify for breach of contract and attorney's fees).

53. Gorelick Interview, supra note 38.

54. Bohatch Mehle Interview, supra note 8.

55. Jamie Gorelick E–Mail to Author, August 25, 2004.

Gorelick helped Bohatch with her communications with Louis Paine. She recalls that she "advised her on how to respond to the firm's objections to her having raised this complaint, and I advised her on her options in terms of where to bring a suit and generally about the sort of whistleblower cause of action. I do recall that one of her goals was to make sure that if it were not to work out to continue at Butler & Binion, then she would want to have an adequate amount of time to relocate."[56]

Under the terms of the partnership agreement, any claims against the Butler partners had to be litigated in Harris County, Texas. Gorelick and Bohatch discussed the possibility of disputing the Texas location, but they concluded that they were unlikely to prevail and that such a lawsuit would waste Bohatch's time and money.[57] Gorelick "called just about everyone [she] knew in Houston to get recommendations," until she found Houston lawyer Eliot P. Tucker, who then represented Bohatch until all the appeals ended in the Texas Supreme Court. [58]

2. Bohatch's Trial Lawyer, Eliot Tucker

Tucker took Bohatch's case on a contingency fee basis, while Bohatch paid the expenses throughout the litigation. Tucker believed that Texas partnership law favored Bohatch and that she could do as well in Texas as in Washington, D.C. They discussed potential problems. Would a Texas jury support Bohatch, a single, female, Catholic, Ohio native who had attended New York's Manhattanville College, graduated from Washington's Georgetown University and Catholic University School of Law, begun her legal career as a prosecutor in Ohio, become a partner in the D.C. office of a prominent Houston firm, and didn't speak like a Southerner? Tucker concluded he "never had a case that he thought was going to be as appealing to a jury"[59] because "there was a strong sense in Texas that you don't cheat people. I felt people in Houston would applaud what she did. People in Texas always talk about doing what was right, and I never saw anyone do a better job of doing what was right than Colette. So I thought I had an enormously appealing case."[60]

Tucker was right about Colette Bohatch and the Texas jury. She was "a superb and stunningly good witness," as the damages award reflected.[61] Because "the Client is always Exhibit A to somewhere near the end of the alphabet," Tucker credited Bohatch for the jury's verdict.[62]

---

56. Gorelick Interview, supra note 38.

57. Bohatch Mehle Interview, supra note 8.

58. Gorelick Interview, supra note 38.

59. Author's Interview of Eliot P. Tucker, May 27, 2004.

60. Id.

61. Id.

62. Id.

Bohatch returned the praise, commenting on how effectively Tucker had presented the evidence to the jury, especially the documentary evidence about the overbilling.[63] The jury understood that you don't make the same length phone call for several days in a row![64] Trial Judge Brister observed that Tucker was "one of the best I saw in 11 years as a trial judge. He looks like an accountant, never questions a ruling, never gets excited, never raises his voice ... and in my experience jurors always gave him every dime he asked for."[65] Bohatch felt relieved and vindicated by the jury's verdict, because "a lot of hard work" had gone into the trial. From the beginning she was actively involved in the lawsuit, attending depositions in D.C. and Texas, and traveling to Houston for the trial, in addition to paying all litigation expenses from her own pocket.[66]

Tucker was mistaken ("on all three levels"), however, in believing that the Texas judges would also support his upstanding client with her "absolute regard for the truth."[67] The ethics emphasis of the trial court diminished as the appeals courts focused on the duties of partners.[68]

3. Legal Theories of the Trial

a. Wrongful Discharge

Most employment agreements involve employment-at-will contracts that allow employers to fire employees for any reason and without cause. If Bohatch's employment was at-will, she could not prevail in wrongful discharge litigation against Butler & Binion. Some state courts, however, have recognized limitations on at-will employment.[69] In some circumstances, workers may sue in tort for their firing under the tort of retaliatory or wrongful discharge.[70] Illinois, for example, recognizes the tort of retaliatory discharge where the employee's discharge contravenes a clearly mandated public policy.[71] In a 1991 case that involved a lawyer whistleblower (an in-house counsel who reported his client's dangerous dialyzers to the FDA), however, the court dismissed the retaliatory

---

63. Bohatch Mehle Interview, supra note 8.

64. Id.

65. July 27, 2004 E-mail from (Texas Supreme Court) Justice Scott A. Brister to Author.

66. Bohatch Mehle Interview, supra note 8.

67. Tucker Interview, supra note 59.

68. See generally Bohatch, supra note 46.

69. See generally Clyde W. Summers, Employment at Will in the United States: The Divine Right of Employers, 3 U. Pa. J Lab. & Emp. L. 65 (2000).

70. See generally Elletta Sangrey Callahan & Terry Morehead Dworkin, The State of State Whistleblower Protection, 38 Am. Bus. L. J. 99 (2000).

71. Palmateer v. International Harvester Co., 85 Ill.2d 124 (1981).

discharge lawsuit because the public policy of protecting the public's safety was "adequately safeguarded" by the Rules of Professional Conduct.[72] In other words, the court reasoned that the attorney should not be rewarded with tort damages, because he was already obligated to report misconduct by the bar's professional rules. As the court explained, "all attorneys know or should know that at certain times in their professional career, they will have to forgo economic gains in order to protect the integrity of the legal profession."[73] A dissenting justice complained that the court's holding was unrealistic because fidelity to the bar rules does not provide sufficient incentive for attorneys to report misconduct and thus provides an "inadequate safeguard" for the public's well-being.

Other states, however, have disagreed about what circumstances merit a tort exception to the at-will doctrine,[74] especially for lawyers and in-house counsel.[75] Bohatch hoped that Texas would allow a wrongful termination lawsuit for Butler's retaliation against her report of McDonald's overbilling.

Another method of getting around the at-will bar is to bring suit on a contract theory. In a 1992 New York case, *Wieder v. Skala*, an associate in a law firm was fired after he reported the misconduct of another attorney in the firm to the state bar association.[76] The Court of Appeals did not allow Wieder to sue for the tort of abusive or wrongful discharge, because it believed it was the legislature's job to extend statutory protection to whistleblowers, not the court's job to grant them common law protection.[77] Nonetheless, the Court of Appeals permitted Wieder's breach of contract cause of action to proceed on the theory that there was an implied obligation of good faith and fair dealing that limited the firm's ability to fire Wieder. The implied term is that both the associate and the firm must conduct themselves in accordance with the ethical standards of the profession.[78] If the law firm had fired Wieder

---

72. Balla v. Gambro, 584 N.E.2d 104, 109 (Ill. 1991); see also Jacobson v. Knepper & Moga, P.C., 706 N.E.2d 491 (Ill. 1998) (declining tort of retaliatory discharge for an associate in a law firm).

73. Id. at 110.

74. Callahan & Dworkin, supra note 70, at 105.

75. See generally Crews v. Buckman Laboratories, 78 S.W.3d 852 (Tenn. 2002); Burkhart v. Semitool, Inc., 5 P.3d 1031 (Mont. 2000); GTE Products Corp. v. Stewart, 653 N.E.2d 161 (Mass. 1995); General Dynamics Corp. v. Rose, 876 P.2d 487 (Cal. 1994); McGonagle v. Union Fid. Corp., 556 A.2d 878 (Pa. 1989); Willy v. Coastal Corp., 647 F.Supp. 116 (S.D.Tex. 1986).

76. 609 N.E.2d 105 (N.Y. 1992).

77. Id. at 110.

78. Id.

for complying with his ethical obligations, then it breached its implied obligation of good faith and fair dealing, the court reasoned.

Bohatch's claim for wrongful termination for retaliatory discharge was dismissed by trial judge Scott Brister on summary judgment because Texas law does not permit a cause of action for a private employee whistleblower. In *Sabine Pilot*, the Texas Supreme Court recognized only a "very narrow exception" to the employment-at-will doctrine, allowing a cause of action only for the "discharge of an employee for the sole reason that the employee refused to perform an illegal act."[79] The court later declined to recognize an exception to at-will employment for "private employees who are discharged for reporting illegal activities."[80] (In 2001, the implications of the same *Sabine Pilot* precedent became prominent after Sherron Watkins alerted Kenneth Lay to questionable accounting practices at Enron.)[81] In 1993, the Texas precedents did not help Bohatch. Judge Brister allowed Bohatch to amend her petition to allege facts sufficient to meet the Texas standard. She argued that Butler had required her to participate in the illegal billing of Pennzoil and hence his conduct fell within the *Sabine Pilot* exception. [82]Although Tucker made some attempts to fit her situation within the wrongful discharge case law, Butler had not asked Bohatch to perform an illegal act; as Tucker noted, "No one had asked Colette to record untrue hours or sign off on the bill."[83] Butler won the summary judgment motion on retaliatory discharge.

The Texas court was equally unreceptive to the breach of contract claim, according to Tucker:

> We cited the *Wieder* case but did not argue that there was a duty of good faith and fair dealing based on contract—the partnership agreement, in this case. Except in the context of first party insurance litigation, the Texas courts have consistently and repeatedly rejected arguments that contracts create an implied obligation of good faith and fair dealing. That argument succeeded in that context because of the unequal bargaining power between an insurance company and an individual insured. It was also a very different court that bought that argument. Furthermore, since *Sabine Pilot v. Hauck*, the Supreme Court has rejected every effort to argue that

---

79. Sabine Pilot Serv., Inc. v. Hauck, 687 S.W.2d 733 (Tex. 1985).

80. Winters v. Houston Chronicle Publ. Co., 795 S.W.2d 723, 724 (Tex. 1990).

81. See E-mail from Carl Jordan to Sharon Butcher, August 24, 2001, available at http://energycommerce.house.gov/107/hearings/02142002Hearing489/tab18.pdf (concluding that Watkins did not have a whistleblower suit under Texas law).

82. Plaintiff's First Amended Petition in the District Court of Harris County, Texas, 234th Judicial District, No. 91–53813, filed April 3, 1992.

83. Tucker Interview, supra note 59.

any non-statutory limitations on employment at will exist. Arguing either theory to that court would have likely evoked eye rolling, I believe.[84]

It was gradually becoming apparent that the ethics issue had no legal home; this whistleblower could find no remedy in whistleblower law.

b. Tort and Contract based on the Partnership Agreement

Unlike the Illinois and New York lawyers, however, Bohatch was a partner in a law firm, not an in-house counsel or an associate. She could therefore argue that partners had a higher duty not to engage in retaliatory discharge. The partnership agreement gave rise to claims in both tort and contract law. In effect, the agreement created fiduciary duties for the Butler partners—duties that Bohatch would argue they breached. The partnership was also a contract, including terms governing the dismissal of a partner—terms that Butler breached in terminating Bohatch. Judge Brister allowed the case to proceed on those two theories: breach of partners' fiduciary duties (tort), and breach of the partnership agreement (contract).

The key tort issue was whether partners had a fiduciary duty not to expel a partner who reported misconduct. According to Brister, the case "was about ethics, which is why I submitted the breach of fiduciary duty question (and got reversed)."[85] He "would not have guessed at the time that the partners involved owed no fiduciary duty to each other" in these circumstances.[86]

The absence of a fiduciary duty, however, was the central argument of Butler's trial lawyers, Larry Knippa and Joseph Kral, which succeeded on appeal.

4. Butler's Trial Lawyers, Joseph Kral and Larry Knippa

Louis Paine called the law firm of Knippa and Kral after he received Gorelick's about Colette Bohatch. Following the firm's advice, Butler & Binion formally expelled Bohatch from the partnership on October 21, 1991. This formal notification complied with the terms of the partnership agreement, and became important to the assessment of Bohatch's contract damages.[87] Because of the notification, Judge Brister ruled that Bohatch could collect damages only up to October 21.[88] Accordingly he granted summary judgment for Butler on breach of fiduciary duty and

---

84. E–Mail from Eliot Tucker to Author, July 29, 2004.

85. Brister E–Mail, supra note 65.

86. Brister E–Mail, supra note 65.

87. Author's Telephone Interview of Joseph Kral, July 12, 2004.

88. 905 S.W.2d at 600.

breach of contract after that October date, denying her claim of $1,500,000 for post-October 21 damages.[89] Bohatch was thus unable to recover the lost earnings of the difference between her salary at Duncan & Allen and her higher salary at Butler. Tucker criticized the judge's ruling while acknowledging that he had made a mistake in dealing with Butler. "We decided we would make an effort before filing the lawsuit, to write to Butler and ask them to reconsider and put her back on the job. That proved to be a mistake. Not only did they not put her back, they then went through the right procedures."[90] Tucker complained the ruling denying damages after October 21 was "ridiculous": "It's as if you hit someone and broke their leg and then three weeks later you come to the same red light and now you've done the right thing by not hitting them at this second trip to the intersection."[91] By contrast, Judge Brister took the view that a Texas employee could not claim damages for constructive discharge: "if the firing wasn't wrongful (and the Texas Supreme Court said it was not because it complied with the firm contract), she was not entitled to future damages."[92]

Knippa and Kral split the trial work. Kral knew before trial that the facts looked bad; he expected a jury to sympathize with Colette Bohatch. Hence the jury verdict "was not unexpected; in fact it was anticipated."[93] Kral thought Bohatch appeared as "a presentable witness, who looked like an aggrieved, injured person, like an employee as opposed to a partner in a law firm." Louis Paine agreed that the jury never understood that Bohatch was a partner and not an associate, and thus awarded her damages as an aggrieved employee.[94] After all, "jurors are usually sympathetic to people they perceive to be underdogs."[95]

Because the facts were against them, Kral and Knippa focused on the law, arguing that the case was about a narrow issue in partnership law, not about ethics and whistleblowers. Kral "read every case he could find" on Texas partnership law, and concluded over and over again that Butler owed no duty to Bohatch. "Under the facts we believed that duties owed by a partnership to a partner were very limited. Their claims were much too broad for what a partner's duties were."[96] Kral's

89. Appellant's Brief in the Court of Appeals for the Fourteenth Supreme Judicial District, No. 14–93–00903–CV, February 28, 1994, at 43.

90. Tucker Interview, supra note 59.

91. Id.

92. The Court of Appeals did not address this issue because it did not remand for a new trial, 905 S.W.2d at 608.

93. Kral Interview, supra note 87.

94. Paine Interview, supra note 26.

95. Brister E–Mail, supra note 65.

96. Id.

hopes rested with the appellate judges; "I always have faith in the appellate courts on a matter of law."[97] During the trial, he did everything he could to preserve the partnership issue for the appeal.

Even Kral, however, did not anticipate the $4 million in punitive damages against the three partners. He took the jury's award of over $1 million in damages against Hayden Burns (who had merely investigated the initial allegations) as further proof that no one could have won the case with the jury.[98] The Butler partners saw the verdict differently. They were unpleasantly surprised by the high damages assessed against them, and were critical of their trial lawyers' performance. They hired different lawyers for the appeal.[99]

In retrospect, Kral would like "to convince every ethics professor in the world that Bohatch is not an ethics case."[100] He disagrees that Bohatch was a whistleblower dismissed for reporting misconduct; instead she was fired because she was "an unproductive worker" who stayed at Butler while not billing any time for ten months.[101] Moreover, he insisted that before she reported McDonald, her billable hours were declining and Chapman was unhappy with her work. Chapman testified about his dissatisfaction with Bohatch's work for Pennzoil.[102] Gorelick disagreed with both Kral's facts and his conclusion:

> As I understand it, she was very productive until they told her she could no longer work on Pennzoil and provided her no other work to do. It's a little bit circular to say that she was unproductive, if what they're saying is that she didn't do any work after they took her off the case that had been her full-time occupation.[103]

Kral established one important legal basis for the appeal when he objected to Question 2a of the jury instructions, which asked:

> "Was there a breach of fiduciary duty owed by Defendants to Colette Bohatch that proximately caused damages to Colette Bohatch?"

> "Breach of fiduciary duty" means a failure to act fairly, honestly, in the utmost good faith, with undivided loyalty, or with full disclosure of all material information. Termination of a partner in accordance

97. Kral Interview, supra note 87.

98. Id.

99. Paine Interview, supra note 26.

100. Kral Interview, supra note 87.

101. Id.

102. See September 23, 1992 Deposition of John Chapman, p. 12, lines 1–10 (first criticism of Bohatch's work was in summer 1989).

103. Gorelick Interview, supra note 38.

with the Partnership Agreement does not constitute a breach of fiduciary duty.[104]

The jury had answered yes. Kral objected that this instruction was improper and that the trial court should have identified the four specific duties of partners under Texas law rather than a general duty of loyalty. He argued that his client could not win under this partnership defini- tion; the "undivided loyalty" term was "almost like you can never terminate a partner."[105] Kral thought the Court of Appeals got it right when it went "straight down the line" on denying the breach of fiduciary duty claim.[106]

C. The Appeals.

Bohatch and Tucker hired Victor Thomas to write the briefs for the appeals; Tucker made the oral argument in the Supreme Court. Butler & Binion hired Richard Countiss to represent the firm; David Holman represented the three partners who were assessed punitive damages. The Butler partners hired two lawyers because of a possible conflict of interest about the entire partnership's liability for the individual part- ners' damages. Countiss and Holman never ran into an actual conflict, however; they submitted their briefs together, edited each other's briefs, and split the oral argument in the Supreme Court.[107]

At the end of the trial, Bohatch had accepted the remittitur of the punitive damages to $237,141 in lieu of a new trial. She appealed the remittitur as well as the trial court's grant of summary judgment to Butler on the wrongful termination claim.[108] On the latter point, she attempted to fit her facts within the *Sabine Pilot* exception by arguing that she "was unacceptably forced to choose between continuing to participate in the sending of fraudulent invoices, exposing herself to both criminal and civil liability, or risking discharge by reporting the activi- ty."[109] Butler & Binion countered that those facts did not fit the narrow *Sabine Pilot* exception of being asked to do something unlawful.[110] Because Bohatch asked the court to review this issue only if a new trial was granted, the appeals courts never addressed the merits of her

---

104. Bohatch, 905 S.W.2d at 601.

105. Kral Interview, supra note 87.

106. Id.

107. Author's Interview with Richard Countiss, Houston, Texas, May 6, 2004.

108. Appellant's Brief in the Court of Appeals for the Fourteenth Supreme Judicial District, No. 14–93–00903–CV, February 28, 1994.

109. Id. at 45.

110. Appellees'/Cross–Appellants' Brief in the Court of Appeals for the Fourteenth Supreme Judicial District, July 6, 1994, No. 14–93–00903–CV, at 68–69.

lawsuit for wrongful termination.[111] This whistleblower's case thus did not provide a precedent on whistleblowing or the law of retaliatory discharge.

Butler cross-appealed the breach of fiduciary duty claim, arguing that the trial court had misunderstood the law of partnership and discovered a breach of fiduciary duty where none existed. That partnership issue (i.e., whether partners owed a fiduciary duty not to expel a partner who reports misconduct) was a question of first impression for the Texas courts. Under both Texas common law and the Texas Uniform Partnership Act, partners owed the following fiduciary duties to each other: (1) full disclosure of all matters affecting the partnership; (2) accounting for all partnership profits and property; and (3) refraining from competition with the partnership.[112] Recall that Kral had argued that the "undivided loyalty" language of the jury instruction was much too broad.[113] The Court of Appeals gave him and the appellate lawyers a narrow and focused ruling on partnership law when it concluded that, although "partners have a general fiduciary duty not to expel other partners from the partnership in bad faith," bad faith "means only that partners cannot expel another partner for self-gain."[114] Despite the jury's verdict for the plaintiff, as well as Bohatch's argument that Butler had profited from maintaining Pennzoil as a client and taking over Bohatch's partnership interest, the Court of Appeals concluded that there was insufficient evidence that Butler's partners intended to act for self-gain.[115] Accordingly, the appellate court dismissed the fiduciary duty claim and allowed Bohatch to recover only part of her contract damages, not the full amount awarded by the trial court.[116]

Bohatch's appellate specialist Victor Thomas thought this rejection of the self-gain argument was "completely wrong" because the court should have allowed all reasonable inferences to be drawn in favor of the jury's verdict.[117] He and Tucker submitted an application for writ of error to the Texas Supreme Court to hear the case. Because the partnership issue was "clearly an issue of first impression," Thomas was "very confident" the court would take the case; he was "stunned" when

111. Bohatch, 905 S.W.2d at 608.

112. Bohatch, 905 S.W.2d at 602 (citations omitted).

113. See supra notes 104–106 and accompanying text.

114. 905 S.W.2d at 602 (emphasis added).

115. Id. at 603.

116. Id. at 606. The Court subtracted $22,000 from the jury's original award of $57,000 because it ruled that she had been properly notified of her reduction of her partnership interest for 1990.

117. Author's Interview with Victor Thomas, Houston, Texas, May 21, 2004.

they rejected the application.[118] The litigants did not quit; Bohatch, Tucker and Thomas decided to "be creative and do something different to try and grab the court's attention" with a new Motion for Rehearing.[119] Bohatch later explained why she pushed the Supreme Court to hear her case, even though she had prevailed on the contract issue in the Court of Appeals:

> I wanted a decision on the ethics issue. I was not going to give up no matter how bad the decision was going to be. I felt I wanted the court to step up and render their decision so it would be on the record—good or bad, they had to go on the record. I was hoping we would prevail on that and there would be a good standard out there.[120]

As a result of their deliberations and with a little "inspiration from God," Thomas submitted an unusual new Motion for Rehearing. The motion was written as an interview of Bohatch, Tucker and Thomas, conducted by a reporter from a fictional "National Association of Corporate Consumers of Legal Services."[121] The motion urged the court to recognize the ethical implications of the case and its importance to consumers who were at risk of being overbilled if whistleblowers were denied protection. Thomas had never written such a brief before, but it was effective.[122] Butler's lawyer, David Holman, did not think the court would pay attention to it. He filed a letter acknowledging that the brief was "creative," but insisting that it did not offer new reasons for the court to hear the case.[123] Nonetheless, Holman reports, the court "grant-

---

118.   Id.; 39 Tex. Sup. Ct. J. 725 (June 14, 1996).

119.   Id.

120.   Bohatch Mehle Interview, supra note 8.

121.   Thomas Interview, supra note 117; Motion for Rehearing of the Court's Denial of Colette Bohatch's Application for Writ of Error in the Supreme Court of Texas, No. 95–0934, July 26, 1996.

122.   Thomas Interview, supra note 117. I asked both Texas Supreme Court Justices Craig Enoch and Nathan Hecht about this unusual brief. Although they did not remember this specific brief, both acknowledged that the Court occasionally does grant motions for rehearing because of an effective and unusual brief. Justice Enoch explained that, if a lawyer loses the original application for writ of error, it makes sense to try a new approach on the second, especially if the lawyer knows how to use humor appropriately. (He added that good humor is much more effective than berating the Court for not granting review the first time). Justice Hecht observed that 99% of the motions either complain that the Court didn't read the brief (so here it is one more time) or they call the Court "complete idiots," for letting the issue go by. Of course neither one of those motions is going to get a very favorable treatment! "It is the motion that comes in and says okay we took our best shot, thought this would be important—we were wrong—but this is important—not making reality sufficiently clear, let us try again—that works." Author's Telephone Interview of Justice Craig Enoch, July 26, 2004 and of Justice Nathan Hecht, July 27, 2004.

123.   August 15, 1996 Letter from David W. Holman to the Honorable Justices of the Texas Supreme Court, 95–0934, filed August 22, 1996.

ed the review and set the case for oral argument completely out of the blue," without even getting a response from Holman.[124] Holman then responded in kind; his brief imagined a conversation between the judge and a briefing attorney debating the merits of the case and poking fun at the odd Thomas motion.[125]

Bohatch also commissioned amicus briefs on her behalf. She went to the law library on weekends to read law review articles related to her case and spent hours tracking down amici. A brief on partnership duties was submitted by Professor Robert Hamilton because Bohatch and her attorneys hoped that the Texas court would be influenced by the respected University of Texas law professor's partnership expertise. On one trip to the library, she discovered the Wieder case involving the law firm associate whistleblower from New York. She called Wieder, who told her about Southern Illinois University School of Law Professor Leonard Gross's brief on his behalf. Bohatch called Gross, who submitted a brief joined by six other professors.[126] Because of his victory in Wieder, Gross expected to succeed in Bohatch; her case "looked every bit as strong as Wieder's."[127] His amicus brief argued that Bohatch did not have to show self-gain by the partners; bad faith included expulsion for reporting misconduct. The professors warned that "[t]he right of any client not to be overcharged may be rendered meaningless if the lawyers who have the basic information on whether overcharging has occurred cannot come forward without risk of being terminated without adequate recourse."[128] Moreover, on the whistleblower point, the professors distinguished the Texas precedents. For non-lawyer whistleblowers, the courts should defer to the legislature. For lawyer whistleblowers, however, there was no need for deference, because the courts regulate attorney conduct.[129]

When the Bohatch briefs were submitted, Chief Justice Thomas R. Phillips and Justices Nathan L. Hecht, Priscilla R. Owen, Rose Spector,

---

124. 40 Tex. Sup. Ct. J. 725 (June 14, 1996); Author's Interview of David Holman, July 23, 2004. Under the Texas Rules in effect at that time, Holman was not under any obligation to file a response unless the court requested one.

125. Respondents Paine, Burns and McDonald's Reply Brief in the Supreme Court of Texas, No. 95–0934–CV, November 15, 1996.

126. Bohatch Mehle Interview, supra note 8. Professors Richard L. Abel (University of California at Los Angeles School of Law), David J. Luban (University of Maryland School of Law), Gary Minda (Brooklyn Law School), Ronald D. Rotunda (University of Illinois College of Law), Theodore J. Schneyer (University of Arizona College of Law), and Charles W. Wolfram (Cornell Law School) joined Gross on the brief. 977 S.W.2d at 553; Brief of Amicus Curiae in the Supreme Court of Texas, No. 95–0934, February 2, 1996.

127. Author's Telephone Interview with Leonard Gross, April 20, 2004.

128. Brief of Amicus Curiae, supra note 126.

129. Brief of Amicus Curiae in the Supreme Court of Texas, No. 95–0934, February 2, 1996 at 11.

Raul A. Gonzalez, Gregg Abbott, James A. Baker, Craig T. Enoch, and John Cornyn sat on the court.[130] Justice Abbott recused himself because he had worked for Butler & Binion.[131] Tucker made the oral argument for Bohatch, while Countiss and Holman split their time on behalf of Butler & Binion. Holman argued the breach of fiduciary duty and Countiss addressed the contract. Holman's main strategy was to claim that Butler had behaved ethically and honorably throughout its dealings with Ms. Bohatch:

> She sounded like a whistleblower who had been harmed, but that's not exactly what happened. It seemed to me that the firm had done everything right—they investigated it, went through and told the corporation about the overbilling, asked the client to look into it, had objective people investigate it.[132]

During the oral argument, Holman tried to keep the focus on the fact that "the firm didn't do anything wrong," and indeed had "done everything properly."[133]

The court issued its decision on January 20, 1998.[134] Justice Enoch delivered the opinion of the court, joined by Justices Gonzalez, Owen, Baker, and Hankinson. Justice Hecht concurred, while Justice Spector, joined by Chief Justice Phillips, dissented. Justice Enoch's opinion provided a clear, simple rule that, because partners "have no duty to remain partners," there is no duty "not to expel a partner who reports suspected overbilling by another partner."[135] Justice Hecht concurred to make the point that partners may (in other circumstances) owe a fiduciary duty to partners who accurately report misconduct, but that Bohatch's report was incorrect. Justice Spector dissented; in her view, partnerships may dismiss partners who report misconduct but may be liable for damages when they do so. The court upheld the breach of contract damages of $35,000 plus attorney's fees and interest. Butler

---

130. Deborah Hankinson replaced Cornyn on October 28, 1997, after the oral argument in Bohatch but before the opinion was issued.

131. After the Court set oral argument, Eliot Tucker sent a letter to Justice Priscilla Owen, asking her to recuse herself on her own motion because he had heard from a neighbor that she had represented Pennzoil when she was a lawyer at Andrews and Kurth. Tucker Interview, supra note 59; November 11, 1996 Letter from Eliot P. Tucker to Justice Priscilla R. Owen. The usual procedure is for attorneys to file a recusal motion, not a letter. Countiss Interview, supra note 107. The Court's clerk responded to Tucker that lawyers' correspondence should not be directed to individual justices and responded that Justice Owen would not recuse herself. November 13, 1996 Letter from John T. Adams, Clerk of the Supreme Court of Texas, to Eliot P. Tucker.

132. Holman Interview, supra note 124.

133. Id.

134. Bohatch v. Butler & Binion, 977 S.W.2d 543 (Tex. 1998).

135. Id. at 545 (emphasis added).

paid Tucker just under $500,000, which covered the contract damages, expenses and attorneys' fees.[136] From that award, Tucker paid Bohatch her damages and reimbursed her for expenses.[137]

Holman was "elated" to win; it was an important professional moment for him.[138] When the Court of Appeals has held in your favor, he explained, the Supreme Court is usually granting review to reverse.[139] Although Bohatch prevailed on the breach of contract issue, Butler's lawyers felt victorious in avoiding the higher tort award with its punitive damages.[140] Managing partner Louis Paine was somewhat less elated, because the damages were not covered by the firm's insurance. In retrospect, Paine noted that his lawyers could have fought harder on the contract issue, but also acknowledged that he could have followed some of his partners' advice and settled the case before it went all the way to the Supreme Court.[141]

Under the majority's analysis, the only remedy for Bohatch's whistleblowing arose from the odd circumstance that the partnership had failed to give her written notice of a change in her compensation. Although Bohatch won the contract claim, she did not receive the ethics precedent that she had hoped to establish:

> From an ethics standpoint, it's a loss, but on the contract a win. As far as the long-term effects of the case, the ethics thing was disappointing, but I still think that you have to get a decision from the court. That's what they're paid for, to make decisions in hard cases. I don't like the decision but I wanted to make them make the decision.[142]

The case was hard because, as appellate attorney Countiss explained, there was a "true dilemma" at its core, the debate between ethics and partners that had dogged the parties throughout the litigation:

> I think Ms. Bohatch had the right to complain as she did, but under the contractual agreement, contract, and the law of partnership, the partners had the right to ask her to leave the firm. I say that

---

136. Holman Interview, supra note 124.

137. Tucker Interview, supra note 59.

138. Holman Interview, supra note 124.

139. Id.

140. Countiss Interview, supra note 107.

141. Paine Interview, supra note 26. The participants reflected that it was unlikely that the case would settle. For Bohatch, it was important to get an ethics precedent on the books; the partners, especially the three who were assessed punitive damages, wanted to remove the stain on their reputation that such a judgment suggested. According to Thomas, "Colette didn't want to settle," and Paine stated: "I don't like to settle cases." Thomas Interview, supra note 117; Paine Interview, supra note 26.

142. Bohatch Mehle Interview, supra note 8.

recognizing that the dilemma posed by that arrangement is a true dilemma. What happens to [whistleblowers] when they do what they think is right and get kicked out of a law firm? On the other hand, what happens to a partnership if you have partners who don't trust each other, or don't like each other? That's the dilemma.[143]

IV. The Whistleblower's Dilemma

"How could the bar have a rule requiring a lawyer to report and not protect that partner?" asked Colette Bohatch Mehle.[144]

Whistleblowers are not usually popular; pejorative labels—rat, tattletale, snitch—make this clear. They frequently suffer severe losses in their professional and personal lives after they report misconduct.[145] Bohatch's story illustrates many of the difficulties that whistleblowers confront. She reported the misconduct on July 15; only one day later her Pennzoil assignments were taken away and her previous work for Pennzoil was called into question.[146] By August she was asked to leave the firm. The other Butler partners overlooked McDonald's billing and Bohatch's pre-reporting accomplishments, while accusing Bohatch of being unable to attract new clients for the law firm and to find a new job. Her partners and their lawyers, moreover, soon identified three theories to support their argument that Bohatch was not a true whistleblower. First, they asserted that she had been part of a cabal (with Richard Powers) to overthrow McDonald and acquire the Pennzoil representation for herself.[147] Second, they attributed her complaint against McDonald to her vindictive response to his and Chapman's criticism of her work. They claimed she had blown the whistle to protect herself from poor work evaluations. Third, they pointed to a minor office dispute between Bohatch and McDonald about the misdelivery of an

---

143. Countiss Interview, supra note 107. See, e.g., Margaret Kline Kirkpatrick, Partners Dumping Partners: Business Before Ethics in Bohatch v. Butler & Binion, 83 Minn. L. Rev. 1767, 1798 (1999) (Court "should have created an exception to the employment-at-will rule for whistleblowing partners and associates on the basis of the public policy of encouraging ethics in the legal profession."); Lindsay M. Oldham & Christine M. Whitledge, The Catch–22 of Model Rule 8.3, 15 Geo. J. Legal Ethics 881, 882 (2002) (explaining that striking the balance against whistleblowers leaves them without an incentive to report misconduct: "Currently, if a lawyer is fired for reporting misconduct, he will have little success in recovery through a suit for retaliatory discharge. Conversely, there is little to fear for a failure to report misconduct.").

144. Bohatch Mehle Interview, supra note 8.

145. See generally Terance D. Miethe, Whistleblowing at Work: Tough Choices in Exposing Fraud, Waste, and Abuse on the Job (1999).

146. Powers stated that Chapman and McDonald had expressed some disappointment with her work before July 1990; both testified to weaknesses in some of her work for Pennzoil.

147. See supra notes 44–45 and accompanying text.

important item of Bohatch's mail as the reason for the report to Paine. After McDonald had given a cavalier response to her request that her mail be delivered properly, they argued that she decided to get even by reporting him to Paine.[148] As Holman recalls, "Bohatch was not the saint. She admitted that at the time she brought up overbilling allegations she was upset and pissed off with McDonald because of the mail. She admitted that on the stand."[149] Countiss agrees: "You have to reach hard to reach the conclusion she was a whistleblower."[150]

Bohatch vigorously disputed all three arguments. The alleged cabal with Richard Powers is inconsistent with his steadfast refusal to support her after the report to Paine. Bohatch believes that the law firm discredited her by telling Pennzoil that, <u>after</u> McDonald and Chapman criticized her work, she retaliated by reporting McDonald. Finally, she rejected the mail complaint as ridiculous. It was not misdelivered mail that persuaded Bohatch to complain about McDonald; rather, she was genuinely troubled by observing McDonald's work hours in the office next door. She pondered her responsibilities because of the D.C. Bar's new reporting rules. She reported him because she was "raised to do the right thing." Bohatch identified several influences that persuaded her to persist in doing the right thing during the long years that the case dragged on. She had an "old style Catholic upbringing" that taught her right from wrong. She was a student leader in high school and knew it was important to set a good moral example. She had learned by the moral example of other people to choose well. Finally, she did not want to disappoint her family by failing to do the right thing when she had an obligation to do so.[151]

Bohatch suffered as whistleblowers often do. Her trauma after being asked to leave the firm so impressed the jury that they awarded her $250,000 for mental anguish damages. The job market was very tight when she started looking for a new job in 1990. Her level of seniority and expertise made it difficult for her to find a new position. She was also in an awkward situation because she carried the "stigma" of revealing her dispute with Butler to potential employers. Although she was hired by Duncan & Allen in September 1991, she faced "seven lean years" there as she paid for the litigation expenses while working at a less lucrative job as a Duncan contract partner. She also spent her free time on evenings and weekends at the library, working on her case. How did she withstand the pressure of losing her job and fearing she would

---

148. Appellees'/Cross–Appellants' Brief in the Court of Appeals for the Fourteenth Supreme Judicial District, July 6, 1994, No. 14–93‑00903–CV, at 10.

149. Holman Interview, supra note 124.

150. Countiss Interview, supra note 107.

151. Bohatch Mehle Interview, supra note 8.

remain unemployed? Bohatch explained that every whistleblower "needs a safe harbor," and that her safe harbor was to consider a return to Ohio, where she had begun her legal career, to set up a new law practice there.[152]

Bohatch and her lawyers argued that the courts needed to extend legal protection to whistleblowers in order to protect the profession and encourage reports of misconduct. A more negative perception of whistleblowers prevailed in the Supreme Court of Texas, however. In interviews, both Justices Enoch and Hecht expressed concern about extending broad legal protection to whistleblowers who may be vindictive (or simply wrong). As Enoch explained,

> If you're going to accuse someone of being unethical, then you ought not be insulated from the consequences if you're wrong, because you can do harm, you can ruin someone's reputation by an accusation. You can't make it as easy as possible to report misconduct and insulate [the whistleblower] from being wrong.[153]

Justice Hecht echoed Enoch's argument. In Texas, protective whistleblower legislation originally looked like a good idea until the state "started getting tagged for huge damages," and it became easier and cheaper not to fire a whistleblower, even a vindictive or incorrect one.[154] When asked about dissenting Justice Spector's proposal—that the firm release the partner but compensate her for her damages—he replied, "At least in the abstract you'd have to worry, particularly in a law firm where it's awfully easy to accuse a lawyer of unethical conduct given the play in the rules. You could be reporting anyone for anything and then having to pay them damages."[155] The Texas justices thus engaged the same argument that had split the Illinois Supreme Court in 1991: do the bar's reporting rules provide sufficient incentive and reward for attorneys to report misconduct that threatens the public's well-being?

The ABA's long debates about proposed amendments to the Model Rules on confidentiality and reporting, as well as Congress' passage of the Sarbanes–Oxley corporate responsibility legislation, confirm that questions about attorney-whistleblowers continue to perplex and divide the legal profession. In 1998, the Texas Supreme Court's decision offered three alternatives for handling law partner whistleblowers who report misconduct: no legal protection when they report misconduct (Enoch); possible legal protection if their allegations are correct (Hecht); or damages for good faith whistleblowers, including Bohatch (Spector). The

---

152. Id.

153. Enoch Interview, supra note 122.

154. Hecht Interview, supra note 122.

155. Id.

justices disputed the implications of those approaches for the enforcement of the ethics rules. Enoch insisted that the decision did not excuse
lawyers from failing to report misconduct.[156] Spector countered that this
position dissuaded whistleblowers. Indeed the primary reason she dissented was her belief that the court's first job was to uphold and
reinforce the bar's professional standards.[157] "I dissented because it was
in fact the court that is responsible for the integrated bar; we're
supposed to uphold the ethical standards and we should bear some
responsibility to clients and the bar to transcend ordinary business
relationships."[158] Justice Hecht believed that the majority was "too black
and white" and the dissent was "too one-sided."[159] He accused Enoch of
ignoring the ethical argument completely and taunted Spector about the
quotation from Huckleberry Finn: "[she] assumes incorrectly that the
only 'recourse' is an action for damages. Twain suggests that righteousness has its own rewards."[160] For many whistleblowers, as for Colette
Bohatch, righteousness must be its sole reward.

Lost in the debate about rewards and incentives for reporting
misconduct, however, was the ethical problem that had first provoked
the whistleblower's dilemma, namely the difficulty of detecting attorneys' overbilling of clients.

V. The Ethics of Billing

"If Bohatch had been able to better substantiate her claim, she may
have fared better in the Texas courts."[161]

Colette Bohatch's worries about McDonald's overbilling began when
she contrasted the time he spent in the office next door with the
numbers reported on the firm's billing records. While she estimated he
worked three to four hours per day, the records reflected 10–12.[162] His
daily diaries, with their "same as" entries that violated the firm's billing
policies, confirmed her fears that he was working fewer hours than he

---

156. 977 S.W.2d at 547.

157. Id. at 561; Author's Telephone Interview of Justice Rose Spector, August 25,
2004; see also Bruce Hight, Ruling on Ethics Favors Law Firms, The Austin–American
Statesman, January 23, 1998, at D1. ("Walter Borges, a spokesman for Texas Citizen
Action, said the clients of law firms should worry about the ruling because it will
discourage lawyers from reporting overbillings.").

158. Spector Interview, supra note 157.

159. Hecht Interview, supra note 122.

160. 977 S.W.2d at 558.

161. Whitledge, supra note 152, at 889.

162. Colette Bohatch's Reply Brief to Butler & Binion et al.'s Cross–Points, in the
Court of Appeals for the Fourteenth Supreme Judicial District, October 31, 1994, No. 14–
93–00903–CV, at 14.

billed. Even Louis Paine confirmed that McDonald was "terrible" about keeping time.[163]

> He never kept time, never kept it on a basis. He was one of the people we had to pass a rule that if you didn't turn your time it, you didn't get paid. He never was very particular about the way he kept his time. . . . McDonald was the worst, I believe, I have ever seen.[164]

Bohatch did not see the actual bills to Pennzoil because McDonald prepared them.[165] At trial, Tucker presented the daily diaries, the firm's billing records, and the bills to Pennzoil.

> The bills do not reflect which lawyers or paralegals did the work, contain no line-by-line description of the work, contain no recitation of the number of hours worked and no indication when the work was done (other than the billing period, which is often <u>several</u> months). The bills contain only a general description of the work done and a total sum owed. In some years there is only one total, in other years there are subtotals by each general description of the projects.[166]

Tucker supplemented those billing materials with Bohatch's testimony about how long McDonald spent on certain items of work, especially on reading new FERC orders and cases. The jury heard that he spent twenty-five hours reviewing a ten-page court decision; between 65 and seventy hours reading a two-page FERC decision and preparing a six-page pleading; and thirty-five hours on a 15–page decision. Some entries for reviewing a FERC order in December 1989 predated the actual date of issuance of the order.[167]

The jury did not hear Professor Geoffrey Hazard's testimony about McDonald's violation of normal billing practices and procedures or, for that matter, the testimony of any other billing expert. Judge Brister excluded both plaintiff's and defendants' billing experts because "there are no experts on common knowledge." Instead, the judge said <u>he</u> would

---

163.   Paine Deposition, supra note 7, at p. 100, line 6.

164.   Id. at p. 100, lines 10–18 and p. 103, lines 1–2.

165.   Bohatch estimated that Pennzoil had been overbilled by about $25,000 per month. Because some of the monthly bills totaled about $25,000, Butler argued that she was incorrect in her allegations of overbilling. She countered that because the bills were not prepared on time every month, it was the total amount of bills and not the monthly amount that was most significant.

166.   Colette Bohatch's Reply Brief to Butler & Binion et al.'s Cross–Points, in the Court of Appeals for the Fourteenth Supreme Judicial District, October 31, 1994, No. 14–93–00903–CV, 5–6.

167.   Id. at 12–14

tell the jury about the common knowledge "that padding bills is wrong, even for lawyers."[168] This ruling was not appealed.

Even before the trial started, the Butler partners had rejected Bohatch's complaint because Pennzoil's representatives expressed their satisfaction with the bills. While she still worked for Pennzoil, Bohatch complained to Paine that he should use a different method of evaluating the bills, similar to the kind of analysis she later presented at the trial:

> What would be more telling would be an evaluation of the reported hours based on (a) the facial plausibility of his original time records, (b) the time the activities he reported could conceivably have taken, even if actually conducted, and (c) the compatibility of his reported time with his extensive and demonstrable out-of-office personal activities during the work day (e.g., attendance at a six-week photography course during business hours).[169]

Paine insisted, however, that, despite numerous requests, Bohatch never provided documentation of the alleged overbilling to the firm. Paine testified that he never saw the daily diaries until the trial.[170]

Bohatch also criticized Pennzoil's representatives for never undertaking a similarly detailed analysis of McDonald's billing records. Both Shaddix and Chapman testified that they saw no problems with McDonald's billing, and Kral said Shaddix was his best witness.[171] Bohatch, however, argued that Shaddix and Chapman did not want to make themselves look bad by renouncing the man whom Shaddix had recommended for Butler & Binion's D.C. office. "Mr. Shaddix and Mr. Chapman had every incentive to cover up or disregard Mr. McDonald's theft. Their reluctance to investigate the matter is shown by their failure to ask for any back up to these bills that contain almost no information or support."[172] According to Richard Edmonson (Chapman's supervisor at Pennzoil who also reviewed the bills), however, Pennzoil never reviewed a lawyer's timesheets when considering the fairness of the amount billed.[173]

---

168. Brister E–Mail, supra note 65 (emphasis in original).

169. 12/27/90 Letter to Paine, supra note 23.

170. Appellants Paine, Burns and McDonald's Reply Brief in the Court of Appeals for the Fourteenth Supreme Judicial District, January 20, 1995, No. 14–93–00903–CV, at 6.

171. Kral Interview, supra note 87.

172. Colette Bohatch's Reply Brief to Butler & Binion et al.'s Cross–Points, in the Court of Appeals for the Fourteenth Supreme Judicial District, October 31, 1994, No. 14–93–00903–CV, at 7.

173. Author's Telephone Interview with Richard Edmonson, May 4, 2004; see also William G. Ross, Kicking the Unethical Billing Habit, 50 Rutgers L. Rev. 2199, 2207–08 (1998) ("Many clients also may encourage disreputable billing tactics insofar as they

In addition to the testimony of their Pennzoil clients, Butler & Binion attempted to offer evidence from another source, namely a D.C. Bar report that "exonerated" John McDonald of the underlying charge of overbilling. Louis Paine and John McDonald had reported Bohatch's allegations against McDonald to the D.C. Bar Association. At trial, Butler offered a D.C. Bar report into evidence. It concluded that bar officials "investigated the matter and found that there were no ethical violations."[174] Bohatch argued that the report was hearsay, and did not reveal "what was reported to the bar or what issue was resolved by the bar, or what information, if any, the bar relied upon to reach its conclusion."[175] Judge Brister denied Butler's request to enter the Bar's report into evidence because it was irrelevant to the underlying law-suit,[176] and the Court of Appeals upheld his ruling, stating that "whether there was in fact a violation of those rules is irrelevant and inadmissible" to Bohatch's claim that she was fired for reporting a violation of the rules.[177] That report on John McDonald is not available for review;[178] the D.C. Bar rules do not permit the release of any record of the investigation. Deputy Bar Counsel Eugene Shipp explained, however, that D.C. Bar investigations do not "exonerate" individual lawyers.[179] They either find violations of the rules or dismiss complaints. McDonald was never sanctioned for billing misconduct.[180]

On Bohatch's side of the billing issue is the jury's verdict; on Butler's side are the D.C. Bar investigation and the testimony of Penn-

---

probably do not care whether attorneys bill their time ethically if they receive satisfactory services at what they regard as a reasonable fee.").

174. Respondents Paine, Burns and McDonald's Reply Brief in the Supreme Court of Texas, November 15, 1996, at 6.

175. Bohatch Brief in Response to Conditional Cross–Application for Writ of Error in the Supreme Court of Texas, No. 95–0934–CV, November 15, 1996, at 25–27.

176. Brister E–Mail, supra note 65 ("I excluded it because it was up to the jury to decide what had occurred, and a[] bar committee's opinion would only tend to prejudice their doing so.").

177. 905 S.W.2d at 607.

178. Although the bar report should be attached to the pleadings (see Countiss Interview, supra note 107), I could not find copies of it in either the Houston or Austin case files. The D.C. bar cannot release the report because of Rule 11, Section 17 of the D.C. Court of Appeals Rules Governing the Bar, see Author's Telephone Interview of D.C. Deputy Bar Counsel Eugene Shipp, July 14, 2004.

179. Id. Bohatch later filed her own complaint about McDonald with the D.C. bar, but she withdrew the complaint right after she filed her lawsuit in October 1991. "She says the bar counsel sought additional information from her but that she declined to submit it because it could have hurt her litigation position. The Office of Bar Counsel says only that it has not taken any public disciplinary action against McDonald." See Amy Boardman, Partner Was Fired After Reporting Alleged Misbilling; Whistleblower Seeks One More Hearing, Legal Times, September 16, 1996, at 2.

180. Shipp Interview, supra note 178.

zoil. The case confirms the difficulty of identifying and policing billing misconduct. First, it is difficult for outsiders to discover inaccurate timesheets and hourly reports.[181] Second, lawyer deception or misrepresentation may occur even when clients consent to what appear to be reasonable bills.[182] Third, clients may focus on their general satisfaction with the attorney instead of the particulars of his or her billing.[183] As Jamie Gorelick observed, "You can have [someone] who may well be capable of binding the client but if the practices are inappropriate in any event or dishonest, that should not absolve someone under the ethics laws of liability for that conduct."[184]

Such general difficulties with preventing and detecting billing misconduct, however, did not persuade the majority of the Texas Supreme Court to allow damages to a law firm partner who makes a good faith report of billing misconduct. Bohatch had demonstrated that the daily diaries were sloppy and the jury had awarded a verdict on her behalf. Why should Pennzoil's consent to the bills affect the outcome of her case? For Justice Hecht, who ruled that an incorrect whistleblower does not have a cause of action for breach of fiduciary duty, client consent was the crucial proof that the billing was acceptable. A lawyer might have a

---

181. See, e.g., William G. Ross, The Ethics of Hourly Billing By Attorneys, 44 Rutgers L. Rev. 1, 11 (1991) (there is "no practical manner of verifying the accuracy of most time records"; this situation "creates rich opportunities for fraud"); Lisa G. Lerman, Blue–Chip Bilking: Regulation of Billing and Expense Fraud by Lawyers, 12 Geo. J. Legal Ethics 205, 209 (1999) ("Billing fraud is far more difficult to detect than expense fraud, unless the lawyer is reckless enough to bill more than twenty-four hours per day. But regulation of this type of conduct is very difficult because no one except the lawyer really knows how much time was spent and how much was billed. Because this arena involves such a wide degree of personal discretion, those tempted to cheat may perceive, quite accurately that the odds of apprehension are close to zero."); Gerald F. Phillips, The Rules of Professional Conduct Should Provide Guidance to Attorneys With Respect to Billing Clients, 15 No. 1 Prof. Law. 2 (2004) (" 'The billing procedures used by most firms practically invite attorneys to commit the 'perfect crime.' The padding of bills is almost impossible to prove since there is no objective way to measure, except within very broad limits, the amount of time that one needs to spend on any particular task.' ").

182. See generally Lisa G. Lerman, Scenes from a Law Firm, 50 Rutgers L. Rev. 2153, 2181–82 (1998) (identifying the inadequacies of client consent for appropriate billing; describing "consensual deception" and "consensual misrepresentation"); Ross, supra note 181, at 11 ("corporate clients rarely question the veracity of individual billing entries, much less accuse attorneys of fraud").

183. Lerman, Blue–Chip Bilking, supra note 181, at 274–75 (Clients "may not have known that they were being bilked. Some of them were apparently pleased with the legal services that they were receiving, and were not concerned about how the bills were calculated. Many of these were large corporate clients, accustomed to paying large legal bills to multiple firms every month. The corporate representatives who reviewed the bills were not personally responsible for the payments, and may have been less careful about reviewing the bills than they would have been if they were spending their own money.").

184. Gorelick Interview, supra note 38.

good faith belief that his client will win a summary judgment motion, he reflected, but if the client loses, the lawyer is wrong and has displayed poor judgment. In the same way, Bohatch was wrong when she predicted, based on the diaries, that the client would find something unacceptable with McDonald's billing, and Butler was justified in firing her for her bad judgment. Another whistleblower might have a lawsuit, but not Colette Bohatch.

By contrast, Justice Spector submitted that the Bohatch case "started out as ethics case about reporting misconduct and wound up as one about how to bill."[185] "The case highlights how the hourly way law firms bill doesn't make sense. Everything is done on this hourly rate, but the truth is that it doesn't reflect the value of the underlying services."[186] The difficulty of proving billing misconduct compounded the whistleblower's dilemma, and ultimately defeated her case in the Texas Supreme Court.

VI. Epilogue

Butler & Binion. Butler had 170 lawyers in 1989, the year that Colette Bohatch was promoted to partner. The firm began its decline in the early 1990s; its size dropped to 25 lawyers in 1999 and it dissolved in December 1999.[187] According to Paine, although paying nearly $500,000 in damages to Bohatch in 1998 was "not a happy day," it had no impact on the partners' decision to liquidate.[188] Instead, he believes that Butler was "a mid-sized firm that ran into typical problems of mid-sized firms" in the 1980s and 1990s. Butler tried but failed to find a large merger partner.[189] Hayden Burns agrees that Butler's downfall was not directly caused by the Bohatch litigation. The firm had structural and management problems, and was "living on borrowed time."[190]

After Butler closed, Paine opened a Houston-based office of the Dallas firm Glast, Phillips & Murray and is a member there today. Burns is a partner in another Houston firm.[191] John McDonald and Richard Powers did not respond to requests for interviews for this chapter; both are now partners in D.C. law firms.[192]

---

185. Spector Interview, supra note 157.

186. Id.

187. Angela Ward, Butler & Binion on the Ropes, Texas Lawyer, October 11, 1999, at 1; Laura Goldberg, Sunset for Law Firm of Butler & Binion; 19th-largest Legal Partnership Here to Close, The Houston Chronicle, December 4, 1999, at 2.

188. Paine Interview, supra note 26.

189. Ward, supra note 187.

190. Burns Interview, supra note 6.

191. Burns, Wooley, Marseglia & Zabel, L.L.P

192. McDonald is a partner at Jackson Kelly and Powers is a partner at Dorsey & Whitney.

Bohatch. As noted earlier, Bohatch ended up with Duncan & Allen, which she described as a "simpatico, nice group of lawyers." Bohatch is grateful that those lawyers were "struck by the ethics part of her case" and were very supportive of her and her career for many years. She worked as a contract partner for Duncan from September 1991 to 1995. The firm did utilities work, but their expertise was in electric utilities, while Bohatch's specialty was natural gas. In 1995, after Duncan decided to discontinue its gas work, she continued to work in their offices as her "own profit center," not as a contract partner. Duncan's lawyers continued to be generous; they sent work her way whenever someone needed a regulatory attorney who specialized in gas. Her practice there had a regulatory and transactional focus on the procurement and transportation of natural gas for utility and industrial clients.[193] Although Bohatch was happy at Duncan, she acknowledged having "seven lean years" as she worked there while financing the expenses of her litigation.

Colette Bohatch Mehle remained in Duncan's offices until February 2003, when she opened her own practice, The Mehle Law Firm, with her husband Roger Mehle, on Connecticut Avenue in the District of Columbia.[194] Bohatch met Mehle in Butler's D.C. office, where his law firm (Royer, Mehle & Babyak) rented space within the Butler offices. Bohatch married Mehle in 1998, the same year that the Supreme Court decided her case. The Mehle Law Firm provides "counseling and representation in the energy and banking and finance fields, and in securities and other commercial litigation."[195]

" 'What's the use you learning to do right when it's troublesome to do right and ain't no trouble to do wrong, and the wages is just the same?' "[196] According to Colette Bohatch Mehle, you do the right thing because it's the right thing to do.

---

193. http://www.mehlelaw.com

194. Bohatch Mehle Interview, supra note 8.

195. http://www.mehlelaw.com

196. Bohatch v. Butler & Binion, 977 S.W.2d 543, 558 (Tex. 1998).

*

3

Travails in Tax: KPMG and the Tax Shelter Controversy[†]

Tanina Rostain

In the fall of 2003, the Senate Permanent Subcommittee on Investigations conducted hearings on the extensive tax shelter activities of KPMG, a Big Four accounting firm.[1] As the hearings revealed, from the late 1990s into the next decade, KPMG devoted significant resources to developing and mass marketing hundreds of abusive tax shelters. These products were designed to enable their purchasers—typically high wealth individuals and Fortune 500 companies—to avoid paying taxes on the huge financial gains they enjoyed during the stock market boom. Abusive tax shelters deprived the Treasury of tens of billions of dollars in lost tax revenue.[2] KPMG, which made hundreds of millions of dollars from its

[†] Tanina Rostain, Professor of Law, New York Law School. Thanks to Terry Cone, Denny Curtis, Leandra Lederman, Deborah Rhode, Hana Rostain, Judith Resnik and Richard Schottenfeld for comments on an earlier draft, and to Michael Andrescavage and Ryan Weber for their research assistance. I am especially grateful to Mike Hamersley who spent many hours describing his experiences to me, providing context for the thousands of documents made public by the Permanent Subcommittee on Investigations, and providing detailed comments on this chapter.

My account of Hamersley's experiences is drawn from the complaint in his lawsuit against KPMG, his testimony in the Senate Finance Committee, his interview for the television show Frontline, and numerous interviews I conducted with him in early 2004. None of Hamersley's allegations have been tested in court.

1. See U.S. Tax Shelter Industry: The Role of Accountants, Lawyers, and Financial Professionals, Hearings before the Permanent Subcommittee on Investigations of the Committee on Governmental Affairs, United States Senate, 108th Cong,. (First Session), November 18 and 20, 2003, Volumes I–IV. In addition to thousands of pages of documents, the subcommittee released a detailed report, Minority Staff Report of the Permanent Subcommittee on Investigations, U.S. Tax Shelter Industry: The Role of Accountants, Lawyers, and Financial Professionals: Four KPMG Case Studies: FLIPS, OPIS, BLIPS, and SC2, reproduced in id. Vol.1 at 145 ["U.S. Tax Shelter Industry"]. For a description of the legal environment, the economic incentives driving the tax shelter market, and the role of promoters and outside legal advisers, see Joseph Bankman, The New Market for Tax Shelters, 83 Tax Notes 1775 (1999); see also Janet Novack & Laura Sanders, The Hustling of X–Rated Tax Shelters, Forbes (Dec. 14, 1998).

2. See U.S. Tax Shelter Industry, supra note 1, at 146. One particularly successful product, marketed to twenty-nine corporations and estimated to have earned the firm $20

tax shelter business, has by no means been the only large accounting firm involved. During the last few years, government investigations and lawsuits brought by the IRS and former clients have exposed the tax shelter activities of Arthur Andersen, PriceWaterhouseCoopers, Ernst & Young, and Deloitte.[3] But KPMG may be the firm in the most trouble. After its tax shelter activities came to light, the Justice Department launched a criminal investigation, with some thirty current and former partners and employees as subjects.[4] Even after disbanding its tax shelter practice and replacing several high level partners involved, the firm was forced to enter into a deferred prosecution agreement, under which it agreed to pay a fine of nearly half a billion dollars. Eight former partners have been indicted, with more indictments likely.[5]

Although KPMG is an accounting firm, it was lawyers at the firm, as at the other former Big Five, who were the main players in the shelter industry.[6] During the late 1990s, large numbers of lawyers joined ac-

---

million in fees, cost the Treasury $1.7 billion. *See* KPMG Shelter Shaved 1.7 Billion off Taxes of 29 Large Corporations, Wall Street Journal, June 17, 2004, at A1.

3. See, e.g., Doe v. Ernst & Young LLP, Case No. 02C–6306 (N.D. Ill. 2002); United States v. KPMG LLP, 237 F. Supp.2d 35 (D.D.C. 2002); United States v. Arthur Andersen, LLP, 2003 WL 21956404 (N.D. Ill. 2003); PwC Pays IRS for Not Following Shelter Rules, Bowman's Accounting Report, Jul.1, 2002; Cassell Bryan–Low, Unhappy Returns: Accounting Firms Face Backlash Over the Tax Shelters They Sold, Wall S.J. Feb. 7, 2003, at A1; Jeremy Kahn, Do Accountants Have a Future? Fortune (Mar. 3, 2003) 115.

Although the Big Five accounting firms led the development and promotion of tax shelters, they were not the only participants. Second-tier accounting firms, investment banks, and law firms have all been involved in promoting tax shelters. See Cassell Bryan–Low, Unhappy Returns: Accounting Firms Face Backlash Over the Tax Shelters They Sold, Wall St. J., Feb. 7, 2003, at A1; Sheryl Stratton, ITS Gets John Doe Summons for Grant Thornton, Updates Shelter Stats., 2003 TNT 209–2; David Cay Johnston, I.R.S. Seeking Buyers' Names in Tax Shelters, N.Y. Times, June 20, 2003, at C1; Cassell Bryan–Low, Moving the Market: Jenkens & Gilchrist Agrees to Pay $75 Million in Tax Shelter Case, Wall St. J., Mar. 8, 2004, at C3.

4. Cassell Bryan–Low, KPMG Tax Shelter Probe Grows; US Classified 30 as Subjects, Wall St. J., March 5, 2004, at A2.

5. See Cassell Bryan–Low, Audit Firms Face Heavy Fallout From Tax Business, Wall. St. J., Feb. 25, 2004, at A1; Jonathan Weil, KPMG's Chief of Finance Quits as Probes Go On, Wall. St. J., July 7, 2004, at A3; Sheryl Stratton & Karla L. Miller, KPMG Sacrifices Tax Leadership in Ongoing Shelter Controversy, Tax Notes Today, Jan. 13 2004, available at 2004 TNT 8–1; see Deferred Prosecution Agreement, available at http://www.us-doj.gov/usao/nys/pressrelease2005.html; Tax Fraud Indictment—Stein et al., available at http://www.usdoj.gov/usao/nys/pressrelease2005.html.

6. See, e.g., Susan Beck, The Trojan Accountant, Am. Law., Nov. 1999, at 18; Anna Snider, Taking a Look inside the Big Five, N.Y.L.J., Sept. 7, 1999, at S11; John T. Lanning, KPMG Recruiting Pitch: *Practice Tax*, Legal Times, Sept. 6, 1999, at S42; Amy Boardman & Carrie Johnson, Accounting for Competition: As Tax Lawyers Jump to the Big Six, Rivalry Grows between Attorneys, Accountants, Legal Times, Feb, 3 1997 at 1; Big Five Court Tax Attorneys: Many Make Leap As Accounting Firms Work to Expand Their Legal Reach, Crain's N.Y. Bus., March 22, 1999, at 13; Ernst & Young Scores Another Top Tax Lawyer, The Recorder, March 25 1999, at 1; Tax Report, Wall St. J., Feb. 2, 2000, AT A1; BIG FIVE PAYS TOP DOLLAR FOR TAX PARTNERS—ESPECIALLY KPMG, THE NAT'L L.J., Nov. 6, 2000, AT B8.

counting firms, lured by their rapidly expanding tax services. Many were recruited directly from school; others were well-established partners at corporate law firms, tempted by the enormous income potential of tax product work.

It was also a lawyer who finally exposed KPMG's shelter activities. In the summer of 2002, Michael Hamersley, a tax lawyer who had worked at the firm for four years and was a few weeks shy of partnership, refused to sign off on the tax treatment of a transaction that was part of a KPMG audit of a Fortune 500 company. Pressured to destroy documents related to the audit, which he believed was fraudulent, Hamersley contacted federal authorities. His cooperation in a government investigation during the subsequent year brought the details of KPMG's shelter business to light.[7]

KPMG's fall from grace offers a cautionary tale about the risks of law practice in large professional organizations in the twenty-first century. On an institutional level, it illustrates how business rationality can displace professional norms, a process accelerated at KPMG by its enormous size, organizational structure, and deeply conformist culture. Once a well-regarded accounting firm, KPMG was quick to trade on its reputation to develop a thriving, highly lucrative tax shelter practice. In its eagerness to become an industry leader in the shelter market, the firm engaged in a variety of evasive tactics to avoid detection by the IRS—tactics that may now land its principals in prison. During the past decade, some large law firms, competing with accounting firms for business, have been eager to emulate their size, organizational style and service delivery model.[8] KPMG's story should cause managing partners at law firms to think twice before borrowing the accounting firm model.

On an individual level, the KPMG story provides a lesson in the growth of self-knowledge and personal accountability. Hamersley insisted on maintaining his objectivity and managed to avoid the processes of group-think and self-rationalization that overcame his colleagues. On the occasions when he was asked to review dubious tax schemes, Hamersley did not hesitate to articulate his concerns. But his main goal after he became aware of the firm's tax shelter activity was professional survival: As he describes it, his plan was to avoid direct involvement in the firm's

---

7. See Michael Hamersley v. KPMG, LLP, et al., Superior Court of the State of California, L.A. County June 23, 2003, available at 2003 TNT 124–5 ["Hamersley Complaint"]; Michael Hamersley, Written Testimony before the United States Senate Finance Committee (October 21, 2003), available at 2003 TNT 204–35 ["Hamersley Senate Testimony"].

8. See, e.g., Robert Rosen, "We're All Consultants Now": How Change in Client Organizational Strategies Influences Change in the Organization of Corporate Legal Services, 44 Ariz. L. Rev. 637 (2002); Randall S. Thomas, et al., Megafirms, 80 N. Car. L. Rev. 115, 136–52 (2001).

unethical and unlawful behavior, make partner, and then leave. The firm refused to let him off so easily, insisting that he engage in questionable practices as a rite of passage to partnership. In hindsight, Hamersley wishes he had heeded the warning signals and gotten out earlier, before he was put to the choice of either engaging in behavior he believed was criminal or becoming a whistleblower and risking his career, reputation, and economic security in the process.

Tax Services and Accounting Firms

Tax services have been a staple of accounting work since the income tax laws were enacted at the turn of the twentieth century.[9] Historically, however, the large American accounting firms built their reputations around auditing. Beginning in the late nineteenth century, railroads seeking to raise capital brought in independent auditors to certify their financial condition. As more and more businesses adopted the corporate form, the demand for independent audits increased. The role of audits was institutionalized with the enactment of the securities laws during the New Deal, which granted the auditing franchise to the accounting profession.[10]

The major accounting firms first gained prominence as a result of the work of influential leaders–Robert Montgomery at Lybrand, Ross Bros., and Montgomery; George May at Price Waterhouse; Arthur Andersen and later Leonard Spacek at Arthur Andersen—who were fiercely committed to safeguarding the integrity of the audit process.[11] May, an Englishman widely considered the founder of American accounting, championed the rights of shareholders to unbiased and rigorous financial reporting. Long before it was thought to compromise auditor independence, he refused to have financial interests in clients. He also made it a point never to sit on their boards or socialize with them.[12]

---

9.   See, e.g., John L. Carey, The Rise of The Accounting Profession: From Technician to Professional I 1896–1936 67–71 (1969); Michael Chatfield, A History of Accounting Thought 207–08 (1974). As Chatfield notes,

> By requiring written records to support the determination of taxable income, the tax law made accountancy mandatory and vastly increased the work of public accountants. CPAs had the immediate problem of helping thousands of businessmen who had never felt the need to make financial statements, and who now got their first statistical view of their total operations.

Id. at 207.

10.   See Chatfield & Vangermeersch, The History of Accounting: An International Encyclopedia 238–39 (1996); Mike Brewster, Unaccountable: How Accounting Firms Forfeited The Public Trust 77–80 (2003).

11.   Id. at 50–62 3, 62–63.

12.   Id. at 61, 69.

In the early days, tax and other auxiliary services were not considered a threat to auditor independence. Accounting firms were intimately familiar with the financial details of their clients' businesses, so it was natural that they would prepare their tax returns. Offering supplemental tax advice geared toward minimizing the tax effects of future transactions was accepted practice.[13] With their knowledge of individual clients' affairs and their large client base, firms were similarly well-positioned to provide managerial consulting advice.[14] During the course of audits, accountants would often uncover problems and inefficiencies that they would then help their clients repair. None of these services, offered on the side, were thought to jeopardize the objectivity required for performing audits.[15]

Between the 1930s and 1970s, Arthur Andersen & Co; Lybrand, Ross Bros. & Montgomery; Haskins & Sells; Ernst & Ernst; Arthur Young & Co; Peat, Marwick, Mitchell & Co.; Touche, Ross & Co; and Price Waterhouse & Co. became ensconced as the "Big Eight" of the American accounting profession.[16] During the 1930s, the firms carved up the business world among themselves, each specializing in certain industries.[17] Arthur Andersen, which had its roots in Chicago, emphasized traditional manufacturing industries; Price Waterhouse was the auditor of choice for blue chip companies.[18] Through multiple mergers with smaller firms in the 1950s, the Big Eight developed a national presence. By the end of the decade, each firm had offices in all major U.S. cities and many smaller ones.[19] Client billings ranged from $17 million dollars

---

13. Id. at 103–04; Walter E. Hanson, Peat, Marwick, Mitchell & Co.: 80 Years of Professional Growth 13 (1978).

14. Brewster, supra note 10, at 103–04; Hanson, supra note 13, at 13.

15. Brewster, supra note 10, at 56–57. The issue of whether providing managerial advisory services to audit clients impaired auditor independence did not emerge until the 1960s. See Wallace E. Olson, The Accounting Profession, Years of Trial: 1969–1980 207; Gary J. Previts & Barbara D. Merino, A History of Accountancy in the United States: The Cultural Significance of Accountancy 338–40 (1998).

16. Charles W. Wootton & Carl M. Wolk, The Development of the "Big Eight" Accounting Firms of the United States, 1900 to 1990, 19 The Accounting Historians Journal 1, 16–17 (1992). By the 1980s, the identities of the Big Eight had shifted somewhat. They were Arthur Andersen; KPMG Peat Marwick; Ernst & Whinney; Coopers & Lybrand; Price Waterhouse; Arthur Young; Deloitte Haskins & Sells; and Touche Ross. Chatfield & Vangermeersch, The History of Accounting: An International Encyclopedia 75 (1996); Mark Stevens, The Accounting Wars 27 (1985).

17. Charles W. Wootton & Carl M. Wolk, The Development of the "Big Eight" Accounting Firms of the United States, 1900 to 1990, 19 The Accounting Historians Journal 1, 11–12 (1992).

18. Brewster, supra note 10, at 117.

19. Wootton & Wolk, supra note 17, at 14–16.

for the smallest to over $40 million for the largest.[20] The firms' growth
continued during the 1960s. By 1968, Peat, Marwick, Mitchell & Co., the
largest measured by U.S. billings, enjoyed revenue in excess of $125
million, while Arthur Young, the smallest, billed $57 million.[21]

Beginning in the late 1960s, however, audit work began to experience pressure from several directions. A landmark appellate decision
upheld the convictions of three accountants at Lybrand, Ross Bros. &
Montgomery accused of filing misleading financial statements with the
SEC.[22] *Continental Vending*, as the case became known, was the first to
suggest that accountants had a responsibility to identify corporate fraud.
It opened a floodgate of litigation. As businesses began to fail during the
economic downturn of the early 1970s, the accounting firms were hit
with a steady flow of lawsuits by the government and corporate shareholders claiming financial reporting abuses. Meanwhile, the SEC began
threatening to take a more assertive regulatory stance toward auditing.[23]
Audit work was also experiencing pressure from within the industry. In
1973, the American Institute of Certified Public Accountants (AICPA),
under threat of litigation by the Federal Trade Commission, was forced
to lift its prohibition on competitive bidding for audits.[24] A few years
later, the AICPA was also compelled to abandon its bans on advertising
and soliciting other firms' clients.[25] The large firms, which had earlier
enjoyed an informal understanding that they would not compete for each
others' clients, now found themselves in audit price wars. As corporate
mergers and acquisitions also mounted, there were fewer companies left
to audit, and competition for audits intensified further.[26]

Accounting firms began promoting their consulting services, because
consulting offered new sources of revenue, did not appear to pose
significant litigation risks, and went largely unregulated. During the
1980s, while audit fees were flattening, those from consulting services
grew.[27] By the 1990s, revenue from non-audit services equalled or
exceeded that from audit services.[28]

---

20. *Id., at* 16.

21. *Id., at* 17.

22. See United States v. Simon, 425 F.2d 796 (2d Cir. 1969), cert. denied, 397 U.S.
1006 (1970).

23. Brewster, supra note 10 , at 117–121, 131.

24. Id. at 136; Previts & Merino, supra note 15, at 397.

25. Brewster, supra note 10, at 136; Previts & Merino, supra note 24, at 397.

26. Brewster, supra note 10, at 11.

27. The Big Eight: 1979 to 1989: A Review of their Rankings 3 (Public Accounting
Report 1990).

28. See James D. Cox, *Reforming the Culture of Financial Reporting: The PCAOB
and the Metrics for Accounting Measurements*, 81 Wash. U. L.Q. 301, 310 (2003); Previts &
Merino, supra note 15, at 400.

With the success of consulting, a sales approach took over the large firms. The audit was repackaged to emphasize how it could uncover information that was useful for management to run the business.[29] If, in earlier days, an auditor's responsibility was providing reliable financial information to help investors, now it was keeping management satisfied. "Value-added" became the mantra at firms.

The value driven focus that invaded the large firms was a boost to tax services. From the late 1980s on, revenue from tax services steadily increased.[30] Decoupled from return preparation or "compliance" services, tax consulting services were offered to supplement other services provided to clients. Until the 1990s, however, tax work typically consisted of advising individual clients about how to structure transactions to minimize their liability. Tax professionals offering such planning advice might take aggressive, even highly aggressive, positions in their interpretations of law—but their focus remained on advising individual clients about actual business deals.[31] The advice was designed for a specific client and was related to a client's business dealings.

In the mid–1990s, however, the large firms adopted a more proactive and standardized approach to tax planning and began to devote significant resources to developing standardized tax products, a shift that was spurred in part by changes in the rules governing the types of fees firms could charge for tax services. Until the 1990s, accountants were prohibited from charging audit clients contingency fees in tax matters.[32] In 1991, responding again to antitrust concerns, the AICPA changed its rule to permit some contingency fees in tax matters.[33] In the late 1990s, the limitations on contingent fees were loosened further.[34] The large firms read these developments as permitting them to charge performance-based fees, calculated as a percentage of the client's tax savings. Whereas firms had been limited to an hourly rate or a flat fee, now they could charge the equivalent of a commission for each tax product sold. All of a sudden, tax professionals could imagine earning incomes at the same level as those enjoyed by investment bankers and corporate lawyers during the Wall Street boom. By the end of the decade, the tax products market had exploded. Between 1995 and 2001, the U.S. tax practices of

---

29. Previts & Merino supra note 15 at 398; Brewster, note 10, at 179.

30. The Big Eight, supra note 27, at 4, 8.

31. Interviews with Michael Hamersley (spring 2004).

32. Previts & Merino supra note 15, at 339.

33. AICPA Code of Professional Conduct ET Rule 302.01 (adopted May 1991); Kahn, supra note 3.

34. Ruling No. 24 under the Rule of Conduct 302: Investment Advisory Services, 5–99 J.A. 138.

KPMG, Deloitte & Touche, Ernst & Young, and PriceWaterhouseCoopers more than doubled their revenue, from 2.4 to 5.6 billion dollars.[35]

KPMG

The rise of KPMG paralleled that of the other major accounting firms. Peat Marwick was founded in 1911 and specialized in providing audit and tax services to banking and financial institutions.[36] During the 1950s, the firm was the most aggressive and innovative of the Big Eight, emerging as the largest and highest grossing accounting firm in the United States.[37] The firm grew by buying up small firms at a rapid pace and by expanding its consulting services. To provide integrated services to clients in different sectors, it reorganized its staff along industry groups, blurring the lines among auditors, tax specialists and consultants.[38] In 1987, Peat Marwick joined forces with a second-tier firm to become KPMG Peat Marwick, the biggest accounting firm in the world at the time.[39] This was the first in a series of consolidations that turned the Big Eight into the Big Six.[40] (The merger between Price Waterhouse and Coopers Lybrand in 1998 brought the number down to five; Arthur Andersen's bankruptcy, to four.) Over the next ten years, consulting and tax services continued to expand.[41]

By the late 1990s, the firm's tax product efforts were in full swing. Under the forceful leadership of Jeff Stein, a lawyer who rose through the ranks to head tax operations, the firm was eager to position itself as an "industry leader" and had decided to commit significant resources to designing and marketing generic tax "solutions" to be sold to multiple clients.[42] The firm hired a substantial sales force, paying it commissions

---

35. Nanette Byrnes & Louis Lavelle, Death, Taxes and Tax Shelters, Business Week, Jan. 27, 2003, at 35.

36. Brewster, supra note 10, at 115.

37. Brewster, supra note 10, at 112.

38. Brewster, supra note 10, at 181.

39. Chatfield & Vangermeersch, The History of Accounting: An International Encyclopedia, supra note 10, at 75; U.S. Tax Shelter Industry, supra note 1, at 166.

40. Brewster, supra note 10 at 176.

41. Bowman's Accounting Report Vol. 14 (March 2000) at 2. In 2000, KPMG separately incorporated its management consulting services group and sold off a twenty percent interest. Thomas, supra note 8, at 166.

42. Id. at 167; Cassell Bryan–Low, Audit Firms Face Heavy Fallout from Tax Business, supra note 5; memorandum from Jeffrey M. Stein to U.S. Tax Professionals, dated April 18 2000, re: KPMG Tax Financial Results, reproduced in United States Tax Shelter Industry Vol. 3, supra note 1, at 2068–69; KPMG Tax Practice: Our Strategic Blueprint, Powerpoint presentation (September 2000), reproduced in United States Tax Shelter Industry Vol. 3, supra note 1, at 2070–2100; Tax Innovation Center FY 2001 Business Plan / *FY 2002*, reproduced in United States Tax Shelter Industry Vol. 3, supra note 1, at 2121–33.

on products sold.[43] It also engaged in a lawyer-hiring spree, recruiting aggressively at law schools and attracting partners away from traditional corporate law practices with multi-million dollar deals.[44] By 2001, the firm's tax practice employed some 10,000 tax professionals and brought in approximately $1 billion in revenue, having increased 45% over the previous four years.[45]

Tax Product Development and "Speed to Market"

In the late 1990s, the firm established a new "Tax Innovations Center," to spearhead the development of new tax products.[46] The center maintained a data bank of new tax ideas and set yearly goals for new submissions to the bank—for the firm as a whole, and for each of the firm's functional groups.[47] To boost proposals, the center tracked and publicized internally the number of ideas submitted by each group. In addition, tax partners and managers in the firm's different functional groups were paid bonuses to develop tax products to sell to their specific clientele.[48]

The most promising ideas went through a lengthy and expensive development and approval process.[49] Tax products can be extraordinarily complex, often combining layers upon layers of partnerships, corporations and trusts, exotic financial instruments, and multi-million dollar loans. Developing a viable product—one that would sell to clients and might arguably pass muster with the IRS—required the participation of numerous tax and other specialists within the firm. Professionals from outside the firm also provided advice on myriad legal, investment,

---

43. See Jeffrey M. Stein, Tax Sales Organization and Telemarketing, memorandum to KPMG Tax Partners, dated 30, 1998, reproduced in United States Tax Shelter Industry Vol. 3, supra note 1, at 2174–79; "The Blueprint" National BDM Tax Sales Initiative: Objectives, Roles and Responsibilities, reproduced in United States Tax Shelter Industry Vol. 3, supra note 1, at 2189–2209 (undated); Tax Business Development Stub Fiscal Year 2001 and Full Fiscal Year 2002 (15 Months Beginning July 1, 2001 and ending September 30, 2002) Compensation Plan and Agreement, reproduced in United States Tax Shelter Industry Vol. 3, supra note 1, at 2210–20.

44. Lanning, supra note 6; Geanne Rosenberg, Big Five Pays Top Dollar for Tax Partners—especially KPMG, Nat'l L.J., Nov. 6 2000, at B8 (partners offered in $2 million range).

45. U.S. Tax Shelter Industry, Vol. 1, supra note 1, at 166–67.

46. Around 1999, KPMG renamed tax "products" tax "solutions" to suggest that the strategies were driven by actual business transactions.

47. U.S. Tax Shelter Industry, Vol. 1, supra note 1, at 172–73.

48. Hamersley interviews (Spring 2004).

49. U.S. Tax Shelter Industry, Vol. 1, supra note 1, at 174–75; Tax Solution Deployment and Development, KPMG Tax Services Manual–US (May 2002), Chapter 24, reproduced in United States Tax Shelter Industry, Vol. 4, supra note 1, at 3086–92.

finance, and accounting questions, as well as logistical support.[50] To the external world, the firm's development process was advertised as one that would guarantee the legitimacy of the product. Internally, however, the development process was driven less by quality concerns and more by profitability and speed to market.

As part of the development process, experts in the firm's Department of Professional Practice for Tax (DPP–Tax) had the responsibility of reviewing products to make sure they complied with applicable legal rules and the firm's internal standards. For a product to be approved, the partner in charge of DPP—Tax had to be persuaded that, if a transaction found its way to court, it would "more likely than not" be upheld.[51] This assurance, provided in the form of a KPMG opinion letter to the client, was necessary to market tax products. The accounting firm's opinion letter, together with a similar opinion letter from an outside law firm, could be produced down the road to show a taxpayer's good faith, thereby deflecting possible penalties if the IRS discovered and challenged the transaction.[52] In addition, it served to reassure a client that the tax avoidance scheme was legitimate.

Opinion letters are the stock in trade of tax lawyers. Although opinions will devote tens of pages to technical tax issues, often the critical question comes down to whether a taxpayer had a business reason for engaging in a transaction or was solely motivated by tax considerations.[53] Since the 1930s, a handful of overlapping judicial doctrines have developed to distinguish between bona fide business and investment ventures and abusive tax shelters.[54] These doctrines seek to find a balance between two countervailing principles underlying the American tax system: On one hand, taxpayers are allowed to arrange their affairs to minimize their taxes; on the other, they are not entitled to tax benefits obtained through formal manipulations of tax law that were not intended by Congress.[55] As deals have become increasingly complex, it has become more and more difficult to tell when they are motivated by business rather than purely tax considerations. To be legal, tax products must resemble, as much as possible, bona fide investments.

---

50. Id. at 175.

51. Id. at 175.

52. See Joseph Bankman, The New Market for Tax Shelters, 83 Tax Notes 1775, 1778–79 (1999).

53. Id. at 1782.

54. See, e.g., Helvering v. Gregory, 293 U.S. 538 (1934).

55. The most famous articulation of these principles is by Judge Learned Hand, sitting on the Second Circuit Court of Appeals, in his opinion in *Gregory*. See Gregory v. Helvering, 69 F.2d 809, 810–11 (2d Cir. 1934).

But if they entail significant financial risk, clients will not be interested in buying them.[56]

In late 1998, Stein and the other heads of the tax services group identified a hot new product intended for sale to high-wealth individuals with large capital gains. Stripped of its complex technical features, "Bond Linked Issue Premium Structure" (BLIPS) involved a series of complex arrangements, engineered by its developers to create a façade of investment purpose. Ultimately, BLIPS permitted a taxpayer to take a large deduction resulting from a prepayment loan penalty that the taxpayer did not actually incur.[57] In February 1999, the heads of the tax services practice were eager to get BLIPS to market. (The fee to the firm for BLIPS would be approximately 1.25% of the tax loss claimed.) Emphasizing the "marketplace potential" of the product, they pushed for speedy review.[58] Although some of the tax professionals responsible for approving the product had qualms that the deal lacked economic substance, by the end of April the firm was poised to issue a more-likely-than-not opinion and launch the product.[59]

---

56. See Bankman, supra note 52, at 1797.

57. BLIPS worked something like this: A taxpayer with $20 million to shelter sets up a shell corporation called a limited liability company. She gives this corporation cash in the amount of 7% of the amount to be sheltered—which comes out to $1.4 million. This money will go to paying the fees of KPMG and of the other participants in the transaction. A part also goes to an investment program that is the purported raison d'être of the transaction. In the next step, a bank makes a seven-year loan of $50 million to the corporation. Because the taxpayer is willing to pay an above market rate, the bank will credit her with an additional $20 million loan premium. Under the terms of the loan, there are severe restrictions on how it can be used. In addition, the taxpayer is required to maintain collateral in cash or liquid securities, equivalent to 101% of the loan, at the bank.

Presidio, an investment advisory firm whose principals are former KPMG partners, now enters the picture. It forms a partnership with the taxpayer and her shell company called a strategic investment fund. The taxpayer's company contributes its assets and ends up with a 90% interest in the investment fund. With the consent of the bank, the company assigns the loan to the investment fund. The fund uses the dollars to buy euros while obtaining a guarantee that it can convert the euros back to dollars within 60 days. (It also creates a semblance of investment activity by using a small amount of money—never more than the taxpayer contributed—to short foreign currencies pegged to the U.S. dollar.) The loan is supposed to last seven years. If the taxpayer continues to participate in the investment fund she will be required to put more money at risk over time. If, however, the taxpayer pulls out early—at 60 days for instance—she is subject to a prepayment penalty equivalent to the $20 million premium originally loaned by the bank. Because of the way the loan has been structured, the taxpayer can now claim that her investment in the partnership was equivalent to $20 million (plus the original $1.4 million) and take a $21.4 million loss on her tax return. See U.S. Tax Shelter Industry, Vol. 1, supra note 1 at 255–65. (Inside KPMG, BLIPS was known as a "loss generator." Id. at 255.)

58. E-mail dated 2/10/99 from John Lanning to multiple KPMG tax professionals re: BLIPS, reproduced in United States Tax Shelter Industry, supra note 1 at 654.

59. U.S. Tax Shelter Industry, Vol. 1, supra note 1, at 178.

But doubts about the shelter resurfaced. In late April, Mark Watson, a partner in the national office and the chief technical expert assigned to review BLIPS, attended a meeting during which an outside investment advisor acknowledged that "the probability of actually making a profit from this transaction" was "remote."[60] Watson, an accountant by training, also came to doubt whether a bona fide loan was involved since the bank maintained complete control over the proceeds and repayment schedule in the deal. Even assuming the loan was bona fide, Watson had serious concerns that the taxpayer would not be viewed as the borrower. Acknowledging that he was "going to catch hell," he e-mailed his concerns to Larry DeLap, the head of the DPP–Tax, who in turn forwarded it to the leaders of the tax practice.[61]

The tax practice leaders were not pleased. In an e-mail to the BLIPS group in early May, John Lanning, a lawyer and vice-chair of tax practice, wrote that he was "amazed that at this late date (must now be six months into this process) our chief ... technical expert has reached this conclusion ... What gives? This appears to be the antithesis of 'speed to market.' Is there any chance of ever getting this product off the launching pad, or should we simply give up—"[62] A few days later, Philip Wiesner, the head of the national tax office, complained that it was very late in the process to revisit a prior decision on a technical issue.[63]

Later that same day, Wiesner sent an e-mail to the tax partners involved in BLIPS, urging approval. "Many people" had "worked long and hard" to craft an opinion that met the more-likely-than-not standard. The question of investors' actual motive—whether they reasonably thought they would make a profit—could be deferred to implementation. KPMG's "reputation," moreover, would help market the transaction. For Wiesner, the business decision came down to whether the firm's fees were sufficient to offset the risks of potential litigation. "My own recommendation" he wrote, "is that we should be paid a lot of money here for our opinion since the transaction is clearly one that the IRS would view as falling squarely within the tax shelter orbit." It was "time to shit and get off the pot" he emphasized.[64]

---

60. Id. at 178.

61. E-mail dated 5/4/99 from Mark Watson to Larry DeLap, reproduced in United States Tax Shelter Industry, supra note 1, at 622.

62. E-mail dated 5/8/99 from John Lanning to four KPMG tax professionals, reproduced in United States Tax Shelter Industry, supra note 1, at 626.

63. E-mail dated 5/10/99 from Philip Wiesner to various WNT tax professionals, reproduced in United States Tax Shelter Industry, supra note 1, at 3468.

64. E-mail dated 5/10/99 from Philip Wiesner to various tax professionals re: BLIPS, reproduced in United States Tax Shelter Industry, supra note 1, at 625–26.

"I think it's shit OR get off the pot," Stein shot back in an e-mail that day. "I vote for shit."[65] Nine days later, Larry DeLap approved the sale of BLIPS.[66]

When it came time to implement BLIPS, the firm had to make sure that each purchaser characterized the decision to participate as an investment strategy. Clients were required to sign a representation, drafted by KPMG, that they had "independently reviewed the economics underlying" the deal and "believed that there was a reasonable opportunity to earn a reasonable pre-tax profit."[67] Given the extraordinary complexity of the transaction, it was questionable whether a typical client could grasp its underlying economics. Clients' representations that they could reasonably anticipate making a "reasonable profit" were equally implausible.[68] Every client nevertheless was required to make these specific representations so that the firm could rely on them in issuing the more-likely-than-not opinion letters that accompanied each sale.

In February 2000, after the first sixty-six purchasers of BLIPS had promptly liquidated their positions and taken tax losses, Wiesner wondered whether the firm could continue to rely on these representations in upcoming deals. He suggested that it might be time to "close the books" on BLIPS.[69] But even after DeLap, whose job was to enforce tax practice standards at the firm, concluded that the sale of BLIPS should stop, KPMG kept selling.[70] By the end of the run, 186 taxpayers had bought BLIPS and claimed a tax loss.[71] The product, which earned the firm $53 million, is its biggest revenue producer known to date.[72] In September 2002, the IRS listed BLIPS as an abusive tax shelter.[73] Neither KPMG nor purchasers of BLIPS have sought to defend the strategy in court.[74] BLIPS is estimated to have cost the Treasury at least

65. E-mail dated 5/10/99 from Jeff Stein to various tax professionals re: BLIPS, *reproduced in* United States Tax Shelter Industry, supra note 1, at 624.

66. United States Tax Shelter Industry, supra note 1, at 182. In his interview with the staff of the subcommittee, DeLap declined to say that he had personally concluded that BLIPS met the requirements of the IRC. He approved the sale of BLIPS because the national tax office had completed its review. Id. at 184.

67. Id. at 156, 212–213.

68. Id. at 212–13.

69. Id. at 213–14.

70. Id. at 214–15.

71. Id. at 255.

72. Id.

73. IRS Notice 2000–44 (2000–36 IRB 255) (9/5/00) at 255.

74. U.S. Tax Shelter Industry, supra note 1, at 185.

$1.4 billion in uncollected tax revenue.[75]

KPMG's Marketing Efforts

By 2000, the firm had in place an extensive infrastructure to sell tax shelters. After a product made it through the firm's development process, it was assigned to a "National Marketing Champion."[76] Champions were charged with assembling a team from various field offices to lead marketing efforts in different regions of the United States.[77] To assist Champions in market planning and execution, the firm provided marketing professionals and research. KPMG identified potential clients by mining its tax and audit client lists, and extracting information from computer databases compiled to prepare clients' tax returns, among other methods. Marketing champions could also use a large telemarketing center maintained by the firm in Fort Wayne, Indiana.[78]

Tax partners throughout the firm were expected to participate in the sales effort. Management's approach mixed upbeat motivational messages with threats and negative pressure. In February 2000, Wiesner instructed the firm's US tax partners to defer "non-revenue producing activities" for the next five months and concentrate on selling products with significant revenue potential. Quoting Stein, the e-mail exhorted: " 'We are dealing with ruthless execution—hand to hand combat— blocking and tackling.' Whatever the mixed metaphor. Let's just do it."[79] Assurance partners were also pressured to pitch tax products to their audit clients. According to the firm, cross-selling shelters to audit clients would increase its "market penetration." [80]

To make its products more attractive, KPMG emphasized that legal opinions from purportedly independent law firms were available.[81] In the case of one product, the firm even agreed to pay a law firm a fee each time the law firm's name was mentioned during a sale, regardless of whether the firm provided an opinion.[82] It also used insurance as a marketing tool, mentioning in its sales pitch that insurance companies

---

75. Id. at 147.

76. See KPMG Tax Deployment Champion Manual: A Process Guide for National & Area Deployment Champions (July 2002), *reproduced in* United States Tax Shelter Industry. VOL. 3, supra note 1, at 2136–47.

77. U.S. Tax Shelter Industry, supra note 1, at 189.

78. Id. at 152, 189–90, 198.

79. E-mail dated 2/3/00 from Philip Wiesner to US–WNT Tax Partners, *reproduced in* United States Tax Shelter Industry, supra note 1, at 460–62.

80. U.S. Tax Shelter Industry, supra note 1, at 194–95.

81. Id. at 200.

82. Id. at 200–01.

would be willing to insure the tax benefits of a product at a small premium.[83]

KPMG's marketing efforts may have reached a peak with SC2, a product that targeted Subchapter S corporations and turned out to be one of the firm's top revenue producers in 2000 and 2001.[84] As with BLIPS, tax professionals at the firm identified several significant defects with SC2 during the review process.[85] Nevertheless, it was approved for sale. When SC2 was launched in March 2000, area "Champions" around the country were exhorted to "SELL, SELL, SELL!!"[86] A few months into the effort, a tax professional in Houston learned that his office was "behind" and that management expected "significant value added fees by June 30." "The heat is on" he warned his office.[87] The firm culled internal, public, and commercial databases, and contacted professionals within the firm, clients, and other referral sources to compile lists of thousands of potential clients. These names were passed on to the telemarketing center, which made thousands of cold calls to promote SC2.[88]

When it came to persuading buyers, KPMG did not shy away from the hard sell. A June 2000 memo, entitled "Sticking Points and other Problems" offered pointers on how to deal with recalcitrant clients.[89] If a client thought it was "too good to be true," the seller was to remind him or her that the product had gone through an extensive review—including by specialists at the firm who were ex-IRS employees. The client was also informed that many sophisticated clients had already bought the product, and at least one outside law firm was available to provide a legal

---

83. Id. at 201.

84. Id. at 266–67. SC2 ("S–Corporation Charitable Contribution Strategy") permitted a Subchapter S corporation to shelter a significant portion of its income by "allocating," with little or no distribution, the income to a charitable organization. In the shelter, the S–Corporation issued and then donated non-voting stock, with very low fair market value, to the charity, typically making the charity a 90% owner of the corporation. In addition, the corporation and the charity entered into a redemption agreement to require the corporation to buy back the stock. While the charity owned the stock, the corporation "allocated" most of its income to it without distributing it. According to the KPMG opinion letter provided with the shelter, the corporation could claim a deduction for the donated shares in the year the "donation" took place. It also did not have to pay taxes on the income allocated to the charity. Id.

85. Id. at 187–88.

86. E-mail dated 2/18/00 from Richard Rosenthal to multiple KPMG tax professionals Partners, *reproduced in* United States Tax Shelter Industry, supra note 1, at 413.

87. E-mail dated 4/21/00 from Michael Terracina, KPMG office in Houston, to Gary Choate in the Dallas KPMG office, reproduced in United States Tax Shelter Industry, supra note 1, at 463.

88. U.S. Tax Shelter Industry, supra note 1, at 194–98.

89. "SC2–Meeting Agenda" and attachments, dated 6/19/00, reproduced in United States Tax Shelter Industry, supra note 1, at 483–85.

opinion.[90] If the client needed to "think about it," the memo recommended three approaches:

> *The "Get Even" approach*: Contact the client again right around the time a large estimated tax payment is due, when she or he is likely to be "extremely irritated";
>
> *The "Beanie Baby" approach*: Tell the client the firm has established a cap on the product that is quickly filling up;
>
> *The "Break–Up" approach*: Tell the client that because the cap has been reached, the client should no longer consider purchasing the product. (For obvious reasons, this one was risky and could only be used in a limited number of cases, where the client could be expected to fall for the ruse.)[91]

The memo also offered strategies to do end runs around "stubborn outside counsel" who had advised against purchasing the product.[92]

The efforts to market SC2 were so extensive that one tax partner in December 2001 complained that the firm was "intent on marketing the SC2 strategy to virtually every S corporation with a pulse."[93] With all this activity, he worried, the IRS would "get wind" of the product. He expressed concern that the widespread marketing of SC2 (which had originally been intended for a small number of Subchapter S corporations) was likely to bring KPMG and SC2 "unwelcome attention" from the IRS, which was bound to mount a "vigorous (and at least partially successful) challenge."[94]

During the eighteen months it was on the market, SC2 was sold to fifty-eight Subchapter S corporations, generating $26 million in revenue.[95] In April 2004, the IRS classified SC2 as a potentially abusive tax shelter.[96]

Avoiding Detection by the IRS

In its efforts to secure its lead in the tax shelter market, KPMG engaged in evasive maneuvers so that its products would fly under the IRS's radar screen. The firm's tactics included disregarding tax shelter registration rules, advising clients to use impermissible reporting mecha-

---

90. Id. at 483.

91. Id. at 484–85.

92. Id. at 485.

93. E-mail dated 12/20/01 from William Kelliher to David Brockway, WNT head, reproduced in United States Tax Shelter Industry, supra note 1, at 607.

94. Id.

95. U.S. Tax Shelter Industry, supra note 1, at 266.

96. Jonathan Weil, IRS Puts Shelter Sold by KPMG on "Abusive List," Wall S.J.,April 2, 2004, at C6.

nisms in their tax returns, and resisting enforcement summonses by the IRS.

Tax practice leaders apparently took a breezy attitude toward any disclosure requirements that might stand in the way of sales. Under the tax laws, promoters are required to register transactions that have certain tax shelter characteristics so that the IRS can more easily identify them and review their legality.[97] Without the registration requirements, the only way that the Service would be able to discover abusive tax shelters would be to burrow deep into a taxpayer's returns as part of an audit—a complex and labor intensive exercise that would overconsume meager IRS resources. Over the years, KPMG never registered any tax products, taking the public position that the tax "solutions" it offered were not "tax shelters" that fell within the registration requirements, but legitimate investment strategies.[98]

Internally, the decision not to register products was apparently driven by a different calculus. In the spring of 1998, the firm was developing OPIS, or "Offshore Portfolio Investment Strategy," a product that was intended for high-wealth individuals, and that had significant profit potential.[99] In an e-mail to Jeff Stein, Gregg Ritchie, a tax professional at the firm, explained the business reasons that OPIS, even if it fell within the registration requirements, should not be registered with the IRS.[100] His view was based on the "immediate negative impact on the Firm's strategic initiative to develop a sustainable tax products practice and the long-term implications of establishing . . . a precedent in registering such a product." More specifically, Ritchie wrote, "the financial exposure to the Firm" was "minimal" since any penalties from noncompliance were much smaller than potential profits. At most, they would represent 14% of fees earned. Other promoters were not registering their products, so registering the product would put KPMG at a "severe competitive disadvantage" given "industry norms." In addition, there had been "a lack of enthusiasm on the part of the Service to enforce" the registration provisions. Lastly, Ritchie noted, there was a lack of guidance as to how the registration requirements should be interpreted. All told, he concluded, "the rewards of a successful marketing [of OPIS] far exceed the financial exposure to penalties that may arise."[101]

---

97.   See I.R.C. § 6111.

98.   United States Tax Shelter Industry, supra note 1, at 168, 235.

99.   OPIS stands for "Offshore Portfolio Investment Strategy." Like BLIPS, it was a "loss generator." Id. at 185.

100.   Memorandum dated 5/26/98 from Gregg W. Ritchie to Jeffrey N. Stein, entitled "OPIS Tax Shelter Registration," reproduced in United States Tax Shelter Industry, supra note 1, at. 3245–47.

101.   Id.

Not everyone at the firm took the view that OPIS should not be registered.[102] But in the end, Stein and Lanning decided against registering OPIS, which went on to earn the firm $28 million during the two years it was on the market (before it was identified as a potentially abusive tax shelter by the IRS).[103]

KPMG's concern with avoiding detection extended to the advice it provided clients about how to report gains and losses related to OPIS on their tax returns. To minimize information that might alert the Service to OPIS on clients' tax returns, a number of KMPG tax professionals advised clients to effect these transactions through grantor trusts so that they could add and subtract their gains and losses at the grantor trust level and then report a single capital gain or loss on their returns.[104] This "netting" technique would conceal the specific loss being claimed in connection with the tax shelter. When Watson discovered that clients were being advised to use this approach, he made clear his opinion that the practice was illegal. As he wrote in an e-mail, "[w]hen you put the OPIS transaction together with this 'stealth' reporting approach the whole thing stinks."[105] In a second e-mail, he was even more explicit: "I believe we are filing misleading, perhaps false, returns by taking this reporting position."[106]

Watson's recommendation should have prevented KPMG's tax professionals from advocating this technique.[107] The OPIS deployment team decided, however, to leave the decision whether to advise a client to engage in "netting" to individual partners.[108] Earlier, some tax professionals at the firm had advised their clients to use the same netting technique to avoid alerting the IRS to their BLIPS transactions.[109] When the IRS invalidated BLIPS in September 2000, it issued a stern warning that "[i]n addition to other penalties, any person who willfully conceals the amount of capital gains and losses [through grantor trust netting], or who willfully counsels or advises such concealment, may be guilty of a criminal offense."[110]

---

102. U.S. Tax Shelter Industry, supra note 1, at. 235

103. Id. at. 172

104. Id. at 238.

105. E-mail dated 9/2/98 from Mark Watson to various KPMG tax professionals re: "FW: Grantor Trust Memo," reproduced in United States Tax Shelter Industry, supra note 1, at 3798.

106. E-mail dated 1/21/99 from Mark Watson to various KPMG tax professionals, re: "Grantor Trust Reporting," reproduced in United States Tax Shelter Industry, supra note 1, at 3779.

107. U.S. Tax Shelter Industry, supra note 1, at 239.

108. Id.

109. Id.

110. IRS Notice 2000–44 (2000–36 IRB 255) (9/5/00) at 256.

KPMG engaged in other evasive tactics in response to summonses the IRS had served on the firm in early 2002 requesting the firm to identify clients who had purchased various tax shelter products. In response to one summons, relating to SC2, the firm failed to identify all the clients who had purchased the strategy.[111] In response to another summons, which related to a shelter marketed between 1998 and 2000 under the name Short Option Strategy, the firm insisted to the IRS that its involvement was limited to preparing clients' tax returns and that it had fully complied with the summons.[112] It was not until more than a year after the summons was issued that the firm produced documents showing that it had been actively involved in designing and marketing the shelter in question.[113] The firm's initial denial of its participation may have been an attempt to run the three-year statute of limitations that normally applies to the IRS's ability to disallow tax benefits claimed by purchasers of the transaction.[114]

In response to yet other IRS summonses, the firm claimed that the documents sought fell variously under the statutory accountant-client, attorney-client, and work product privileges.[115] In a decision granting an enforcement action brought by the IRS, the D.C. District Court found that the firm had intentionally mischaracterized the documents it claimed were privileged. As the court noted, "KPMG appears to have withheld documents summoned by the IRS by incorrectly describing the documents to support dubious claims of privilege."[116] The court concluded that overall, "KMPG is misrepresenting its unprivileged tax shelter marketing activities as privileged communications."[117] After reviewing the history of the case, the court had arrived at the "inescapable conclusion that KPMG has taken steps since the IRS investigation began

---

111. See e-mail from Ken Jones to various KPMG tax controversy service professionals, "TCS Weekly Update" dated 4/19/ 2002, reproduced in United States Tax Shelter Industry Vol. 3, supra note 1, at 2388. This e-mail was forwarded to Jeff Stein by a colleague who was "watching [Stein's] back" and who wondered whether "[g]iven the sensitivity of this situation should we be putting all this in print?" See Message 4044 from Wendy Klein to Jeffrey M. Stein dated April 22, 2002, reproduced id.

112. See Third Declaration Michael A. Halpert, dated 12/04/03, United States v. KPMG LLP Misc. No. 02–295 (TFH) ¶ ¶ 7 & 8, reprinted at 2003 TNT 239–17.

113. Id., at ¶ 8; Petitioner's Objections to Reports and Recommendations of Special Master, United States v. KPMG LLP Misc. No. 02–295 (TFH) ¶ 17, reprinted at 2003 TNT 239–16.

114. Id. at 18.

115. United States v. KPMG LLP, 316 F. Supp. 2d 30 (D.D.C. 2004).

116. Id. at 38.

117. Id. at 44.

that have been designed to hide its tax shelter activities."[118] In the proceeding to enforce the IRS summonses, the Service had argued that KPMG had engaged in obstruction of justice, a charge that was in substance accepted by the district court.[119]

Mike Hamersley

The government's efforts to uncover KPMG's tax shelter activities were greatly facilitated by Mike Hamersley, a tax lawyer at the firm who decided to become a whistleblower in 2002. A year later, after he was put on administrative leave, he sued the firm for retaliation and defamation. In his complaint he alleged that in the spring of 2002, he was assigned to work on the tax aspects of an audit that he came to believe was fraudulent.[120] During the summer, he spent sleepless nights struggling with whether he should disclose KPMG's activities to federal authorities. But the firm finally made the decision easy. According to his complaint, toward the end of the summer, a tax partner instructed him to discard his notes, which cast serious doubt on the validity of the audit.[121] Concerned that he was being implicated in conduct he believed to be criminal, Hamersley believed that he had no choice but to contact the government.[122] Hamersley, who had received "exceptional" performance evaluations throughout his tenure, was up for partnership.[123] His wife had just given birth to their first child.[124]

A 1995 Georgetown law graduate, Hamersley had come to KPMG after a brief stint at Ernst & Young.[125] After graduating, Hamersley had decided to work for Ernst & Young over a traditional law firm. During law school, Hamersley had taken several tax courses with a view to specializing in the area. The summer of his second year he worked at the accounting firm and came away impressed. Ernst & Young was eager to enhance the profile of its tax practice and had recently recruited a number of leading tax partners away from their law firms. The firm enjoyed a corporate client base many times that of most law firms and a

---

118.   Id. at 37–38.

119.   Petitioner's Objections to Reports and Recommendations of Special Master, supra note 113, ¶ 6; United States v. KPMG, 316 F. Supp. 2d 37–38.

120.   Complaint in Michael Hamersley v. KPMG, LLP et al., Superior Court of the California (L.A. County 9/10/2003), Case No. BC 297905, ¶ ¶ 19–48 ["Hamersley Complaint"].

121.   Id. at ¶ 42.

122.   Written Testimony of Michael Hamersley in the United States Finance Committee (October 21, 2003) ["Hamersley Testimony"], p. 8.

123.   Hamersley Complaint, ¶ ¶ 10–12.

124.   Hamersley interviews (spring 2004).

125.   Id.; Hamersley Testimony, supra note 122, p.1.

professional tax staff of thousands.[126] For Hamersley, who had earned an M.B.A. before law school, the firm offered the opportunity to use his business background and develop a highly specialized tax niche. Starting salaries for lawyers at accounting firms, which had once lagged significantly behind those at law firms, were also starting to catch up.[127]

Hamersley joined Ernst & Young's Washington National Tax Department, specializing in mergers and acquisitions (M & A) tax.[128] Shortly after he started, he began to notice changes in the provision of tax services toward what he calls the "productizing" of tax.[129] Traditionally, the modus operandi in corporate tax practice had been reactive to clients' requests. But in the late 1990s, the tax group at Ernst & Young, like those at the other accounting firms, realized that developing tax products could be an effective strategy to serve its many similarly situated clients. To Hamersley, the efficiency gains were obvious. In Hamersley's words, a products approach was preferable to having "three people on the same floor researching the same issue."[130] Complex processes, such as analyzing the acquisition costs of a company, benefited from standardization. Having gotten a sense of this potential, Hamersley was eager to combine product development with individual client-based services.[131] After a few years, Hamersley moved to the seemingly more dynamic M & A tax practice at KPMG, where he hoped to do both products and client-based work.

As a junior person in KPMG's National Tax Practice, Hamersley was not exposed to the discussions surrounding BLIPS and other tax shelters. The partners involved in developing these products held the information "pretty close to the vest" and access was limited to a "need-to-know" basis.[132] The official reason the firm gave for such restrictions was fear that information would be leaked to competitors. The unofficial reason, Hamersley realized in retrospect, was that "this was some pretty ugly stuff."[133] Hamersley sometimes saw a "Tax Product Alert" about a new product or heard a description. Deferring to the more senior tax practitioners at the firm, he naively assumed that even the most technically aggressive products—i.e. those that heavily shaded the law to reach

---

126. Hamersley interviews (spring 2004).

127. Id.

128. Id.; Front Line: Tax Me if You Can: Interview of Mike Hamersley, available at www.pbs.org/wgbh/pages/frontline/shows/tax/interviews/hamersley.html. ["Frontline Interview"].

129. Frontline Interview, supra note 128.

130. Hamersley interviews (spring 2004).

131. Id.; Frontline Interview, supra note 128.

132. Hamersley interviews (spring 2004); Frontline Interview, supra note 128.

133. Hamersley interviews (spring 2004); Frontline Interview, supra note 128.

a favorable result—could be implemented legally. He never imagined that KPMG would sign off on transactions with knowledge that material facts were being omitted, concealed or misrepresented.[134] On a few occasions, he was asked by tax partners to research whether a specific type of transaction had been ruled on by the IRS or a court. If he reported back that the transaction had been disallowed, his supervisor would thank him, and he would not hear about the matter again.[135]

The pictured changed in 2000 when Hamersley was promoted and moved to the Los Angeles field office. A hard-working and talented corporate tax lawyer, Hamersley was considered a rising star at the firm.[136] In late 1999, he was offered a promotion to senior management if he relocated to L.A. The firm assured him that, if things continued on course, he would be made a partner within two fiscal years, and would eventually take over the direction of the Los Angeles M & A tax practice.[137] Thrilled, Hamersley packed up and moved with his wife to L.A.[138]

In the field, the blitz of tax product marketing would have been hard to miss. In his new office, Hamersley was surrounded by members of the firm's Stratecon Practice, which was established to develop and market the firm's most aggressive tax shelters to corporate clients. Several of Stratecon's members in L.A. had once been part of Deloitte's tax shelters marketing group (known internally as the "Predator" group).[139] Hamersley continued to work on client service matters, but he began to hear about details of corporate tax shelters being promoted by Stratecon. At first, Hamersley attributed the aggressive salesmanship to the "Wild West" atmosphere of the office. But over time he began to realize that the push to market tax shelters came directly from the firm's senior tax leadership.[140]

In L.A., tax service engagement partners would occasionally show Hamersley the descriptions and legal opinions on tax products marketed by Stratecon. These partners, who were under significant pressure to give Stratecon access to their clients, sought out Hamersley's advice to help them understand the strategies and their purported tax benefits.[141] Frequently, implementation of these shelters depended on dubious rep-

---

134. Hamersley interviews (spring 2004); Frontline Interview, supra note 128.

135. Hamersley interviews (spring 2004).

136. Hamersley Complaint ¶ ¶ 8–10.

137. Id. at ¶ 9.

138. Hamersley Interviews (spring 2004).

139. Hamersley Complaint ¶ ¶ 15, 16; Frontline Interview, supra note 128.

140. Hamersley Complaint at ¶ 17. Hamersley Interviews (spring 2004).

141. Id.

resentations drafted by KPMG relating to buyers' reasons for entering into a transaction. Hamersley did not hesitate to voice his concerns. At one point, he was advised by a partner in a closed-door meeting to "shut-up about this tax shelter stuff or these guys will keep you from getting promotions or salary increases."[142] Over the next two years, Hamersley managed to avoid direct involvement in tax products, but he persisted in raising questions about their legality.[143]

Hamersley was particularly troubled by the firm's practice of selling highly aggressive tax shelters to audit clients and allowing them to include the tax benefits on their financial statements. KPMG's tax shelter promoters would team with audit partners, who received financial bonuses for facilitating sales to their clients. Frequently, audit partners would later sign off on the financial statement treatment of the tax shelter based solely on a tax opinion provided by the tax partner who had developed or marketed the transaction. This practice severely compromised auditor independence, since the audit partner was not relying on an objective evaluation of the tax shelter, but on the opinion of the very person who had argued that the product was legitimate at the time it was approved.[144]

The XYZ Audit

Matters came to a head in the summer of 2002. Earlier that year, KPMG won the audit of a major company. (The company, whose identity is confidential, is referred to in court filings as XYZ Corporation.) XYZ Corporation had been a client of Arthur Andersen, but following that firm's indictment in connection with the Enron debacle, it retained KPMG to re-audit its last three years of financial statements to assure investors that it was in sound financial condition. Unknown to investors, the partner at Arthur Andersen who had overseen the original audit was now at KPMG and was effectively in charge of the re-audit. During the years in question, XYZ had engaged in aggressive tax shelters—including some that had been listed as potentially abusive by the IRS—whose financial statement treatment had been approved by this partner. KPMG had also sold nearly identical tax shelters to its clients. During the course of the re-audit, tax partners at KPMG were eager to sell additional tax products to XYZ.[145]

In mid–2002, Hamersley was asked to review the proposed disposition of stock owned by XYZ in a Special Purpose Entity partnership. XYZ

---

142. Hamersley Complaint ¶ 17; Hamersley Interviews (spring 2004).

143. Id.; Hamersley Complaint ¶ 18.

144. Id. at ¶ 18. Hamersley Interviews (spring 2004).

145. Hamersley Complaint ¶ 20.

planned to claim a $450 million tax loss in connection with this sale.[146]
As auditor of XYZ, KPMG could not permit the company to take a
financial statement benefit for this loss without also taking a reserve,
unless it arrived at "should" level of certainty—70%—that the tax
treatment of the transaction would be upheld if the IRS challenged it in
court. The standard for audit opinions to avoid having to require a client
to reserve for a contingent liability is more stringent than the more-
likely-than-not standard that applies to tax shelter opinions.[147] After
reviewing the transaction, Hamersley concluded that KPMG could not
reach a "should" level of certainty.[148]

Over the next days, tax partners involved in the re-audit searched
for ways to get around the problem.[149] The stakes were high both for
XYZ, which stood to lose several hundred million dollars if it was unable
to take the tax loss, and for KPMG, which stood to lose millions of
dollars in fees if the firm was fired because it could not get "comfortable" with XYZ's position.[150] After one of the partners found a ruling by
the IRS that rejected the approach KPMG was proposing on a parallel
set of facts, the tax partners informed XYZ corporation that it did not
look as if the firm would be able to reach a "should" opinion.[151] XYZ's
vice president of tax became very upset during the conversation and
made it clear that XYZ would have to restate its earnings if KPMG did
not sign off on the tax treatment favored by the company.[152]

The next morning, Hamersley received an e-mail from Richard
Bailine, the tax partner to whom he reported on the audit, informing
him that after further conversations with XYZ corporation, the firm
concluded that it was able to reach a "should" level of certainty.[153] Later
that day, he left Hamersley a voice mail admitting that he and the other
partners were looking at the matter through "rose colored glasses."[154]
When Hamersley spoke by phone with Bailine and another tax partner
the next day, Bailine started off by saying that he had gotten a call that
the client would fire the firm unless it got comfortable with the company's position.[155] After revisiting the merits with Bailine and the other tax
partners involved, Hamersley remained unpersuaded and informed them

---

146.   Id. at ¶¶ 26, 27.
147.   Id. at ¶ 27.
148.   Id. at ¶ 28.
149.   Id. at ¶ 30.
150.   Id. at ¶ 29.
151.   Id. at ¶ 30.
152.   Id. at ¶ 32.
153.   Id. at ¶ 33.
154.   Id.
155.   Id. at ¶ 34.

that Bailine would have to write the analysis supporting the firm's favorable conclusion.[156]

Over the next few weeks, Hamersley continued to worry about the audit and voice his concerns to other partners.[157] In mid-July, he was called into a meeting by Michael Burke, the Western managing partner of the firm's tax practice. When Burke grilled him about the tax aspects of the audit, Hamersley reiterated his concerns. Burke chided him, telling he was "naïve" and was now "playing with the big boys."[158] A few days later, another partner warned Hamersley at a private lunch that if he persisted in raising questions about the XYZ audit, he was not going to make partner.[159] Later that month, Burke stopped by to talk to Hamersley about the audit. During the conversation, Burke emphasized that KPMG's job was not to ferret out problems, but to be partners with audit clients. When Hamersley responded that the firm owed a fiduciary obligation to the shareholders of publicly owned companies, Burke became furious and started to yell at him.[160]

Having informed the tax partners involved of his views, Hamersley believed that he had extricated himself from the XYZ audit. Recognizing that his prospects for partnership were now slim, he immersed himself in other work and began to look for an exit strategy.[161] But the firm would not let him off so easily. In late summer 2002, after KPMG had signed off on XYZ's financial statements, Hamersley was asked to write an opinion supporting the firm's tax treatment of the company's sale of its interest in the Special Purpose Entity partnership.[162] Hamersley objected that he had already informed his superiors that he was not capable of justifying the position claimed by the firm.[163] After he showed the partner involved the memorandum he had written describing the problems with the XYZ audit, he was repeatedly instructed to remove the negative information.[164]

On July 30, 2002, Section 802 of the Sarbanes–Oxley Act, which provides for a ten year prison term for destroying corporate audit papers, had become effective.[165] After reviewing the Act and consulting with a

---

156. Id.

157. Id. at ¶ 35.

158. Id. at ¶ 36.

159. Id. at ¶ 38.

160. Id. at ¶ 40.

161. Hamersley Inteviews (spring 2004).

162. Hamersley Complaint, ¶ 46.

163. Id.

164. Id. at ¶ ¶ 46, 50.

165. 18 U.S.C. §§ 1519 & 1520.

private lawyer, Hamersley concluded that destroying information relating to the XYZ audit, as he had been instructed, could subject him to
criminal prosecution.[166] He decided it was time to contact government
officials.[167]

Aftermath

When the firm discovered that Hamersley was cooperating with the
government, it put him on administrative leave, cut off his access to his
clients, e-mail, and files, and forbade him from coming to the office.[168] A
rumor began to circulate in the firm that Hamersley was unable to work
because he had mental health problems.[169]

In June 2003, Hamersley filed a lawsuit against KPMG in California
state court, contending that the firm had defamed him and retaliated
against him for his whistleblowing activities.[170] KPMG tried, unsuccessfully, to have all the pleadings and records in the suit put under seal.
The firm also tried to force Hamersley to go into arbitration.[171] In
January 2004, the suit settled "amicably" for an undisclosed amount.[172]

In the summer of 2004, Hamersley accepted a position with the
California Franchise Tax Board. Two years earlier, California had enacted new laws to strengthen its capacity to investigate and prosecute tax
shelters.[173] Hamersley serves in the abusive tax shelter task force, which
was created pursuant to the legislation.

During their testimony before the Senate Permanent Subcommittee
on Investigations, representatives of KPMG insisted that BLIPS and
other products were investment strategies and not tax shelters, that the
firm was not a tax shelter promoter, and that all of its tax products
complied with applicable law and regulations.[174] After the hearings,
KPMG apparently changed course. Since January 2004, the firm has
removed or obtained the resignation of many of the tax partners in-

---

166. Hamersley Complaint ¶ 46.

167. Hamersley Testimony, supra note 122, at p.1–2, 8.

168. Hamersley Complaint ¶ ¶ 58, 60, 62, 63.

169. Id. at ¶ 57.

170. Hamersley Complaint.

171. See Defendants' Motion to Seal and Defendant's Motion for Arbitration in
Hamersley v. KPMG LLP. , et. al. (Case No. BC297905). KPMG considered its work
proprietary and required employees to sign comprehensive confidentiality agreements.

172. Hamersley Interviews (spring 2004).

173. Faranak Naghavi, et al., Legislation and Audits: Changing Trends, 34 The Tax
Adviser 755 (2003).

174. See, e.g., Testimony of Jeffrey Eischeid before the Senate Permanent Subcommittee on Investigations in United States Tax Shelter Industry vol. I, supra note 1, at 32–
55.

volved in its tax shelter activities.[175] After extensive negotiations with the Justice Department, KPMG entered into a deferred prosecution agreement, under which it accepted responsibility for developing, promoting and implementing fraudulent tax shelters. It also agreed to pay a $456 million fine. Eight former partners were indicted with more likely to follow.[176]

Pursuant to Sarbanes–Oxley, the SEC proposed more stringent auditor independence rules that would limit the tax services that accountants could perform for their audit clients.[177] The accounting firms objected strenuously to any limitation, citing the long history of accountants providing accounting and tax services together without risk to their independence.[178] Under the final rule enacted in 2003, a firm can provide any tax service to an audit client subject to approval by the client's audit committee.[179] In the wake of the tax shelter revelations, however, the Public Accounting Oversight Board, which is charged under Sarbanes–Oxley with overseeing audits of publicly traded companies, adopted new auditor independence rules that restrict firms' participation in selling tax shelters to their audit clients.[180] Donald Nicolaisen, the Chief Accountant at the S.E.C., also clarified that, contrary to the position of the Big Four accounting firms, under current regulations, they are not permitted to charge contingency fees in connection with tax services provided to audit clients.[181]

---

175. See David Cay Johnston, Changes at KPMG After Criticism of Tax Shelters, N.Y. Times, Jan. 13, 2004, at C1; Sheryl Stratton & Karla L. Miller, KPMG Sacrifices Tax Leadership in Ongoing Shelter Controversy, Tax Notes Today (Jan. 13 2004) *available at* 2004 TNT 8–1; see also Laurie Cohen, Prosecutors' Tough New Tactics Turn Firms Against Employees, Wall St. J., June 4, 2004, at A1.

176. See Deferred Prosecution Agreement and Tax Fraud Indictment—Stein, et al., available at http://www.usdoj.gov/usao/nys/pressrelease2005.html.

177. See Proposed Rule: Strengthening the Commission's Requirements Regarding Auditor Independence, Securities Act Release No. 8154 (December 2002), 67 FR 76779–76817.

178. See, e.g, Comments of PriceWaterhouseCoopers re: File No. S7–49–02, (Dec. 26, 2002) available at www.sec.gov/rules/proposed/s74902/pricewater1.htm; Comments of KPMG LLP re: File No. S7–49–02, (January 9, 2003) available at www.sec.gov/rules/proposed/s74902/kpmg1.htm; Comment Letter of Deloitte & Touche LLP on the Commissions Proposed Rule Implementing Sections 201, 202, 203, 204, and 206 of the Sarbanes–Oxley Act of 2002, available at www.sec.gov/rules/proposed/s74902/deloitte1.htm.

179. See SEC Final Rule Strengthening the Commission's Requirements Regarding Auditor Independence, 17 CFR Parts 210, 240, 249 & 274, 68 FR 6006, 60616–17 (February 5, 2003).

180. See New PCAOB Rules Target Tax Shelters (July 28, 2005), available at 2005 TNT 145–5.

181. Jonathan Weil, Moving the Market: SEC Rejects Accountants' Effort To Loosen Rules Governing Fees, Wall St. J., May 24, 2004, at C3.

In 2003, the Treasury enacted more stringent disclosure and registration requirements to strengthen the Service's ability to discover tax shelters.[182] At the prodding of the organized tax bar, it has also strengthened the standards that apply to more-likely-than-not opinions.[183] IRS investigations and enforcement actions and lawsuits by former clients are ongoing. In October 2004, Congress enacted the JOBs Act, which contains numerous provisions intended to curtail tax shelter activity.[184] In early 2005, a district court approved an $85 million settlement of a class action brought by clients against the law firm Jenkens & Gilchrist in connection with its tax shelter activities.[185]

Conclusion

What lessons might new lawyers draw from Hamersley's experience? Choosing to work at professional organizations that value dissent and constructive dialogue is a start. KPMG's hierarchical and highly conformist culture made it difficult for employees to question tax shelter activity and encouraged them to engage in "group think." Hamersley's experience is also a reminder that lawyers, no matter how junior, should have faith in their own judgments and not simply defer to more senior lawyers on ethical issues. The fact that "everyone else is doing it" in an organization or particular sphere of practice is never, of itself, a sufficient justification for engaging in questionable conduct.

The KPMG story also illustrates the continued importance of the institutions of professionalism. Many of the principal players in the firm's tax practice were lawyers who used their tax expertise outside the confines of traditional lawyer-client relationships. Although precise numbers are hard to come by, a growing number of law graduates are finding it advantageous to renounce law practice in favor of characterizing themselves as consultants or legal experts. In claiming that they are not practicing law, "law specialists" seek to sell their expertise outside the strictures of professional regulation. The KPMG saga signals some of the

---

182. See Treas. Reg. §§ 1.6011–4; 20.6011–4; 25.6011–4; 31.6011–4; 53.6011–4; 54.6011–4; and 56.6011–4, reprinted at 68 FR 10161 (Mar. 4. 2003) (taxpayer disclosure requirements); Treas. Reg. § 301.6111–2 reprinted at 68 FR 10170 (Mar. 4. 2003) (registration of confidential tax shelter requirements); Treas. Reg. § 301.6112–1 reprinted at 68 FR 10173 (Mar. 4. 2003) (list maintenance requirements); Treas. Reg. § 1.6664–4 (accuracy related penalties), reprinted at 68 FR 75126 (Mar. 4. 2003).

183. Circular 230, 31 CFR Part 10 § 10.35, Dep't of the Treasury, Regulations Governing Practice Before the Internal Revenue Service, 69 FR 75839–45 (December 20, 2004). For a discussion of the role of the organized tax bar, see Tanina Rostain, Sheltering Lawyers: The Organized Tax Bar and the Tax Shelter Industry (forthcoming 2005, Yale Journal on Regulation).

184. The American Jobs Creation Act of 2004, Pub. L. No. 108–357, 118 Stat. 1418 (2004).

185. See Final Judgment and Order of Dismissal of Claims against Jenkens & Gilchrist (February 18, 2005) in Denney, et al. v. Jenkens & Gilchrist, et al. (S.D.N.Y.), published at 2005 TNT 34–12.

risks of this strategy. By divesting themselves of a professional persona of a lawyer, law specialists may end up caring less about the law.

*

4

In the Pink Room*

Stephen Gillers

Trial lawyers have been compared to actors, performance artists, playwrights, and directors. All comparisons are valid, to a point. Unlike playwrights, lawyers cannot make up information, but short of lying or suborning perjury, trial lawyers can do a great deal to influence their audience—the jury. Whatever adverse testimony a trial lawyer cannot explain away or counter with competing testimony, she will seek to contextualize in a way that benefits the client or, failing that, harms him as little as possible. The trial lawyer will do that in cross–examination and in the two speeches to the jury—the opening statement and summation—that bracket a trial. She will use all the tools of play acting, to the extent of her ability, including gesture, facial expression, sarcasm, rhetorical questions, word choice, simile and metaphor, silence, tone, and volume. Her opponent will do the same, constructing a different narrative with the same body of evidence. A trial can, in fact, be seen as a contest between dueling narratives. Duelists are not ordinarily inclined to aid each other. Yet litigation, like traditional duels, does have rules and a few of them do require a lawyer to assist an opponent's case even if it means harming her own. Given the adversarial nature of trials, and the natural desire of lawyers to win, these rules are not always honored. In the following story, they were not.

I

The Grand Concourse runs four and a half miles north-south in the borough of the Bronx, City of New York. Designed in the 1890s, 180 feet wide, it was meant to allow horse drawn carriages quick access to parks in the borough's north. Today, there is nothing about the Concourse that can be called grand. Tourists are unlikely to visit it unless they have a keen interest in urban planning or Art Deco apartment buildings. Unless they are students of neo-classical architecture, tourists are also unlikely to visit the nine story Bronx County Courthouse. Built in 1934 and designated a city landmark in 1996, it occupies a full city block toward the southern end of the Concourse. But tourists may have read about the

---

* Many of the facts in this chapter come from briefs, transcripts, and other documents on file with the author, and from interviews. Other sources are cited in footnotes.

courthouse. This is where Sherman McCoy, the "Master of the Universe" in Tom Wolfe's novel "Bonfire of the Vanities," faced trial for homicide. It is also where, in 1978, David "Son of Sam" Berkowitz pled guilty to murder.[1] Of less prominence, but not without drama, this is where, on September 6, 1984, Alberto Ramos was indicted for raping a five year old girl at a Bronx day care center and where he went on trial the following May.

In January 1984, Alberto Ramos was a 21–year old student at Hostos Community College, and an aspiring teacher, when a friend told him about a part-time job as an aide at the Concourse Day Care Center. The center operated under the authority of the Human Resources Administration (HRA), a city agency. On Friday, February 17, Ramos was assisting Fernie Skerrit in a class of five year olds. He was alone with the children during nap time. Some of the children talked and Ramos put masking tape vertically over their mouths as a reminder to be quiet. O. was one of those children. When Mrs. Skerrit returned to the classroom, she removed the tape and admonished Ramos. The taping, which Ramos admitted, showed bad judgment, but that seemed to be the end of it. But it was not the end of it. Suspicions, and then accusations, from O.'s family led to two investigations—one by HRA and one by the police. These in turn led to the allegation that Alberto Ramos raped O. in the bathroom adjoining the classroom during Mrs. Skerrit's absence, and then to his indictment and his trial in May 1985.

The jury learned that Fernie Skerrit's classroom was called the Pink Room. Skerrit testified that at 1 p.m. on February 17, 1984, she took her forty-five minute lunch break during the children's nap time. An aide, Margaret Alieu, left work ten minutes later. Ramos was then alone with the children in the Pink Room for 15 minutes, possibly longer. O., six years old at trial, testified that in this interval Ramos put tape on her mouth and took her into the adjacent bathroom, closing the door. In the bathroom, O. said, Ramos put his "thing" in "my kitty cat," using anatomically correct dolls to illustrate what she meant. Initially, O. said that both she and Ramos were standing when this happened, a physical impossibility, but on further questioning O. testified that Ramos was kneeling. O. then returned to her cot. Patricia Wilson, another student in the class, also testified. She said Ramos took O. into the bathroom and closed the door and that when O. came back to her cot she was crying. When Skerrit returned to the classroom at 1:45, she said she saw the tape on O.'s mouth. She asked O. why it was there and O. replied that "Alberto put it there" because she was talking. She did not seem upset.

Redell Willis, O.'s grandmother, told the jury that she picked O. up at the daycare center that Friday afternoon. O. had tears in her eyes but

---

1. Mario Merola, Big City D.A. 189 (1988).

did not say why. At home, O. said her "kitty cat" hurt. Esterlita Harvin, O.'s mother, testified that she returned from her night job at one or two a.m. Saturday. O. was still awake and Harvin gave her a bath. She noticed that O.'s panties had stains and detected a foul odor from her genital area. Harvin told the jury that she noticed redness and bruises in the vaginal area and consulted her mother, who noticed the same. Harvin worked two jobs. She had to report to one of them that Saturday morning and to her second job immediately thereafter. When she came home on Sunday at two a.m., the redness was still there. She took O. to Bronx Lebanon Hospital, where O. told a nurse that Efrain, a boy in her class, caused the bruises. At trial, O. testified that she had named Efrain because she didn't want the doctor to know about Alberto.

At the hospital, O. was examined by Dr. Paraclet Louissaint, who did not testify but whose record of the examination became a trial exhibit. Louissant recorded that he found O.'s hymen slightly opened and some redness in the genital area. He concluded that "the irritation could have been caused by 'almost anything, including bathroom play with another child or ... masturbation.' "[2] Louissaint referred O. to the pediatric clinic, where she was seen by Dr. Annette Vasquez the following Tuesday. Vasquez testified that O. had been "sexually abused." She based her opinion on her examination of O., the medical records, and conversation with O. "Basically," she told the jury, "because she [O.] gave such an accurate description of everything that happened." Two days later, O.'s mother and grandmother informed the director of the Concourse Day Care Center of Vasquez's conclusion and Ramos was fired the next day for taping the mouths of children. Informed as well of Vasquez's opinion, Ramos denied that he had abused O.

The defense called two witnesses. Christina Gonzalez, the assistant director at the day care center, testified that she had encountered Alberto in the hall outside the Pink Room at about 1:25. He was arranging a bulletin board. Gonzalez asked Oscar Rojas, another aide, to look in on the Pink Room while Ramos came to her office. Ramos was in Gonzalez's office for ten to fifteen minutes. She offered him a permanent job. Gonzalez said Ramos left her office at 1:45 or 1:50. Oscar Rojas also testified. He was the friend who told Ramos about the job at Concourse. He told the jury that he saw Ramos in the hall outside the Pink Room at 1:25. He looked in on the Pink Room between 1:30 and 1:55 as Gonzalez instructed. Rojas admonished Ramos for taping the mouths of children. Ramos did not testify. He had no criminal record.

In summation, Diana Farrell, the prosecutor, argued that this evidence proved Ramos's guilt beyond a reasonable doubt. After summariz-

---

2. Ramos v. City of New York, 729 N.Y.S.2d 678, 682 (1st Dept. 2001).

ing O.'s testimony and Vasquez's opinion, Farrell asked some powerful rhetorical questions:

> She [O.] sat in that chair and she told you that it was Alberto. It was difficult for her because she came over here and she showed you with these dolls and she pulled down their pants and showed you where the kitty cat was and showed you where his thing was and then told you he put his thing in her kitty cat and then she went on to tell you that the way he did it was he was kneeling and pulled her onto him and that he put it in a little bit and went in and then he pulled it out and is this the type of thing a child makes up? She wasn't telling you that Santa Claus had come to her house with fairies or about—about any nursery rhymes. She was telling you that a man, Alberto, had put his penis into her, into her kitty cat, into her vagina. A five year old describing it for you, showing you how it was done. That's the type of thing that a five year old child makes up?

The jury deliberated less than a day. It asked to rehear the Vasquez testimony. On May 20, 1985, it convicted Alberto Ramos of raping O. His reaction was immediate. "I want to die," he screamed. "Kill me. Kill me." Ramos was remanded to custody. On June 12, he was given the maximum sentence, eight to twenty-five years in prison. The judge expressed regret that the law did not permit him to impose a life sentence. "It is difficult to comprehend the enormity" of the crime, the judge said. "One must be completely puzzled in trying to understand how he could have been so cruel, so insensitive, so inhumane as to put a child through that degradation."[3] Ramos lost his appeals to higher state courts.[4]

Prison is especially hard on inmates convicted of abusing children. Ramos's case, and other child sex abuse prosecutions in the Bronx around the same time, received headline treatment in the tabloids. Word naturally reached the prisons and jails of New York State. So when Ramos was incarcerated, he was already known as a "baby raper." He was verbally abused by court officers, guards, administrators, nurses, and doctors. Other inmates beat him. He was threatened with death. As he would later testify, in the prison hierarchy, "I was the lowest of the lowest piece of garbage that walked the jailhouse. I was viewed as a piece of—I was viewed as garbage." On several occasions he was sexually abused by other inmates in exchange for protection or on threat of being cut.

---

3.   25 Years for Rape of Girl, 5, at Center, N. Y. Times, Jan. 13, 1985, at B4.

4.   People v. Ramos, 508 N.Y.S.2d 130 (1st Dept. 1986), app. denied, 506 N.E.2d 550 (N.Y. 1987).

In the summer after Alberto Ramos was convicted, O.'s mother sued the Concourse Day Care Center and the City of New York for her daughter's injuries. The center was insured. The insurance company hired a law firm. The firm retained an investigator to collect evidence. His name was Anthony Judge. The civil case dragged on for five years. A settlement agreement, reached in October 1990, gave O., then eleven years old, a series of staggered payments. She was to receive $5000 immediately, $15,000 on each of her eighteenth through twenty-first birthdays, $25,000 on her twenty-fifth birthday, $50,000 on her thirtieth birthday, and a monthly payment of $1100 for life (with annual increases of three percent) starting when she turned twenty-one. An additional $21,618 was to be deposited in a trust account for O. immediately, which she could withdraw with interest when she reached eighteen. The insurance company also paid $100,000 for O.'s legal fees.

II

This might have ended the story except for Anthony Judge. In the course of his investigation, Judge discovered documents in HRA files that were not given to Ramos and that led Judge to believe that Ramos was innocent. "I was astounded to read what I read," Judge would tell the *New York Times* in 2004.[5] But Judge was not free to give the documents to Ramos without an agreement from the firm's clients. They did agree, and Judge gave the documents to Flor Cupelis, Ramos's mother. Of course, the documents were of no use without a lawyer to interpret them and evaluate whether they might provide a legal basis for challenging Ramos's conviction. By this time, 1991, Ramos had been in prison nearly six years. Cupelis told her son what Judge had given her. He told her whom to call.

About a year after he was sentenced, Alberto Ramos was incarcerated at the Clinton Correctional Facility in Dannemora, New York, a maximum security prison near the Canadian border, about 300 miles from New York City. There he met four other men in a special unit that included inmates convicted of child sex abuse: Nathaniel Grady, a Methodist minister; Albert Algarin; Jesus Torres; and Franklin Beauchamp. The five had other things in common. All protested their innocence and all had been convicted in the Bronx within a two-year period, at a time when the country was seeing a rash of child sex abuse prosecutions.[6] The five convictions were big news in New York City and beyond. The Bronx District Attorney who brought these cases was Mario

---

5. Disciplinary Action Is Rare After Misconduct or Mistakes, N. Y. Times, Mar. 21, 2004, at A1.

6. Ramos v. City of New York, 729 N.Y.S.2d at 682. See generally, Dorothy Rabinowitz, No Crueler Tyrannies: Accusation, False Witness, and Other Terrors of Our Times (Free Press 2004).

Merola. Formerly a New York City councilman, he was elected to the
Bronx post in 1973. In "Big City D.A.," his autobiography, Merola wrote
with pride about the sex crime prosecutions in his office and about the
difficulty of proving cases where the victim is a child. "The crime is so
horrendous that sometimes jurors—and even we—need overwhelming
proof before we can accept that the accused has done what the children
say he or she has done. We look for more evidence than even the law
requires—and the law, in my opinion, is pretty tough."[7] Merola explained how he sought this proof. It was necessary, he explained, to win
the trust of young children who are asked to testify in court:

> I've been accused of giving them candy. I plead guilty. I give
> them candy, I stroke them, I kiss them. We try everything
> humanly possible to relax them.... But let me tell you, when it
> comes to situations like this, you can't put words in the kids'
> mouths. Kids tell the truth. And if it takes hugging and candy
> to relax them enough to tell the truth, I'm all for it.[8]

While Merola's book discusses his prosecution of each of the men Ramos
met at Clinton, he does not mention Ramos.

Grady was forty-seven in 1984 when he was convicted of abusing
three-year-olds during nap time at his church day care center. He was
sentenced to forty-five years in prison. The three other men Ramos met
at Clinton were in their twenties. All had worked at a day care center
run by the Puerto Rican Association for Community Action (PRACA). By
1991, when Anthony Judge gave Ramos's mother the documents he had
uncovered, state courts had already freed the three PRACA defendants
on the ground that the indictments against them were legally defective
under New York law. The indictments did not provide adequate notice of
the charges, making it unreasonably difficult to defend against them.
Beauchamp's case reached the highest state court in 1989.[9] Algarin and
Torres had their convictions overturned in lower courts the following
year.[10] Mario Merola did not live to see the loss of these convictions. He
died in 1987.[11] His autobiography was published a year later. Robert
Johnson, a criminal court judge elected to replace Merola in 1989, chose
not to retry the PRACA defendants although he was free to do so.

Grady's case took longer. On appeal, his lawyer had not raised the
grounds that freed the PRACA defendants. As far as the state courts

---

7. Big City D.A., supra n.1 at 205.

8. Id. at 216.

9. People v. Beauchamp, 539 N.E.2d 1105 (N.Y. 1989).

10. People v. Algarin, 560 N.Y.S.2d 771 (1st Dept. 1990); People v. Torres, New York
Law Journal, Dec. 11, 1990, at 24.

11. Mario Merola, 65, Prosecutor in the Bronx for 15 Years, Dies, New York Times,
Oct. 28, 1987, at A1.

were concerned, that meant Grady had forfeited the right to raise these issues. His only hope was to claim ineffective assistance of counsel, a violation of the Sixth Amendment that would excuse the lawyer's failure. Grady challenged his conviction on ineffectiveness grounds in federal court and won. The federal court ordered the state to hear Grady's appeal or free him.[12] Johnson chose the second option. He conceded the validity of Grady's legal claim.[13] Grady was freed in 1996, after more than a decade in prison.

Torres, Beauchamp and Grady had one more thing in common. The same lawyer eventually secured their freedom. So it was perhaps predictable that when Ramos's mother told him about the documents that Anthony Judge gave her, he told her to call Joel Rudin.

III

Many law students have some idea of the career they want to pursue. But their goals are often vague and subject to change. As graduates, they may work at law firms or government law offices while their preferences come into sharper focus. Chance plays a role too, both in the kind of legal work that happens to come their way and in the senior lawyers with whom they are assigned to work. A much smaller group of law students know exactly how they want to spend their professional lives. Among them are the few who want to defend criminal cases. They may go to a public defenders office for experience before joining a small firm or starting a practice with friends or alone. Joel Rudin wasn't a member of this small group when he started New York University School of Law after a year as a reporter in New England, but that soon changed. While in law school, he worked for a prominent New York defense lawyer and took a job with him after his 1978 graduation. He left three years later and in the ensuing decade worked solo or in small partnerships. In 1991, Rudin was on his own when Cupelis asked him to review the documents that Anthony Judge had given her.

Today, Rudin's ninth floor corner office is across the street from Carnegie Hall in Manhattan. The view from one window looks up Seventh Avenue to a sliver of Central Park. Rudin is an easygoing man with a quick smile and no suggestion, other than his curly gray hair, that he has crossed fifty. He has a quality common to many successful trial lawyers: he often pauses an extra beat before responding in a conversation, as if analyzing sentences for latent ambiguities that he must clarify in order to avoid imprecision.

In taking Ramos's case, Rudin faced significant legal hurdles. New information often turns up after a trial, sometimes many years later.

---

12. Grady v. Artuz, 931 F. Supp. 1048 (S.D.N.Y. 1996).

13. People v. Grady, 675 N.E.2d 1240 (1st Dept. 1997).

That's unremarkable. The question for Rudin was whether the documents from Cupelis provided a legal basis to challenge the conviction. Principles established in two cases from the early 1960s gave Ramos his best chance. Both required a prosecutor, who ordinarily has superior investigative resources, to give a defendant information in his files that could help the defendant at trial. Alberto Ramos would have had no reason to know the cases of Luis Rosario and John Brady. But each played a pivotal role in his life.

More than twenty-five years before Alberto Ramos's trial, Luis Rosario and two other men were accused of murdering a Manhattan restaurant owner in the course of a robbery. Rosario was convicted and on appeal he raised one issue only. Three prosecution witnesses had made pretrial statements about the crime that were either in writing or transcribed. After each witness had testified, Rosario's counsel asked to see that witness's pretrial statement for possible use on cross-examination. The trial judge, in accordance with New York law at the time, reviewed the statements privately and gave defense counsel only those portions of each statement that were, in the judge's view, inconsistent with the witness's testimony. On appeal, Rosario argued that he was entitled to the entirety of each statement on the subject of the witness's testimony so that his lawyers could decide for themselves whether and how the statements might be useful in cross-examining the witness.[14]

The New York Court of Appeals agreed. Variance with trial testimony, it held, was not the only reason a defense lawyer might wish to see a pretrial statement.

> Even statements seemingly in harmony with such testimony may contain matter which will prove helpful on cross-examination. They may reflect a witness's bias, for instance, or otherwise supply the defendant with knowledge essential to the neutralization of the damaging testimony of the witness which might, perhaps, turn the scales in his favor. Shade of meaning, stress, additions or omissions may be found which will place the witness's answers upon direct examination in an entirely different light.[15]

Nor was a trial judge best positioned to identify the value of a pretrial statement:

> Furthermore, omissions, contrasts and even contradictions, vital perhaps, for discrediting a witness, are certainly not as apparent to the impartial presiding judge as to single-minded counsel for the accused; the latter is in a far better position to appraise the

---

14. People v. Rosario, 173 N.E.2d 881 (N.Y. 1961).

15. Id. at 883.

value of a witness's pretrial statements for impeachment purposes.[16]

In New York today, criminal defense lawyers routinely ask for
"*Rosario* material" as a shorthand way to describe a prosecution witness's pretrial statements. As the years pass, fewer and fewer lawyers
will remember the *Rosario* case itself. They are especially unlikely to
recall that while Rosario won his argument, and thereby gained a certain
immortality, he lost his appeal. The Court affirmed his murder conviction after concluding that there was no "rational possibility that the jury
would have reached a different verdict if the defense had been allowed
the use of the witness' prior statements."[17] The variations in the prior
statements, the Court said, were "of a most inconsequential character"
and the other evidence of guilt was strong, including Rosario's confes-
sions to friends and the authorities.[18]

Two years after the New York Court of Appeals decided *Rosario*,
John Brady's case came before the United States Supreme Court. Brady
and a companion, Boblit, were separately tried in Maryland for murder
in the course of a robbery. Brady, who was tried first, testified and
"admitted his participation in the crime,"[19] but sought to avoid a death
sentence by arguing that Boblit committed the murder. Boblit had
admitted as much but the prosecution did not provide this statement to
Brady, whose lawyer learned about it only after Brady was convicted and
the jury had sentenced him to death. In a challenge to both his
conviction and sentence, Brady claimed that he was constitutionally
entitled to Boblit's admission to use in his defense.[20] The Supreme Court
held, in an opinion by Justice William Douglas, that Brady was not
entitled to Boblit's statement for use at trial, where it would not have
been admissible, but that he was entitled to use it at the sentencing
hearing, where it could affect the jury's decision whether to impose a
death sentence.[21]

Justice Douglas quoted from a 1954 speech by Simon Sobeloff, when
Sobeloff (later a federal circuit judge) was Solicitor General of the United
States:

> The Solicitor General is not a neutral, he is an advocate;
> but an advocate for a client whose business is not merely to
> prevail in the instant case. My client's chief business is not to

---

16. Id.

17. Id. at 884.

18. Id.

19. Brady v. Maryland, 373 U.S. 83, 84 (1963).

20. Id. at 89.

21. Id. at 87.

achieve victory but to establish justice. We are constantly reminded of the now classic words penned by one of my illustrious predecessors, Frederick William Lehmann, that the Government wins its point when justice is done in its courts.[22]

And then, in a single sentence, Douglas set down a constitutional principle that dramatically changed the obligations of every prosecutor in the United States:

> We now hold that the suppression by the prosecution of evidence favorable to an accused upon request violates due process where the evidence is material either to guilt or to punishment, irrespective of the good faith or bad faith of the prosecution.[23]

John Brady, like Luis Rosario, has also attained a certain immortality, at least in the legal canon. Today, defense lawyers routinely ask for *Brady* material, or make *Brady* motions, without necessarily knowing the details of Brady's case or that Brady's own victory extended only to a new sentencing hearing, not a new trial. Over the years, the Supreme Court and lower courts have filled in some of the details of a prosecutor's *Brady* obligations. For example, the defense request cited in *Brady* may not be required, depending on the exculpatory nature of the evidence.[24] But the holding remains undisturbed. In fact, it has also been preserved in ethical rules for lawyers. Model Rule 3.8(d) of the American Bar Association, widely adopted in some form, imposes a duty on prosecutors that is broader than the *Brady* rule:

> The prosecutor in a criminal case shall ... make timely disclosure to the defense of all evidence or information known to the prosecutor that tends to negate the guilt of the accused or mitigate the offense, and, in connection with sentencing, disclose to the defense and to the tribunal all unprivileged mitigating information known to the prosecutor, except when the prosecutor is relieved of this responsibility by a protective order of the tribunal.

In New York, site of the Ramos prosecution, Disciplinary Rule 7–103(B) stated:

> A public prosecutor or other government lawyer in criminal litigation shall make timely disclosure to counsel for the defendant, or to a defendant who has no counsel, of the existence of evidence, known to the prosecutor or other government lawyer,

---

22. Id. at 88 n.2.

23. Id. at 87.

24. See, generally, Robert Hochman, Brady v. Maryland and the Search for Truth in Criminal Trials, 63 U. Chi. L. Rev. 1673 (1996), which explores post-*Brady* developments.

that tends to negate the guilt of the accused, mitigate the degree of the offense or reduce the punishment.

IV

To get the benefit of *Brady* and *Rosario,* Rudin had to satisfy two legal burdens. He had to persuade the courts, first, that the prosecutor had the documents that Anthony Judge had discovered in the HRA files; and second, that there was some likelihood that if the defense had been given the documents, the verdict would have been different. This second burden is particularly thorny. It requires the courts to reconstruct a past event (the trial), that was itself an attempt to reconstruct a past event (the alleged crime), in order to determine the effect that the missing information would have had on the jury's view of the prosecutor's proof of that crime. Through witnesses and documents, and subject to the rules of evidence, juries get information about the past. Always, that information is incomplete. Gaps are inevitable. Also, some of the evidence may be contradictory because witnesses honestly perceive or remember differently. Sometimes witnesses lie. It is the jury's job to decide which purported facts are true. Lawyers want juries to view the facts and fill in the evidentiary gaps in a light that is best for their clients. In summations, lawyers offer the jury competing interpretations of the information it heard. They tell different stories about the evidence. In a criminal case, this does not mean that the jury must decide whose story is true. Jurors are asked only to decide whether the interpretation offered by the defense lawyer causes them to have a reasonable doubt about the prosecution's story. So in 1991, Rudin had to persuade a judge in the Bronx, and eventually higher judges, that the story Ramos could have offered the jury with the withheld information would have created a reasonable doubt of his guilt and changed the verdict.

But how confident should a court be that with the information the verdict would have been different? Courts will not overturn a conviction simply because a different outcome is conceivable. The defendant has a higher burden than that. Luis Rosario established an important legal right, but he did not get the new trial he wanted because the evidence of his guilt was strong. John Brady did not get a new trial either (only a new sentencing hearing) because the withheld information would not have been admissible in evidence at trial. The defendant's burden has been described in various ways. In New York, some cases have said that a defendant challenging his conviction after his appeals are done must show "a reasonable possibility" that he would not have been convicted if the withheld evidence were available to him. Other cases have imposed a higher burden, linguistically at least, by requiring "a reasonable probability" of a different result. But before Rudin would even be allowed to argue the likelihood that the documents would have changed the verdict, he had to meet the first burden. He had to prove that the Bronx District Attorney's Office ("the BDAO") had the HRA documents, because under *Rosario* and *Brady* the BDAO, not HRA, had the legal obligation to turn them over. It's an obligation imposed on lawyers—not third parties. Anthony Judge found the documents in HRA's files.

Rudin learned that in February 1984, within days of O.'s accusation of sexual abuse, HRA investigated the charge, as legally required, and quickly concluded that it was not credible. At this time, HRA still understood that O. was accusing her classmate, Efrain. But in March, O.'s mother approached HRA to say that O. had named a substitute teacher as the person who had sexually abused her. HRA caseworker Irene Jarvis and her supervisor Robert Wilson reopened the investigation, and interviewed O. and Ramos, among others. In April, Wilson and Jarvis handwrote a draft report concluding that there was no credible evidence of sexual abuse. That conclusion was based in part on various documents in their file. But the conclusion was ultimately revised, apparently at the direction of their superior who had not been part of the investigation, to say that O.'s claim of sexual abuse was "indicated." A final report with the revised conclusion was then sent to the district attorney. A police investigation ensued, ultimately leading to Ramos's arrest, indictment and trial amid extensive publicity. What HRA did not then send the district attorney were the documents that led Wilson and Jarvis to reject O.'s charge or their handwritten draft report with a contrary conclusion. Except for the handwritten draft, which was never located, these were among the documents Anthony Judge discovered (as a court later described them):

1. Notes dated February 22 of a day care teacher, Mrs. Skeritt, which report that the child masturbated openly and exhibited herself to others [Document A].

2. A memorandum dated February 23, 1984 of the New York City Human Resources Administration (HRA). It reports Mrs. Mendonez, the director of the day care center, called HRA indicating that the teachers and directors were doubtful of the child's accusation against a five year old boy; that the child watches late night HBO movies; that the child plays with dolls, placing them in intercourse positions with movement [Document B].

3. An undated HRA investigation report relating that the director and teachers of the day care center were interviewed and it highlights that the child masturbated openly at the school [Document C].

4. A handwritten letter dated February 22, 1994 by Mary Pizarro, an assistant group teacher, indicating that the child was "sexually wiser," "always masturbating." [Document D].

5. An HRA report dated April 25, 1984 relating that members of the day care center staff observed the child masturbating [Document E].

6. A letter by R. Wilson dated May 3, 1985 addressed to the District Attorney stating, "Enclosed please find the case material on the [O.] file ... " [Document F].[25]

In addition, Anthony Judge discovered a day care center log (called Document G in the court opinion) showing that O.'s aunt, not her grandmother, had picked O. up on the day of the alleged incident. O.'s grandmother had testified that she had picked O. up and that O. had tears in her eyes.

Still, none of these discoveries was likely to help Ramos unless Rudin could prove that the prosecutor had received the documents before or during trial. Ordinarily, a prosecutor cannot be faulted for withholding exculpatory material that she does not have or know about. Investigation revealed that the prosecutor's file contained Documents C, D, E and F in 1991. The prosecutor's file also contained information from the HRA investigation that Anthony Judge had not uncovered, including this note of an HRA interview with O.:

[W]hen asked what Mr. Ramos did to her, she said "he taped my mouth." When asked what else he did, she said "nothing— taped my mouth."[26]

But the question remained whether the presence of these documents in the prosecutor's file in 1991 was enough to persuade a court that they were there back in 1985, when Ramos was tried. Day care center witnesses would later testify that they gave the prosecutor Document G, the sign in log, before trial. That left Documents A and B. The evidence would establish that after Diana Farrell was assigned to the Ramos case in the spring of 1985, she visited HRA's offices and spoke with Robert Wilson, the supervisor in charge of its investigation. She asked him to send her the agency's file. Document F was proof that Wilson mailed the file, including Documents A and B, on May 3, 1985. But Wilson sent it third class. The district attorney's office received it on May 17, just three days before the trial ended.

On October 17, 1991, using the documents from Anthony Judge, and citing *Brady* and *Rosario*, Rudin asked the court to vacate Ramos's conviction. The BDAO resisted. Farrell, the prosecutor, denied having seen the HRA documents or knowing how any of them had ended up in the file in 1991. Ramos was returned to the courthouse, since renamed

---

25. People v. Ramos, N.Y. Law J., June 3, 1992, at 24.

26. People v. Ramos, 614 N.Y.S.2d 977, 981 (1st Dept. 1994).

for Mario Merola,[27] for a hearing in April and May 1992. On June 1, Justice John Collins issued his opinion. He concluded that Documents A through E and G were in the BDAO file during the trial. Further, these documents constituted *Rosario* or *Brady* material or both. Last, he concluded that there was "a reasonable probability" that the failure to provide these documents "contributed to the verdict." Recalling that in summation Diana Farrell had asked "where else the child could have learned such conduct," Justice Collins wrote, "Now after this hearing, we know the answer to that question."

> If the defense had possessed document A, they could have demonstrated that Mrs. Skeritt was untruthful or mistaken at the trial when she testified that the child had never masturbated openly. Through investigation and the use of documents B, C, D and E the defense could have refuted the theory of the People and the testimony of the doctor that the child could only have described her molestation by reason of experiencing it. Through the use of document G, the defense could have established that the grandmother and mother's testimony was either untruthful or mistaken. Contrary to their testimony, records indicate that the grandmother did not pick up the child on the day of the incident, hence she didn't see the child crying and didn't report any incident to the mother which led to the mother's examining the child and taking it to the hospital.[28]

Alberto Ramos was freed the next day after seven years in prison.

Justice Collins's opinion does not end the story however. The BDAO chose to appeal. It argued that Ramos had not in fact proved that the documents were in its files during the trial (as opposed to 1991) and that in any event they were not exculpatory. For example, responding to the evidence that O. had "plac[ed] dolls in intercourse positions with movements," which Justice Collins wrote could have been used to show the child's precocity about sex, the BDAO offered a reason why this information was not exculpatory: "By placing the dolls in close proximity she could have been simulating wrestling or some other activity."

In affirming Justice Collins two years later, the appellate court also explained how the withheld documents could have enabled Ramos to offer the jury a different explanation—to tell a different story—from the one the prosecutor argued in summation:

> [The undisclosed evidence] overwhelmingly demonstrated that the child's ability to accurately describe sexual behavior long pre-dated the date of the alleged incident and that she had

---

27. In Memory of Merola, Newsday, Feb. 27, 1988, at 15.

28. People v. Ramos, N.Y. Law J., June 3, 1992 at 24.

extensive knowledge of sexuality derived from obviously inappropriate exposure to sexual information at home. This was particularly crucial in light of the inconclusive nature of the medical evidence and Dr. Vazquez' testimony that her conclusion that the child had been sexually abused was primarily based on this young child's ability to describe what had happened. . . .

The undisclosed documents demonstrating the child's prior knowledge of sexual matter and her prior conduct with regard to the use of anatomically correct dolls would have sharply undercut the basis of both the doctor's opinion and the argument made on summation.[29]

Then the appellate court, in an opinion by Justice Betty Ellerin, went further. It held that it was "unlikely," based on all of the evidence, that Ramos could ever have been lawfully prosecuted for sexually assaulting O. But, "unfortunately," it added, it did not then have the power to dismiss the indictment entirely. So the BDAO was free to retry Ramos.[30] But by now it realized the case was over. Retrial was impossible. On November 10, 1994, the BDAO formally asked Justice Collins to dismiss the indictment on the ground that "no reasonable cause exists to continue this prosecution." The request was granted.

V

Dismissal of the indictment does not end the story. It has one final chapter. Before turning to it, though, a side note that appears in no court opinion: Two days after the indictment was dismissed, the press reported that when O. was eight years old, she claimed that she had been snatched and raped by a "tall man" while on her way to the store. As she had initially testified at Ramos's trial, O. said that both she and the man were standing. A medical examination disproved her claim and she recanted. "She said her mother never believes anything she tells her," a police officer said, adding that O. made up the story because she was afraid her mother would be angry that her clothes were soiled.

Exoneration, while important, left one unanswered question: Who should pay for Alberto Ramos's seven years in prison? To that question Rudin next turned. The answer would take nearly a decade in coming.

Justice Collins did not find that the BDAO intentionally deprived Ramos of his legal rights. He found instead that its "handling of the matter" was "cavalier and haphazard."[31] He did not have to address HRA's conduct because it was not relevant to the issues before him. But

---

29. People v. Ramos, 614 N.Y.S.2d at 982–983.

30. Id. at 984.

31. People v. Ramos, N.Y. Law J., June 3, 1992 at 24.

the agency was also to blame. When it told the BDAO that sexual abuse was "indicated" and named Ramos, it did not concurrently provide the exculpatory information in its file. It did so later, but by then the trial was imminent or in progress, and the BDAO did not stop to revisit the legitimacy of its prosecution. Looked at most charitably, then, a terrible injustice was done because of bureaucratic incompetence, not evil intention. Professionals in two fields bungled their responsibilities and a man who could not legally have been prosecuted in 1984 if all the facts were known at the time (as the BDAO ultimately admitted) spent most of his twenties in prison as a "baby raper."

There is, of course, no way to compensate for seven years unjust imprisonment, no way for Ramos to recover the twenty-second through twenty-ninth years of his life and relive them outside prison walls. So any compensation, though inadequate, must be monetary. But who would pay? None of the individuals whose conduct contributed to Ramos's conviction were likely to have that kind of money. Only New York City had it. Rudin's challenge was to find a legal theory that would hold the city responsible for the conduct of HRA and the BDAO. Two theories were most promising. The first was to charge the HRA with malicious prosecution under New York tort law when it held back exculpatory documents in its initial referral to the BDAO. The city would then be liable for the misconduct of its agency. The court accepted this theory. The second theory reached the city via the dereliction of the BDAO. This theory relied on a federal civil rights law creating a right to damages when a person acting under color of state law (that is, with official authority) deprives someone of his or her federal rights. Rudin could claim that the BDAO had withheld documents to which Ramos was constitutionally entitled under *Brady*. The courts had already said so when they freed Ramos.

The argument presented one serious problem, however. A municipality is not liable for the constitutional violations of its employees unless they are implementing a policy of the municipality itself. A city can establish policy through its laws or regulations or simply through the decision of a high official. Farrell, the line assistant who prosecuted Ramos, had no authority to make policy.[32] Rudin had to prove that it was the policy of her office to violate the *Brady* rights of defendants. Of course, Rudin was not going to find a smoking gun memo from Mario Merola or other high BDAO officials stating such a policy. But without a policy, the *Brady* violation would simply be the mistake or misconduct of a single trial attorney and the city would have no liability for it.[33] Ramos would get nothing.

---

32. Monell v. City of New York, 436 U.S. 658 (1978).

33. Farrell herself had immunity from civil liability. People v. Ramos, 729 N.Y.S.2d at 687.

Rudin argued that a policy can exist, at least for purposes of establishing municipal liability, by silence or a failure to act no less than through an explicit assertion.[34] To gather such proof, Rudin first identified all cases both during and after Mario Merola's tenure when lawyers in the BDAO were criticized by trial or appellate courts either for *Brady* violations or for using misleading or inflammatory evidence or arguments, whether or not the convictions were overturned. During the Merola era alone, Rudin discovered thirty-two opinions in which trial or appellate courts criticized a Bronx prosecutor on one of these grounds. One prosecutor was criticized in three of these cases within a four year period. In 1982, the appellate court reversed a manslaughter conviction, citing this prosecutor's "persistent misconduct" during summation. Three years later, it reversed another manslaughter conviction, faulting the same prosecutor's "willful and deliberate" misconduct. A year later, it reversed a third manslaughter conviction, calling the misconduct "pervasive," "egregious," "deliberate," and "reprehensible." Rudin wanted to know whether the BDAO ever punished this prosecutor or any of the other prosecutors whose conduct the courts had criticized. (None had ever been publicly disciplined by the court committee responsible for lawyer discipline.) Absent such punishment, Rudin claimed, Merola would have established a policy of acquiescence in prosecutorial misconduct, including *Brady* violations, through inaction. He argued that given Merola's stature, his acquiescence would equal a policy of the city. In a brief supporting his theory of municipal liability and arguing for the right to see the disciplinary records of lawyers on Merola's staff whose conduct was the subject of judicial criticism, Rudin wrote: "The BDAO's failure to take adequate remedial action against the prosecutors involved in these cases would be powerful evidence of the existence of an unlawful policy or practice of tolerating and thereby encouraging such misconduct."

In 2001, the same appellate court that had affirmed Justice Collins's 1992 decision acknowledged that a policymaker's "deliberate indifference" to constitutional rights can support municipal liability. Justice Peter Tom wrote:

> Deliberate indifference may be shown by the policymaker's choice from among various alternatives, not to fully train employees when "in light of the duties assigned to specific officers or employees the need for more or different training is so obvious, and the inadequacies so likely to result in the violation of constitutional rights, that the policymakers of the city can reasonably be said to have been deliberately indifferent to the need." Similarly, the standard may be met circumstantially by

---

34. City of Canton, Ohio v. Harris, 489 U.S. 378 (1989).

evidence that the municipality had notice of, but repeatedly failed to make any meaningful investigation into, charges that employees were violating citizens' constitutional rights.[35]

The court held that a jury could infer deliberate indifference at the BDAO from, among other evidence, its failure to discipline prosecutors "for *Brady* or other violations," its failure to discipline Diana Farrell in the Ramos case itself, and most remarkably, the BDAO's "strident opposition" to Ramos's effort to overturn his conviction based on the undisclosed evidence.[36] Central to Rudin's need to prove his case, the court said he was entitled to learn of any "internal discipline or other remedial action taken" against prosecutors whose misconduct was the subject of judicial criticism.[37]

In the following months Rudin learned the breadth of the problem. From 1975 to 1996, a period spanning both the Merola and Johnson administrations, courts criticized Bronx prosecutors seventy-two times for *Brady* violations or for using inflammatory or misleading evidence or argument. In sixty-two of those cases the misconduct was a factor leading to reversal of the conviction. Convictions in eighteen of the seventy-two cases involved *Brady* violations and all were overturned. Fourteen prosecutors were cited multiple times. Yet each of the cited prosecutors continued to receive promotions and raises. Only once in these twenty-one years, according to Rudin's review of the records, did the BDAO discipline a prosecutor—suspending him without pay for a month, after which he received promotions and raises.[38] Questioned about this pattern by the *New York Times* in 2003, the BDAO said that not all discipline may be reflected in the records Rudin reviewed. The BDAO "takes even unfounded allegations of prosecutorial misconduct very seriously," the district attorney's counsel told the *Times*.[39] Coming from any law office, but especially from a prosecutor's office, that unspecific answer is woefully inadequate. The BDAO's failure is not merely, not even principally, the failure of a single trial lawyer. It is an institutional failure. The BDAO had the duty, as do all law offices, to adopt formal systems to insure that its lawyers behaved ethically and to detect deviance from professional norms early, before damage is done.[40]

The new information Rudin discovered, coupled with the appellate court's endorsement of both of Rudin's key theories of liability, spurred

---

35. Ramos v. City of New York, 729 N.Y.S.2d at 694 (quoting City of Canton v. Ohio, 489 U.S. at 390).

36. Id. at 695.

37. Id. at 696.

38. Prosecutors Not Penalized, Lawyer Says, N. Y. Times, Dec. 17, 2003, at B1.

39. Id.

40. See Model Rule 5.1(a); New York Disciplinary Rule 1–104.

the city to settle. In December 2003, nearly twenty years after the fifteen or so minutes that Alberto Ramos spent alone with his class in the Pink Room, the city offered Ramos $5 million, which it "believed to be the largest false-conviction award in the city's history."[41] Ramos accepted. He wanted something else, too, but he never got it. "I am still very angry," he said after the settlement was announced, "that no one from the district attorney's office, no city official, has come up yet to the plate and stepped up and admitted wrongdoing."[42]

VI

Where incompetence locked Ramos up for seven years, chance and human decency freed him. Technically, of course, Ramos was freed because the indictment was dismissed. But even that came too late. The BDAO earnestly resisted undoing the harm it had caused. It opposed Rudin's initial motion to vacate the sentence when it should have recognized the miscarriage of justice. And then it appealed Justice Collins's decision, delaying closure for two more years, years in which Ramos lived under the threat, however remote, of an appellate reversal and a return to prison.

So it is not entirely accurate to say that the system corrected itself. Rather, vindication for Ramos was the result of a series of fortuities. It was fortunate that O. sued the city and the day care center. It was fortunate that the law firm hired to defend the suit asked Anthony Judge to investigate the facts rather than assume, as it easily could have, that the conviction established the facts. It was fortunate that Anthony Judge found the HRA documents. It was fortunate that Judge sought and got permission to give them to Ramos and that Ramos got a persistent and careful lawyer to represent him. And it was fortunate that Justice Collins took the time to scrupulously evaluate the new evidence and follow where it led.

Of course, the BDAO and HRA are not solely at fault. Ramos's trial lawyer did not discover the HRA files either. Perhaps he can be excused because the BDAO had made an "express promise to obtain and turn over all relevant HRA documents."[43] But even if that promise entitled him to assume integrity from other lawyers, it was a mistake, as we have now learned, to rely on the BDAO's (and HRA's) attention to their professional duties. The police department, which investigated Ramos following the HRA referral, also behaved poorly, though not unlawfully.

---

41. City Gives $5 Million to Man Wrongly Imprisoned in Child's Rape, N. Y. Times, Dec. 16, 2003, at B1.

42. All Things Considered, 2003 Westlaw 65514148 (Dec. 16, 2003).

43. People v. Ramos, 614 N.Y.S.2d at 982.

It failed to discover the HRA files and provide them to the BDAO before the indictment.

In the end, though, the BDAO is most blameworthy. It is run by lawyers, after all, men and women expected to know their legal and ethical obligations. As lawyers and prosecutors, they had primary responsibility to insure accuracy, keep their promises, and exercise great care. Instead, the office behaved irresponsibly, both during the Ramos prosecution and in pressing on for more than two years after the HRA documents were unearthed and even after Justice Collins's harsh opinion. Its justification for taking the appeal is breathtaking. "The judge is attributing to our office knowledge of certain documents that we did not have," a spokesman for District Attorney Johnson said in 1992 to explain the decision.[44] That comment, with its focus on the BDAO's reputation as the motivating concern, shows no awareness that the unearthed documents destroyed the legitimacy of Ramos's conviction whatever BDAO's "knowledge." And that comment, along with Rudin's discovery that failure to punish unprofessional conduct continued after the Merola era ended, means the office may not have learned its lesson. It could happen again.

---

44. Man Freed After Serving 7 Years for Rape, N. Y. Times, Jun. 3, 1992, at B1.

5

United States v. Kaczynski: Representing the Unabomber

Michael Mello*

A. The Unabomber's Pen Pal

The first letter from the Unabomber arrived out of the blue. One morning in July, 1998, the letter just showed up in my Vermont Law School mailbox. It was in a white, legal-sized envelope, addressed to me, with Kaczynski's name, prisoner number, and return address in the upper left-hand corner. My initial instinct was that the letter was a gag engineered by one of my friends from my days as a Florida capital public defender. Still, the envelope, and the letter it contained, seemed authentic. I recognized his cramped, painfully precise handwriting, and the envelope contained all the appropriate prison stamps, such as the prison mail room's date stamp.

Theodore Kaczynski wrote to me because, several months previously, I had written a couple of newspaper op-ed pieces questioning whether his lawyers and judge were about to deny him his day in court. How Kaczynski learned about these op-ed pieces, and how he got my address, I have no idea. But there it was, in blue ink, very legibly printed: Kaczynski's request for copies of the two op-ed pieces.

I replied that I was willing to correspond with him, but that he needed to understand two things up front. The first was that I was writing a book about his case; this meant I couldn't be his lawyer. The second was that nine winters previously, a man I loved like a father—federal appellate judge Robert S. Vance—was murdered by a mail bomb. I worked as Judge Vance's law clerk for the year following my graduation from law school in 1982. He was far more than a boss, however; in the years following my clerkship I came to rely upon his wisdom, guidance, and experience. He became my friend and my father in the

* Professor of Law, Vermont Law School. In the interest of space, I have not included footnotes in this chapter. Citations may be found in Michael Mello, The United States Versus Theodore John Kaczynski: Ethics, Power and the Invention of the Unabomber (1999); Michael.Mello, The Non–Trial of the Century: Representation of the Unabomber, 24 Vermont Law Review 417 (2000).

law. A few days before Christmas 1989, a racist coward with a grudge against the federal judiciary mailed a shoebox sized bomb to judge Vance. The bomb detonated in the kitchen of his home on the outskirts of Birmingham, Alabama. Judge Vance had been a genuine hero of the race wars in Alabama during the 60s and 70s. I mourn him every day. I miss him every day. His assassin now lives on Alabama's death row and, although I have spent a large portion of my life as a lawyer defending death row prisoners, when Judge Vance's killer is executed, part of me will cheer.

I mentioned Judge Vance's murder in my letter to the Unabomber because I wanted to be clear that I harbor a special venom in my heart for people who kill by sending bombs through the U.S. mails. That's what the Unabomber did. For nearly two decades, the Unabomber designed, and mailed, increasingly deadly bombs. Judge Vance, and the mailbomb that murdered him, are never far from my mind whenever I think or write about the Kaczynski case. Every aspect of my thinking about the Unabomber case was influenced, in some immeasurable way, by the fact and the means of Judge Vance's murder. Ted Kaczynski needed to know that.

After writing Kaczynski about my book and my judge, I fully expected never to hear from him again. But I did hear back again, and promptly. Kaczynski and I remained in touch, by letter and by phone, for more than a year after he first contacted me. The stack of materials he sent me is two feet tall and runs more than 2,000 pages. Although we've never met, we have exchanged about 150 pieces of mail and spoken by phone several times.

At first, the correspondence was almost exclusively about my book, but it soon turned to Kaczynski's legal hopes. In the early fall of 1998, Kaczynski asked me to try to find him a lawyer to represent him on a motion to vacate his guilty plea. I agreed, not realizing how hard that would be. As fall wore on, and I was unable to find the right lawyer for the Unabomber, it began to look as though I might come up empty. So Kaczynski asked me to work on a Plan B—to draft a motion attacking the guilty plea that he would file on his own, pro se. I agreed to write a draft, and three Vermont Law School students—Jason Ferriera, Ingrid Busson, and Rich Hentz—stepped forward to help. These three students volunteered their time—a lot of their time—to this project. These students worked their tails off on this project, yet they earned no money, no class credit, and no recognition from the law school. Although not lawyers yet themselves, these three exemplified the best in the calling that they were about to enter. I've never been prouder of law students.

Thus, we worked on two fronts. I still searched for a good lawyer—a seasoned lawyer with the experience and expertise to do the job right.

And the students and I researched and wrote a draft motion that Kaczynski could file in the event that no lawyer could be recruited. In December 1998, both efforts reached a culmination of sorts. We found Kaczynski a lawyer, one of my old law school professors. And we finished the draft pro se motion. I sent the draft to Kaczynski and to his new lawyer with a huge sigh of relief, confident that Ted was in good legal hands.

But it wasn't meant to be. As Kaczynski describes in his motion to vacate his guilty pleas, on April 3, three weeks before the filing deadline, the lawyer I had recruited backed out of the case. It was too late for new counsel to come in, and given the delays in the U.S. mails, it was too late for Kaczynski to run a draft past me or another lawyer. So he wrote the motion himself. He dusted off the draft my students so conscientiously prepared; he wrote the 123–page motion by hand, and he filed it. Our draft, which was designed to be a safety net of sorts, in case Kaczynski found no lawyer, served its purpose.

When District Judge Garland Burrell denied Kaczynski's motion to set aside his guilty plea, I called the prison to give him the bad news. Kaczynski's prison counselor agreed with me that it would be better for Kaczynski to hear of the denial from me rather than hearing it on the 6:00 news. As always, he took the result in stride, and we spent most of the conversation discussing where to go from there. At Kaczynski's request, I drafted an application for permission to appeal to the Ninth Circuit. That concluded my involvement in the litigation.

The Ninth Circuit granted Kaczynski permission to appeal. On the merits, the court split 2–1 in favor of affirming the guilty plea and sentence.

Most of what the public knows about the Unabomber case is wrong. But not for lack of media coverage. The media presence at the Unabomber's non-trial was massive. Seventy-five news organizations set up a center dubbed "Club Ted" near the Sacramento courthouse where the trial was to have been held. Media tickets to the courtroom went for $5,000 apiece, according to reporter Tom Nadau.

The mainstream media, despite its thorough and generally excellent daily coverage of Kaczynski's interaction with the criminal justice system, largely bought into Kaczynski's lawyers' spin on his travails. In particular, the daily press—which did not have access at the time to the court records upon which I rely—seemed to accept unquestionably these principles: (1) Kaczynski was a paranoid schizophrenic; (2) his lawyers acted properly in raising a mental illness defense regardless of their client's vehement objections; and (3) Kaczynski himself, not his lawyers, was responsible for the disruption of his trial. The chaos into which Kaczynski's trial plunged was blamed on Kaczynski's alleged manipulation of the judicial process, rather than on his lawyers' ultimately successful manipulation and control of their client.

I believe this popular wisdom is wrong on all counts. First, I do not believe that the existing public record supports a conclusion that Kaczynski was suffering from any serious or organic mental illness, much less that he was so mentally ill that his lawyers' hostile takeover of the Unabomber defense was justified. My point is not to criticize the daily press; the reporters did the best job possible with the limited facts available to them. However, transcripts of the closed door meetings between Kaczynski, his lawyers, and the judge, present a different, more accurate picture of the Unabomber and his lawyers. That picture suggests that Theodore Kaczynski was unquestionably competent to stand trial and therefore was competent to make important decisions about his case. Kaczynski understood exactly what he was giving up in foregoing a mental health defense. And for him it was worth it, even though it virtually guaranteed a death sentence—which also was acceptable to him.

Second, I do not believe that Kaczynski's lawyers had any legitimate right to force their mentally competent client to stake his life on a mental illness defense. As long as he followed their instructions, the Unabomber's attorneys never doubted that he was mentally competent to stand trial. The fact that Kaczynski was mentally competent to stand trial meant that he was competent—and constitutionally entitled—to make important decisions about his defense: how to plea, whether to testify, whether to appeal, and whether to raise a mental illness defense. Given Kaczynski's decision months before trial that a mental illness defense was unacceptable to him, his lawyers were ethically obligated to either (a) honor their competent client's wishes, or (b) withdraw as Kaczynski's attorneys in time for another defense lawyer—one willing to follow his client's instructions—to take over the Unabomber's defense, and to do it at a time that gave the new lawyer time to prepare for trial.

Third, I believe that Kaczynski's lawyers, not Kaczynski himself, were responsible for disrupting the Unabomber trial. In the months leading up to the trial, Kaczynski's lawyers kept him uninformed about the defense they planned to raise. By the time Kaczynski figured out what his lawyers had planned, it was too late for him to change lawyers or, the judge ruled, to represent himself. Cornered by his lawyers and the judge, Kaczynski had only two ways to prevent his court-appointed lawyers from portraying him as a madman: to kill himself or to plead guilty. On the eve of his capital trial, Theodore Kaczynski made a serious suicide attempt. Then, failing suicide, Kaczynski was left with only one way to prevent being publicly cast as mentally ill. He pled guilty.

Based principally on court documents and published accounts by first-hand observers of the events described, this is what I believe happened in the Theodore Kaczynski case.

B. The Crazy Hermit and His Lawyers

Soon after Kaczynski's arrest, the court determined that he lacked the money to hire a defense lawyer and therefore appointed Montana federal public defender Michael Donohue to represent him. Kaczynski described forming a quick and close relationship with Donohue. Five days after Kaczynski's arrest, the well known attorney J. Tony Serra wrote Kaczynski a letter in which he offered to represent him. Serra wrote: "My personal belief systems prompt me to volunteer my services to you.... I have done many cases with similar symbolic content. I would serve you loyally and well." Serra told Kaczynski that he viewed the case "as one where [Kaczynski's] ideology would be the crux of the defense (not insanity; not a 'whodunit')." After reviewing the letter, Kaczynski decided to continue to work with Donohue. However, Kaczynski remained in touch with Serra.

When it became clear that Kaczynski would be tried in California, federal public defender Quin Denvir was appointed lead counsel. Denvir asked the judge to appoint Judy Clarke, a passionate opponent of capital punishment, as co-counsel, which he did. A third lawyer, Gary Sowards, later joined the defense team. Sowards, a prominent specialist in mental illness defenses, seemed to be in charge of that aspect of the Kaczynski defense. Sowards had a leading role in selecting the defense mental health experts, and, like any good criminal defense lawyer, Sowards knew how to select experts who would give him the diagnosis he wanted.

Within the small community of experienced capital defense lawyers, Denvir, Clarke and Sowards are widely regarded by their peers as among the most competent. Long-time opponents of capital punishment, Denvir, Clarke and Sowards have for a professional lifetime put their principles first. Denvir and Clarke could have made far more money in private law practice. Both are federal public defenders—*capital* public defenders—by choice, and they are two of the best in the business.

According to the *Washington Post*, long in advance of trial—perhaps as early as May 1996—prosecutors and defense lawyers had agreed that Kaczynski was mentally competent to stand trial. The defense lawyers were right: Kaczynski clearly was competent to stand trial. Four decades ago the Supreme Court articulated the legal test for competency: To be tried, a criminal defendant must possess "sufficient present ability to consult with his lawyer with a reasonable degree of rational understanding" and a "rational as well as factual understanding of the proceedings against him." Theodore Kaczynski obviously met this test.

Beginning before his arrest, and continuing until after he pled guilty in January 1998, Kaczynski's family portrayed him as seriously mentally ill. After Kaczynski's arrest on April 3, 1996, the Kaczynski family's lawyer cited Kaczynski's alleged mental illness as a reason the government ought not seek the death penalty in the case. "In his correspondence," the family's lawyer wrote to the prosecutor, "Ted projects his own feelings of anger, depression and powerlessness onto society at large—a society of which he has never really been a member. He blames these ill effects on a wide variety of external factors, including childhood classmates, teachers and his family as well as the media, chemical and electronic mind control, education, science and technology."

On November 12, the first day of jury selection in the Kaczynski case, the *Wall Street Journal* published an article headlined *Alleged Unabomber's Attorneys Press For "Mental Defect" Defense*. The article cited Kaczynski's lead defense attorney as saying that his client's refusal to be examined by prosecution psychiatrists might be due to paranoia.

On November 30, the Newark, New Jersey *Star-Ledger* published a story headlined *Contrary Kaczynski Hampers Defense*. The newspaper reported that "Kaczynski, based on claims put forward by his attorneys, suffers from a classic case of paranoid schizophrenia, an irreversible disease characterized by a preoccupation with one or more delusions, or with frequent hallucinations related to a single theme." The definition of the disease listed in the leading professional textbook of psychiatrist disorders states: "The combination of prosecutory and grandiose delusions with anger may predispose the individual to violence."

As a result of this extensive publicity, everyone seemed to know about the defense Kaczynski's lawyers were preparing for him—everyone, that is, except their client. He would first learn it during jury selection.

The process of selecting a jury was prolonged, beginning on November 12 and running through December 22. Because of the extensive pretrial publicity the case had received, and the need to "death qualify" the jury (i.e., to weed out prospective jurors whose personal feelings about capital punishment might prevent them from fairly considering the sentencing evidence), 600 jurors were summoned; of these, 450 jurors filled out extensive questionnaires. One hundred-eighty-two jurors were brought into court for individual questioning by the prosecution, defense and judge. Only at that point did Kaczynski learn that his lawyers intended that mental illness would be a significant feature of his trial.

It appears that prior to November 21, 1997, Kaczynski was not present in court during a single hearing on any of the motions surrounding the defense counsel's filing of the notice of intent to rely on expert psychiatric evidence. On November 21, 1997, the court directed lawyers for the defense and prosecution, as well as Kaczynski himself, to meet and confer concerning the extent to which the defendant would allow himself to be examined. At that hearing, defense counsel advised the court that they "were willing to speak with Mr. Kaczynski and encourage him to engage in any testing which the government experts find necessary." The court questioned Kaczynski at the conclusion of the proceedings.

On November 25, the judge addressed the government's motion to preclude expert mental defect evidence during jury selection; at that point, according to news reports, Kaczynski became noticeably agitated. He became agitated because he had just discovered that his lawyers had released a psychiatric report to the prosecution and public. He slammed his pen down on the defense table, where it skittered.

Kaczynski's surprise and anger during jury selection seemed genuine to perceptive observers. And if, as Kaczynski asserts, he was kept in the dark about trial strategy, this is consistent with one model of capital defense lawyering, where the idea is to "manage"—i.e., control—the client who resists following the attorneys' best judgment. Recalcitrant clients who insist on fruitless strategies may bend to arguments, threats, promises or other forms of pressure. Almost always, such techniques succeed in persuading clients whose lives are at risk to try and minimize the risk.

By keeping their client in the dark about the defense they planned to present, Kaczynski's lawyers precluded his ability to exercise certain options available to any criminal defendant. Kaczynski could have replaced his court-appointed lawyers with a lawyer willing to present the defense he wanted. Such an attorney, J. Tony Serra, was in fact ready and willing to do exactly that. Or, Kaczynski could have exercised his constitutional right to act as his own lawyer at trial, if he had adequate time to do so.

As it turned out, Kaczynski later tried to exercise both of these options—but Judge Burrell ruled that he did so too late. The judge ignored the fact that the *reason* Kaczynski made his lawful requests "too late" was because his own court-appointed attorneys manipulated him into that position, forcing his hand at a critical moment in the proceedings.

On December 5, 1997, the Montana cabin Kaczynski had built and lived in for more than two decades arrived, on a flatbed truck, in Sacramento for his trial. The truck, towing the cabin shrouded in a tarp, had departed Montana three days earlier. The driver, fearful of leaving his rolling cargo unguarded, slept in the truck for two nights and even ate his meals there; the driver made the 1,110-miles journey driving only at night. The truck arrived trailed by a media caravan. According to the

Associated Press, Kaczynski's lawyers paid to have the cabin transported to Sacramento to provide the trial jury with a window into his mind. The lawyers "say it is the most tangible proof that Kaczynski is mentally ill." Until needed as a defense exhibit at the trial, Kaczynski's Montana home would be kept at Mather Field, an old Air Force base near Sacramento.

The media drumbeat continued that Kaczynski's attorneys knew their client was mentally ill. The *Washington Post* reported that "the lawyers for Theodore Kaczynski have a problem, and the problem is their client. His attorneys believe Kaczynski is mad. So do at least two psychiatrists they hired." The message that Kaczynski was crazy influenced the way the outside world perceived and understood the coming battles between Kaczynski and his attorneys. Who would favor a madman's attempt to control his defense? Who would not support the poor lunatic's lawyers' attempts to call the shots and save his life? Kaczynski's attorneys took on a heroic role in the media. Soon, when the centrifugal forces of Kaczynski's resistance to his lawyers' pressure would tear the defense apart, who would side with the madman and against his lawyers? By now, the *New York Times* was speculating about the existence of "a serious conflict between Mr. Kaczynski and his lawyers over trial strategy." The day before, the judge had held an unusual closed door meeting with Kaczynski and his counsel, without any prosecutors present. The judge said afterward that the meeting "involved matters of attorney-client confidentiality."

C. Behind Closed Doors: A Fragile Truce

In early December, Theodore Kaczynski wrote a series of letters to the judge, prompting him to hold a series of extraordinary closed door meetings with Kaczynski and his lawyers, from which the prosecutors were excluded. Although the meetings focused on the deteriorating relationship between Kaczynski and his attorneys, they also dealt with Kaczynski's mental competency to stand trial. The competency issue and the representation issue were closely linked, at least in the minds of Kaczynski's lawyers. During the meetings, it became evident that the defense lawyers equated Kaczynski's "mental incompetence" with his resistance to their determination to portray him as mentally ill.

On December 18, there occurred an "unexpected" (as described by the court reporter who recorded it) closed door session between the judge and Kaczynski's lawyers. The judge, defense counsel and Kaczynski were present; the prosecutors were not. At that hearing, lead defense attorney Quin Denvir spoke of "a major problem" that had come up between Kaczynski and his lawyers. Denvir told the judge: "You just need an opportunity to explore with Mr. Kaczynski and counsel where things are and try to figure out where to go from here. We are all unhappy and sad to be in this position, but we are in the position." Denvir also addressed the issue of his client's mental competency to stand trial. Denvir said: "We are not requesting a hearing or inquiry into the issue of competency," and, second, that "as to the question of competency, we were fairly confident that Mr. Kaczynski understood the nature of the proceedings and the role of counsel and the Court and that we had been able to, up to that time, to accommodate his mental illness in preparing and presenting the defense."

Defense counsel also addressed, apparently for the first time, their views on the appropriate allocation of decision-making power and responsibility between attorneys and their clients. A footnote to their brief noted that prevailing American Bar Association standards on the control and direction of a case provide that "certain decisions relating to the conduct of the case are ultimately for the accused and others are ultimately for defense counsel." The ABA standards provide that the decisions are to be made by the accused (after full consultation with counsel) include what pleas to enter, whether to accept a plea agreement, whether to waive jury trial, whether to testify in his or her own behalf, and whether to appeal. However, the text of defense counsel's brief argued that "the decisions whether to ... present a defense based on ... defendant's mental condition [as it] bears on guilt fall squarely within the category of strategic decisions that ultimately must be decided by trial counsel." Thus, defense counsel argued that they, not a client concededly competent to stand trial and to make the important decisions in his case, had the authority to stake Kaczynski's life on a mental illness defense.

Kaczynski himself disagreed, and he said so in a series of letters to the judge. In the first, Kaczynski set out three possible options that could satisfactorily resolve the conflict he was having with his lawyers: (1) proceed with current counsel under certain conditions; (2) obtain substitute counsel; or (3) represent himself, "preferably with an attorney appointed to provide [him] with advice." After receiving these letters, the judge ordered the secret, in-chambers meeting with Kaczynski and his lawyers; the prosecutors were excluded from these meetings. The meetings ended up taking two days.

The court observed that the closed-door meetings were necessary "to make an inquiry adequate for the court to reach an informed decision about Kaczynski's concerns with appointed counsel's representation. These concerns involved attorney-client communications." The court also sought to make clear that defense counsel were not questioning Kaczynski's competency. In addition, the court determined that there was "no need to give Kaczynski the warnings required [in order for him to discharge his defense counsel and represent himself at trial]."

On December 22, the court held another closed door hearing. There, Kaczynski accused his lawyers, particularly Gary Sowards, of deceiving him about their intent to use a mental illness defense. The defense lawyers did not exactly admit to their client's allegations, but they did not exactly deny them, either. The lawyers were evasive; Kaczynski was not. At the December 22 hearing, Kaczynski and his attorneys, with the court's assistance, reached an agreement over the mental illness defense. Kaczynski's lawyers would abandon their efforts to present expert evidence in support of a "mental disease or defect" at the guilt/innocence phase, but they reserved the right to present such evidence at the penalty phase. Kaczynski's lawyers may have been displeased about this compromise, but it did create the possibility of delaying the conflict for a while.

The question of Kaczynski's mental competency to stand trial also arose at the December 22 hearing, at least hypothetically. The judge ruled that there was no evidence that Kaczynski was incompetent; rather, the court stated, *"I personally have no doubt about your competency,"* and, *"I feel that Mr. Kaczynski is competent."*

The following exchange occurred (with my italics added):

THE COURT: I feel that Mr. Kaczynski factually and legally understands everything that has occurred during the proceedings against him; that he understands he has to make choices. One of the choices that he apparently has made is the abandonment of the [mental illness] defense. That abandonment may very well end up with a guilty verdict in this case.

You understand that?

THE DEFENDANT: Yes, sir.

THE COURT: But based upon the intelligent approach he has used in dealing with the issue, the eloquent manner in which he has voiced his opinions, it just *seems clear to me that he would rather risk death than to assert that as a defense.* Not to say that that's a necessary result—

THE DEFENDANT: (Nods head up and down.)

THE COURT:—because you would have to go to the sentencing phase. But it just seems that the only way he would have a chance of avoiding a guilty verdict . . . would be to assert the [mental illness] defense. But he's willing to give that up.

THE DEFENDANT: Yes. Yes, sir.

THE COURT: *But I don't see his abandonment of that defense as something that evidences incompetence.*

As to Kaczynski's ability to "understand the nature and consequences" of the trial proceedings—the core of mental competency to
stand trial—Kaczynski's lead defense counsel said, *"I don't think there's
any doubt about that."* Denvir explained what he *meant* when they
suggested, always hypothetically, that Kaczynski might possibly be incompetent: "our feeling ... is that any discussion of competency was
merely raised in the context of if Mr. Kaczynski were to proceed with
what he wanted to do in representing himself. I think that's what raised
the question ... *So any questions of competency were raised only on the
hypothetical that he was going to seek to have us discharged and
represent himself."*

As the prosecutor put it later, "the defense argument goes something like this: that in part the defendant is not competent, or they
question his competence, because he refuses to go along with the defense
that they have chosen. They have kind of equated his refusal with
[in]competence."

This circular reasoning cannot be right, and it isn't. Professor
Richard Bonnie is correct that "disagreement with counsel is not, in
itself, evidence of incompetence. Counsel's advice may ... fail to take
adequate account of the defendant's values and preferences ... unless
the defendant is decisionally incompetent, his preferences bind the
attorney." In fact, "the purpose of the competence requirement is to
establish the minimum conditions for autonomous participation. From
this standpoint, the necessary conditions are ordinarily satisfied if the
client is aware that she has the prerogative to decline the attorney's
advice, and is able to understand the nature and consequences of the
decision."

The transcript of the December 22 hearing demonstrates that the
negotiated truce between Kaczynski and his lawyers was tentative and
provisional. The judge said: *"Why don't we try it this way first, to see if it
works. And if you have difficulty with it, I think you know how to reach
me."*

Thus, two days of closed door meetings addressing Kaczynski's
competency and his relationship with his attorneys had produced a
fragile truce. At the guilt/innocence phase of trial, defense lawyers would
not present expert evidence that Kaczynski was mentally ill, and on that
understanding he would continue with those lawyers. Also, because
Kaczynski had agreed not to fire his attorneys, they would not challenge
Kaczynski's competency to stand trial.

The truce didn't last, and probably couldn't, given the fundamentally antithetical positions taken by Kaczynski and his lawyers. Four days
after the lawyers' abandonment of plans to raise a mental illness defense
at the first phase of Kaczynski's bifurcated trial, his lawyers notified the

prosecution that if Kaczynski were convicted, they "plan to try to spare him a death sentence by arguing in the penalty phase that he is mentally ill." Further, defense counsel told the prosecution informally that they intended to introduce lay testimony at the guilt phase of trial to demonstrate Kaczynski's alleged mental illness. For example, the defense might show the jury photographs of Kaczynski "before and after" he became a hermit in the wilds of Montana. Kaczynski did not learn of these developments until the evening of Sunday, January 4, the night before the trial was scheduled to begin.

Thus, notwithstanding the withdrawal by Kaczynski's lawyers of their notice of intent to introduce *expert* evidence about Kaczynski's mental illness at the first phase of Kaczynski's trial, the lawyers still planned to present *non-expert* evidence of Kaczynski's mental condition. The stage was set for another confrontation between Kaczynski and his counsel over who controlled the case.

D. The Truce Collapses, and the Unabomber Tries to Fire His Lawyers

On what had been scheduled as the opening day of Theodore Kaczynski's capital murder trial, the drama began the instant Kaczynski entered the courtroom. There, in the front row, with his arm draped around their 80–year-old mother Wanda, was Ted's brother David. The *Washington Post* reported that "it is believed to be the first time the two brothers have been face-to-face since David alerted the FBI two years ago that his brother might be the elusive Unabomber." Kaczynski, refusing to acknowledge the presence in court of his brother and mother, sat with his back to them. Wanda and David held hands and wept, as Ted sat only a few feet away from them.

Also in the courtroom, on the front row behind the prosecution table, sat two survivors of the Unabomber's bombs: Charles Epstein and David Gelernter. David Gelernter, a Yale computer sciences professor, had been outspoken in his views that Kaczynski was an evil coward who deserved to die.

Just after the judge took the bench to begin the trial, Kaczynski addressed the judge. Kaczynski, dressed in a bulky knit sweater and blue pants (an observer would later write that he looked "more like an aging grad student ... than the wild-haired hermit who was arrested nearly two years ago,") clutched an envelope as he spoke. Kaczynski said: "Your honor, before these proceedings begin, I would like to revisit the issue of my relations with my attorneys. It's very important."

The judge ushered Kaczynski and his lawyers into his chambers for meetings that dragged on so long that the jurors were sent home. For the next four-and-a-half hours, Kaczynski and his counsel met with the judge in closed session. The *New York Times* observed that "it was clear from the defense lawyers' remarks, in a brief courtroom session after the closed door proceeding, that Mr. Kaczynski was continuing to rebel against his lawyers' efforts to portray him as insane." According to the redacted transcript of the January 5, 1998 meeting, it was here that the question of Attorney J. Tony Serra's taking over Kaczynski's defense was raised. Serra, who had inspired a 1989 movie, *The True Believer*, starring James Woods, is a long-time radical lawyer known for his unpopular clients, his ponytail, and his marijuana habit. Serra's clients have included Hell's Angels and Black Panthers. He also successfully represented two inmates on death row. According to news reports, Serra's office had a resume painting him as as a legal "warrior" who has served his profession well, intent on "defending society's outcasts" and who believes the 1960s were the "golden age of law."

The judge asked Kaczynski: "What is your goal, Mr. Kaczynski, your ultimate goal as far as Mr. Serra is concerned?" Kaczynski's reply was redacted, according to the transcript, "for attorney-client privilege and representation matters." The judge noted that one issue on the table "is a presentation issue focused on a change of counsel, possible change of counsel, at this stage of the proceeding.... What I think I should do is maybe appoint another lawyer to assist Mr. Kaczynski with what he has characterized as a conflict-type issue. I'm saying that in front of you. And then that way he would have a lawyer to communicate with the court on these types of issues. He could communicate either personally or through a lawyer ... I don't foresee that the communications that Mr. Kaczynski has just related should be communication that should cause a breakdown in the attorney-client relationship."

Denvir as lead defense counsel replied: "It may be, though, your honor, to Mr. Kaczynski it has caused that or could cause that if it's confirmed. I think that's what he may be conveying to you. I'm not sure ... your honor, one thing I think Mr. Kaczynski has said is that he would like to know whether Mr. Serra would in fact be available to represent him, and the court might consider having—calling Mr. Serra or having us call him to see if he could make himself available on short notice to resolve that question for Mr. Kaczynski."

The judge then asked Kaczynski: "Do you want me to communicate with Mr. Serra's office, Mr. Kaczynski, as your attorney has indicated?" Kaczynski responded: "I think that would be a very good idea." Lead defense attorney Denvir then asked Kaczynski: "Would you like that? Would that be helpful?". Kaczynski responded: "Yes, it would." The court then held a telephone conversation off the record. The judge then observed, "His office doesn't open until around 9:00. The message center that receives messages for the office didn't have a pager number or any other means of communicating with the people in the office."

While waiting for Tony Serra's office to open, Denvir opined that the problem between Kaczynski and his lawyers wasn't simply a failure to communicate. It was more basic than that. Denvir: "I think without going into a lot of detail about it, I think that what you have termed a communication problem may be a much deeper one that goes into the representation problem. I think that Mr. Kaczynski's feelings may be that there is a much more fundamental breakdown in the attorney-client relationship. I'm not sure of that and—." Kaczynski: "Yes."

A moment later, the court told Kaczynski: "You have fine lawyers. I've seen a lot of lawyers appear in front of me in criminal cases ... " Kaczynski: "Your honor, I do not question my attorneys' abilities." The court: "Okay." The court asked whether Kaczynski or his lawyers had "any problems if I call a [new] lawyer right now? ... I am thinking about appointing another lawyer." Attorney Denvir replied, "I think it would be very helpful. I think Ted would like that." Kaczynski interjected: "I think that would be good."

The judge raised the question of delay, saying to Kaczynski: "I'm assuming that when I communicate with Mr. Serra's office, it's possible that this matter could be resolved and we could proceed on with the trial...." But Kaczynski responded: *"I don't think it's likely that the matter can be resolved that easily. My lawyers have suggested that I should make it clear to you what I want. And what I'm looking for is a change of counsel."*

Not long afterward, the court said: "I just spoke to a secretary in Tony Serra's office.... She could not verify whether or not he's even going to come in the office. She thinks it's possible that he's on vacation right now and couldn't give me details about that." Later, the court received a message from Serra's office, that he was abroad, and no one was sure exactly when he would be back. The attorney sending the message further stated that Serra was interested in the case but had a conflict with the federal defender's office and unequivocally withdrew his offer to represent Mr. Kaczynski because of the conflict.

However, the judge came up with the name of another attorney to represent Kaczynski in his dealings with his current counsel and with the court: Kevin Clymo. Attorney Clymo arrived, met with the group, met with Kaczynski, and reported back: "In my conversations with Mr. Kaczynski, I do not get the impression that he has a desire to represent himself...." For his part, Kaczynski stated, " ... [T]he possibility of change of representation or representing myself is still very, very nebulous. There's still no definite intention there. It's just a possibility that may arise after present discussions continue. So I don't think change of counsel is yet the issue, though it may become an issue."

While Kaczynski was out of the room, the judge told defense attorneys Denvir and Clarke: "I wanted to chat with you about that [mental competency] issue, because it's my discernment that you had previously indicated that if Mr. Kaczynski took a position that frustrated the defense you were going to assert on his behalf, that maybe that would indicate the need for a competency hearing. And I'm assuming, based on everything I heard, that Mr. Kaczynski may not agree with the defense you are asserting—at least you contemplate asserting...." Attorney Denvir: " ... There's the possibility, in my mind at least, of the need for a competency hearing, but I'm not in a position, I don't think we are, to tell the court that it is necessary at this time. We may know better after we explore the communication questions and these other questions with Mr. Clymo and Mr. Kaczynski to advise you in that regard." When attorney Clymo reported that he was making progress, but needed more time, Clymo suggested that, "with regard to these proceedings in open court, I think it would be appropriate to continue to have Ms. Clarke and Mr. Quin [Denvir] represent Mr. Kaczynski's interest with the government in public on the record. Is that all right with you?" Kaczynski: "That's agreeable to me."

Kaczynski's sense of the matter was that Clymo was in effect acting as an advocate *for* his lawyers (Denvir and Clarke) and *against* Kaczynski. To Kaczynski, Clymo's role seemed to be to persuade Kaczynski to accept what his attorneys wanted rather than vice versa. Among other things, Kaczynski claims, Clymo tried to frighten him away from requesting representation by Tony Serra; Clymo went so far as to say he would have doubts about Kaczynski's mental stability if he asked to be represented by Serra.

The judge then denied a motion from the prosecution seeking to preclude Kaczynski from introducing non-expert testimony to show that he had a mental defect. The judge's order implied that Kaczynski's attorneys would be allowed, over their client's vehement objection, to rely on non-expert testimony in evidence to establish that Kaczynski suffered from a mental defect.

The redacted transcripts of the closed-door meetings are confusing and disjointed. One plausible interpretation is that Kaczynski had agreed to continue with his current counsel in control of the defense. Another, equally plausible interpretation is that Kaczynski had put the court and his lawyers on notice that their control of his defense was unacceptable. My own best guess is more complicated. I think Kaczynski, his lawyers and his judge were all honestly seeking a compromise that would allow the trial to proceed. They all came away from the meetings with very different perspectives about what they thought had been agreed upon in those meetings. When subsequent events exposed the fault-lines of those rival interpretations, the Unabomber defense team fell apart.

The pressure on Kaczynski to acquiesce in what his lawyers and judge wanted him to do must have been intense. He was alone. He was isolated. He was a prisoner. He was vulnerable. He must have found it all but impossible to resist the pressure from his lawyers and the judge who had appointed them to represent him. The strain was beginning to show. During the closed-door meetings with the judge on January 7, Kaczynski indicated that he was simply too tired to argue his own case and had no choice but to continue with his lawyers. He said, "Your honor, if this had happened a year and a half ago, I would probably have elected to represent myself. Now, after a year and a half with this, I'm too tired and I really don't want to take on such a difficult task."

At the conclusion of this, the second day of closed-door meetings, Kaczynski stated in open court, for the first time, that he did not want his lawyers to pursue a mental health defense. But the judge told Kaczynski several times that his attorneys are "in control" of his case and that they would be allowed to introduce non-expert testimony about Kaczynski's alleged mental state.

Although Judge Burrell announced in open court that Kaczynski had agreed to proceed with his present lawyers, the court also explained that he had received a communication from J. Tony Serra, offering to represent Kaczynski for free. Serra wrote: "If he is successful in recusing his present attorneys, I'm willing to serve on his behalf," according to a note the judge read in court, and "I wish him well whatever way it goes." Then, still in open court, Kaczynski told the judge, "I think I would like to be represented by [Serra] . . . since he had agreed he was not going to pursue a mental health defense." Kaczynski added that Serra would be able to meet with him next week, but conceded "he would need considerable time to prepare."

Treating Kaczynski's request as a motion to substitute his present counsel with Serra, the judge told Kaczynski, "the motion is denied." The judge reiterated his prior rulings that it was too late for Kaczynski to change lawyers, reminding Kaczynski that a jury had been selected, witnesses were ready to go, and the trial was about to begin. The *Washington Post* described Kaczynski's reaction: "The alleged Unabomber looked at the judge for an instant, and then began rapidly writing on his legal pads." During the afternoon proceedings in open court, Kaczynski was "alternatively scribbling on his legal pads, shoving notes at his attorneys, or whispering animatedly at them. His brother, David, and mother, Wanda, attended the session. But Kaczynski did not look at them."

Also on January 7, the prosecution filed a brief arguing that the decision to pursue or forego a particular line of defense belonged to the defendant as long as he was mentally competent to stand trial. The prosecution argued that because the Sixth Amendment to the Constitution grants to the accused personally the right to raise his defense, "the government believes that the decision to forego a legally available defense rests with the defendant," rather than with the attorney for the defendant. The prosecution explained: "Any absence of a finding that the defendant is [mentally] incompetent, which defense counsel and the court have expressly and repeatedly rejected, the government sees no reason why the defendant cannot decide whether to pursue a mental defect defense during both the guilt and penalty phases of trial, as long as he is fully advised as to the wisdom of doing so and the potential consequences of ignoring his attorneys' advice. Once the defendant makes a knowing and intelligent decision concerning the defense he wishes to pursue, however, the government sees no reason why current counsel cannot continue to represent him. Aside from differences over the mental defect defense, there can be no doubt that counsel has been able to represent the defendant vigorously. Indeed, whatever the disagreement between the defendant and his counsel, it is unlikely that substitute counsel could put on a more effective defense or more vigorously represent the defendant."

The judge was unmoved. He informed Kaczynski that counsel controlled "major strategic decisions" in the case, including the decision whether to put on non-expert mental health testimony; Kaczynski said: "I've become aware that legally I have to accept those decisions whether I like them or not. So I guess I just have to accept them."

My view is that the prosecution's brief was correct and the judge's rulings were wrong, although not entirely implausible under the law. What was missing from the judge's reasoning was his failure to ask the question: In the months leading up to jury selection, did Kaczynski's lawyers keep him in the dark about the defense they were determined to raise? If not, then it was plausible for the court to refuse to allow Kaczynski to change the rules now, on the eve of trial. But, if the lawyers had misled their client as he asserted, then the fairest course would be to do one of two things: (1) require the lawyers to follow their mentally competent client's decisions about what defense to raise, or (2) dismiss the jury, put the trial on hold, and replace Kaczynski's attorneys with lawyers more compatible with Kaczynski's values and beliefs. Since delay appeared out of the question for this relentless judge, the most reasonable option was to ask Kaczynski and his lawyers the questions: what did Theodore Kaczynski know about his lawyers' plans, and when did he know it? If the judge ever asked these questions, it does not appear on the transcripts of the public court records.

By the end of the day of January 7, 1998, Theodore Kaczynski must have felt especially alone. On the eve of trial for his life, his only institutional allies in the courtroom—his lawyers—had kept him in the dark. Now, the judge had authorized his lawyers to raise the issue of mental illness anyway, regardless of their client's wishes. Firing his lawyers and representing himself was still an option, but for the legally unschooled Kaczynski it must have been a terrifying one. He never wanted to represent himself; he wanted his lawyers to provide the assistance of counsel guaranteed him by the Constitution. Also, the judge didn't seem to want him to represent himself; although the law gave Theodore Kaczynski the right to represent himself, the judge might just deny him that right—and, if so, there would be nothing he could do to prevent his attorneys from portraying him as mentally ill.

E. Meltdown

Sometime during the night of January 7, Theodore Kaczynski tried to kill himself in his jail cell. He tried to hang himself with his underpants. Kaczynski's attempted suicide seemed to many observers the final confirmation of his mental illness. I don't think so. Consider it from Kaczynski's point of view. Under the circumstances, suicide was the only rational option open to him. He was utterly alone. His lawyers had betrayed him by keeping him in the dark until it was too late for him to replace them or to defend himself at trial without a lawyer. The law-challenged judge seemed poised to refuse even to allow him to exercise his constitutional right to fire those lawyers and represent himself. For the next few months, he would have to sit in court, listening to his own lawyers inexorably build a case that he was mentally ill—and there was absolutely no way he could stop it. Except for suicide.

Kaczynski's attempted suicide also was a communication directed at his lawyers. Kaczynski claims that his counsel told him that suicide was acceptable if he found life imprisonment unacceptable. The response conveyed by his hanging was equally to the point: Your defense is unacceptable. Yet Kaczynski's lawyers never got the message in their client's communicative act. Their determination to represent Kaczynski as mentally ill remained undeterred.

I followed the meltdown of the Kaczynski defense from my home in Vermont, a continent away from the Unabomber trial in Sacramento. I don't like to second-guess the tactical decisions made by trial lawyers in capital cases (especially high profile capital cases), particularly when I respect the lawyers as much as I do Kaczynski's lawyers; those lawyers always know facts about their case that can't be known by outside observers or commentators at the time. Still, the Unabomber's lawyers seemed to me to be denying their client his day in court.

Thus, I did something I have never done before: I wrote about a high-profile capital case that was still in trial. In the Rutland, (Vermont) *Herald*, and later in the *National Law Journal*, I published op-ed pieces arguing that Theodore Kaczynski was being denied his day in court by his own lawyers. I think I understood why Kaczynski's attorneys had seized control of his defense: they were trying to save his life—from himself, if necessary. But, it seemed to me, by saving his body by any means necessary, his well-intentioned lawyers were destroying his life and his life's work, his manifesto.

From my far-off observation perch in Vermont, I wondered who would crack first: Kaczynski or his lawyers. I didn't think Kaczynski would; he had already sacrificed so much for his political ideology, and I didn't see him giving it all up now to stake his life on a mental illness defense he abhorred. And, given that Kaczynski was obviously competent to stand trial, I couldn't see Kaczynski's lawyers abandoning him to represent himself rather than allow him to control the direction of his own defense. Yet, as the Unabomber non-trial entered its next level of weirdness, that's exactly what his lawyers seemed to do.

Over the past weeks, Kaczynski's choices had been narrowing progressively. Now, he had only one realistic option to avoid the mental illness defense: fire his lawyers and represent himself. Kaczynski clearly did not want to serve as his own attorney; he wanted—and understood that the Constitution guaranteed him—the *assistance* of counsel in presenting to his jury, as a defense against capital punishment, an ideological defense rather than a mental illness defense. But, if representing himself was the only way to avoid a mental illness defense, that was what he would do. Kaczynski hoped that the law gave him the right to fire his lawyers and represent himself. Kaczynski understood the law better than his judge understood it.

When court convened at 8:00 a.m. on January 8, neither the trial judge nor the lawyers were aware of the suicide attempt the night before. The judge had said that opening statements would begin that morning, and the prosecutors were preparing to lead off. During the morning's proceedings, no mention was made of Kaczynski's suicide attempt. Around half an hour after court opened on January 8, defense attorney Judy Clarke noticed a red mark on Kaczynski's neck. That was the first inkling Kaczynski's lawyers had of the suicide attempt, but they did not learn of the facts until after the hearing concluded. The proceedings began, however, not with opening statements, but with Clarke's announcement that Kaczynski now wanted to represent himself. It was, the lawyer said, Kaczynski's "very heartfelt reaction to the mental defense, a situation which he simply cannot endure." He "has lived with this fear all his life," she said, "that he would be described as mentally ill." He would prefer to conduct his own defense and he was ready to proceed immediately.

As for the defense lawyers, Clarke explained that they could not, consistent with their ethical responsibilities, continue as Kaczynski's attorneys if they were forced to forfeit a mental illness defense. The lawyers did not explain how their ethical duties allowed them to abandon a capital client on the day of trial—a client they had represented for a year and a half, a client who asserts they had kept him firmly in the dark about their intentions until it was too late for him to do anything other than represent himself. According to Kaczynski, what had happened was simple: in their game of chicken with their client, Kaczynski's lawyers had counted on him blinking. He didn't. As Clarke told the judge that Kaczynski insisted on representing himself, Kaczynski's mother Wanda wept, and his brother David appeared shaken.

On the other hand, perhaps Kaczynski's lawyers were gambling that the judge would not allow them to withdraw at this late date—that the judge would, in other words, deny their client his constitutional right to self-representation. The judge had already ruled that counsel, not the client, controlled the defense. Good defense lawyers know their judges, and these were two very good defense lawyers. They might well have been counting on the possibility that the judge might ignore the law and refuse to allow Kaczynski to represent himself at the trial.

Such a ruling would have been attractive to the defense lawyers—indeed, it would have given their client an insurance policy of sorts. The lawyers would remain on the case and in control of the defense; if their mental illness defense worked, and Kaczynski's jury voted to spare his life, then he would be sentenced to life imprisonment. If their mental illness defense failed, and the jury sentenced Kaczynski to death, then the judge's erroneous ruling (that Kaczynski did not have a right to self-representation) would require the appellate courts to throw out Kaczynski's conviction and order a whole new trial: a second bite at the apple. Either way, the lawyers stood to win by the judge ruling wrongly that Kaczynski could not represent himself at trial. Either way the client "wins," but at the price of day after day listening to his own lawyers portray him as a paranoid schizophrenic.

This entire scenario depends, of course, on the judge's willingness to disregard the law and deny Kaczynski his constitutional right to self-representation. As it turned out, that's exactly what the judge would do in the end.

Kaczynski's lawyer stressed, again and again to the judge, that Kaczynski was ready to proceed with the trial *"without any delay."* The defense lawyer emphasized: "Mr. Kaczynski has advised us he is ready to proceed [as his own lawyer] *today*. His request to proceed on his own behalf *would not delay the [trial]."* And: It is *"not Mr. Kaczynski's request that anything be delayed* ... He is prepared in the sense that he feels he has no choice [but] to go forward today. *He is not asking for any delay.*" And: "I know the timing is a question when a delay is involved. But that is not his position. His position is he will go forward on his own behalf [today] ... *He is prepared. He is not asking, as the [prosecution] is, for any delay.*"

I belabor this point—that Kaczynski was not seeking any delay of his trial—because, as subsequent events showed, the judge didn't get it. But the judge, on his own initiative, ruled that Kaczynski's mental competency to stand trial and to represent himself would have to be examined and decided. The trial would have to be delayed, again.

The judge's impatience was palpable. The court said Kaczynski had told him "categorically" that he did not want to represent himself—a bit of an overstatement, and one that understandably left Kaczynski "shaking his head in disagreement." Then the judge seemed to soften, acknowledging that he may have forced Kaczynski into it by ruling that he could not prevent his lawyers from presenting a mental illness defense.

The judge threatened to send Kaczynski to a mental institution for thirty days of observation unless Kaczynski cooperated with the psychiatric exam. Kaczynski agreed to cooperate. The message of the judge's anger and his actions could not have been lost on Kaczynski. One need not be paranoid to understand what was going on: The judge was angry at Kaczynski for exercising his constitutional right of self-representation. None of the lawyers in the case seriously believed that Kaczynski was even arguably incompetent to stand trial.

Why, then, did the judge order another delay in the trial for a psychiatric examination that had a foregone outcome? I don't know, because I can't read the judge's mind. However, I suspect that he was trying to buy himself some time to figure out what to do about Kaczynski's invocation of his right to self-representation. It should have been an easy call: Kaczynski had invoked his right, and he was ready to proceed with the trial "without any delay"—immediately. The judge should simply have granted Kaczynski's request and let the trial begin. Or, he could, and I believe *should*, have dismissed the jury and given Kaczynski—or J. Tony Serra—time to prepare to present the defense to which Kaczynski was entitled. That, however, was unacceptable to this judge, who seemed almost obsessed with his felt need to proceed. Indeed, he seemed oblivious to the risk that his rulings had made a guilty verdict extremely vulnerable to reversal by an appellate court, which would mean more delay—a retrial with a new jury.

The judge appeared determined to search until he found a plausible ground for preventing Kaczynski from serving as his own lawyer. Journalist William Finnegan suggested a possible explanation. As he saw it, the court seemed haunted by the experience of Judge Lance Ito in the

O.J. Simpson trial, and was determined not to allow the Unabomber trial to become a prolonged circus. Honoring Kaczynski's right to self-repre-sentation—and his right to put on an ideological defense—would have risked bringing upon Judge Burrell the wrath that had befallen Judge Ito. In short, even if his rulings laced the trial record with error that would require reversal by an appellate court, at least the proceedings in Burrell's court *would* be dignified—with the defense lawyers firmly in control of their potentially disruptive client.

Thus, perhaps the judge needed time to think. He needed the time-out from the trial to come up with a credible reason for denying Kaczynski his constitutional right of self-representation—preferably some reason that could be blamed on Kaczynski himself, and not upon his attorneys.

At the time the judge ordered the psychiatric evaluation, he was unaware that Kaczynski might have attempted suicide. After court had been recessed, the Sacramento sheriff's department announced that U.S. Marshals had reported at midmorning that Kaczynski had a red welt on his neck; he also had arrived at the federal courthouse the preceding day wearing his jail uniform without his underwear. Every day before court began, Kaczynski changed from his jail uniform into civilian clothes. He was also strip-searched. According to the *Washington Post*, Kaczynski told the U.S. Marshals he had lost his underwear in the shower after they noticed it missing. Eventually, the underwear was found inside a smaller plastic bag inside Kaczynski's trash can. According to a sheriff's department spokesman, "The underwear appeared to be stretched." Until the suicide attempt, he said, Kaczynski had been a "model prison-er."

Outside the courtroom, reporters asked Kaczynski's lawyers why he now appeared willing to cooperate with psychiatric testing. Lead defense attorney Quin Denvir gave a blunt answer: "He has no choice."

On the afternoon of January 9, the judge gathered the parties together to see if they could agree on "a psychiatrist to conduct a study and examination of Mr. Kaczynski to determine his competency to stand trial." The court said that the examination would occur in the Sacra-mento jail only if Kaczynski cooperated: "If he's not going to cooperate, he will be on a plane, and I will fly him to a psychiatric institution immediately." Kaczynski would be examined by North Carolina prison psychiatrist Dr. Sally Johnson, who had tested the competency of John Hinckley, the man who had attempted to assassinate President Ronald Reagan. Dr. Johnson planned to spend five days meeting with Kaczynski, evaluating the records in his case, and writing a report, which was to be sealed. Given the low threshold for finding competency to stand trial, no knowledgeable observer expected Kaczynski to be found incompetent.

Certainly his lawyers didn't—they had conceded months ago that their client was indeed competent to stand trial. Although the court reasoned that Kaczynski's suicide attempt would be "significant to a determination of the competency issue," he had ordered the exam before learning of the attempt. His initial reason was Kaczynski's invocation of his right of self-representation. Like Kaczynski's lawyers, the judge equated Kaczynski's resistance to the mental health defense as possible evidence of mental incompetency. So long as Kaczynski had followed his lawyers' instructions, neither his lawyers nor his judge questioned his competency to stand trial.

Accordingly, the court issued an order stating that "the gist of the conflict between Kaczynski and his counsel relates to whether a mental status defense should be asserted and communications attendant to that defense." The court found that "while this conflict [has] presented problems, it has not resulted in a total lack of communication." The court explained that substitution of J. Tony Serra would "be inappropriate in the circumstances" because Kaczynski's request for Mr. Serra was untimely and because Kaczynski's conflict with current counsel was not "so great that it will result in a total lack of communication, thereby preventing an adequate defense."

Both the trial judge and the media made clear whom they felt was to blame for the disruption of the trial. According to a *New York Times* reporter, Kaczynski had "reduced his trial to chaos."

Dr. Sally Johnson ran a marathon psychiatric examination of Kaczynski, questioning him for twenty-two hours, on eight separate occasions, over five days. Johnson also reviewed transcripts of Kaczynski's conversations with his lawyers and the judge, and studied the reports of the defense and prosecution experts, along with other material provided by both the prosecution and the defense. A sheriff for the Sacramento Sheriff's Office reportedly said that interactions between Kaczynski and Dr. Johnson had been calm, that Kaczynski was cooperating with the testing, and that "things are going smoothly." Dr. Johnson submitted her 47 page written assessment to the judge at 9:00 pm on Saturday, January 17. The judge scheduled a telephone conference for the following Tuesday.

During this latest delay in the proceedings of the Kaczynski trial, his lawyers and prosecutors reopened conversations about a guilty plea. The *New York Times* reported that the "sticking point" in the negotiations was Kaczynski's insistence that he be allowed to appeal the court's rulings on certain pretrial motions. At least one such ruling, allowing the government to use at trial Kaczynski's private diaries, was a very strong appellate issue for Kaczynski.

The prosecution filed a brief asking for a hearing on issues concerning Kaczynski's representation. Given that Kaczynski was mentally competent to stand trial, the brief noted that the court would face difficult questions about who would decide whether to present a mental defect defense. The purpose of the prosecution's brief was to set forth the government's understanding of the court's options, and to recommend that the court instruct defense counsel to follow their client's wishes. The brief explained: "Based on the events of January 8, 1998, it appears that the defendant will assert his constitutional right to represent himself if the court rules that defense counsel may put on a mental defect defense of any kind during the guilt phase of trial. If the defendant, after proper warning from the court, knowingly and intelligently asserts his [right to represent himself at the trial] and is willing to proceed to trial immediately," the prosecution believed that the court must grant the defendant's request to represent himself.

The brief urged the court to direct defense counsel to follow their client's wishes concerning the mental defect defense. If they sought to withdraw, "the court would have the discretion to deny their request. . . . In addition, the court would have recourse through its civil contempt power to enforce its decision if defense counsel continued to refuse to represent the defendant under these circumstances. Should the court hold counsel in contempt, they would have the right to appeal, to challenge the court's conclusion that they must follow the defendant's instructions."

F.   The Psychiatric Evaluation

Dr. Johnson stated in the cover letter to her report, "It is my opinion that, despite the psychiatric diagnoses [of paranoid schizophrenia] described in the attached report, Mr. Kaczynski is not suffering from a mental disease or defect rendering him mentally incompetent to the extent that he is unable to understand the nature or consequences of the proceedings filed against him or to assist his attorneys in his own defense."

The press reported that Dr. Johnson had diagnosed Theodore Kaczynski as suffering from paranoid schizophrenia. The *New York Times*, citing "a lawyer who had consulted on the case and had read the report," informed its readers that Dr. Johnson's report had "concluded" that Kaczynski "suffers from serious mental illness, including 'schizophrenia, paranoid type.' " The *Washington Post* lumped Dr. Johnson in with the defense psychiatrists who had collectively "concluded Kaczynski suffers from the grandiose fantasies and delusional rage of an unmedicated paranoid schizophrenic in deep denial." The Associated Press wrote that Dr. Johnson had "diagnosed [Kaczynski] as a paranoid schizophrenic."

This was not quite right. In fact, Dr. Johnson made a *provisional* diagnosis that Kaczynski suffered from paranoid schizophrenia and paranoid personality disorder. Like the mental health experts hired by the defense lawyers, the linchpin where Dr. Johnson hung her diagnosis of Kaczynski as schizophrenic was her conclusion that his politics were a delusional architecture, not a philosophy.

Dr. Johnson's report, despite the mass of detail, rested on two dubious propositions. The first was that Kaczynski's politics were a delusion rather than a philosophy, and that his decision in the early 1970s to return to nature indicated mental illness. The second was that Kaczynski blamed his parents for his discontent and unhappiness as an adult—an idea expressed every day in countless psychiatrists' offices across America. Like the mental health experts hired by Kaczynski's defense lawyers, Dr. Johnson's report reveals as much about her own values as it reveals about the mental health of Theodore Kaczynski.

Dr. Johnson was undoubtedly under tremendous pressure to find Theodore Kaczynski mentally ill in some way. The defense lawyers wanted this outcome for obvious reasons. The judge also must have wanted it, because a crazy Kaczynski would provide the judge with more ammunition for denying Kaczynski's right of self-representation. The prosecution also wouldn't have been displeased with a finding of some sort of mental illness, because then the judge might keep Kaczynski's lawyers in control of the defense. The media and public had already decided that Kaczynski was crazy.

In the Tuesday conference with the judge, Kaczynski's lawyers reiterated the obvious point that they had conceded since 1996: that their client was mentally competent to stand trial. Because prosecutors had always maintained that Kaczynski was competent, this latest concession by Kaczynski's lawyers resolved the issue without any ruling from the judge.

Given that Kaczynski's lawyers *never* doubted his competence to stand trial, Kaczynski had the right to decide the objectives of his own defense. As Professor Richard Bonnie notes, "unless the defendant is decisionally incompetent, his preferences bind the attorney ... disagreement with counsel is not, in itself, evidence of incompetence. Counsel's advice may ... fail to take adequate account of the defendant's values and preferences." The "client's prerogatives to define the basic objectives of representation and to select the main theory of defense lie at the core of the idea that the client acts as the principal and the attorney as the agent in legal representation. This means that the attorney must accede to the client's wishes in regard to these fundamental choices."

G. The Unabomber's Lawyers Play Chicken With the Court and With Their Client

Under the law, the judge's decision on Theodore Kaczynski's assertion of his right of self-representation should have been a no-brainer. Dr. Johnson, the defense lawyers, and the prosecution all agreed that Kaczynski was mentally competent to stand trial. That meant that Kaczynski was also mentally competent to make the important decisions about his defense—including whether to forgo the aid of a lawyer—so long as he was warned and understood the risks and disadvantages of self-representation. It does not matter that the judge might think the defendant is making a self-destructive choice. The law is that it is the *defendant*'s decision to make, not the judge's.

In order for the court to deny the defendant's clear constitutional right of self-representation, the judge would have to find a procedural technicality. The procedural flaw that the court invoked was delay: Kaczynski had waited too long to invoke his right of self-representation, and his invocation of that right was designed to delay the trial.

The judge's reasoning flatly contradicted the public record in the case. Kaczynski had invoked his right to self-representation more than a week earlier, at the latest—on January 8. At that time, as Kaczynski's lawyers had hammered home again and again, Kaczynski was seeking *no* delay: He was ready to go ahead with the trial *immediately*. The government's January 21 brief summarized the relevant history as follows:

> Thus, as the government understands the record, the defendant first raised the issue that later caused him to invoke his [right of self-representation] on December 22, before the jury was impaneled. He had no reason to assert his [self-representation] rights at that time because he believed the issue was resolved to his satisfaction. Presumably, the defendant learned that the issue was not resolved to his satisfaction on or after January 2, 1998, when the government filed a motion to preclude the defense from using non-expert testimony to show a mental defect defense. The defendant then immediately raised the issue again with the court when he next appeared in court on January 5, 1998. In camera proceedings followed. During these proceedings the defendant learned that the issue would not be resolved to his satisfaction. The redacted transcripts of these proceedings indicate that at one point on January 7, the defendant was informed by the court that he had the right to represent himself, but the defendant declined to do so. The next day, the defendant, through counsel, invoked his right to represent himself in open court. As the government understands the

sequence of events in this case, we cannot say that the defendant's assertion of his right to represent himself was untimely
or for purposes of delay.

The defense agreed with the prosecution—a fairly uncommon event
in a hard-fought capital trial. The defense's brief agreed that Kaczynski
was not trying to delay the trial: he said he was ready to proceed
immediately when, on January 8, he first asked publicly to represent
himself. In their January 21 brief, Kaczynski's defense attorneys argued
that his request to represent himself "was timely because the request
was made before the jury was empaneled and sworn.... Moreover, *the
request was clearly not made to delay the trial since Mr. Kaczynski
announced he was ready to proceed with the trial as scheduled and did
not seek any delay.... Mr. Kaczynski first moved to represent himself on
January 8, 1998, and he has not wavered in this request*." [emphasis
added]

Denvir and Clarke threatened to withdraw from the case if the court
ordered them to follow their client's instruction and thus "forgo what
counsel believes is the only viable defense in favor of one that would lead
to Mr. Kaczynski's conviction and execution." Indeed, according to some
observers, including one *New York Times* reporter, the brief implied that
defense counsel might engage in civil disobedience if ordered to allow
their client to control his defense.

Kaczynski's lawyers also argued that the "prosecution takes the
unprecedented step of asking the court to order defense counsel on a
capital case to forgo counsel's own judgment of the best defense to
present at trial, and requests instead that counsel be ordered to follow
the wishes of a defendant, whom experts have diagnosed as suffering
from paranoid schizophrenia, on the choice of a defense that will assist
the prosecution in convicting and executing the defendant." The defense
lawyers continued: "The decisions whether and how to present a mental
status defense in the guilt phase (other than an insanity defense) and
what witnesses to call in the penalty phase of a capital trial fall squarely
within the category of strategic decisions that ultimately must be decided
by trial counsel." Further, "the government's argument that defense
counsel would not render ineffective assistance in this case by following
the defendant's wish that no mental health evidence be presented at
trial is a red herring. It means little that defense counsel might pass
muster under the minimal standards of performance required under the
Sixth Amendment if counsel should decide to accede to a defendant's
request not to present certain evidence at trial.... It is unconscionable
for the government to ask the court—in a capital case—to order defense
counsel to forgo the only defense that is likely to prevent the defendant's
conviction and execution. In fact, the government's improper interfer-

ence with defense counsel's choice of a defense and relationship with Mr. Kaczynski infringes his Sixth Amendment right to counsel."

H. Judgment Day

What turned out to be the final day of the Unabomber's non-trial began with the by-now predictable ruling by the judge that Kaczynski had made his request to act as his own attorney too late. The court held that allowing Kaczynski to represent himself would amount to providing him with a "suicide forum." In the judge's view, Kaczynski must have known that his public defenders planned to portray him as mentally ill; therefore the court found that Kaczynski's request was too late.

The judge began his opinion by criticizing Kaczynski for sending him a letter. The letter, dated January 21, covered two areas: Kaczynski's desire to represent himself; and his views on his counsels' filing of the notice of intent to rely upon mental health experts at sentencing. Although the court had in the past received letters from Kaczynski regarding these matters, this time he found it "an inappropriate ex parte communication with a jurist" because "it contained advocacy which should have been made through counsel." The judge added that "Mr. Kaczynski does not represent himself, at least not yet." The opinion then acknowledged that: "A criminal defendant has a Sixth Amendment constitutional right to self-representation if it is timely asserted and the assertion is not a tactic to secure delay." In the court's view, Kaczynski's request to proceed pro se failed to satisfy this standard.

On the matter of timeliness, the court found that "Kaczynski's first unequivocal request for self-representation occurred on January 8, 1998, seventeen days after the jury had been empaneled. Although the subject of self-representation was discussed several times over the course of the ex parte, in camera proceedings [between December 18 and January 7] Kaczynski never made a statement that could even remotely be construed as an *unequivocal* request to represent himself." Of course not: Kaczynski never *wanted* to represent himself; he wanted—and was entitled, as a matter of federal constitutional law—to be represented with the assistance of counsel. His decision to represent himself was a last resort. Before January 8, Kaczynski hoped to be able to work out some sort of compromise with his lawyers. Only when that proved impossible—on January 7—did he ask to represent himself, and to proceed with the trial "without any delay."

In addition to ruling that Kaczynski's request for self-representation was untimely, the judge held that it was a "tactic to secure delay." In effect, the judge reasoned that Kaczynski's willingness to proceed "without any delay" did not really mean "without any delay." "Although Kaczynski did not accompany his request [to represent himself] with a motion [for delay to allow him time to prepare], granting Kaczynski's request at this stage will undoubtedly result in a substantial impediment to the orderly process of this capital case." In the court's view, Kaczynski would need time to prepare—something Kaczynski emphatically was not asking for—and granting him that time would require selection of a new jury. The judge then explained that Kaczynski must have known that his lawyers intended to raise a defense against capital punishment based on his mental illness. At the end of his ruling, the judge did acknowledge "the paramount principle at the heart of [the right of self-representation], ... the freedom of the accused to personally manage and control his own defense in a criminal case." But in this case, "if Kaczynski abandons the mental health defense, he will forgo the only defense that is likely to prevent his conviction and execution." That would convert his courtroom into a "suicide forum." Quoting from the *dissenting* opinion—*i.e.*, the losing side—of the leading Supreme Court case on self-representation, *Faretta v. California*, the judge reasoned that the "system of criminal justice" cannot be used as "an instrument of self destruction."

However, what the *majority* of the Court had to say in that landmark case is more to the point. Many legal doctrines are unclear and difficult to apply. The right of self-representation is not one of them. The right has been well established since 1975, when *Faretta* reached the Supreme Court. In that case, the defendant, Anthony Faretta faced charges of grand theft. He was dissatisfied with the California state public defender the court assigned to represent him, and also requested to represent himself instead. The judge, after initially allowing self-representation, held a hearing to determine Faretta's ability to conduct his own defense. The court then ruled that Faretta must be represented by the public defender. He was, and the trial resulted in a conviction. The Supreme Court granted certiorari to determine whether a defendant "has a constitutional right to proceed *without* counsel when he voluntarily and intelligently elects to do so. Stated another way, the question is whether a state may constitutionally hale a person into its criminal courts and there force a lawyer upon him, even when he insists that he wants to conduct his own defense." The Court ruled that "a state may not constitutionally do so."

In so holding, the majority reasoned that the "right of self-representation—to make one's defense personally—is ... necessarily implied by the structure" of the constitutional source of the right to counsel, the Sixth Amendment. "The right to defend is given directly to the accused; for it is he who suffers the consequences if the defense fails." The Sixth Amendment itself speaks of the "assistance" of counsel. The Supreme Court explained that:

an assistant, however expert, is still an assistant. The language and spirit of the Sixth Amendment contemplate that counsel, like the other defense tools guaranteed by the Amendment, shall be an aid to a willing defendant—not an organ of the state interposed between an unwilling defendant and his right to represent himself personally.

To thrust counsel upon the accused, against his considered wish, thus violates the logic of the Amendment, the Supreme Court continued. In such a case:

> counsel is not an assistant, but a master; and the right to make a defense is stripped of the personal character upon which the Amendment insists. It is true that when a defendant chooses to have a lawyer manage and present his case, law and tradition may allocate to counsel the power to make binding decisions on trial strategy in many areas. This allocation can only be justified, however, by the defendant's consent, at the outset, to accept counsel as his representative. [An] unwanted counsel 'represents' the defendant only through a tenuous and unacceptable legal fiction. Unless the accused has acquiesced in such representation, the defense presented is not the defense guaranteed him by the Constitution for, in a very real sense, it is not *his* defense.

In Faretta's case, the Supreme Court recognized that virtually all defendants would be better off with counsel; the old saw, "the person who represents himself has a fool for a lawyer," is firmly rooted in the experience of most criminal attorneys. Still, the court in *Faretta* justly concluded that free will should trump paternalistic choice which "must be honored out of that respect for the individual which is the lifeblood of the law."

Kaczynski's choice was not honored and no trial took place. Immediately after the judge's rulings, Denvir approached the bench and stated: "Your Honor, Mr. Kaczynski would like to offer the government that he would plead guilty ... if the government would withdraw the death penalty notice. We have not been authorized to make that offer before." All the lawyers needed was an hour, defense counsel said, "just an hour." The judge initially refused, but then relented with a warning: "You'd better do it before an hour."

With that deadline in view, the defense team then met privately, to work out terms of the plea agreement. For the first time, Kaczynski agreed to plead guilty with no strings attached, except a reprieve from a death sentence. The plea negotiations apparently took less than an hour.

Cornered by the judge's erroneous rulings, and by his own lawyers' apparent willingness to disobey even a court order to allow him to take control of his own case, Kaczynski finally caved in to the pressure.

Kaczynski pleaded guilty. The plea agreement provided that, "in return for the defendant's guilty plea, the government agrees that it withdraw the Notice of Intent to Seek the Death Penalty . . . " During the process of pleading guilty, Kaczynski acknowledged publicly that he was the Unabomber, responsible for the series of bombings between 1978 and 1995, throughout the United States.

Kaczynski plead guilty in this way:

THE COURT: Mr. Kaczynski, please state your full and true name for the record.

THE DEFENDANT: Theodore John Kaczynski.

THE COURT: How old are you?

THE DEFENDANT: Fifty-five years old.

THE COURT: How far did you go in school?

THE DEFENDANT: I have a Ph.D in mathematics.

THE COURT: What is your occupation?

THE DEFENDANT: That's an open question right now. My occupation, I suppose, now is jail inmate.

THE COURT: Okay. What past occupations have you held?

THE DEFENDANT: I was once an assistant professor of mathematics. Since then I have spent much time living in the woods in Montana and have held a variety of unskilled jobs.

THE COURT: Have you ever been treated for any mental illness or addiction to drugs of any kind?

THE DEFENDANT: No, your Honor.

. . .

THE COURT: Mr. Kaczynski, are you fully satisfied with the counsel, representation and advice given you in this case by Mr. Denvir and Ms. Clarke as your attorneys?

(Discussion off the record between Ms. Clarke and Mr. Kaczynski).

THE DEFENDANT: I am satisfied except as reflected otherwise in this record.

THE COURT: You need to explain that, sir.

THE DEFENDANT: All right, your Honor.

You know that I have had certain dissatisfactions in my relationship with my counsel. And those dissatisfactions are reflected in the record. Apart from those dissatisfactions that are reflected in the court record, I have no other dissatisfactions with my representation by counsel.

(Discussion off the record between Mr. Denvir and the defendant.)

THE DEFENDANT: I am willing to proceed for sentencing with present counsel.

THE COURT: My understanding of your dissatisfaction with present counsel is that there was a disagreement as to the assertion of the mental status defense and you had some problems with present counsel concerning communications surrounding the presentation of mental status-type evidence.

THE DEFENDANT: Yes, your Honor.

THE COURT: Is that what you are referencing?

THE DEFENDANT: Yes, your Honor. That is what I am referring to.

THE COURT: Are you referring to anything other than that?

THE DEFENDANT: No, your Honor.

THE COURT: Is it your understanding that your attorneys had discussions with the attorneys for the Government in this case concerning your change of plea?

THE DEFENDANT: Yes, your Honor.

THE COURT: Does your willingness to plead guilty result from those discussions?

THE DEFENDANT: Yes, your Honor.

THE COURT: Are you entering this plea of guilty voluntarily because it is what you want to do?

(Discussion off the record between Ms. Clarke and the defendant.)

THE DEFENDANT: Yes, your Honor.

William Finnegan described the close of the hearing:

Next, the prosecutors laid out some of the facts that they would be prepared to prove at trial. The recitation lasted nearly an hour. It was gory—shrapnel piercing a heart, hands blown off—and what was particularly horrifying were decoded "lab notes" from Kaczynski's journals, in which he recorded the results of his "experiments." "Excellent" was his judgment on the swift, bloody death of Hugh Scrutton, a young computer-rental-business owner. "A totally satisfactory result," he wrote of the murder of Thomas Mosser, a New Jersey father of two.

After each horror story—and all sixteen bombings were described—the Judge asked Kaczynski, "Do you agree with the factual representation just made by the Government's attorney?"

And Kaczynski answered, in a clear, unreadable tone, "Yes, your Honor."

Relatives of Kaczynski's victims who were in court wept. As her son confessed publicly for the first time, Wanda Kaczynski wept as well. She and her son David leaned into one another for comfort. Ted Kaczynski studiously ignored them, as he had done from the outset of the proceeding.

Why did the parties agree to the plea bargain? The prosecutors, no doubt, agreed for the reason they gave: Kaczynski, for the first time, was willing to plead guilty and spare the government the enormous expense of trial. They may also have been worried that legal errors by the trial judge, especially his denial of Kaczynski's right of self-representation, would have rendered any verdict of guilt highly vulnerable to reversal on appeal. The reasons the defense lawyers jumped at the plea bargain were also obvious. From the start, counsel had identified their goal as a life sentence. The plea gave them that. Less clear was why Kaczynski accepted the agreement. Perhaps he wanted to avoid the death penalty. Perhaps he wanted to prevent his lawyers from portraying him as mentally ill; that's what he said. Perhaps both reasons, combined with exhaustion and isolation, came into play.

In reporting on the plea, the press repeated, with plodding predictability, their misstatement that Dr. Johnson had diagnosed—as opposed to *provisionally* diagnosed—Kaczynski as a paranoid schizophrenic. The *Washington Post* wrote that Dr. Johnson had "concluded" that Kaczynski "suffers from the grandiose fantasies and delusional rage of an unmedicated paranoid schizophrenic in deep denial." *Time* magazine, in an article headlined *Crazy Is As Crazy Does*, reported that Dr. Johnson had "found that he was a delusional paranoid schizophrenic." The *New York Times* reported that after Dr. Johnson had "diagnosed [Kaczynski] as a paranoid schizophrenic," Kaczynski's "struggle seemed more and more to highlight the legal system's difficulties in dealing with the mentally ill." A *Times* editorial maintained that Johnson's "sealed report, according to people who have seen it, says that he suffers from schizophrenia and has delusions of persecution that can lead to violence. Dr. Johnson's diagnosis is in accord with the defendant's own [sic] psychiatric experts, who have said he is severely mentally ill."

Formal sentencing was deferred until May 1998. Between the time Kaczynski pleaded guilty in January, and his formal sentencing in May, he continued to be represented by public defenders Quin Denvir and Judy Clarke; during this time, he did not challenge the legality of his guilty plea or the manner in which his lawyers represented him. Kaczynski's lawyers objected to the prosecution's filing of a brief on sentencing, which the judge overruled. The prosecution's sentencing brief is a singularly powerful document on the harm wrought by Kaczynski's bombing campaign, and the methodical records Kaczynski himself kept about that campaign.

On May 4, 1998, Theodore Kaczynski was formally sentenced to four life terms plus thirty years—life imprisonment without possibility of parole, ever. On that day, Kaczynski spoke. He also listened—to the statements by people he had maimed and families of those he had killed. "May your own eventual death occur as you have lived, in a solitary manner, without compassion or love," said Lois Epstein, whose husband was disfigured by one of Kaczynski's bombs. "Lock him up so far down that, when he dies, he will be closer to hell," said Susan Mosser, whose husband's body was torn apart by one of the Unabomber's bombs.

When it was Kaczynski's turn to speak, the following dialogue occurred:

> THE COURT: Does the defendant wish to make a statement before I pronounce sentence?
>
> THE DEFENDANT: Yes, your Honor.
>
> Your Honor, may I come to the podium?
>
> The COURT: You may.
>
> THE DEFENDANT: My statement will be very brief.
>
> A few day ago the government filed a sentencing memorandum, the purpose of which was clearly political. By discrediting me personally, they hope to discredit the ideas expressed by the Unabomber. In reality, the government has discredited itself. The sentencing memorandum contains false statements, distorted statements and statements that mislead by omitting important facts.
>
> At a later time I expect to respond at length to the sentencing memorandum and also the many other falsehoods that have been propagated against me.
>
> Meanwhile, I only ask that people reserve their judgment about me and about the Unabomb case until all the facts have been made public.

THE COURT: Let the record reflect Mr. Kaczynski has finished making his statement and returned to counsel table.

The victim impact evidence was not the aspect of the prosecution's brief that seemed to trouble Kaczynski the most. What bothered the Unabomber was the brief's use of his private diary: The diary passages quoted in the brief portrayed Kaczynski not as a principled neo-Luddite warrior trying to protect society from technology, but rather as a petty, childish murderer who killed to extract "personal revenge" (words he had used) on the kinds of people who annoyed him: women who rejected him; business travelers who flew in the planes above his home; campers who wandered onto his property. This petulant misanthrope, the prosecution argued in its sentencing brief, was the *real* Theodore Kaczynski.

The Unabomber promised an eventual reply: "At a later time I expect to respond at length to the sentencing memorandum. Meanwhile, I hope the public will reserve judgment against me and all the facts about the Unabomb case until another time." At that later time, Kaczynski implied, he will show the world the *real* Theodore Kaczynski—when he gets the day in court denied to him by his lawyers and the judge.

*

6

Spaulding v. Zimmerman: Confidentiality and its Exceptions

Roger C. Cramton[1]

I. *SPAULDING* REVISITED

A. *The Lessons of* Spaulding

It is August 1956 in rural Minnesota and two cars are speeding toward one another to a fatal rendezvous at a country crossing with no stop signs. The collision resulted in one of the gems of law teaching, *Spaulding v. Zimmerman.*[2] David Spaulding, a twenty year old minor, was seriously injured as a passenger in a car driven by John Zimmerman, which collided with one driven by Florian Ledermann. Spaulding's father brought suit on his behalf against the drivers and parent-owners of the two vehicles. The three medical experts who treated David Spaulding did not discover that Spaulding, in addition to a severe brain concussion, broken clavicles, and chest injuries, had incurred an aneurysm of the aorta—almost certainly caused by the accident—that threatened his life. The physician retained by the Zimmermans' defense lawyers, Dr. Hannah, discovered and reported this injury and its life-threatening character to one of the defense lawyers shortly before the parties were to meet to discuss settlement:

> "The one feature of this case which bothers me more than any other ... is the fact that this boy of 20 years of age has an aneurysm, which means a dilatation of the aorta and the arch of the aorta.... Of course an aneurysm or dilatation of the aorta in a boy of this age is a serious matter as far as his life. This aneurysm may dilate

---

1. Roger C. Cramton is the Robert S. Stevens Professor of Law Emeritus, Cornell Law School. This essay draws heavily on a comprehensive treatment of the same subject: Professional Secrecy and Its Exceptions: Spaulding v. Zimmerman Revisited, 83 Minn L. Rev. 63–127 (1998) [with Lori P. Knowles], with the consent of the authors and the Minnesota Law Review. The author may be contacted by e-mail to: roger-cramton@postoffice.law.mail.cornell.edu.

2. 116 N.W.2d 704 (Minn. 1962).

further and it might rupture with further dilatation and this would cause his death."

Spaulding's lawyer, Roberts, who had been in practice only a short time, did not make a formal request for Dr. Hannah's injury report; nor did he ask questions about it at a settlement conference held just prior to the scheduled date of trial. At that conference in 1957, Spaulding's claim was settled for $6,500. The defense lawyers, knowing that Spaulding and his lawyers were unaware of the aneurysm, did not disclose it or make representations concerning the scope of Spaulding's injuries. Because Spaulding was a minor at the time of the settlement, his lawyer was required to petition the court to approve the settlement. The petition included only the injuries known to Spaulding and his lawyer. The court approved the settlement and entered judgment.

Nearly two years later, during a physical examination required by Spaulding's army reserve status, the aneurysm was discovered. Surgery was immediately performed. Spaulding, now an adult, then sought to set aside the earlier settlement, arguing mutual mistake of fact, and, after the defense lawyers revealed that they had known of the aorta aneurysm all along, fraudulent concealment from Spaulding and the court.

The trial court held that the defense lawyers had no duty under ethical or procedural rules to disclose to the adverse party the information of which they alone were aware. Nevertheless, the settlement was set aside. Under Minnesota law the court had discretion to rescind a minor's personal injury settlement when the petition seeking its approval did not fully and accurately state the minor's injuries. Once the parties had agreed on a settlement, they were no longer in an adversarial relationship with respect to the court's approval of the settlement. The defendants, when they concealed Spaulding's aorta aneurysm from the court, took a "calculated risk" that the court might subsequently exercise its discretion to set aside the settlement. On appeal, the Supreme Court of Minnesota, in a terse and legalistic opinion, upheld the trial court's exercise of discretion.

Two generations of law teachers and students have discussed this rich case on the basis of the limited facts and holdings contained in the trial court's memorandum and the state supreme court's brief affirming opinion. Emphasis is usually placed on the tension between the obligations of the lawyer's adversary role and the moral obligations of an actor to protect third persons from harm: Is a lawyer acting for a client required to protect a client's confidential information even if doing so risks the sacrifice of an innocent human life?

A careful analysis of the case in the law school classroom reaches three conclusions: First, the settlement would not have been set aside if Spaulding had reached the age of majority when it was made. Second, the ethics and procedural rules in effect in 1957, in Minnesota or elsewhere in the United States, did not require (and probably prohibited) the defense lawyers, without their clients' consent, from disclosing Spaulding's life-threatening condition to him. And third, under the ethics and procedural rules in effect in nearly all states today, the defense attorneys' obligations (or non-obligations) to Spaulding are the same.[3]

The *Spaulding* case forces law students to grapple with the harsh reality that the lawyer's partisan role in the adversary system, reinforced by the narrow exceptions to the professional duty of confidentiality, sometimes prevents a lawyer, without the consent of the client, from doing the right thing: telling Spaulding that he has a life-threatening condition that needs immediate attention. And it is easy to discover or imagine other fact situations in which the lawyer's duty of confidentiality is in severe tension with ordinary morality. *Spaulding* is the classic setting for two fundamental queries of a life as a lawyer: Can a good lawyer also be a good person? And, within the professional conduct codes as they are today, how may a good lawyer ensure that a morally decent course of action is followed?

If we look at the second question first, it leads to discussion of the duties and opportunities that a lawyer has in relating to a client. Three key principles stand out: communication, counseling, and ultimate deference to client.

Clients retain lawyers to obtain legal assistance. To provide it, the lawyer needs to be fully informed concerning the client's situation and objectives. The first step in communication is listening to the client, the second involves inquiry by the lawyer into the relevant facts and law, and the third involves informing the client of lawful courses of action that may achieve the client's objectives. These duties are succinctly stated in Rules 1.1 (competence), 1.2 (scope of representation),1.3 (diligence), and 1.4 (communication) of the American Bar Association's Model Rules of Professional Conduct. These ABA rules provide the

---

3. A lawyer is permitted to disclose confidential information to an adversary in litigation only when required by law (e.g., in response to a proper discovery request), when the client consents or the use of the information advances the client's interest, or when disclosure is permitted or required by an exception to the confidentiality protection. If the client intends to commit a crime likely to result in death or bodily injury, all states today either require or permit disclosure. See Attorneys' Liability Assurance Society, Ethics Rules on Client Confidences, reprinted in Thomas D. Morgan & Ronald D. Rotunda, 2004 Selected Standards on Professional Responsibility, pp. 144–155 [hereinafter, "ALAS Confidentiality Memorandum"] and n. 36, infra, discussing California law. In Spaulding, however, no client intended to commit a crime of any kind. The defense lawyers, observing an adversary ethic, merely failed to seek the clients' consent to disclose information that might have halted the advance of a life-threatening condition.

framework for the disciplinary codes governing lawyers in all but a small number of states.

Communication slides imperceptibly into counseling.[4] The lawyer-client relationship is a joint endeavor that normally involves a legal and moral dialogue in which client and lawyer learn from one another. The ethics rules require the lawyer to inform the client of alternative courses of action (Rule 1.4(a)(1)), and to defer to the client's choice of a lawful objective (Rule 1.2(a)). The rules require the lawyer to give "candid advice" and "exercise independent judgment," and permit the lawyer to include moral and other considerations in that advice (Rule 2.1).

Many lawyers believe that client-lawyer conversations should be largely or totally limited to "legal" matters, on which lawyers have special expertise. But what is "legal" in character, or relevant to sound "legal advice," cannot be so easily cubby-holed. Even the choice not to discuss "policy" or "moral" or other concerns is a moral choice with moral implications. Properly conceived, justice is not solely the product of governmental institutions, procedures and actions—the grist of laws and lawsuits. Justice is a gift that good people give to each other by the way they treat one another at all times and places, in and out of the courtroom.

A focus on lawyer-client interaction offers an opportunity to explore a common but erroneous assumption that lawyers often have concerning clients—that clients are ruled by selfishness and are less moral than their lawyers. It also focuses attention on a lawyer's broad discretion to use the threat or actuality of withdrawal in a last-resort effort to persuade an obdurate client to avoid repugnant conduct. Model Rule 1.16, somewhat more broadly than the corresponding Model Code provision, permits a lawyer to withdraw when "the client insists upon taking action that the lawyer considers repugnant or with which the lawyer has a fundamental disagreement," even though withdrawal may have an adverse effect on client interests.

In the backdrop is a larger question, to which I will turn in the second portion of this essay: Do the profession's confidentiality rules give lawyers sufficient discretion to disclose information to protect the superior interests of third persons when the client insists on an immoral course of conduct threatening serious harm to others?

Spaulding highlights several important aspects of the law and ethics of lawyering: First, the unwillingness of lawyers, judges and the organized profession to talk openly and seriously about the situations in which threats of harm to third persons justify a breach of the lawyer's most sacred duty, that of confidentiality to client. Second, the reality,

---

4. See Deborah Rhode, Ethics in Counseling, 30 Pepperdine L. Rev. 602 (2003).

again shrouded in professional and judicial silence, that the attorney's adversarial role permits the lawyer to behave in an immoral or amoral way. Third, the importance of amoral dialogue between lawyer and client about the ends and means of representation, especially when substantial interests of third persons are threatened. Fourth, the ubiquity of conflicts of interest and the threat they pose to client representation and to the public interest in just outcomes. In *Spaulding*, for example, the reality that defense counsel is selected, directed and paid by the liability insurer creates a risk that defense counsel may ignore the insured, deferring to the economic interest of the insurer, who controls repeat business. And finally, the truth that the duties and obligations of lawyers often find more concrete expression in procedural and other law applicable to a particular situation than they do in the profession's codes of legal ethics.

B.   *What Really Happened in* Spaulding?

The record on appeal and conversations with surviving parties, family members, and lawyers provide several significant details that illuminate the *Spaulding* case.[5]

- The crash of the Ledermann and Zimmerman vehicles late in an August day at a rural crossroads in Minnesota involved eleven members of the Ledermann, Zimmerman, and Spaulding families, and one additional person. One passenger in each car was killed; most of the others were seriously injured.

- The six occupants of the Ledermann family car were on their way to the county fair. Florian Ledermann, age 15, was driving on a farm permit; his sister, Elaine, costumed for the 4–H dress review, was killed. The six occupants of the Zimmerman car were the owner and five of the employees of a road construction company. David Spaulding and his father, as well as John Zimmerman (the driver, nineteen years old), were co-employees of the business operated by John's father. Zimmerman, as the employer, was providing a ride home at the end of the workday. John Zimmerman and David Spaulding were acquaintances and probably friends.

- The Ledermann and Zimmerman families each suffered tragic losses. The family members were in the position of being both plaintiffs and defendants; doctrines of contributory and imputed

---

5. In addition to the reported decision and the record on appeal, this account relies on a newspaper article on the accident, 2 Killed Friday in Car Collision, Park Region Echo (Alexandria, Minn.), Aug. 26, 1956, at 1. Several of the lawyers who participated in the case and the trial judge, who had been elevated to the Supreme Court of Minnesota when the case was decided by that court, were interviewed by telephone. Surviving family members who could be located provided details of the incident and its effect on their lives.

negligence impaired the monetary value of their claims against each other. Spaulding's claim was not similarly burdened because Minnesota did not have a guest statute restricting the liability of an auto owner or operator to an injured passenger.

- The lawsuits arising out of this tragedy were settled at a joint settlement conference. The liability insurers paid a total of $40,000, of which Spaulding's share was $6,500. Spaulding's settlement was signed about ten days before his twenty-first birthday. At the time, the Minnesota limit on wrongful death recovery was $15,000, and auto liability coverage limits of $50,000 per accident were common.

- The parties, who lived in a rural farming area reminiscent of Garrison Keillor's Lake Wobegon, apparently did not contemplate any recovery beyond the policy limits. Attitudes toward litigation in this relatively close-knit farming community were different than those prevalent in American society today. Moreover, as indicated earlier, the claims of the two families against each other put them in the position of being both plaintiffs and defendants. Under these circumstances, the parents in each family were reluctant to make claims against the personal assets of the other for social, cultural, and economic reasons (i.e., fear of reciprocal exposure).

- The individual defendants did not participate in the settlement conference or approve the settlements, which were agreed to by their liability insurers. In a situation in which settlement would be within insurance policy limits, the defense lawyers viewed the insurers as the only real parties in interest.

- Nor were the individual defendants informed by their lawyers of Spaulding's life-threatening condition. Dr. Hannah's report was mentioned to at least one of the insurers, but the available evidence suggests that the Zimmermans' defense lawyers did not meaningfully consult representatives of their clients' liability insurers as to whether Spaulding's condition should be disclosed to him prior to settlement. The defense lawyers probably made the decision not to disclose on their own.

- Upon remand to the trial court from the Minnesota Supreme Court, David Spaulding, now an adult, settled his claim of additional damages for an unknown amount.

The implications of these additional facts are: (1) The moral obligations of a driver whose conduct has caused a friend's life-threatening injury are strengthened by the employment relationship between David Spaulding and the Zimmermans; and (2) the Zimmermans' defense lawyers, under the circumstances, considered the insurers as their sole or primary client, failing to inform their individual clients of the risk to David Spaulding's life.

C. *The Professional Failures in* Spaulding

Spaulding is a case of multiple professional failures:

Spaulding's inexperienced lawyer, Roberts, was negligent in failing either to request Dr. Hannah's report or to question the defense lawyers about its content prior to settlement. This failure jeopardized Spaulding's life. The potential recompense for such a failure is insufficient, because even if Spaulding or his successors discovered it, and even if they could find a lawyer to bring a malpractice suit, Roberts probably lacked malpractice coverage or personal assets sufficient to pay an award.

Dr. Hannah, who expressed his concern about the "serious" condition that threatened Spaulding's life, was an "examining physician" rather than a "treating physician" and thus did not have a full doctor-patient relationship with Spaulding. Nevertheless, Dr. Hannah had a moral obligation at the time to inform Spaulding of the dangerous condition he had discovered. Under today's law, this moral obligation has ripened into a professional and legal duty exposing Dr. Hannah to professional liability.

The defense lawyers, Arveson and Rosengren, when their conduct is viewed in hindsight and on the assumption that they decided against disclosure without consulting either the individual defendants or the insurers, behaved monstrously. They violated fundamental legal and moral obligations they owed to their individual clients and the insurer who retained them and controlled the defense, including (1) the duty to inform them of an important matter so that they could exercise the decision-making authority that the law of lawyering vests in clients; and (2) the moral obligation to provide their clients with sound advice as to what they should do under the circumstances.

Professional failure, because it occurs quite frequently and is both a personal and an institutional problem, deserves more attention than it gets. Some years ago Charles Bosk wrote a fine book on professional failure as encountered by surgeons.[6] Bosk recognized that we all make mistakes—some of which may cause serious harm—and that these instances of departure from professional standards of due care are enlarged by practice structures and professional ideologies. One of these is the built-in conflict of interest of insurance defense counsel; another is the attitude that clients are only interested in winning, and so need not be consulted about moral issues. Bosk's thesis, as suggested by his title,

---

6. Charles L. Bosk, Forgive and Remember: Managing Medical Failure (1979).

"Forgive and Remember," is that we should forgive ourselves and our professional colleagues for their and our inevitable imperfections, while remembering, and striving to correct, the circumstances, conditions and inattentions that lead to professional failure.

In the *Spaulding* case, I believe the defense lawyers were influenced by the authoritarian and paternalistic pattern of practice that was more common in the 1950s than it is today.[7] This professional attitude was combined with a common practice of viewing the insurers as essentially the sole client, and by another attitude assuming that insurers were only interested in saving money, even at the cost of a human life. Therefore, it was convenient and efficient for the defense lawyers, without consulting either the individual defendants or the insurers, to decide the question on their own.

If the defense lawyers had told John Zimmerman and his parents about the threat to Spaulding's life, what would they have done? Spaulding was an employee of the Zimmerman family enterprise, a co-worker of John Zimmerman, and probably a friend. Both the Zimmerman and Ledermann families had lost a young member of their families in the accident. It is improbable that they would knowingly allow their family tragedies to be visited upon the Spaulding family, even if preventing this would cost them more money (an unlikely event at a time and place when settlements within the policy limits were the standard practice).

Most people do the right thing under such circumstances and insurance personnel who adjust and settle liability claims are ordinary people doing ordinary work. Why do law students and lawyers assume that corporate actors are only interested in company profits and are totally lacking in moral sensitivity? Yet many law students and lawyers assume that most clients, when consulted, will make a selfish choice. Imputing selfish goal simplifies the lawyer's work by allowing her to shirk the hard work of client counseling.

Lawyers have a terrible habit of fitting client objectives into a simplified framework—an assumed world in which clients are governed only by selfish concerns—and then deciding matters for them as if the clients were moral ciphers. An interesting study by Marvin Mindes provides empirical support for the view that clients and lawyers have quite different views concerning what clients want from lawyers.[8] Clients

---

7. See, e.g., Douglas E. Rosenthal, Lawyer and Client: Who's in Charge? (1974); and Mark Spiegel, The New Model Rules of Professional Conduct: Lawyer–Client Decisionmaking and the Role of Rules in Structuring the Lawyer–Client Dialogue, 1980 Am. Bar Found. Res. J. 1003.

8. Marvin W. Mindes, Trickster, Hero, Helper: A Report on the Lawyer Image, 1982 Amer. Bar Found. Res. J. 177.

want a caring and helping lawyer, but lawyers commonly believe that clients want a trickster who is more likely to win. This misapprehension, which distorts and short-circuits their counseling efforts, is part of the macho, self-centered focus of law school and legal culture.

The first and most important lesson of *Spaulding*, then, is one of counseling: taking the client seriously as a person, communicating with and advising the real client not a client stereotype, and engaging in a moral dialogue in which lawyer and client can learn from each other how to act decently in an unredeemed world.

A second lesson emerges from what has just been said. It is fashionable today to lament the decline of professional standards over time and to mourn the passing of a golden age of lawyering in which lawyers were more civil to each other and more public-spirited than in today's era of "commercialism." The facts of *Spaulding* suggest that in a number of important ways, things have gotten better rather than worse. Procedural rules in some state and many federal courts require disclosure to the opposing party of basic litigation documents and witnesses. Today's better trained and more competent trial bar would ask for Dr. Hannah's report or, more informally, pin the defense lawyers down on its content. And today's professional rules as well as evolving practice require defense lawyers retained by a liability insurer to consult with the insured, even when the insurer controls the defense and may settle without the insured's consent. The lawyer-client relationship today, even in the individual-client sector of the profession, is more participatory and less authoritarian than was the case forty years ago. Every era has its problems and some evils are perennial,[9] but some solace can be derived from recognizing that institutional and other changes have improved many aspects of client representation.

D.   Who Among Us Will Do The Right Thing?

Suppose the defense lawyers in *Spaulding* had informed their individual clients and their insurer of the threat to Spaulding's life and had strongly advised that this information be communicated to him. The universal experience of lawyers is that most clients most of the time will

---

9. One perennial problem, evident in Spaulding and many other cases, is the general unwillingness of judges to engage in candid discussion of ethics rules and their moral component. In Spaulding neither the trial judge nor the appellate court discussed the relevant ethics rules or considered their moral dimension. Nor were they willing to criticize the conduct of any of the lawyers involved, other than an implicit criticism of Roberts for his failure to discover the medical report. Most judges are former trial lawyers and identify with the difficulties of the role. In Spaulding the trial judge, elevated to the state supreme court at the time of the appeal, had an additional inhibition: a professional acquaintance with the defense lawyers. The unwillingness of courts to discuss and enforce the constraints of ethics rules, especially when it would involve criticism of the conduct of specific lawyers, is a continuing and important form of professional failure.

accept the lawyer's advice because they believe it is sound, and because the attorney retains an aura of professional authority.

But clients as well as lawyers can sometimes be moral monsters. Perhaps in the *Spaulding* case itself, or another one like it, the moral delinquency flows from clients who spurn their lawyers' advice and refuse to do the right thing. What should a good lawyer do when that situation arises? There are three possibilities: (1) withdraw from the representation if that is possible, but without preventing the client from harming third party interests, perhaps with the unknowing assistance of another lawyer; (2) participate in immoral conduct by doing the client's bidding; or (3) engage in conscientious disobedience of the profession's rules.

The *Spaulding* facts do not present a situation in which withdrawal would be required by the ethics rules. However, withdrawal is generally permissible under Rule 1.16(b) so long as it will not have a material adverse effect on the client. Moreover, the rule permits withdrawal, even if it will have a material adverse effect on the client, if "the client insists upon taking action that the lawyer considers repugnant or with which the lawyer has a fundamental disagreement." But if the question arises on the eve of trial, as in *Spaulding,* or during trial, the court is likely to reject the lawyer's request, forcing the lawyer to continue the representation.

In any event, a silent withdrawal does not resolve the tension between being loyal to the client and protecting the interests of others. Silent withdrawal leaves the client in the lurch, and does not remove the harm. Withdrawal is often more of a "flight" response—an easy escape from a difficult situation—than a solution to a difficult moral dilemma.

The choice between withdrawing or performing the client's dirty work, permissible when doing so will not assist the client's criminal or fraudulent conduct, is made easier by the opportunity to blame the problem on others. When things go wrong, and sometimes they do, the typical response is a "circle of blame" in which each actor blames the problem on other participants. Consider the recurrent corporate frauds that have engaged our attention during the early years of the twenty-first century. The principal actors—corporate managers—invariably assert that the directors approved their actions, and that competent and respected accountants and lawyers structured the transactions, provided advice and opinions concerning them, and approved the company's securities disclosures. The directors, on the other hand, argue that they were kept in the dark by the managers, and that they relied on the accountants' certifications and the lawyers' opinions. The accountants and lawyers repeat the same arguments and blame each other. And so on, around the circle of blame.

The events in *Spaulding* might have gone differently. Suppose David Spaulding had died from a dilatation shortly after the settlement, and someone leaked to the press the information that Dr. Hannah and the defense lawyers had known of the danger to his life and had not acted to prevent his death. At that point, the defense lawyers (and those justifying their choice of withdrawal or continued representation) might have attempted to deflect blame by pointing the finger at the plaintiff's lawyer, Roberts, and at Dr. Hannah. Recall that Roberts had failed to request Dr. Hannah's report, or, absent a formal discovery request, failed to ask pointed questions of the defense lawyers concerning its content prior to settlement. He thus arguably departed from prudent and customary standards of care and, in theory at least, would be liable for malpractice. Dr. Hannah, as the examining physician and not a treating physician, might also be liable today (but probably could not have been held liable at the time).

Even assuming that Spaulding's successors might recover damages against lawyer Roberts or physician Hannah, this does not solve the moral dilemma. The case is not about money, but turns on questions of life and death. Blaming Spaulding's lawyer or one of the physicians who examined him does not excuse the inaction of those who might have prevented another person's death.

If the threatened harm was as serious and as likely to occur as that in *Spaulding*, I would like to think that most any lawyer, including myself, would take the third path of conscientious disobedience. But ordinary human beings, including lawyers, should not be put in the position of risking their livelihood or careers by doing the right thing. Professional rules should not require that lawyers be heroes. Exceptions to the professional duty of confidentiality should be broad enough to permit a lawyer to take action necessary to prevent serious (and usually irreparable) harm in situations when failure to do so is clearly condemned by ordinary morality.

Thus the most important lesson of *Spaulding* is that the professional rules permitting a lawyer to disclose otherwise confidential information need to be reformed.

II.   REFORMING THE LAW OF PROFESSIONAL SECRECY

A.   The Social Purposes of Professional Secrecy

Two bodies of law confer a large degree of justifiable secrecy on information acquired by lawyers in the representation of clients: the attorney-client privilege and the professional duty of confidentiality.[10]

---

10. A third and more recent doctrine—the work product immunity of procedural law—protects information prepared by a lawyer in anticipation of litigation. This important

The attorney-client privilege of evidence law, the oldest of the privileges recognized by the common law, prevents the admission into evidence of a confidential communication between a client and a lawyer made for the purposes of obtaining legal advice. By encouraging the client to communicate all relevant information—even facts that are intimate, unpleasant or embarrassing—the privilege puts lawyers in a position to offer the client sound legal advice in counseling and effective advocacy in litigation. Clients, it is assumed, will choose among lawful alternative courses of action advised by the lawyer. Conduct will be channeled along law-abiding lines, and the goals of the adversary system will be advanced by sound representation of all parties.

The functions and purposes of the attorney-client privilege also determine its limits. The privilege is intended to further *lawful advice and conduct*. When the client, concealing his illegal intent and objective, consults a lawyer to commit or continue a crime or fraud, the privilege evaporates. The crime-fraud exception to the attorney-client privilege, recognized in all jurisdictions, is supported by two fundamental propositions of the profession's historic traditions and of state ethics codes: first, in all jurisdictions a lawyer is prohibited from counseling or assisting a client in unlawful conduct; second, in the vast majority of jurisdictions, a lawyer is permitted to disclose confidential information to prevent the client from committing or continuing a crime or fraud.

The professional duty of confidentiality is broader in scope and application than the attorney-client privilege. The duty applies in all times and places, not only when a tribunal seeks to compel a lawyer or client to testify concerning privileged communications. A lawyer, as an agent of the client, may not disclose or use information gained in the agency relationship to the disadvantage of the client. Agency law combines this broad prohibition, applicable in all settings and times, with a general exception that permits disclosure when the superior interest of another exists. Because the lawyer-client relationship deals with highly sensitive and important client interests, such as reputation, property and freedom, the profession has justifiably concluded that a greater degree of confidentiality is required than in other agency relationships. But the central moral tradition of the profession has always permitted the lawyer to disclose confidential information to prevent a client crime or fraud. In addition, the dominant tradition until the late 1970s has required the lawyer to disclose confidential client information to rectify a client fraud on a third person or a tribunal when the lawyer's services were used to perpetrate the crime or fraud.

---

aspect of lawyer secrecy is largely governed by the same principles of waiver and disclosure applicable to the attorney-client privilege and the professional duty of confidentiality.

B. Disclosure to Prevent or Rectify a Client Crime or Fraud

The policies and purposes that justify the professional duty of confidentiality in the first place argue strongly for a permissive exception to that duty corresponding to the client-fraud exception of the attorney-client privilege. If a lawyer is required to testify to a client communication, otherwise privileged, when the client has sought the lawyer's advice and services to further a fraud on a third person, a concomitant discretion to disclose without testimonial compulsion should be recognized under the professional duty of confidentiality. Neither the legal profession nor society as a whole should tolerate a regime in which lawyers may be used by clients as a means of carrying out a crime or fraud.

Permissive disclosure in this context reinforces the lawyer's duty to provide only *lawful* assistance and advice to clients, giving the lawyer a last-resort weapon and increased leverage in dealing with a client embarked on a fraudulent course of conduct.[11] Moreover, a lawyer's failure to take reasonable steps to prevent or rectify client fraud is likely to lead to civil liability. If insolvency and litigation occur in the aftermath of the fraud, the client's confidentiality will inevitably disappear.[12] In August 2003, the ABA provided this guidance by amending Rule 1.6 to permit a lawyer to disclose confidential information to prevent a prospective crime or fraud and to rectify an ongoing client fraud in which the lawyer's services have been used.

While it is possible to reach the same result by expanding the self-defense exception to include a proactive rather than reactive disclosure,[13]

---

11. See Geoffrey C. Hazard, Jr., Rectification of Client Fraud, Death and Revival of a Professional Norm, 33 Emory L.J. 271, 292 (1984): "the law cannot license some of its subjects, least of all 'lawyers,' to assist in the commission or concealment of serious legal wrongs, such as fraud." See also Geoffrey C. Hazard, Susan P. Koniak & Roger C. Cramton, The Law and Ethics of Lawyering, 282–89 (3d ed. 1999) (discussing the tortured history of the ABA's handling of client fraud prior to 1999).

12. A successor in interest of the client, such as a bankruptcy trustee, is likely to waive any privileges in an effort to recover assets for the insolvent entity. See, e.g., Commodity Futures Trading Comm'n v. Weintraub, 471 U.S. 343 (1985), holding that the successor in control of an entity client can waive the entity's attorney-client privilege over the objections of the officers who consulted with the entity's lawyer. If waiver does not occur, the crime-fraud exception of the attorney-client privilege may be successfully invoked by a showing that the client consulted a lawyer to obtain advice concerning the commission of a crime or fraud. See, e.g., United States v. Hodge & Zweig, 548 F.2d 1347 (9th Cir. 1977). Finally, if the lawyer is charged by defrauded persons, the lawyer is likely to reveal information relying on the self-defense exception. See, e.g., Meyerhofer v. Empire Fire & Marine Ins. Co., 497 F.2d 1190 (2d Cir. 1974).

13. The ABA Committee on Ethics and Public Responsibility, unsuccessful in 1991 in obtaining an amendment broadening the exceptions to confidentiality of Model Rule 1.6(b), interpreted the rule to permit limited disclosure by a lawyer who learns that her client is using her services to perpetrate a fraud on a third person. See ABA Formal Op. 92–366

or to interpret the prohibition on assisting client criminal or fraudulent conduct as creating an implied exception to confidentiality, guidance to lawyers is best provided by a forthright exception to the professional rule dealing with confidentiality. Similarly, the "noisy withdrawal" possibility buried in a comment to Model Rule 1.6 prior to August 2003 is insufficient, because it is inconsistent with the text of the rule itself, which forbids disclosure. Withdrawal and disaffirmance of tainted opinions or representations will also be ineffective in situations in which there are no legal opinions or lawyer representations to be withdrawn or when the victim of the fraud fails to understand the hidden meaning of the signal. Lawyers deserve more explicit guidance from rule-makers.[14]

The ABA partially abandoned the dominant tradition in 1974, when DR 7–102(B)(1) of its Model Code was amended to prohibit, rather than require, the disclosure of confidential information to prevent or rectify a client crime or fraud perpetrated on a third person or a court. Fortunately, only a small number of states adopted this amendment. A broader retreat occurred in 1983 when the ABA, in recommending adoption of the Model Rules of Professional Conduct, eliminated the exceptions to confidentiality that had paralleled the crime-fraud exception to the attorney-client privilege, while preserving the lawyer's permission to disclose confidential information when it served the lawyer's own interest: to defend against accusations of wrongdoing made against the lawyer or to collect a fee.

Under the rule adopted in 1983, confidential information could be disclosed to protect third-party interests in only three situations: (1) to prevent fraud on a tribunal (Rule 3.3(a)(3), which required disclosure); (2) "to prevent the client from committing a criminal act that the lawyer believes is likely to result in imminent death or substantial bodily harm," (a limited permission under Rule 1.6(b)(1)); and (3) to correct a "material fact when disclosure is necessary to avoid assisting a criminal or fraudulent act by a client" and disclosure is not prohibited by Rule 1.6 (Rule 4.1(b)).

(1992) (relying on provisions of the rules prohibiting unlawful assistance and requiring withdrawal, along with the "noisy withdrawal" language of comment [15] of Rule 1.6, to prevent prospective client fraud).

14. Commentators and ABA insiders have criticized the ABA's position as incoherent, confusing, and unworkable. See Hazard, Koniak & Cramton, The Law and Ethics of Lawyering, supra n. 8, at 297–300; Ronald D. Rotunda, The Notice of Withdrawal and the New Model Rules of Professional Conduct: Blowing the Whistle and Waving the Red Flag, 63 Ore. L. Rev. 455 (1984); ABA Committee on Ethics and Professional Responsibility Report to House of Delegates, 7 Law. Manual Prof. Conduct 256, 258 (Aug. 28, 1991) (confidentiality provisions of Model Rules were "unworkable" and unfairly exposed lawyers to potential civil liability and criminal prosecution).

On the central question of whether an attorney may disclose confidential information to prevent a client from committing a criminal fraud likely to result in injury to the financial interest or property of another, state high courts have emphatically rejected the position taken by the ABA in 1983. In 2002, when the ABA again considered the question, thirty-eight states permitted disclosure in this situation, and four states required it. However, when rectification of a past crime or fraud is involved, the number of disclosure states drops sharply, with sixteen permitting disclosure and two requiring disclosure.

Developments during the past five years evidence a resurgence of the central moral tradition of the legal profession. In 2000, after more than a decade of consideration, the American Law Institute's Restatement (Third) of the Law Governing Lawyers adopted an influential recommendation. Section 67 provided that a lawyer may use or disclose confidential client information when the lawyer reasonably believes that its use or disclosure is necessary to prevent, rectify or mitigate a client crime or fraud that threatens or has caused substantial financial loss when the client has used the lawyer's services to further the crime or fraud.

In the same year, the ABA appointed the Ethics 2000 Commission to evaluate and recommend changes in the Model Rules suggested by the various states' rules and the positions taken by the ALI in its Restatement. In 2002 the Commission recommended that the ABA amend Rule 1.6(b) to add exceptions to confidentiality substantially the same as those recognized by the ALI. The Commission's recommendation on this subject was defeated in a close vote of the ABA House of Delegates in February 2002, but the recommendation was given new life by the massive corporate frauds and failures of 2002–2003. Substantially the same language was adopted by the ABA in August 2003 in response to the recommendation of the ABA Task Force on Corporate Responsibility.

The many changes made in the ABA Model Rules in 2002–2003 have led a great many states to reconsider their ethics codes. There are hopeful signs that on this and other issues the central moral tradition of the legal profession will be affirmed, and disclosure will be permitted or required when a client has used the lawyer's services in perpetrating a crime or fraud on a third person or a tribunal.

The final development of significance is the inclusion of a provision in the Sarbanes–Oxley Act of 2002[15] that authorizes the Securities and

---

15. 15 U.S.C. § 7201 et seq. See Roger C. Cramton, George M. Cohen & Susan P. Koniak, The Legal and Ethical Duties of Lawyers After Sarbanes–Oxley, 40 Villanova L. Rev. 260 (2004) [hereinafter "Duties After Sarbanes–Oxley"] (discussing up-the-corporate ladder reporting of material violations of law, permissive "reporting out," and other

Exchange Commission (SEC) to regulate lawyers who represent issuers of publicly-traded securities. Section 307 of the Sarbanes–Oxley Act provides a general authorization to the SEC to promulgate "minimum standards of professional conduct for attorneys appearing and practicing before the Commission in any way in the representation of issuers." The section also directs the SEC to promulgate a regulation requiring a lawyer to report evidence of a material violation of securities or other law by the company or its agents to the chief legal counsel or chief executive officer of the company and, if that counsel or officer does not appropriately respond, to go up the corporate chain of command until the company makes an appropriate response. This SEC rule—often referred to as the "reporting up" rule—was adopted on January 23, 2003 and became effective on August 5, 2003.

Section 205.3(d)(2) of the SEC's regulation permits a lawyer to disclose confidential information related to the representation to the extent that the lawyer reasonably believes necessary "(i) To prevent the [client] from committing a material violation that is likely to cause substantial injury to the financial interest or property of the [client] or investors; . . . or (iii) To rectify the consequences of a material violation by the [client] that caused, or may cause, substantial injury to the financial interest or property of the [client] or investors in the further-ance of which the attorney's services were used." The provision—often referred to as the "reporting out" or "noisy withdrawal" proposal—is similar in substance to that of ABA Rule 1.6(b)(2) and (3) as amended in August 2003. The SEC action preempts state ethics rules that are inconsistent with it, including, in the SEC's view, the minority of states that prohibit a lawyer from exercising discretion to disclose in the situations covered by the SEC rule.[16]

In summary, desirable currents of change provide promise that permissive disclosure of confidential information to prevent or rectify a client's crime or fraud on a third person will become the law of most states.

C. Disclosure to Prevent Death or Substantial Bodily Harm

Once a fraud exception to the professional duty of confidentiality is recognized, reinforcing the policies and purposes that justify lawyer

---

questions raised by current ethics rules and the adopted and proposed rules of the SEC implementing § 307 of the Sarbanes–Oxley Act)

16. See Duties After Sarbanes–Oxley, supra n. 15, at pp. 169–80 (arguing that the SEC intended to preempt conflicting state ethics rules and that its adopted rule permitting disclosure in certain situations does in fact preempt inconsistent state rules; the contrary views expressed in a Washington interim ethics opinion and a California bar letter are rejected as unsound). The Washington State Bar opinion warned Washington lawyers that they might be disciplined for disclosing information that is permitted to be disclosed under § 205.3(d)(2) of the SEC regulation.

secrecy, the remaining task is to determine whether there are other third-party interests that justify a sacrifice of confidentiality.

Four situations provide vehicles for considering the circumstances that should permit a lawyer to disclose confidential information to prevent threatened harm to human life or bodily integrity:

- Spaulding-*type scenarios*: The attorney informs the client of crucial information unknown to the opposing party (e.g. Spaulding's medical condition) and the client instructs the attorney not to disclose.

- *The death row and wrongful incarceration scenarios*: A client accused of an unrelated charge informs his lawyer in plausible detail that he was responsible for a crime for which an innocent person is awaiting execution on death row[17] or is serving a lengthy sentence.

- *The threatened collapse of a building or other natural disaster*: The client, who owns a large apartment building located on an earthquake fault line in a major city, receives the detailed report of an architectural engineer to the effect that the building structure is inadequate to withstand even a modest earthquake. An event of this character at the location involved occurs approximately every six years. When the quake occurs, it is extremely likely that the building will collapse with substantial loss of life. The client asks the lawyer for advice about his options. The lawyer advises the client that no current law requires the owner to report the danger to public authorities, warns the client of potential civil liability if the building collapses, and recommends that the client take prompt steps to inform tenants and reconstruct the building. The client, concluding that the costs of rebuilding are too great, decides to do nothing and directs the lawyer to remain silent.

- *Threatened violence on the part of the client or someone associated with the client*: Suppose a lawyer is defending a client whose business is at risk in commercial litigation. The client tells the lawyer that her husband, enraged at the tactics of the opposing party, plans to kill the opposing party's lawyer. The lawyer's contact with the spouse persuades the lawyer that the spouse's threats are likely to be carried out. The client, however, is

---

17. The death-row scenario is a "hard case" that arises only rarely. However, the scenario illustrates a situation that, prior to the ALI's adoption in 2000 of a rule permitting disclosure when "necessary to prevent reasonably certain death or serious bodily harm to a person," was not covered by the exceptions to confidentiality of any state.

unwilling to consent to disclosure to the potential victim or the police.[18]

These situations have two common features: human life is at risk and, under current state ethics codes, disclosure is generally not permitted.[19] Should ethics rules permit disclosure in these and other situations in which the lawyer knows that death or physical harm is likely to result unless the lawyer discloses the threat?

Virtually all the states recognize that under certain circumstances, an attorney is warranted in disclosing confidential client information when a person's life is at risk of severe harm. The problem is one of defining those circumstances. There is also agreement that disclosure should not occur unless certain predicate conditions are met; these are: (1) the facts known to the lawyer, after adequate inquiry and investigation, must give rise to a reasonable belief that disclosure is necessary to prevent someone's death or serious bodily injury; (2) the lawyer should consult the client about the intent to disclose unless it is not feasible under the circumstances, such as when the client's plausible threat to kill himself or a third person may be triggered rather than avoided by consultation; (3) no other available action is reasonably likely to prevent the threatened harm; and (4) the disclosure is limited to what is reasonably necessary to prevent the threatened consequence. In the following discussion, the reader should assume that these qualifications have been satisfied in each instance.

The confidentiality provisions of most existing ethics codes impose a number of limiting conditions that make them inapplicable to situations of the type mentioned. Existing rules generally limit disclosure to situations in which an act of the client is involved. They exclude situations in which the threatened act is that of a third person, such as a spouse or associate of the client, and harm resulting from a natural event of which the client has special knowledge, as in the building collapse scenario. The requirement may also exclude situations in which

---

18. This scenario involves a fact situation not contemplated by nearly all state versions of Rule 1.6(b). A more typical example involves a client who threatens violence against the opposing party or lawyer, or against the judge or other adjudicatory official. Those situations, which are contemplated by the common exception to confidentiality for a client's intended criminal act threatening harm to third persons, are much more common. Matrimonial lawyers and criminal defense lawyers, among others, attest to the reality of the violent client. Existing ethics rules generally permit disclosure because a prospective crime by the client is involved. Moreover, when the criminal act is directed at the judge, another adjudicatory official, or a juror, disclosure is usually required (see Model Rule 3.3(a)(3) and (b)).

19. A few exceptions to this statement may now be found. See, e.g., the Massachusetts version of Rule 1.6(b), which permits disclosure "to prevent the wrongful execution or incarceration of another," and the 2002 version of Model Rule 1.6(b)(1), which permits disclosure to prevent imminent and reasonably certain death or physical injury to another.

there is a failure to act (an omission), as opposed to an affirmative act. Moreover, under most ethics codes, the client's act must be criminal in character.

In the scenario based on *Spaulding*, the client's refusal to consent to disclosure fails to meet these requirements. Even if the failure to disclose would qualify as a "client act," it does not constitute a prospective or ongoing crime or fraud. Yet the moral considerations that justify disclosure have great force in this situation. Moreover, the fact that such situations very rarely occur means that the overall objective of preserving clients' confidences will not be jeopardized.

Similarly, the client's refusal to permit disclosure to save the life of an innocent person from execution or continued incarceration does not involve a prospective crime. Although the moral dilemma of conflicting obligations to the client and a third person is a difficult one, ethics rules should provide discretion to disclose when wrongful execution or incarceration is reasonably certain to occur.

In the building collapse situation, disclosure would be prohibited under current rules because there is no client criminal act that threatens deadly harm. Indeed, there is no client act at all, only the client's special knowledge that a natural event that will cause death is foreseeable and probable. The requirement in Model Rule 1.6(b)(2) that the threat be "imminent" is also not satisfied. Protection of innocent life again justifies disclosure.

Finally, in the scenario where the client's spouse is planning murder, existing exceptions do not apply because the client is not the actor. Yet the situation is morally identical to those in which the client is the actor, in which current ethics rules permit disclosure.

The rules governing exceptions to confidentiality should be broadened to permit disclosure in all of these situations. First, the preservation of human life clearly has as high a priority in the hierarchy of values as any other objective. Existing professional responsibility codes recognize the high priority accorded the preservation of human life.[20] But their application is unduly limited because of preconditions that are overly broad. Second, a profession that justifiably asks for and receives permission to disclose confidential client information when its own economic interests are at stake (e.g., to collect a fee from a client) cannot take the position that the threatened death or serious injury of another does not justify an occasional sacrifice of confidentiality.

---

20. Today all states and the District of Columbia permit or require a lawyer to reveal confidential client information to prevent a client's criminal act when it is likely to result in death or substantial bodily harm. See ALAS Confidentiality Memorandum, supra n. 3, at Column B (reporting that all jurisdictions except California permit or require disclosure in this situation; for the 2004 change in California, see n. 36, infra).

The Restatement of the Law Governing Lawyers provides guidance to rule makers in reconsidering the exceptions to the professional duty of confidentiality.[21] The largely uncontroversial exceptions to confidentiality are spelled out: confidential information may be used or disclosed: (1) to advance client interests (§ 61); (2) when the client consents (§ 62); (3) when required by law or court order (§ 63); and (4) in the lawyer's self-defense (§ 64). Disagreement about these exceptions is largely confined to the details of drafting.

In situations in which death or personal injury is threatened, the Restatement pioneers by casting aside the narrow conditions of Model Rule 1.6(b)(1) that limit disclosure to protect human life or substantial bodily harm. Section 66 provides that a lawyer, after attempting to persuade the client to do the right thing, "may use or disclose confidential client information when and to the extent that the lawyer reasonably believes such use or disclosure is necessary to prevent reasonably certain death or serious bodily injury to a person." The exception "is based on the overriding value of life and physical integrity" and extends to acts of a non-client, such as a spouse's plausible threat to kill an opposing party, or to knowledge of natural causal events, as in the building-collapse situation. The ALI provision also would permit the defense lawyers in the *Spaulding* scenario to disclose Spaulding's life-threatening condition to him.

In 2002 the ABA's Ethics 2000 Commission recommended that the ABA adopt the position taken by the ALI. In February 2002, the ABA House of Delegates amended Rule 1.6(b) by adding a new exception to confidentiality: A lawyer may reveal confidential information to the extent the lawyer reasonably believes necessary "to prevent reasonably certain death or substantial bodily harm." No client act of any kind is required. The resulting language would permit disclosure in all of the situations discussed above.

D. *Underlying Policy Issues*

The central issues in drafting exceptions to confidentiality involve, first, defining the interests that justify a possible sacrifice of the client's interest in secrecy; second, determining whether disclosure should be permissive or mandatory; third, determining whether limiting language concerning the actor, the victim, or the harm should be included; and

---

21. American Law Institute, Restatement (Third) of the Law Governing Lawyers §§ 61–67 (2000). The confidentiality provisions of the Massachusetts Rules of Professional Conduct (1998) also contain broader exceptions than those of most states. Rule 1.6(b) provides that "A lawyer may reveal [confidential information] ... (1) to prevent commission of a criminal or fraudulent act that the lawyer reasonably believes is likely to result in death or substantial bodily harm, or in substantial injury to the financial interests or property of another, or to prevent the wrongful execution or incarceration of another."

finally, deciding, in connection with client fraud, whether disclosure should be limited to prospective fraud only, and, if rectification is included, whether a duty or permission to disclose should exist only when the lawyer's services are or have been involved.[22]

The major argument against broadening exceptions to confidentiality is that clients will be deterred from confiding information to their lawyers.[23] The lack of candor on the part of clients, it is said, will make it difficult or impossible for a lawyer to give informed advice. The "sound advice" and "sound administration of justice" thought to result from this highly confidential relationship will not be achieved. Moreover, the ability of the lawyer to disclose client information may diminish client trust and adversely affect the quality of the relationship and the single-mindedness with which the lawyer pursues the client's interests. If and when the lawyer informs the client that disclosure is desirable or contemplated, a serious conflict arises between the lawyer and the client. The relationship ends in bitterness and a sense of betrayal.

There are several responses to these arguments. First, some long-standing exceptions to both the professional duty and to the attorney-client privilege have not resulted in the consequences that are feared. The self-defense and client-fraud exceptions involve situations that arise quite frequently, yet there is no evidence that those broad exceptions have had undesirable effects on the candor with which clients communicate to lawyers. It is not clear that a slight broadening of the exceptions in situations that arise less frequently will have any discernible effect.

A great deal of romanticism often surrounds discussion of "trust" and "candor" in the lawyer-client relationship. Studies indicate that mistrust and suspicion are frequently encountered in the relationship; lawyers frequently state that clients are unwilling to reveal embarrassing or sensitive facts, which need to be dynamited out of them. Factors that restrict candor operate in various practice contexts in powerful ways.[24] In the criminal defense field, for example, both lawyer and client may be reluctant to discuss candidly facts relating directly to guilt.

Second, arguments that candor will be discouraged by modest rule changes ignore the fact that both lawyers and clients appear to be

---

22. For discussion of the competing policies governing exceptions to lawyer confidentiality, see David Luban, Lawyers and Justice: An Ethical Study 177–233 (1984); Sissela Bok, Secrets, *passim* (1982), and Deborah L. Rhode, Ethical Perspectives on Legal Practice, 37 Stan. L. Rev. 589, 612–17 (1985).

23. See, e.g., Monroe H. Freedman, Understanding Legal Ethics (1990). Freedman's argument for nearly absolute confidentiality also relies on the special constitutional protections afforded criminal defendants.

24. See, e.g., Robert A. Burt, Conflict and Trust Between Attorney and Client, 69 Geo. L.J. 1015 (1981).

relatively uninformed concerning both (a) the details of exceptions to either the attorney-client privilege or the professional duty of confidentiality, and (b) the relationship of the two doctrines to one another. The available empirical evidence, albeit very limited, suggests that most lawyers and clients expect that confidentiality will be breached when extremely important interests of third persons or courts would be impaired.[25] Nor is there any indication that clients are more candid with their lawyers in jurisdictions that have fewer exceptions to confidentiality than they are in jurisdictions with broader exceptions.[26] Any objective observer must concede that there is insufficient solid empirical evidence to support firm conclusions in either direction. When severe harm is threatened that can be prevented by disclosure, the reality of that more certain interest should be preferred to dubious assumptions about effects on client candor.

What types of clients are likely to be sufficiently informed about the details of exceptions to the attorney-client privilege, the work-product immunity, and the professional duty of confidentiality so that this knowledge will influence their willingness to confide in a lawyer? The answer is clear: this group of informed clients is largely confined to sophisticated repeat players, usually substantial corporations, who may want to use lawyer secrecy to conceal ongoing regulatory violations. This group of clients has many advantages in litigation over those with less resources, experience and staying power.[27] The social value of secrecy versus disclosure is less when one is dealing not with individual citizens encountering law for the first time, but with repeat-player, profit-making organizations that have strong incentives to conceal or delay compliance with regulatory requirements that impose substantial costs.

Third, there is no evidence that exceptions to confidentiality have led or will lead to frequent whistle-blowing on the part of lawyers. Indeed, it is clear that the incidence of whistleblowing by lawyers is astonishingly low given the fact that most or all states require disclosure

---

25. See Fred C. Zacharias, Rethinking Confidentiality, 74 Iowa L. Rev. 351, 377–78 (1989) (discussing attitudes of general public and of lawyers regarding disclosure of confidential information by lawyers).

26. Lawyers today frequently practice across jurisdictional lines. For example, a law firm in the District of Columbia may also handle transactions or litigation for clients in nearby Maryland or Virginia. The District of Columbia prohibits a lawyer from disclosing information to prevent or rectify a client's criminal fraud; Maryland permits a lawyer to disclose in those situations; and Virginia requires a lawyer to do so. Does the attorney-client relationship or the client's candor vary across these jurisdictional lines? There is no evidence of any differences.

27. See, e.g., Marc Galanter, Why the Haves Come Out Ahead: Speculations on the Limits of Legal Change, 8 Law & Soc'y Rev. 95, 97–104 (1974) (discussing advantages of "repeat players," such as corporations, over those with less litigation experience or familiarity with court proceedings).

when a crime or fraud has been perpetrated on a tribunal: Over forty states permit disclosure to prevent a client criminal fraud, and four populous states require disclosure in that situation. Disciplinary proceedings for failing to disclose information when required to do so are virtually non-existent and the same is true for failure to withdraw when withdrawal is required.[28] On the other hand, law firms that took no action to prevent large or massive client frauds involving the use of their services have frequently settled malpractice and third-party liability claims for large and sometimes huge amounts. Available evidence indicates that lawyers who have discretion to disclose almost always decide not to do so, even when that course of action risks civil liability.[29] The objection to rules permitting or requiring disclosure is not that they will lead to professional discipline. Rather, the rules' effect on the likelihood and success of the malpractice and third-party liability claims signify the real risk and, prior to the SEC's implementation of the Sarbanes–Oxley Act, the principal deterrent force.

American lawyers are imbued with a professional ideology that gives dominant place to loyalty to client, treats confidentiality as a sacred trust, and abhors lawyer conduct that constitutes a betrayal of client. Lawyers know that harming a client to protect the superior interest of a third party will lead to the ending of the lawyer-client relationship, probable non-payment of fees, client bitterness, recrimination, potential litigation, and possible loss of repute with other lawyers and clients. They also know that whistleblowers will be shunned both by some clients and by other lawyers. Experience shows that lawyers are extraordinarily reluctant to risk these consequences. The rules should not be drafted so that rule prohibition reinforces this natural risk aversion, with the result that loyalty to client—even a client who is abusing the lawyer's services to cause serious harm to third persons—always prevails

---

28. For a startling recent instance of a major law firm continuing to represent a client known to be engaged in an ongoing criminal fraud, see Duties After Sarbanes–Oxley, supra n. 15, at 733–35 and 817–31 (discussing the Examiner's report in SEC v. Spiegel, Inc., 2003 WL 22176223 (N.D. Ill. 2003), at <http://www.sec.gov/litigation/litreleases/lr18347.htm>).

29. Evidence supporting this assertion comes from the documentary evidence available in numerous court and bankruptcy proceedings since the OPM case in 1983. In some of these cases the report of a magistrate or bankruptcy trustee confirms a determination that the lawyers knew or should have known of the client's criminal fraud. Numerous other cases involve large, and sometimes massive, settlements by a major law firm of malpractice or third-party liability claims alleging negligence in the former and intentional wrongdoing in the latter. When millions of dollars are paid to settle a goodly number of separate cases, it is plausible to infer that at least some of them involved intentional wrongdoing that would violate the ethics rules. See Susan P. Koniak, Corporate Fraud: See Lawyers, 26 Harv. J. Pub. Policy 195, 198–210 (2003), and Koniak, When the Hurleyburly's Done: The Bar's Struggle with the SEC, 103 Colum.L.Rev. 1236, 1239–43 (2003) (both discussing the role of lawyers in corporate frauds).

over the superior interests of others. Moreover, conscientious and highly moral individuals may migrate to areas of practice that are less likely to place them in problematic situations.

The arguments for and against discretion are familiar. A blanket command provides more explicit guidance and, if followed by those to whom it is directed, will lead to more uniform and predictable responses. A clear duty helps avoid the problem of a client being subjected, without advance disclosure, to responses and risks that vary depending on the judgment or conscience of individual lawyers. On the other hand, the situations that arise are often morally complex ones in which practical judgment is influenced by a variety of factors relating to context, personalities, circumstances and relationships. The clarity of the lawyer's knowledge concerning the likelihood of the client's proposed conduct, its illegality, and its threatened consequences varies enormously from case to case.

In the past I have been inclined to support discretionary proposals on the pragmatic ground that they are more likely to commend themselves to lawyers who fear that mandatory disclosure will increase their exposure to liability claims. The recent recurrence of numerous and massive corporate frauds—each involving attorneys who assisted in structuring the fraudulent transactions, provided legal opinions affirming their legality, and approved misleading securities disclosures—has persuaded me that mandatory disclosure requirements are preferable.[30] Professional discipline is not the issue; the disciplinary process has neither the will, experience or resources to pursue charges that a major law firm has failed to withdraw when required to do so and knowingly assisted a corporate client's fraud of investors or third parties. Ethics rules that increase the threat of malpractice or third-party liability are necessary to provide adequate deterrence.

E. Effect of Permissible Disclosure on Client's Attorney–Client Privilege

It should be kept in mind that the ethical propriety of a lawyer disclosing information without the client's consent "tells us nothing

---

30. This conclusion is supported by an important fact that is frequently ignored or unrecognized: In forty-four U.S. jurisdictions, a lawyer who has knowledge of a client's ongoing crime or fraud is required to disclose the fraud when further representation would assist or further the ongoing crime or fraud; in three additional jurisdictions a lawyer may disclose in this situation; and in all jurisdictions, including the two in which disclosure is not permitted, the lawyer must resign. See ALAS Confidentiality Memorandum, Column G, supra n. 3, at 149–50 (concluding in Comment (3) that Rule 4.1(b), when disclosure is permitted or required under Rule 1.6, requires prevention or rectification of the ongoing crime or fraud in this situation). See also, Duties After Sarbanes–Oxley, supra n. 15, at 783–84, 823–24.

about the admissibility of the information disclosed.''[31] The professional
duty of confidentiality and the attorney-client privilege are separate
doctrines although they have overlapping objectives. Disclosure by a
lawyer in a situation permitted by the ethics rule, but without the
client's consent, does not waive the client's attorney-client privilege in
the communication that is privileged. Although the information becomes
known to those to whom it is revealed and may result in harm to the
client, the client retains the right to assert the privilege in any subsequent proceeding whether or not the client is a party. In *Macumber v.
State*,[32] a lawyer reported to public officials that his client had committed
a crime for which another person had been convicted. The disclosure was
viewed as ethically permissible (i.e., not in violation of the lawyer's duty
of confidentiality). Nevertheless, the lawyer's testimony concerning the
client's communication was not admissible in a subsequent hearing
challenging the allegedly wrongful conviction.

In *Purcell v. District Attorney*[33] the Massachusetts Supreme Judicial
Court held that a lawyer's permissible disclosure of information that his
client planned to set fire to an apartment building did not lead to the
conclusion that the lawyer could be required to testify concerning the
client's communication of his criminal intent in a subsequent arson trial.
The client, a maintenance man with an apartment in the building, had
consulted the lawyer about matters relating to loss of his job and
housing. Those communications were privileged and the privilege was
not waived by the lawyer's permitted disclosure of the intended arson
under the ethics code. The harder question was whether the communication concerning the threatened arson was admissible because of the
crime-fraud exception to the privilege, a determination that rested on
whether the client informed the lawyer of the intention to commit arson

---

31.   Purcell v. District Attorney, 676 N.E.2d 436, 438 (Mass. 1997).

32.   State v. Macumber, 544 P.2d 1084 (Ariz. 1976) (reversing conviction and remand-
ing for a new trial, and holding that lawyer's permissible disclosure to authorities of
client's information that he was responsible for a crime for which another person had been
convicted did not waive the client's attorney-client privilege); and State v. Macumber, 582
P.2d 162 (Ariz. 1978) (affirming conviction after second trial; waiver of privilege not
reconsidered because the declaration against interest was properly ruled inadmissible as
unsupported by sufficient circumstantial probability of trustworthiness). In *Macumber*, the
lawyer's decision to disclose was eased by the fact that his client was deceased and could
not be punished for the crime which he had told his lawyer he had committed. See also
State v. Valdez, 618 P.2d 1234, 1235 (N.M. 1980) (lawyer could not testify that his client
had confessed to a robbery for which the defendant had been convicted). *Macumber* and
other cases dealing with the "death-row scenario" are thoroughly and ably discussed in W.
William Hodes, What Ought to Be Done—What Can Be Done—When the Wrong Person Is
in Jail or About to Be Executed?, 29 Loy. L.A. L. Rev. 1547, 1560–81 (1996).

33.   676 N.E.2d 436 (Mass. 1997).

"for the purpose of receiving legal advice" concerning the unlawful conduct.[34]

As Susan Martyn has stated:

> [A] lawyer's discretion to disclose a client intention to commit a serious future crime [gives] lawyers an added incentive to do so when efforts to dissuade the client prove unsuccessful. Lawyers who disclose this confidential information need not worry that it can be used directly against the client in a subsequent proceeding, as long as the client sought legal advice about lawful matters. A lawyer can act to save lives, and at the same time avoid being the instrument of the client's conviction.[35]

CONCLUSION

Spaulding v. Zimmerman is a ghostly metaphor for the silence of lawyers, judges and the organized bar on the moral issues presented by lawyer secrecy. The most extreme case of silence and denial is in California, where leaders of the bar often take pride in the erroneous statement that California's professional duty of confidentiality is an absolute one not qualified by any exceptions.[36] The reluctance of lawyers and judges in and out of the courtroom to talk forthrightly about the morality of lawyer behavior is illustrated by the unwillingness of the trial judge in *Spaulding* to discuss ethics rules or moral principles while stating that the defense lawyers acted in "good faith," presumably meaning that they were not morally accountable because they were only

---

34. On remand in *Purcell*, the defense lawyer was not required to testify against his client. The client's communication of the proposed arson was not one made for purposes of legal advice, unlike those relating to the client's job and housing.

35. Susan Martyn, The Restatement (3d) of the Law Governing Lawyers and the Courts, Prof. Law. 115, 124 (1997 Symposium Issue).

36. In 2003 the California legislature amended the statutory lawyer's oath, Bus. & Prof. Code § 6068(e), by adding a limited exception to confidentiality: an attorney may "reveal confidential information relating to the representation of a client to the extent that the attorney reasonably believes the disclosure is necessary to prevent a criminal act that the attorney reasonably believes is likely to result in the death of, or substantial bodily harm to, an individual." In 2004, the California Supreme Court, on the recommendation of the State Bar, included the same language in Rule 3–100 of the California Rules of Professional Conduct. All other U.S. jurisdictions have permitted or required disclosure in this situation for many years. California continues to be unique in having no statute or rule authorizing disclosure of confidential information in client fraud or other situations, although judicial decisions have supported disclosure to remedy client perjury, prevent fraud on a tribunal, and to establish or defend a claim against a lawyer (e.g., collect a fee, bring a retaliatory discharge claim, or defend a malpractice or other claim involving a lawyer's representation of a client). See generally Roger C. Cramton, Proposed Legislation Concerning a Lawyer's Duty of Confidentiality, 22 Pepperdine L. Rev. 1467 (1995); and Fred C. Zacharias, Privilege and Confidentiality in California, 28 U.C. Davis L. Rev. 367 (1995).

doing their job under the adversary system. The Minnesota Supreme Court stated no view on the law and ethics of the lawyering involved, other than the ambiguous statement that "no canon of ethics or legal obligation *may* have required [defense counsel] to inform plaintiff or his counsel" of the life-threatening condition (emphasis added).

Lawyer participants in *Spaulding* report a macabre dance in which the reality of the case involved—how human beings should behave toward one another when human life is at stake—was skirted. Instead, the parties argued technical matters, such as whether the trial court had the discretion to reopen a minor's settlement and whether a petition to approve a settlement was a joint petition or merely that of the party submitting it. Richard Pemberton, who was new to practice at the time, believes he was asked to brief and argue the case in the Minnesota Supreme Court because his senior partner found the task a distasteful one, as did Pemberton:

> [W]hen I briefed and argued the *Spaulding* case in the Supreme Court, I was within the first few months of legal practice and was attempting to defend a senior partner's handling of the matter in the trial court. After twenty years of practice, I would like to think that I would have disclosed the aneurysm of the aorta as an act of humanity and without regard to the legalities involved, just as I surely would now. You might suggest to your students in the course on professional responsibility that a pretty good rule for them to practice respecting professional conduct is to do the decent thing.[37]

As it turned out, David Spaulding, present whereabouts unknown, did not die of a massive coronary hemorrhage. Almost two years after the settlement, during a military reserve examination, Spaulding's long-time physician discovered the aorta aneurysm and corrective treatment was immediately begun. However, David Spaulding suffered a further injury for which an additional insurance payment is an inadequate measure of compensation. He forever lost most of his voice as a consequence of the delayed treatment of his aneurysm.

Why do lawyers and judges lose their voices when it comes to speaking about moral conduct and exceptions to confidentiality? Why does professional silence greet moral arguments that a good person, including a lawyer, should take reasonable steps to prevent death or substantial injury to third persons? Recent developments suggest that the silence may be lifting. I sincerely hope so.

---

37. Letter from Richard L. Pemberton to Dr. Jay Katz, Professor of Law and Psychiatry, Yale Law School (Nov. 30, 1981).

*

7

Bankrupt in Milwaukee: A Cautionary Tale

Milton C. Regan, Jr.[1]

Introduction

In February 1994, John Gellene was a thirty-seven year-old partner at the prestigious Wall Street law firm of Milbank, Tweed, Hadley and McCloy. He made half a million dollars a year. He was regarded both within his firm and by members of the bankruptcy bar as a brilliant and accomplished lawyer. He was married, had three young daughters, and lived on the Upper East Side of Manhattan. By most standards, he had a successful and rewarding life. A little over four-and-a-half years later, he was in federal prison. What happened?

The facts are relatively straightforward: Gellene failed to disclose to a federal bankruptcy court that his law firm had a potential conflict of interest. The potential conflict existed because Milbank represented both a corporate debtor, Bucyrus Corporation, in its bankruptcy, and Bucyrus's major secured creditor, South Street partnership, in a separate matter. This created the risk that Milbank might provide advice to Bucyrus that would favor its client South Street at the expense of Bucyrus or other creditors. For this reason, Gellene was required to alert the court that Milbank was representing South Street in another matter. This would give the court the opportunity to decide whether the potential conflict was serious enough to disqualify Milbank from representing Bucyrus in the bankruptcy. When Gellene's failure to do this was discovered two years after the bankruptcy, Milbank was forced to return almost $2 million in fees. Furthermore, Gellene was prosecuted and convicted of bankruptcy fraud. He was sentenced to fifteen months in prison and later disbarred.

There are two prevailing explanations for what happened. On one account, Gellene was a rogue lawyer. He had misrepresented for eight

---

1. Professor of Law, Georgetown University Law Center. Adapted from Milton C. Regan, Jr., Eat What You Kill: The Fall of a Wall Street Lawyer (University of Michigan Press 2004). The book is based on, among other sources, interviews with several of the participants both in the Bucyrus bankruptcy and John Gellene's criminal trial, although Gellene himself did not respond to requests for an interview.

years that he was a member of the New York bar, and trial evidence indicated that he had cut corners on other occasions. He also was regarded as something of an intense loner who kept his own counsel and shared little of his workload. In light of this, some observers claim that it's not surprising that Gellene, if he thought he could get away with it, would conceal Milbank's ties to South Street. His habitual dishonesty finally caught up with him.

Another view is that Gellene was simply the fall guy for Milbank Tweed. An influential partner at the firm, Larry Lederman, had represented both Bucyrus and South Street on various matters over the years. The managing partner of South Street, Michael Salovaara, was a long-time friend and client of Lederman's. It was Lederman who suggested that Gellene be in charge of Milbank's work for Bucyrus in the company's bankruptcy. Lederman also was the one who got Gellene involved in working for South Street on another matter. Some have suggested that Lederman masterminded a plan to protect Salovaara's interest in the Bucyrus bankruptcy by arranging for Gellene to represent Bucyrus. Since disclosing Milbank's work for South Street would disqualify the firm from representing Bucyrus, the argument goes, Lederman pressured Gellene to keep quiet. When the scandal broke, Milbank protected Lederman and threw Gellene overboard.

The evidence suggests, however, that the story is more complicated than either account implies. Attributing blame solely to flawed individuals or corrupt organizations rarely captures the subtleties of how ethical misconduct occurs. Furthermore, it offers false reassurance that only moral deviants, not ordinary people, engage in such behavior. A striking amount of wrongdoing can occur in settings populated by people who are generally decent and well-intentioned. Complex features of individual and social psychology can interact in ways that can't always be anticipated.

In the case of John Gellene, there is enough information to sketch out at least the outlines of a plausible explanation that is more complex than the prevailing views. This explanation acknowledges the role of Gellene's personality and character, but also takes into account crucial features of modern large law firm practice. Some of these factors motivated Gellene's behavior, while others helped him rationalize it. John Gellene, in other words, was the protagonist in several different stories, whose intersection combined to send him to jail.

Approaching events in this way suggests that Gellene's story may be less lurid but more sobering than standard explanations imply. Gellene's personality is not dramatically different from other lawyers', and may in fact be functional for succeeding in highly competitive law practices. Furthermore, the features that characterize Milbank Tweed are pervasive in all modern large law firms. In other words, neither Gellene's personality nor the circumstances in which he practiced are unique—nor are the ethical risks that can result from interaction between the two.

The Overachiever's Tale

John Gellene was accustomed to competition and achievement. He grew up in suburban New Jersey about fifteen miles west of New York City. He was the second of six children, four boys and two girls, in a middle-class, devoutly Catholic, Italian–American family. Gellene's oldest sibling was a sister a year older; his youngest was a brother eleven years younger. His parents' marriage was a traditional one. His father was self-employed as a buyer's representative for chemicals used in textile manufacturing, while his mother was a homemaker.

Gellene's father was a hard-driving man who established extremely high standards of achievement for his children, particularly the boys. As the oldest boy, John was especially shaped by these expectations. He was tightly-wound, self-contained, and highly directed. He skipped not one but two grades in school. Despite his youth, fellow students regarded him as intellectually gifted and driven by an intense desire for academic accomplishment. Gellene participated in student government, chess, and debate at DePaul High School, a Catholic school in Wayne, New Jersey. He was a gifted pianist despite having no formal training. On rare occasions, he would use music among friends as a release from the strict self-control that he usually imposed on himself.

Gellene acknowledged that recognition for his intellect was a crucial element of his sense of self-worth. "[N]ot just for my adult life, but before that," he has said, "I've been recognized as a person with gifts of my intellect and my ability to deal with problems."[2] Larry Lederman described his work as "absolutely brilliant."[3] Another Milbank partner reported a client's view that Gellene was the best bankruptcy lawyer in the United States.

Such expectations, however, also were a burden. They left Gellene afraid to admit that he had made any errors, out of fear that this esteem for him would evaporate. "When I am confronted with a mistake," he said, "it is very difficult for me to stand up and say I did a stupid thing."[4] He was, he admitted, someone "who feels that he had to be perfect because that is where I've gotten my view of myself. That is where I've gotten satisfaction. That's where I've tried for better or worse

---

2. Gellene trial transcript (GTT), United States v. Gellene, Criminal No. 97–CR–221, E.D. Wis., Feb. 27, 1998, p. 1218.

3. 1993 Milbank Tweed Compensation Committee Memorandum (CCM), Exhibit 361, Gellene criminal trial, p. B–E4990.

4. GTT, p. 1218.

to have meaning in my life[.]"[5] Adding to the burden was a sense that perhaps Gellene did not deserve the admiration that he seemed to evoke. For many years, he observed, he had acted as if his presumed gift was "an affliction, something that I had to reject, something that I suppose I wasn't worthy of."[6]

Competing for intellectual distinction offered Gellene a way to validate a sense of self-worth. Success in one arena led to opportunities to compete in even more demanding ones. He graduated Phi Beta Kappa and *summa cum laude* from Georgetown, with degrees in philosophy and economics. This opened the door to Harvard Law School, from which he graduated *cum laude*. His performance at Harvard led to a summer position with Milbank Tweed between his second and third years of law school. His work during that summer led to an offer of permanent employment with Milbank, which he accepted. Before he began at Milbank, he served as a clerk to Justice Morris Pashman on the New Jersey Supreme Court. He then embarked on the quest for partnership at Milbank, a prize granted only to a handful of associates each year. With each success, a new challenge arose; with each prize, another appeared on the horizon.

At every step of the way, Gellene had the reputation of being extraordinarily hard-working. Those who knew him in law school recall someone who seemed driven to prove himself. Gellene put in exceptionally long hours even by the standards of students accustomed to punishing schedules. His compulsiveness appeared to be fueled in part by anxiety, prompted perhaps by the fear that he might reveal that he was not as smart as others believed.

Gellene's work habits continued when he joined Milbank Tweed. He initially worked with a group of litigators who did both commercial litigation and bankruptcy work. He found the environment at the firm "extremely competitive."[7] Eventually, he gravitated to Milbank's bankruptcy practice. In an environment of high achievers who spent most of their waking hours at the firm, he stood out as someone who "works like a dog."[8] Gellene described his typical work week as "being in the office ten, twelve, sometimes more hours a day five days a week and then a number of hours in the office on Saturday or Sunday or both."[9] This schedule was in place, he said, soon after he joined the firm. The desire to make partner in a very competitive environment no doubt intensified

---

5. GTT, p. 1220.

6. Transcript of Sentencing Hearing, United States v. Gellene, Criminal 97–CR–221, E.D. Wis., July 24, 1998, p. 131.

7. GTT p. 1119.

8. 1993 CCM, p. B–E4990.

9. GTT, p. 1119–1120.

any predilection he had for immersing himself in his work, despite the fact that as his life unfolded his wife and three young daughters were waiting for him at home.

This pattern of behavior didn't abate, however, after he was named a partner. In 1993, the year leading up to the Bucyrus bankruptcy filing, he billed 3,100 hours through November—a rate that would result in 3,400 hours for the year. In 1994, the projection was just under 3,000 annual hours. Milbank's annual compensation committee reports on Gellene were studded with comments from other partners such as "He works tremendously hard;"[10] "a very hard worker;"[11] "tireless worker;"[12] "overworked,"[13] and "he work[s] fiendishly hard."[14]

Colleagues also describe a lawyer who tended to take too much on himself without delegating responsibility to or involving others. In one of its annual reviews, the Milbank compensation committee told Gellene that "[t]here are concerns about practice management as a result of the heavy burdens that you have taken on yourself[.]"[15] The committee expressed the hope that he would "share the burden with your Partners" and to use associates more effectively in his projects.[16] Barry Radick, co-head of the firm's bankruptcy practice, put it more vividly: "He is a control freak and a loner. He refuses help; we are concerned that he may get himself into trouble because he is working so hard."[17] The compensation committee's 1995 message to Gellene stated that he could accomplish a lot more if he would "develop better working relationships with others[.]"[18] Gellene himself admitted that he was the sort of person who "if I needed help, I wouldn't necessarily reach out for it."[19]

Whatever anxiety Gellene felt was likely aggravated by an experience that underscored just how fragile his position at Milbank could be. Only a few months after earning a partnership at the firm on January 1, 1989, his achievement was in jeopardy. In late May of that year, Milbank was conducting a routine check of the credentials of all its lawyers. It

---

10. Id.

11. 1994 CCM, Exhibit 362, Gellene criminal trial, p. B–E4982.

12. 1993 CCM, p. B–E4990.

13. 1994 CCM, p. B–E4982.

14. 1994 CCM, p. B–E4978.

15. 1994 Feedback Message, in 1995 CCM, Exhibit 363, Gellene criminal trial, p. B–E4974.

16. 1995 Feedback Message, in 1996 CCM, Exhibit 394, Gellene criminal trial, p. B–E4959.

17. 1994 CCM, p. B–E4982.

18. 1995 Feedback Message, in 1996 CCM, p. B–E4959.

19. GTT, p. 1203.

confirmed that he was a member of the New Jersey bar. The firm
discovered, however, that, contrary to his representation, Gellene was
not listed as a member by the New York state bar. This in turn meant
that his claimed membership in the federal bar in New York City was
invalid. In other words, for almost nine years Gellene had practiced law
in New York without a license.

Before he began his clerkship with Justice Pashman on the New
Jersey Supreme Court, Gellene had taken both the New Jersey and New
York state bar examinations in the summer of 1979. A few months later,
he received word that he had passed the New Jersey bar exam and was
then sworn in as a member. About the same time, he learned that he had
passed the New York bar exam. In order to become a member of that
state's bar, however, Gellene had to fill out a thirteen-page application,
provide affidavits from all his legal employers, and arrange for an
interview in Albany with the character and fitness committee of the bar.

After passing the New York bar exam, Gellene simply had not
completed this phase of the process. In all likelihood, his failure was due
to feeling too busy at the time with his clerkship duties to fill out the
forms and make the trip to Albany. When Gellene joined Milbank, the
highly competitive atmosphere of the firm must have reinforced his
perception that his schedule didn't provide him with time to finish the
process. As the *New York Law Journal* noted, "Faced with the pressure
to pile up billable hours, some associates push aside the tedious task of
completing the paperwork necessary to gain admission."[20] As a result,
according to one partner at a major New York law firm, "There's a long
tradition of putting [admission] off in New York."[21]

However Gellene may have rationalized his conduct, Milbank removed him as a partner and granted him a severance payment. At the
time that Gellene's case came to light, the division of the court system
overseeing his status had recently permitted around forty attorneys who
had passed the bar but never finished the application process to take the
steps necessary to gain admission. Gellene was allowed to do the same,
and set about to rectify his failure. He completed the forms and submitted them to the appropriate committee. Despite his earlier violation, the
state accepted his application to be a member of the New York bar. He
was sworn in in March 1990, some ten months after the discovery of his
misrepresentation.

In May, Milbank designated Gellene as "of counsel" to the firm for
the remainder of the year, while Milbank evaluated him and considered
what if any further steps to take. Finally, he was reinstated as a partner

---

20.   Edward Adams, Bar Groups to Curb Unlicensed Lawyers, N.Y.L.J., Dec. 21, 1989,
1.

21.   Id.

at the beginning of 1991. The firm did penalize him, however, by putting him in the class with other lawyers who had been named partner in 1991, rather than returning him to his 1989 class. This meant that his compensation would lag behind others who had been named partner along with him two years earlier.

Thus, what began with minor procrastination due to work demands eventually evolved into misrepresentation. This in turn made it difficult to change course as the years went on. Such behavior clearly was dishonest. At the same time, putting off completing the application process after passing the bar exam was not completely uncommon among associates in major New York law firms. The character and fitness committee to which Gellene eventually submitted his material had compiled a list the previous year of almost 100 individuals in practice who fell into this category, some at prestigious law firms. The committee's secretary said that he was unaware of any case in which a person had ever been denied admission because he or she had performed legal work without completing the application process. This policy of leniency, reported the *New York Law Journal*, "may reflect a recognition of the unintentional hole that some young lawyers dug for themselves when, in the race to pile up billable hours, they failed to complete the paperwork required for admission."[22]

Surprisingly, when Gellene took the steps to gain admission to the state bar, he didn't also take the time to submit an application to be admitted to the federal bar in New York City. In 1994, when filing his application to represent Bucyrus in its bankruptcy, Gellene represented that he was a member of that bar. He believed that this was necessary for him to practice before the federal bankruptcy court in the Bucyrus case. Eventually, prosecutors investigating his disclosure failure in the bankruptcy case discovered this as well. As Gellene has said of gaining admission to the federal bar, "It would have been a very simple thing to do, but I was confronted with the absurd stupidity of not filling out forms that thousands of lawyers fill out year in and year out and I couldn't stand up and say, 'I did this.' I did something stupid so I didn't do it."[23]

At Gellene's trial, it also came to light that, when his disclosure failure was discovered and Burycus had sued Milbank to recover legal fees, he had hidden the suit from his partners at the firm. After receiving the complaint in the case, Gellene let the deadline pass for responding to the claim. This meant that the judge had the authority to enter a default judgment against Milbank. When his partners approached him after hearing a rumor of this, Gellene told them that the

---

22. Id.
23. GTT, pp. 1218–1219.

deadline had not yet passed and that the suit was without merit. Only when evidence continued to mount against him did he break down and confess the truth.

These events have led some observers to explain Gellene's conduct in the Bucyrus bankruptcy as simply the product of his dishonest character. It's clear that Gellene was not forthright in all his professional dealings. His disclosure failure in the bankruptcy, however, doesn't fit the pattern of other instances in which Gellene had cut corners. The latter episodes represent situations in which Gellene put off dealing with an obligation for an unreasonably long period of time. He then lied to conceal his earlier omission. In other words, if Gellene had a character flaw, it was that he tended to lie in order to cover up his past negligence. That surely is not admirable, but is understandable.

Gellene's violation in the Bucyrus case, however, doesn't seem attributable to this flaw. He lied at the outset to deceive the court, not to save himself criticism or embarrassment. That was a different, and arguably more serious, ethical breach. On balance, it seems unpersuasive to claim that Gellene's disclosure failure was merely the product of a man with an impaired moral compass. Gellene had a tendency to cut corners when his inattention got him into a bind. With the Bucyrus case, however, he moved from defensive dishonesty to assertive deceit.

Nonetheless, Gellene's tendency to engage in petty transgressions may have left him at risk to commit more egregious ones. Research indicates that moral behavior to some degree is a matter of habit. The ways people routinely approach and react to circumstances shape them in subtle ways over time, much as continuous incremental changes in the course of a river can eventually shift its course. Gellene's willingness to cut corners on occasion may have eroded some of his resistance to dishonesty. This erosion may have left him without adequate ethical resources to withstand temptation in the Bucyrus case. Gellene's character thus is a part of the story, but it's not the whole story. That requires more attention to the organizational setting in which he worked: the modern large law firm.

The Young Partner's Tale

For most of the twentieth century, Wall Street law firms were characterized by long-term relationships with corporate clients, a gentleman's agreement not to compete for other firm's clients or lawyers, and an "up or out" system in which associates either progressed to partner or obtained positions elsewhere with the help of the firm. Partners generally were compensated according to seniority, so that those who became partners together advanced in lockstep up the compensation ladder. Stable relationships with clients provided a predictable stream of work for everyone, which obviated the need to be aggressive in seeking out new business. Firms thus were insulated in large measure from the vagaries of the market.

During this period, Milbank Tweed was the epitome of a traditional Wall Street firm with ties to the corporate and social elite. From its inception in 1866 as Anderson, Adams & Young, the firm had served as a place "where clients from the upper class could be served by their peers."[24] Crucial to the ability of the firm to play this role was its tie with the Rockefeller family and its enterprises. The firm's largest client was the Equitable Trust Company, which was controlled by the Rockefellers and eventually became Chase Manhattan Bank.

With its close connection to the various Rockefeller interests, lawyers in the combined firm "just waited for the phone to ring with business."[25] One reflection of this tie was that the primary Milbank counsel for Chase and for the Rockefeller family both had permanent positions on the firm's governance committee. As the 1970s began, the Wall Street law firm in general, and Milbank in particular, "offer[ed] its partners security equivalent to IBM." [26]

Significant seeds of change, however, were being sown by new market conditions. Global competition among corporations arose and began to cut into profit margins, creating pressures to reduce labor costs and improve productivity. Companies began to look to mergers and acquisitions as ways to gain economies of scale that would enhance their ability to compete in worldwide markets. In a break with tradition, they even began to launch hostile takeovers of other corporations.

Technological advances also accelerated the forces of competition. New technology reduced the length of time that existing products could be counted on to generate profits, and created entirely new markets requiring wholly new expertise and resources. Changes in investment banking and financial markets also destabilized long-standing operations and relationships. With the deregulation of underwriting fees in 1975, long-term relationships between investment banks and corporations were swept away in a tidal wave of aggressive competition. Banks began to pursue corporate clients by designing ever more novel and complex financial instruments, which they marketed as vehicles for managing risk and improving the bottom line. As capital markets became more globally integrated, these instruments had an increasingly important impact on the economic fortunes of large corporations.

---

24. Ellen Joan Pollock, Turks and Brahmins 34 (1990).

25. Id. at 36.

26. Paul Hoffman, Lions in the Street 51 (1973).

In the 1970s, corporations under pressure to control costs began to rethink their use of legal services. Most notably, they began more directly to rationalize these services by bringing many of them within the corporation. Over the past twenty-five years, in-house legal departments have grown dramatically in size, sophistication, and responsibility. Much of the day-to-day work traditionally performed by outside law firms is now done by lawyers who are corporate employees. This development has reduced the steady flow of work on which large law firms used to rely.

This not only results in the loss of a regular source of income, it also attenuates long-term relationships between firms and their clients. Most major corporations now look to outside firms only for discrete, large-scale transactions or major litigation that can't be fully staffed in-house. Rather than rely on the same firm for all their outside work, in-house counsel now tend to act as savvy consumers who shop around for representation on each matter.

Furthermore, many companies are more concerned with retaining individual lawyers than specific firms. With clients now tending to shop for representation on discrete, often specialized, high-stakes matters, the emphasis is on obtaining lawyers with the most expertise regardless of what firms they may call home. For much of their legal work, corporate clients thus tend to cultivate relationships with particular lawyers rather than particular firms. As a result, partners may move from one firm to another with some confidence that clients will follow them. This has created a phenomenon that was nonexistent a generation ago: an active lateral market for lawyers in which law firms compete with one another for "rainmakers" who can bring along the most business.

Large law firms thus now must face unprecedented fierce competition for both clients and lawyers. All this has required firms belatedly to rationalize their operations much more explicitly along business lines. Firms attempt to keep profits high by creating incentives for partners to generate revenues. Most have abandoned lockstep compensation based on seniority in favor of compensation systems that purport to reward productivity. Lawyers no longer can rely on the firm to supply regular work from clients. Instead, their compensation is determined by the "eat what you kill" system. That is, a partner increasingly is compensated from the work that he himself generates from clients. Furthermore, law firms constantly are on the lookout for lawyers they might lure, smaller firms they might acquire, and peer firms with which they might merge.

These characteristics of the modern large law firm shape the experience and outlook of lawyers within them in important ways. Perhaps most striking is that making partner no longer provides any guarantee of job security. Partners who lag in revenue generation may have their compensation cut, their right to vote taken away, and even be terminated from the firm. Partners therefore must compete for compensation, status, and continued employment in an ongoing tournament. It's not a tournament in the conventional sense, in that there is no single ultimate winner. Indeed, no one is ever assured of winning. Instead, everyone is constantly playing simply to remain in the game. The goal, in other words, is not victory but survival.

The amount of revenues that a partner generates is the main method of keeping score in this tournament. There are two ways that a partner can maximize her score. The first, and preferable, one is to be a rainmaker who brings in clients to the firm. Rainmakers not only get credit for the work they personally do, but also receive some credit for the work that others do for those clients. The more lawyers a rainmaker can keep busy, the better her standing in the tournament, and the greater her compensation and influence within the firm.

Partners who aren't significant rainmakers must maximize their competitive position by working regularly for partners who are. These lawyers are "service partners" who perform work for other partners' clients. Developing a good relationship with a rainmaker allows a non-rainmaker to generate revenues by regularly billing a large number of hours on lucrative matters. A tournament survivor therefore must be a successful entrepreneur and profit center. He must find clients that will generate revenue, either on his own or from rainmakers within the firm.

Milbank Tweed began to be shaken by these forces in the 1980s.[27] The firm's relationship with Chase Manhattan Bank became attenuated as the bank expanded its legal department and moved into lines of business in which other law firms had more expertise. As late as 1985, Milbank received 40% of its revenues from the bank. Three years later, the percentage was half that. Similarly, the Rockefeller family began to rely more on its own stable of lawyers and less on Milbank. Furthermore, several family members cashed out the value of many of the family's real estate holdings, which meant fewer entrepreneurial projects requiring legal assistance.

By the mid–1980s, these changes left many at Milbank anxious that the firm was falling behind in the newly competitive market for legal services. Milbank's profits per partner were $370,000 in 1984, compared with $635,000 for Cravath and $795,000 for newcomer Wachtell, Lipton, where Larry Lederman was at the time. The year before, Milbank had seen its first partner leave for practice at another firm. Milbank did little work for investment banks, which were flexing newly profitable muscle. Furthermore, it had missed the lucrative boom in merger and acquisition practice of the early 1980s, which afforded firms such as Wachtell and

---

27. An excellent account of the firm's evolution is found in Pollock, *supra* note 24.

Skadden, Arps the opportunity to vault into the ranks of the most profitable firms.

In 1984, the Milbank executive committee and its chair, Alexander Forger, began the slow task of convincing partners that Milbank needed to transform itself from a genteel white-shoe firm to an aggressive entrepreneurial business. Matters came to a head at a pivotal firm retreat in March 1986. Despite an emotionally charged debate, partners voted to give the compensation committee authority to modify the lockstep system to take account of performance. When the committee issued its report in October, many were surprised at the sweep of its recommendations. Three partners who were high achievers would constitute a class above their lockstep peers. Three midlevel partners also would receive increases above lockstep. In addition, seven other partners were scheduled to receive such raises beginning January 1, 1987.

More ominously, eight partners received notice that they would not be eligible for lockstep increases, and might even suffer a cut in compensation, if they did not increase their productivity. Finally came the most shocking news: two lawyers who had been partners since 1979 would be leaving the firm. The committee insisted that these partners had not been fired. Many members of the firm, however, believed that "evaluations of the two partners had been handled in such a way that the gentlemen had no other logical—or dignified—recourse than to decide to withdraw from the partnership."[28] In all, about twenty partners either gained or lost compared with what they would have received under lockstep compensation. Increases above lockstep averaged about $75,000, while decreases averaged $100,000.

Many partners were shocked at how aggressively the committee had applied a merit compensation approach. The momentum for change, however, continued unabated. The strategic plan for the firm approved by the partnership in March 1990 emphasized how crucial it was for Milbank to develop expertise in what the plan called "Leading Corporate Transactions."[29] The number one priority of the firm, said the plan, was to develop a well-known "General Corporate/M & A [merger and acquisition]" practice.[30] This was necessary in order to provide the impetus for growth in several other practice areas, secure "above-average profitability growth levels," and to ensure Milbank's status as an elite firm.[31]

---

28. Pollock, supra note 24 at 224.

29. Memorandum to Partners Re: Lawrence Lederman, Oct. 28, 1991, Appendix A: 1990 Planning Report of the Executive Committee and Planning Committee, Exhibit 360, Gellene criminal trial, p. B–E8497.

30. Id. at B–E8495.

31. Id.

The plan directly addressed the issue of firm culture. Bringing in a corporate/M & A group, it said, would make the firm "more aggressive, scrappier, more intense, and more highly charged in its desire to accomplish client objectives."[32] To the extent that some within the firm might be disturbed by such a metamorphosis, they "must face up to the trade off that would appear to be necessary if Milbank is to have any chance of holding its own in competing for the business of large, publicly-held corporations, investment bankers, merchant bankers, and the like which we now seek."[33]

The planning committee report also noted that work on corporate financial restructuring and bankruptcy was in an upswing, and that Milbank was poised to benefit from this trend by virtue of having the fourth largest bankruptcy department in the nation. One obstacle to doing so, however, was the firm's high concentration of creditors in its client base. In order to maximize the benefits of its expertise, the firm needed to move more aggressively into the representation of corporate debtors. Developing more extensive connections with investment banks would be important in achieving this objective.

In 1991, Milbank began pursuing this strategy by beginning its courtship of high-powered corporate lawyer Larry Lederman of Wachtell, Lipton, Rosen, & Katz. Because of his ties to major corporations and investment banks, Lederman had the potential to lead Milbank into the promised land of "Leading Corporate Transactions." His contacts also could open the door to more frequent representation of corporate debtors in bankruptcy. Representing such clients could be very beneficial to a young bankruptcy partner like John Gellene who hoped to stay alive in the Milbank tournament.

By the time that Gellene became a partner at Milbank, the rules of the tournament had changed. Lawyers henceforth could not afford to assume that their firms would provide them with a regular flow of work. They had to take responsibility for that themselves. Furthermore, partnership no longer was a guarantee of job security, but was constantly up for grabs in an ongoing competition.

Gellene therefore couldn't assume that his past performance, or the fact that he was a skilled bankruptcy lawyer, would shield him from competition. He had to develop his own client base to ensure that he continued to generate profits for the firm.

The Rainmaker's Tale

Unfortunately for John Gellene, his personality didn't easily lend itself to the role of rainmaker. His single-minded, sometimes isolating,

---

32. Id. at B–E8497.

33. Id.

concentration was an adaptive trait for winning a prize in the old tournament. It could be a hindrance, however, in the new one. Many of his colleagues found him abstracted and absorbed. Even partners who praised Gellene's work sometimes found him difficult to understand. He is "a bit of an enigma,"[34] said one. John Jerome, his bankruptcy mentor, observed, "He can get depressed but perhaps this is his nature."[35] Another partner described him as bright, talented, and ambitious, but suggested, "He should civilize himself more."[36] None of these attributes translates into the easy social skills useful in marketing legal services to potential clients.

An equally significant obstacle to Gellene becoming a rainmaker was the fact that bankruptcy practice is both episodic and cyclical. Clients who want to reorganize in response to financial distress need the services of bankruptcy lawyers for a specific purpose for a limited period of time. If everything goes well, the client no longer needs your services. This makes it difficult to build long-term client relationships. By contrast, a corporate lawyer has the potential to tap into a steady stream of work on behalf of clients who may need help with matters such as securities issues, taxation, mergers and acquisitions, the sale of assets, transactional work, regulatory compliance, and litigation, to name only a few. Similarly, lawyers who represent investment banks work on behalf of clients that are constantly involved in corporate deals.

In addition to its episodic nature, bankruptcy practice is cyclical. It waxes when the economy is not going well, and wanes when times are good. Events such as the failure of many savings and loans in the 1980s, the collapse of many companies in the early 1990s under the burden of debt incurred in leveraged buy-outs a few years earlier, and the bursting of the Internet bubble after 2000, all intensify demand for bankruptcy services. When the economy recovers, however, that demand can fall off considerably. The amount of work that a bankruptcy lawyer has thus can be subject to influences over which he has little control.

Internal Milbank Tweed memos indicate that Gellene was acutely aware of the difficulty of developing a stable of clients, and feared that bankruptcy work would dry up. At the end of each year, members of the Milbank compensation committee met with partners to discuss the compensation that they would be receiving under the firm's merit-based system. The committee's reports indicate that Gellene consistently expressed ongoing anxiety about the future of the Milbank bankruptcy practice.

---

34.   1990 Comments, in 1991 CCM, Exhibit 392, p. B–E5013.

35.   1991 CCM, p. B–E5012.

36.   1993 CCM, p. B–E4990.

Gellene told the compensation committee, for instance, that he was frustrated by what he perceived as the bankruptcy group's failure to engage in adequate business development efforts. The group had no clients of its own, he fretted, and would remain a practice that simply provided services to others' clients as long as the firm primarily represented financial institutions that periodically had creditor claims in bankruptcy. This was frustrating, since Gellene said that he was at the point in his career when he wanted to develop his own practice.[37]

On another occasion, Gellene told the committee that there had been a decline in bankruptcy business, as restructuring work flowing from the high corporate debt of the 1980s was slowing down. Bankruptcy work, he said, was in danger of becoming a "commodity," implying fierce competition and declining profit margins.[38] There were "too many lawyers for the available business."[39] In another committee report, Gellene was quoted as lamenting that bankruptcy is "a fee-based practice with only episodic opportunities for premium billing."[40] He told the committee that "[t]here is less business and more competition," "[i]t is a little hard to see what is in the pipeline," and "[t]he business has shrunk so much that our people do not see the upside potential for them."[41] As he was finishing a major bankruptcy case, he fretted that the challenge "will be to find adequate new work."[42] Gellene complained that the firm in general, and the bankruptcy group in particular, wasn't adequately responding to these challenges.

The arrival of Lederman at Milbank, however, could open the door to a world that no one else at the firm could offer. Lederman's client roster of corporations and investment banks offered the potential for access to a steady stream of corporate clients who needed help with financial restructuring or reorganization through bankruptcy. Lederman was a prominent symbol of the new order in Wall Street law practice. He had been a major player in dismantling an implicit arrangement in which corporations never attempted hostile takeovers and major law firms didn't compete for clients or lawyers.[43] Milbank had lured Lederman by promising to make him the highest paid partner at the firm. As one lawyer put it, Lederman was the "800–pound gorilla" at Milbank.[44]

---

37. 1991 CCM, pp. B–E5009–5010.

38. 1992 CCM, p. B–E5006.

39. Id. at p. B–E5007.

40. 1993 CCM at p. B–E4986.

41. 1994 CCM, p. B–E4978.

42. 1993 CCM, p. B–E4986.

43. Lederman's background and career are set forth in Lawrence Lederman, Tombstones: A Lawyer's Tales from the Takeover Decade (1992).

44. GTT, p. 465.

Lederman, of course, was the partner who tapped Gellene to work on the Bucyrus bankruptcy. Gellene may have been loath at that point to risk losing the opportunity to work for such an important rainmaker and his client. Might Lederman have relied on that reluctance to press Gellene not to disclose Milbank's work for Salovaara and South Street to the bankruptcy court?

No solid evidence supports this conjecture, and there is some evidence that is inconsistent with it. Milbank's 1993 Compensation Committee Memorandum, for instance, indicates that Lederman mentioned to the Committee Gellene's work both on the Bucyrus bankruptcy and on another matter for Salovaara.[45] Such candor doesn't seem consistent with a desire by Lederman to conceal the simultaneous representation. At the same time, it is difficult to imagine that Lederman was indifferent to whether Gellene made a disclosure that likely would disqualify the firm from representing Bucyrus in its bankruptcy. There is, however, another, more subtle, possibility. Lederman may have approached the situation in a way that Gellene construed as implicitly signaling that Milbank should not disclose its representation of South Street to the bankruptcy court. Sensitive to such a signal, Gellene withheld the information.

Exploring this story requires appreciating that corporate transactional lawyers tend to have a distinctive approach to conflicts issues. Legal ethics rules provide that lawyers may not simultaneously represent clients with actual or potential conflicts of interest unless the lawyer reasonably believes that he will be able to represent both interests adequately, and each client consents to representation by waiving objection to the lawyer's conflict.[46] Client waiver of such conflicts is far more common in transactional than in litigation work. Transactional clients often believe that they can benefit from lawyers' relationships with lenders, underwriters, commercial banks, potential merger or joint venture partners, suppliers, and even competitors. The most able lawyers tend to have the widest network of connections. The existence of this network can lower transaction costs for a client. The lawyer may serve as a reputational intermediary, who makes negotiations go more smoothly because the other parties know and trust him. He may have an especially good understanding of those parties' needs and interests, and thereby be able to devise mutually beneficial terms. The lawyer's set of connections may reduce the client's search costs for financing assistance, and permit it to move more swiftly on time-sensitive matters.

---

45. 1993 CCM, p. B–E4990.

46. See, e.g. American Bar Association, Model Rules of Professional Conduct, Rule 1.7 (2004); New York Code of Professional Responsibility, DR 5–105(c) (2004).

All these potential benefits flow from the fact that a lawyer has relationships with parties who have interests that could potentially conflict with those of the client. Many business clients are willing to take this risk, however, in the belief that the lawyer will instead be adept at finding common ground. They desire the opportunity to draw on the lawyer's stock of "relational capital" to derive benefits that might be unavailable from less conflicted representation. Furthermore, the transactional lawyer's location in a web of interconnected relationships can heighten the importance of reputation, and make informal sanctions an effective deterrent to opportunism or disloyalty. For these reasons, client waiver of conflicts is far more common in transactional than in litigation work. Transactional lawyers thus tend more than litigators to see conflicts rules not as unqualified commands but as default rules—rules subject to bargaining, which apply only if parties don't agree on another arrangement.

With such an orientation to conflicts issues, transactional lawyers may look implicitly to the investment bankers with whom they work as models of how to approach potential conflicts—especially since such bankers enjoy greater power, prestige, and income than do lawyers. Since the mid-1970s, both investment banks and corporate law firms have seen the evaporation of long-term relationships with clients and the emergence of fiercer competition. Many corporate lawyers tend to perceive investment bankers as having been far more forceful and innovative than law firms in responding to such market changes. Successful banks create a complex network of ties with numerous market actors that enable them to identify and respond quickly to opportunities for profitable transactions that can involve billions of dollars. They are immersed even more than transactional lawyers in intricate networks of commercial relationships.   *Investment banks have less stringent conflict of*

Investment banks have been able to promote this aggressive culture *interest* in part because of less stringent conflict of interest restrictions than *restriction* those that govern lawyers. Investment banks have more latitude than lawyers with respect to conflicts because, unlike lawyers, they are not regarded in all cases as fiduciaries for clients. Courts generally will impose fiduciary duties on banks only when a bank is in a "superior position to exert influence or control" over a party.[47] Otherwise, the relationships between investment banks and their clients are governed by the rules that apply to parties involved in arms-length market relationships. By contrast, attorneys are treated as fiduciaries for their clients under all circumstances.

Elite corporate lawyers thus may chafe at conflicts rules that require that they obtain consent from clients before representing potentially

---

47. Brandt v. Hicks Muse & Co., 213 B.R. 784, 789 (D. Mass. 1997).

conflicting interests, even though transactional clients often grant such consent. There is always at least the risk that objection by a single client can prevent them from representing new clients or moving easily into new areas of practice. Transactional lawyers may regard the fiduciary restrictions that are the basis for requiring client consent as anachronistic obstacles to building a successful entrepreneurial law firm. Conflict constraints may seem to rest on an outdated notion that a tie of loyalty binds lawyer and client, when in reality both corporate clients and law firms are involved in multiple relationships. Furthermore, many corporate clients hardly fit the model of the vulnerable party that is the foundation of the fiduciary paradigm. If only subconsciously, large-firm transactional lawyers may seek to emulate investment bankers in their approach to conflicts of interest. This may lead such lawyers to see little need to give clients the opportunity to object to a conflict by disclosing it to them.

For these reasons, Lederman may have been inclined to regard Milbank's simultaneous representation of Bucyrus and Salovaara on unrelated matters as unremarkable. One could easily imagine that, if informed of the conflict, each party would conclude that it would ensure a smooth bankruptcy in which each party's interest was protected. Disclosure in such circumstances thus arguably was of minimal concern.

As an experienced bankruptcy lawyer, however, Gellene knew better. Unlike in transactional settings, bankruptcy conflicts rules aren't simply default rules. They are meant not simply to protect self-interested clients, but to ensure the integrity of the bankruptcy proceedings. That integrity requires that the debtor act as a fiduciary for all parties with claims against it, and that the court monitor the fairness of the bargaining process. This means that disclosure of a conflict is important not simply for the debtor and whatever specific creditors the debtor's lawyer may represent on other matters. Bucyrus and South Street weren't the only parties with an interest in Milbank's potential conflict of interest. The two thousand other Bucyrus creditors also would want to know about it, because they might fear that Gellene would provide advice to Bucyrus that would favor South Street at their expense. Furthermore, Bucyrus and South Street were not free to waive the conflict. If another creditor or the trustee objected to the conflict, the court could disqualify Milbank Tweed despite Bucyrus and South Street's willingness to waive it.

Conflicts rules in bankruptcy therefore have a more categorical status than do conflict rules applicable in a transactional context. Gellene also knew that bankruptcy law requires disclosure of all "connections" with parties with interests in the bankruptcy—not simply potential conflicts of interest. Thus, even if Gellene were satisfied that the firm's ties to South Street represented no conflict, he still had to disclose them.

Gellene, however, likely was extremely sensitive to any signal from Lederman about how to handle disclosure. Lederman was the most powerful partner at Milbank, the main catalyst of a transformation of the firm into an entrepreneurial business enterprise. Gellene was among a relatively select group of lawyers teamed to work regularly with Lederman in an effort to capitalize on Lederman's contacts and expertise. It was in furtherance of this plan that Lederman had gotten Gellene involved in the Bucyrus bankruptcy. Gellene therefore had an interest in maintaining strong ties to Lederman.

Lederman need not have explicitly advised Gellene to withhold information for Gellene to conclude that this is what the senior lawyer wanted. Lederman may have instinctively relied on a transactional lawyer's approach to conflicts and assumed that the dual representation was not a problem. As a result, Lederman may have given disclosure little sustained thought. Alternatively, he may have known that the transactional approach was inappropriate for bankruptcy, but implicitly conveyed the view that bankruptcy rules should not stand in the way of Milbank's dual representation. In either case, Gellene would be bright enough to infer that he should not disclose the firm's relationship to South Street. He may have acquiesced in this tacit message rather than press for a more sharply focused discussion of the issue.

Certain tendencies of subordinates in large organizations may have reinforced Gellene's willingness to defer to what he regarded as Lederman's wishes. First, it's common for such persons to attribute highly positive qualities to those on whom they are dependent. Lederman, of course, was not a bankruptcy lawyer. Gellene, however, may have rationalized that Lederman's vast experience with financially distressed corporations engaged in capital restructuring made him better qualified than even Gellene to decide how best to approach conflicts and disclosure issues. Lederman could see the big picture in a way that Gellene could not. Lederman was a rainmaker and Gellene was not. It might be easy, therefore, for Gellene to conclude that Lederman possessed more wisdom than he on how to proceed.

Second, ambitious subordinates often seek to anticipate what their superiors wish them to do rather than wait for explicit direction. Waiting to act until one has received explicit instructions can be seen as a lack of initiative, which can be fatal to prospects for advancement. Many individuals "can be expected to intuit what orders they would be given and 'follow them in advance.' "[48]

---

48. John M. Darley, How Organizations Socialize Individuals into Evildoing, in Codes of Conduct: Behavioral Research into Business Ethics 13, 25 (David M. Messick & Ann E. Tenbrunsel eds. 1996).

Gellene may have felt that he could anticipate what Lederman's position would be on disclosure. He might fear that if he concluded that disclosure was necessary, or if he waited to act until after consulting Lederman, the senior lawyer might regard him as too cautious to play an important role in future major corporate matters. The best way to carry out what Gellene believed were Lederman's wishes would be to tell him that Milbank would not disclose its ties to Salovaara and South Street to the bankruptcy court. In this way, Gellene may have drifted slowly toward non-disclosure without giving the matter in-depth consideration. At the same time, Lederman could maintain that he relied on Gellene to make the appropriate disclosure.

In sum, the overachieving young partner who needed to maintain his tie with a rainmaker may have felt pressure not to disclose Milbank's potential conflict of interest to the bankruptcy court. This pressure, however, would not necessarily lead him to engage in conduct that he believed was clearly wrong. As with most of us, John Gellene likely needed a way to rationalize that non-disclosure was morally defensible. His role in two other episodes provided an opportunity to do just that.

The Bankruptcy Specialist's Tale

Modern law practice is increasingly specialized. Specialists confront issues and problems in their daily work that differ from those faced by colleagues with other expertise in their firms. Much of law practice consists of informal understandings about matters such as what arguments are considered within the bounds of good faith, acceptable levels of aggressiveness, the scope of disclosure requirements, how to interact with regulatory agencies, and what constitutes due diligence. These and other issues may be resolved differently by lawyers in specialties such as securities, tax, banking, patents, environmental law, and bankruptcy, to name only a few. Conferences and other professional education activities tend to be organized around specific fields of practice, thereby providing opportunities for lawyers to trade ideas and develop common understandings based on shared experience. In addition, lawyers may be subject to rules of practice particular to their specialty. Practitioners thus may have more in common with lawyers in other firms who practice in the same specialty than with many lawyers in their own firms. Over time, the shared experiences of practitioners in a particular specialty lead them to develop norms of acceptable behavior.

Especially significant in John Gellene's case, large-firm corporate bankruptcy lawyers have a distinctive perspective of their own. Until the late 1970s, bankruptcy was practiced mostly by lawyers in relatively small firms who tended to represent only creditors or debtors. That began to change with passage of the 1978 Bankruptcy Act, which made Chapter 11 much more attractive to large corporations. The recession of the late 1970s and early 1980s then generated considerable bankruptcy work. A decade later, bankrupt companies burdened by debt acquired in leveraged deals in the 1980s created even greater opportunities. Large law firms subject to heightened competition for business began to realize that there were lucrative prospects in bankruptcy practice. They began acquiring smaller bankruptcy firms in the hope of capitalizing on this promise.

Large firms entering bankruptcy practice, however, began to encounter difficulties with potentially disqualifying conflicts of interest. Section 327 of the Bankruptcy Code provides that a lawyer applying to the court to represent a debtor must be "disinterested" and may not have an interest "adverse to the estate." Large law firms have hundreds, if not thousands, of clients, many of which are major corporations and financial institutions. Any large corporate bankruptcy may involve thousands of parties with claims on the debtor. It's almost certain that clients of large law firms will be among them. These clients can be characterized as having an interest adverse to the debtor. The debtor would like to minimize payouts while claimants seek to maximize them. Even if a law firm represents these clients in matters unrelated to the bankruptcy, the firm still might be in a position to favor these clients if it also represents the debtor. Thus, if Section 327 is applied literally, it would prevent large law firms from representing the debtor in the vast majority of major corporate bankruptcies.

Large law firms naturally are disturbed by this prospect. Major corporate bankruptcies can bring in millions of dollars in fees, all of which have priority over payments to creditors. Large firms argue that the multitude and dispersion of their offices and clients means that the likelihood that a firm will try to play favorites in bankruptcy is remote in many cases. For example, they suggest, a partner representing a corporate debtor in Seattle may well be unaffected by the fact that a partner he doesn't even know in Frankfurt is representing one of the debtor's creditors in a European merger proceeding.

Firms maintain that disqualification in such cases would serve no real purpose, and would deprive debtors of the benefit of large-firm bankruptcy expertise. As was the case with Milbank and Bucyrus, for instance, many law firms begin representing companies in the period preceding bankruptcy. They help the company in its effort to avoid bankruptcy by restructuring its debt, or they participate in negotiations designed to produce consensus on a plan to submit to the court. Forcing a firm to withdraw once the company files its bankruptcy petition can deprive the debtor of counsel who is familiar with the company and all the other interested parties. Having to hire and bring up to speed new counsel can be both expensive and disruptive in such circumstances.

More generally, large firms argue, strict enforcement of Section 327 would prevent corporations in complex bankruptcies from hiring the law firms best qualified to handle such reorganizations. Since the 1978 Bankruptcy Act made Chapter 11 more attractive to corporations, major companies now use bankruptcy as a business tool. Expertise in business planning, recapitalization, mergers and acquisitions, tax, labor law, environmental regulation, intellectual property, pensions, employee benefits, and other fields has become more important in corporate bankruptcies. Large firms claim that it's more efficient for a debtor to retain a firm with all these capabilities than to hire separate firms to deal with each area of the law.

Large-firm bankruptcy lawyers thus tend to be skeptical that strict application of the bankruptcy conflict rule always serves important ethical purposes. That skepticism is reinforced by the fact that applying conflicts rules in corporate bankruptcy practice can be complicated and difficult. First, large bankruptcies involve thousands of parties, whose relationships can be ambiguous. Prospective counsel for the debtor may represent some of these parties in other matters. Does the fact that those clients are creditors of the debtor automatically make them adverse to the debtor, regardless of how small their claim? What if the debtor is not contesting a creditor's claim? What if the debtor and creditor have reached agreement on a bankruptcy plan before the bankruptcy filing? What if the debtor and creditor are allied against another creditor? Does only the second creditor have an interest adverse to the debtor?

Another feature of bankruptcy makes it even more difficult to identify conflicts of interest in corporate bankruptcies in straightforward fashion. Bankruptcy involves multiple, shifting alliances and rivalries that arise and dissipate as particular issues come to the fore. Bankruptcy expert Nancy Rapoport describes this as the generation of conflicts that are dormant, temporary, and actual. They are dormant, she observes, because "the potential for conflict lies in wait unless and until the right combination of strategy decisions (by several parties) comes into play."[49] Conflicts are temporary because they are issue-specific; once the underlying issue has been resolved, the conflict also is resolved. They are actual in that as long as the triggering issue is active, two are more parties are adversaries toward one another.

This makes it very difficult for a lawyer—and a court—to know at the outset of a case which interests now aligned will diverge, and which interests now opposed will converge. Must a court wait and entertain a series of disqualification motions as different issues arise on which

---

49. Nancy B. Rapoport, Turning and Turning in the Widening Gyre: the Problem of Potential Conflicts of Interest in Bankruptcy, 26 Conn. L. Rev. 913, 924 (1994).

parties become adversaries? Should it rescind a disqualification once the adversity disappears? Or should it try to anticipate which actual conflicts are likely to arise? Adding to the complexity is the fact that creditors often sell their claims to other parties during bankruptcy. This means that creditors that could create conflicts of interest for debtor's counsel may be constantly entering or exiting the bankruptcy.

This state of affairs has led courts to take a variety of positions on whether prospective counsel for the debtor can be disqualified for a conflict of interest. Some courts have held that either an actual or a potential conflict will serve to disqualify counsel. Other courts have ruled that a potential conflict may serve as the basis for disqualification in some cases. Still another court has created a rebuttable presumption that counsel should be disqualified because of a potential conflict. Some courts will disqualify an applicant only if there is an actual conflict. Finally, one court has suggested that the distinction between "actual" and "potential" conflict is not very useful as a guide to disqualification decisions.

Lawyers in big firms believe that this state of affairs creates too much opportunity for the strategic use of disqualification motions or objections to appointment. The Bankruptcy Code says that a law firm can't be disqualified from representing a debtor solely because it also represents creditors of the debtor, unless another creditor or the trustee objects and the court finds that there is an actual conflict. A large corporate firm that wishes to represent a debtor is, to some extent, at the mercy of the other creditors among its clients. If negotiations have proceeded relatively smoothly, those creditors may not file an objection to the firm's application. If negotiations have been acrimonious, or creditors are not completely happy with their proposed treatment, they may object. The same underlying connection between the law firm and its creditor client therefore may pose no problem to representing the debtor in one case and serve to bar it in another, based on factors that have nothing to do with substantive conflict concerns.

However confusing or unfair a lawyer may regard Section 327, this is supposed to be irrelevant to her disclosure duty under bankruptcy law. A lawyer must disclose "all" of her "connections with the debtor, creditors, and any party in interest." She has no discretion to decide whether some connections create only "technical" conflicts that raise no substantive ethical concern. That is for the court to decide, since "[a]n attorney's interest in being employed by the estate could cloud the attorney's judgment regarding what should be disclosed."[50]

Nonetheless, it's easy to imagine that a lawyer's sense of the gravity of her disclosure obligation will be influenced by her perception of the

---

50. In re Tinley Plaza Associates, 142 B.R. 272 (Bankr. N.D. Ill. 1992).

fairness and legitimacy of the conflict provisions of Section 327. The purpose of disclosure, after all, is to provide information that can be used in determining whether an applicant has a conflict of interest that would disqualify her from representing the debtor. If the applicant believes that those rules sometimes lead to arbitrary or unrealistic disqualification, she may not treat compliance with the disclosure rule as a categorical duty.

A lawyer may find support for such a rationalization in court decisions that don't apply Section 327 according to its literal terms. New York and Delaware bankruptcy courts hear the largest proportion of major Chapter 11 cases. Those courts tend to reject a "literalist" reading of conflicts provisions in favor of a "realistic" approach that takes account of the practicalities of large-firm practice to avoid disqualification. Even when a potentially disabling conflict exists, these courts are amenable to resolving it by appointing special counsel to handle matters as to which debtor's counsel has a conflict, and/or requiring a law firm to establish a firewall between lawyers working on the bankruptcy and those working for interested parties in other matters. Neither measure is explicitly permitted in the bankruptcy code, but each appears to be a part of the rules in those jurisdictions.

Large firms regard this approach as based on a more realistic view of bankruptcy conflicts. They claim that it reflects appreciation that large corporations in bankruptcy need the services of large firms. Critics, however, argue that courts that accommodate large firms in this way virtually read conflicts restrictions out of the bankruptcy code. Lawyers and judges in different jurisdictions thus may utilize different conceptual models of bankruptcy conflicts law.

As a result, a large-firm bankruptcy lawyer may conclude that there is less risk in New York and Delaware than in other courts that full disclosure will result in what he regards as an unwarranted disqualification. This may incline him to be more forthcoming with disclosure in, say, New York than Milwaukee. If he believes that a bankruptcy court in Milwaukee is likely to take a "literalist" approach to the conflicts rules, he may be inclined to rationalize that a potentially troublesome connection is merely a "technical" conflict that need not be disclosed.

The evidence suggests that John Gellene was well aware of this possible difference in local bankruptcy cultures. On the morning he left for Milwaukee to finish the work necessary to file the Bucyrus bankruptcy petition, Gellene spoke with Lederman about what he would be disclosing to the court. The disclosure of Milbank's ties to Bucyrus creditor Goldman, Sachs, he said, would create no problems in a New York bankruptcy court. He told Lederman, however, that he could not be certain how a bankruptcy judge in Wisconsin would react. Wisconsin, in other words, might be stricter about conflicts than New York.[51] Reinforcing this suspicion is the fact that the Wisconsin bankruptcy judge pointedly admonished Gellene at one of the hearings on Milbank's application: "New York is different from Milwaukee ... [P]rofessional things like conflicts are taken very, very seriously. And for better or worse, you're stuck in Wisconsin."[52] As a result, Gellene may have suspected that he faced a greater chance of being disqualified in Milwaukee than in New York or Delaware for what he saw as merely a technical conflict.

Gellene might have convinced himself that the conflict was a technical one that posed no threat to his loyalty or independence for at least three reasons. First, others, not he, had done most of the negotiations regarding possible concessions by South Street. Second, Gellene had not undertaken his own work for South Street in an unrelated matter until after that investment fund had agreed to terms of the bankruptcy. Thus, Gellene might argue, there is no way that his representation of South Street could have affected whatever negotiations he had with that creditor about the bankruptcy. Finally, because it had agreed to the plan, South Street's interests were aligned with, not adversarial to, those of Bucyrus. Gellene's work as debtor's counsel to obtain confirmation of the plan would be in the best interests of both parties.

Gellene's possible belief that Milbank's ties to South Street gave rise only to a technical conflict of interest may have permitted him in turn to rationalize that withholding information about these connections was not freighted with moral significance. Disclosure of a merely technical conflict would serve no meaningful purpose. Rather, it would simply reflect compliance with a formalistic regulatory requirement that was out of step with the realities of large-firm bankruptcy practice. In light of the motives that Gellene may have had not to disclose Milbank's representation of South Street, he could have been especially receptive to this rationalization.

Furthermore, because courts generally had not imposed stringent penalties for violations of the disclosure rule at the time of the Bucyrus bankruptcy, Gellene may have treated his decision not to disclose as a calculated gamble. The probability of objection and disqualification as a result of disclosure may have seemed high, which made it preferable not to disclose. The fees that Milbank would receive might well exceed the penalty it would suffer if the failure to disclose were discovered. If Gellene believed that the conflict he was hiding was only a technical one, he might have been more likely to take such an instrumental approach to disclosure.

---

51. GTT, pp. 1181–1184.

52. GTT, p. 916.

In these ways, John Gellene may have been able to rationalize to himself that concealing Milbank's work for Salovaara's interests was not unethical. There is one final piece of the puzzle worth considering. This is that Gellene rationalized that non-disclosure not only was not morally blameworthy, but was morally justified under the circumstances. He may have drawn support for this view from the specific dynamics of the Bucyrus bankruptcy negotiations.

The Advocate's Tale

From the time Gellene began working on the Bucyrus bankruptcy in February 1993, a year before the actual filing, it was a major assignment for him. He was the only Milbank partner with day-to-day responsibility for the project. As such, he served as the primary legal advisor for the company, and he represented Bucyrus in its negotiations with various interested parties. In these roles, he was deeply involved in virtually everything that went on, and came to identify closely with his client.

The course of the bankruptcy negotiations served not only to reinforce that identification, but also to provide Gellene with the sense that he was operating in a relatively stark moral landscape. Two aspects of the negotiations were especially prominent. The first was a sense of urgency that the plan had to be confirmed and Bucyrus emerge from bankruptcy as soon as possible. The second was the emergence of an extremely contentious relationship with Bucyrus's largest unsecured creditor, Jackson National Life Insurance Company (JNL).

If Bucyrus were to enjoy potentially substantial tax benefits, it had to file its bankruptcy plan by the end of 1993 or have it approved by the court by the end of 1994. Added time pressure came from company officials' fears that a protracted bankruptcy process would undermine Bucyrus' position in the market. Because of the long lead time necessary to process orders for the heavy machinery that Bucyrus manufactured, customers and suppliers had to have confidence that the company would be viable in the long run. Competitors evidently were already taking advantage of the bankruptcy filing to raise doubts about Bucyrus' condition. The attempt to put together a plan that the company and its creditors could submit at the time of the bankruptcy filing reflected the hope that the company could emerge from bankruptcy in 90 to120 days.

A second notable feature of the negotiations was the acrimony between Bucyrus and JNL. This began when, a year before filing bankruptcy, Bucyrus announced that it would be suspending interest payments on its debt. JNL contended that the purchase of Bucyrus five years earlier by a group of Bucyrus managers and Goldman, Sachs was on terms that were grossly unfair to Bucyrus. It also claimed that other financing transactions, in which other creditors had acquired claims on

Bucyrus, were part of a fraudulent plan by managers and Goldman, Sachs to milk the company. Moreover, JNL was especially upset that Bucyrus had given South Street a secured interest in its plant equipment that gave South Street priority over JNL in bankruptcy. This transaction occurred after Bucyrus had sold bonds to JNL. The insurance company argued that the Bucyrus deal with South Street had been structured to circumvent limits on Bucyrus's debt that JNL had insisted be a condition of its bond purchase.

For these reasons, JNL consistently maintained that it should be paid in full ahead of all other creditors, rather than being given a proportionate share of what Bucyrus could pay in the bankruptcy. It pressed its claim on several fronts. It refused to join the committee of unsecured creditors negotiating with Bucyrus to obtain agreement on a payment plan to submit to the court at the time the company filed for bankruptcy. Instead, JNL insisted that Bucyrus negotiate with it separately.

JNL also filed a lawsuit against Bucyrus and other creditors that would have had the effect of pushing the company immediately into bankruptcy without a bankruptcy plan in place. Gellene was especially perturbed that JNL had included four individual Bucyrus directors in its complaint. He saw this as an effort to intimidate company officials who would be involved in bankruptcy negotiations. Furthermore, JNL sought to eliminate Bucyrus' exclusive right under bankruptcy law to submit a plan, and moved for the right to propose its own plan instead.

Bucyrus and its other creditors ultimately concluded that JNL was not bargaining in good faith and was simply being an obstructionist. For his part, chief JNL negotiator John Stark believed that Gellene was trying to help Bucyrus stiff JNL. Eventually, negotiations between Bucyrus and JNL reached an impasse. Gellene turned his attention to hammering out an agreement among the other interested parties. He ultimately concluded that the only viable course was to "cram down" a plan on JNL—that is, to gain agreement of all other creditors on a plan and file it with the court over JNL's objection. Once the parties neared such agreement, Bucyrus sent out a draft plan to all creditors except JNL. The printer, however, mistakenly sent a copy of the plan to JNL. JNL was incensed that the company and its creditors would try an end-run around it. It agitated for Bucyrus to file for bankruptcy immediately without a plan. Bucyrus resisted and moved to obtain formal agreement from other creditors on a plan to submit to the court.

JNL was not formally an adversary of Gellene's client Bucyrus, because a corporate debtor in bankruptcy has a fiduciary duty to preserve its assets for the benefit of all its creditors. The interaction between Bucyrus and JNL in the year preceding the bankruptcy filing, however, likely made it more natural for Gellene to think of JNL as a foe. By the time Bucyrus prepared to file its petition and Gellene was ready to request court appointment as the company's lawyer during the proceeding, sharp battle lines had formed: JNL versus everyone else. The company, other creditors, and shareholders regarded JNL as uncooperative and unreasonable. It was clear that JNL intended to do all it could to derail the plan to which Bucyrus and the other parties had agreed. Gellene therefore was in litigation mode when he filed his application with the court to represent Bucyrus in the bankruptcy proceeding.

In these circumstances, how might Gellene regard the prospect of disclosing that Milbank also was representing South Street in unrelated matters? He probably already expected that JNL would oppose his appointment because of Milbank's well-known ties to Goldman, Sachs. Disclosure of the firm's representation of Salovaara and South Street would provide even more potent ammunition to JNL. As Bucyrus' major secured creditor, and thus the creditor first in line in bankruptcy, South Street was a potential target for any creditor that hoped to increase its share under the plan. Furthermore, unlike Goldman, South Street was neither so large, nor its connections to large law firms so pervasive, that it would be difficult to find another qualified firm to replace Milbank. Finally, the fact that Gellene himself had done work for South Street would weigh heavily against his application. For these reasons, if Gellene disclosed the firm's ties to South Street, JNL was certain to oppose Milbank's appointment with vehemence—and probably would prevail.

In the moral calculus that likely emerged for Gellene during these negotiations, Milbank's disqualification would mean that JNL, the party that had behaved so unreasonably during the past year, would gain the upper hand. Bucyrus would have to hire new counsel. That counsel would have to spend valuable time becoming familiar with Bucyrus, the other parties, and the plan. Furthermore, JNL undoubtedly would use this disruption as an opportunity to push for drastic changes in the plan. The more time passed, and the closer the deadline for obtaining tax benefits loomed, the more leverage JNL would have in pushing for concessions. Given the hostility of other parties to JNL, the result might be a bloody mess that would leave Bucyrus beyond repair.

For these reasons, Gellene may have convinced himself that nondisclosure not only was morally unproblematic, but also was morally justified. Milbank's ties to South Street, he might claim, posed no real threat to his ability to represent Bucyrus effectively. Both Bucyrus and South Street wanted the court to confirm the plan as soon as possible. Nonetheless, JNL would seize upon those ties to demand that Milbank be disqualified, with potentially disastrous consequences for Bucyrus. On balance, therefore, Gellene might conclude that disclosing the connection to South Street would not be in the best interest of the estate. Disclosure would add little to the integrity of the bankruptcy process, but could seriously undermine the chance for a timely and successful reorganization.

Conclusion

How can we integrate the various tales in which Gellene was a protagonist? A plausible narrative is that Gellene was motivated not to make full disclosure and then rationalized this as the best choice under the circumstances. Gellene wanted to avoid disclosure because it would lead to disqualification. He wanted to avoid disqualification because he was anxious about his future in a competitive law firm. And he wanted to cultivate a relationship with an important partner—Larry Lederman—who Gellene anticipated would prefer that he not disclose the connection to South Street.

Gellene thus was motivated to treat the bankruptcy disclosure requirement not as an absolute ethical command, but as a rule that called for the exercise of attorney discretion. He was able to rationalize this approach because he believed that strictly applying the rule to large law firms was unfair and did not always serve ethical purposes.

Once Gellene justified weighing the costs and benefits of disclosure rather than automatically disclosing all connections, he was able to reach the conclusion that he preferred. He could convince himself that Milbank's ties to South Street were only a "technical" conflict that raised no serious concern. The benefit of disclosure would be negligible. At most it would serve the abstract purpose of promoting the integrity of the bankruptcy process, while resulting in a disqualification that served no significant ethical end. The cost of disclosure, however, would be substantial. Disqualification would be highly disruptive to Bucyrus, threatening its ability to emerge successfully from bankruptcy. It also, of course, would mean the loss of fees for Milbank, deprive Gellene of a client, and perhaps strain his relationship with Lederman.

Given his motivation not to disclose, Gellene may have underestimated the likelihood that his violation would be detected. Even if it were, however, he could rationalize that courts tended to be lenient about violations. Non-disclosure was a calculated risk that could pay off even if it were discovered.

None of this necessarily occurred on the level of conscious thought. Indeed, rationalizations generally are effective to the extent that they aren't recognized as such. Furthermore, while it may be useful to portray the process as relatively linear, in reality it is much less systematic. Nevertheless, the phenomenon of relying on self-serving biases in making judgments is well established. People strongly motivated to reach a certain outcome often are able to rationalize why that outcome is the most reasonable under the circumstances. In Gellene's case, there were several reasons why he might prefer to conceal Milbank's ties to South Street, and plausible ways that he could justify doing so.

To the extent that this scenario captures the dynamics of what occurred, it offers an account that is more sobering than the story of a self-conscious wrongdoer who deliberately hatched a scheme of misconduct. Were Gellene simply an amoral actor indifferent to ethical demands, the tale might be more graphic but less instructive. The ambitions and anxieties that motivated Gellene's decision, however, likely mirror those of many lawyers in large major law firms. Furthermore, the influences that lent support to his rationalizations are pervasive in the world that these lawyers inhabit. Finally, lawyers are especially adept at constructing rationalizations in support of certain pre-established positions. Indeed, this is a highly valuable trait for someone engaged in representing clients.

The way in which these forces came together in John Gellene's life is of course unique. No other lawyer will ever come to the same end in quite the same way. It would have been impossible to foretell all the influences that ultimately resulted in his conviction. At the same time, it's too comforting to attribute his fall simply to defective character or a corrupt law firm. Far better instead to see it as a cautionary tale about the ethical landscape that highly accomplished lawyers in powerful law firms must navigate at the dawn of the twenty-first century.

8

"What's Sex Got To Do With It?[1]": Diversity in the Legal Profession

Deborah L. Rhode

Nancy Ezold's lawsuit against Wolf, Block, Schorr and Solis-Cohen was the nation's first discrimination case to go to trial against a law firm or any professional partnership.[2] The suit attracted widespread attention, in part because it was the first, but also because so many individuals believed that it typified a serious and pervasive problem, and because they disagreed so passionately and publicly about what the problem was.

> According to a coalition of fifty-five women's rights and civil rights organizations, which filed an amicus curiae brief in support of the plaintiff, this was the classic story of a highly qualified woman who was denied promotion while comparably, or less-qualified men were granted promotion. It is Ms. Ezold's individual story, and that of countless others who experience similar discrimination, that accounts for the "glass ceiling"— the vast statistical disparity between the number of women and minorities entering the work force and the number being promoted to its upper levels.[3]

So too, many leaders of the bar saw this case as a classic story of injustice, but one with different villains and victims. From their vantage point, this litigation was about a woman who could not meet a highly demanding partnership standard, could not believe that she was in any way lacking, and looked for someone else to blame. It was also a story

---

1. The title comes from Loren Feldman, What's Sex Got to Do With It: Partnership on Trial, American Lawyer, November, 1990, at 54.

2. Tamar Lewin, Sex Bias Found in Partnerships at Law Firms, N.Y. Times, November 30, 1990, at B5; Victory in Sex Bias Suit Would Only Do So Much, N.Y. Times, Aug. 21, 1992, at A21.

3. Brief of Amici Curiae of Fifty–Five Organizations In Support of the Petitioner, Petition to the United States Supreme Court for Writ of Certiorari to the United States Court of Appeals for the Third Circuit, Ezold v. Wolf, Block, Schorr, and Solis-Cohen, 1993, at 2.

about those unjustly accused, many of whom had been themselves victims of discrimination and had led struggles against it. In a letter to the National Council of Jewish Women, one of the 55 amicus organizations supporting the plaintiff, the firm's chair Robert Segal detailed the history of Wolf, Block and expressed the frustration of many of its members.

> Our firm was founded in 1903 in part because of anti-Semitism. For many years we were the only large Philadelphia firm that accepted Jews. Many of us, myself included, have been subjected to cruel, direct, personal anti-Semitism. We are, therefore, extremely sensitive to and abhor all forms of discrimination.... Our decision not to admit Ms. Ezold as a partner in our firm was based solely and exclusively on our honest and informed belief that she lacked the requisite legal analytic ability.... Don't let yourselves be knee-jerk kapos for the politically correct.[4]

Such competing accounts are typical of many contemporary disputes about diversity in the legal profession. And the *Ezold* case is an ideal vehicle to understand why. Unlike the vast majority of discrimination claims, which are quietly settled, this lawsuit left a lengthy paper trail that is publicly available. The federal district court that tried the case made detailed findings of fact, and the Third Circuit Court of Appeals reviewed those findings and the underlying record in even greater detail.[5] The Third Circuit's opinion was extensively analyzed in petitions supporting and opposing certiorari by the Supreme Court. Widespread media coverage offers additional information about how the case was understood at the time, and helps to put it in broader context.[6] And, most important, the litigants and lawyers were willing to reflect on their experience for this publication. The litigation as refracted through these multiple lenses illumines the capacities and constraints of law in addressing diversity issues, and how legal employers can best respond.

What also makes this case especially interesting and distinctive is its mixed legacy for all involved. Again, unlike most discrimination lawsuits, both sides felt vindicated. Most of those who called the shots have no

---

4. Robert M. Segal for Wolf, Block, Schorr and Solis–Cohen, to the National Council of Jewish Women October, 20, 1993. The letter was widely quoted in the press. "Kapos" is a reference to Jews who served as concentration camp guards during World War II. Many lawyers at Wolf, Block were distressed by this letter, particularly the concentration camp analogy. Letter from Jerome Shestack, (March 3, 2004).

5. Ezold v. Wolf, Block, Shorr and Solis–Cohen, 751 F. Supp. 1175 (E.D. Pa. 1990); 983 F. 2d 509 (1993), cert. denied, 510 U.S. 826 (1993). The Third Circuit's opinion alone totals almost a hundred printed pages.

6. Profiles appeared on ABC and in the New York Times, Chicago Tribune, LA Times, ABA Journal, and American Lawyer, as well as in all the local newspapers and legal journals.

regrets, but they also paid a substantial price. If there is any clear moral to the story, it is one on which reasonable readers can disagree.

The Background of the Litigation

Nancy Ezold went to law school later in life. She first accumulated some thirteen years of legislative and administrative experience, including work as an aid to Senator Edmund Muskie and as Administrator of the Office of Special Prosecutor of the Pennsylvania Department of Justice. While attending Villanova Law School, she held a part-time job and gave birth to a child. She graduated in the top third of her class, and took two positions involving litigation before joining Wolf, Block in 1983. The trial court found that Seymour Kurland, then chair of the firm's litigation department, told her when she was hired that it would not be easy for her because "she was a woman, had not attended an Ivy League Law School, and had not been on law review."[7] At the time that Ezold joined the litigation department, it had one female partner out of thirty-four; when she left five years later, it had one out of fifty-five. About a quarter of the firm's associates were women. Nationally, although women had accounted for at least a third of law school enrollments for over a decade, and about 37% of the associates at large firms, they held only 11% of the partnerships at those firms.[8]

Wolf, Block had an extensively documented system of performance review. All partners were invited to submit evaluation forms for every associate, although they typically did so only if they had direct knowledge of the individual's capabilities. Senior associates who were within two years of partnership eligibility received annual evaluations; junior associates were evaluated semi-annually. An Associates Committee of ten partners from all the firm's departments reviewed the evaluation forms, and each committee member prepared a "bottom line memo" summarizing the comments for each associate. After considering these assessments, the committee gave evaluations to the associate, and ultimately made partnership recommendations to a five-member executive committee. That committee then made its own recommendations to all voting partners. The full partnership considered only those individuals who were recommended by the executive committee. Ten performance criteria were listed on the form: legal analysis, legal writing and drafting, research skills, formal speech, informal speech, judgment, creativity, negotiation and advocacy, promptness, and efficiency. Ten personal characteristics were also listed: reliability, taking and managing responsibility, flexibility, growth potential, attitude, client relationship, client servicing and development, ability under pressure, ability to work inde-

---

7. 751 F. Supp. at 1177.

8. Brief of Amici Curiae, supra note 3, at 3. Other departments at the firm did have women partners. Interview with Roberta Liebenberg (February 26, 2004).

pendently, and dedication. Lawyers were rated as distinguished, good, acceptable, marginal, and unacceptable.[9]

In 1988, after Ezold had worked in the litigation department for five years, she learned that the firm would not admit her to partnership. However, the domestic relations department suddenly had an opening, and the executive committee chair told Ezold that if she agreed to work in this area, she would be made a partner in another year. Alternatively, she could stay on as a litigation associate and be reconsidered in the future with no assurances of a different decision. Shortly thereafter, Ezold began looking for other employment, Six months later, she took a new position as president of an environmental consulting firm, a former Wolf, Block client, and an of-counsel position with a suburban law firm.

The Court Decisions

Ezold then brought suit under Title VII of the Civil Rights Act, claiming that she had been denied a promotion on the basis of sex.[10] She hired as her lawyer, on a contingent fee basis, Judith Vladeck, a prominent New York litigator with expertise in gender discrimination cases. Wolf, Block retained Mark Dichter, another experienced litigator with one of Philadelphia's leading firms. After unsuccessful efforts to negotiate a settlement, the parties tried the case before Federal District Court Judge James McGirr Kelly. During the thirteen-day trial, lawyers presented testimony by 17 witnesses and thousands of pages of exhibits concerning the relative capabilities of Ezold and male associates who were eligible for partnership, as well as other gender-related issues at the firm. The district court held that gender was a "determining factor in the failure of the Firm to promote Ezold to partnership" and ordered back pay in the amount of $131,784, covering the period from her resignation to the date of judgment. The parties agreed that if the court's decision was upheld on appeal, she would be admitted to partnership.[11]

Wolf, Block appealed the decision and retained Arlin Adams, a recently retired member of the United States Court of Appeals for the Third Circuit, to argue the case. The argument prevailed. A unanimous three-judge panel of the Third Circuit reversed and directed a judgment in favor of the firm. In summarizing its decision, the court noted:

---

9. 983 F. 2d 509.

10. 42 U.S. Code Section 2000e. Ezold also alleged violations of the Equal Pay Act, and claimed that she had been constructively discharged from the firm due to intolerable working conditions. The trial court severed the Equal Pay Act charges and found against her on the constructive discharge claim. Because these issues were highly fact-bound and peripheral to the main point of the litigation, they are not discussed here.

11. 751 F. Supp. 1189; 983 F. 2d at 514.

This case raises important issues that cut across the spectrum of discrimination law. It is also the first in which allegations of discrimination arising from a law firm partnership decision require appellate review after trial. Accordingly, we have given our closest attention, and, after exhaustive examination of the record and analysis of the applicable law, we have concluded that the district court made two related errors whose combined effect require us to reverse the judgment in favor of Ezold. The district court first impermissibly substituted its own subjective judgment for that of Wolf in determining that Ezold met the firm's partnership standards. Then, with its view improperly influenced by its own judgment of what Wolf should have done, it failed to see that the evidence could not support a finding that Wolf's decision to deny Ezold admission to the partnership was based upon a sexually discriminatory motive rather than the firm's assessment of her legal qualifications. Accordingly, we hold not only that the district court analyzed the evidence improperly and that its resulting finding of [a pretextual motive] is clearly erroneous, but also that the evidence, properly analyzed, is insufficient to support that finding and therefore its ultimate conclusion of discrimination cannot stand.[12]

Ezold's request for rehearing en banc was denied without dissent, as was her petition for a writ of certiorari before the United States Supreme Court.

The trial and appellate courts were not in dispute about the legal standard. Under Title VII, the plaintiff has the burden of proving by the preponderance of evidence a prima facie case of discrimination. This requires the plaintiff to show that she was a member of a protected class, that she was qualified for the position, that she was not promoted into a job for which she was qualified, and that nonmembers of the protected class were treated more favorably. After the plaintiff establishes a prima facie case, the burden shifts to the defendant to show a legitimate, nondiscriminatory reason for the employee's rejection. The plaintiff must then show by a preponderance of evidence that the defendant's reasons were a pretext for discrimination.[13]

---

12.   983 F. 2d at 512–13.

13.   983 F. 2d at 522, 751 F. Supp. at 1191. *See* Texas Department of Community Affairs v. Burdine, 450 U.S. 248, 252 (1981). An alternative way for plaintiffs to establish discrimination is by showing that an illegitimate factor had a motivating or substantial role in the employment decision. In these "mixed motive" cases, the burden then shifts to the employer to establish by a preponderance of evidence that it would have made the same decision even in the absence of the impermissible factor. 983 F. 2d, at 522; Price Waterhouse v. Hopkins, 490 U.S. 228, 244–45 (1989). Lawyers for Ezold made it clear that they were electing to try the case on a pretext, rather than mixed motives, theory, 983 F. 2d at 522 (quoting transcript of oral argument). If an employer in a mixed motive case is able to prove at trial that it would have made the same decision without regard to the

The trial court found, and the defendant and appellate panel agreed, that Ezold had established a prima facie case of discrimination by showing that she was qualified for promotion. That finding was based on the favorable evaluations of her work and her score of "good" on the 1988 associates committee summary bottom line memo.[14] The issue on which the courts and parties differed was whether the firm's nondiscriminatory reason for denial of promotion was a pretext. Wolf, Block contended that Ezold did not possess sufficient legal analytical skills to handle the responsibilities of partner in the firm's complex litigation practice. Ezold attempted to prove that this explanation was

> "unworthy of credence" by showing that she was at least equal to, if not more qualified than, similarly situated males promoted to partnership. She also contended that her past treatment at the firm showed Wolf's decision was based on a discriminatory motive rather than the legitimate reason of deficiency in legal analytical ability that the firm had articulated.[15]

The trial judge agreed. The district court found that in the year that Ezold was denied partnership, the partner's memo summarizing her abilities rated her "good" in legal analysis, the same grade that seven of the men promoted to partner had received in that year or in the preceding or subsequent year.[16] The court also found that "in the period up to and including 1988, Ms. Ezold received strongly positive evaluations from almost all of the partners for whom she had done any substantial work," and that "male associates who received evaluations no better than the plaintiff and sometimes less favorable than the plaintiff were made partners."[17]

In reaching that conclusion, the court drew extensively from negative evaluations of male associates who had been promoted to partnership around the same time that Ezold had been rejected. When initially released, the opinion identified these lawyers by name. On request of defense counsel, the names were redacted in the final published opinion, but the original version was reprinted in a local legal journal, and received widespread attention in the Philadelphia community.

Representative adverse comments concerning one associate included:

---

discriminatory factor, then it will avoid all liability, including attorneys' fees. Only with the 1991 amendments to the Civil Rights Act did counsel fees become available based on a showing of mixed motives. See text at infra note 70.

14. 751 F. Supp. at 1191; 983 F. 2d at 524.

15. 983 F. 2d at 525.

16. 751 F. Supp. at 1183–87.

17. 751 F. Supp. at 1182, 1184.

> I really don't think [Associate A] should become a partner. In fact, if he is made a partner, I will never again submit an evaluation on any associate. I don't know how he has lasted this long in the firm.
>
> [Associate A's] writing is dense and mediocre. He missed target dates for completing projects and then slapped together something hurriedly when I complained.
>
> [Y]ou find a lack of professionalism in [Associate A's] ... legal analysis and research.... I believe his intellectual laziness will someday embarrass us.

Other lawyers described the associate as "not real smart," and expressed concerns that he "may not be bright enough."[18]

A number of other attorneys who became partners between 1987 and 1989 received similar evaluations. Associate B was characterized as a "bit of a con man," "very lazy," "more sizzle than steak," and "too slick to instill ... [a] degree of comfort." Associate F reportedly had an "outrageous personality," had "abandoned ship" on a legal matter assigned to him, and had so offended one client (a partner's father-in-law) that the client had changed firms. Associate G was "not a Star," "sloppy at times" and alternately "wishy washy and immature," or overly "confrontational."[19]

> The trial court also found that:
>
> Other instances of conduct by the defendant firm toward Ms. Ezold support the conclusion that the plaintiff was treated differently because of her gender. Ms Ezold was evaluated negatively for being too involved with women's issues in the Firm, specifically her concern about the treatment of paralegals.... In addition, the fact that a male associate had engaged in sexual harassment of female employees at the Firm was seen as insignificant and not worthy of mention to the Associates Committee in its consideration of that male associate for partnership. Ms. Ezold was also evaluated negatively for being "very demanding," while several male associates who were made partners were evaluated negatively for *lacking* sufficient assertiveness in their demeanors. Finally, Ms. Ezold was the target of several comments demonstrating the defendant's differential treatment of her because she is a woman.[20]

Those comments included Kurland's initial warning about her likely difficulties at the firm because she was female and a graduate of a non-Ivy League law school. In addition, when Ezold suggested to another

---

18. Id. at 1184–85.

19. 751 F. Supp. at 1185–86.

20. Id. at 1192. Ezold had expressed concerns that the largely female paralegal staff was being required to work overtime without pay.

partner that gender bias may have adversely affected the quality of her assignments, he responded: "Nancy, don't say that around here. They don't want to hear it."[21]

The Third Circuit Court of Appeals saw the evidence differently. In its view, the trial court had:

> engaged in a pick and choose selection of various comments concerning male associates' personalities, work habits and other criteria besides legal analysis, conducted its own subjective decision process, and then found that male associates who received evaluations no better than Ezold and sometimes less [favorable] were made partners. In so doing, the district court made no references to the many favorable evaluations of the analytic ability of these male associates.[22]

The appellate court then proceeded to summarize favorable evidence concerning male associates and unfavorable evidence concerning Ezold. Adverse comments included:

> I have found her analysis to be rather superficial and unfocused. I am beginning to doubt that she has sufficient legal analytical ability to make it with the firm. She ... can handle routine matters well. However these traits will take you just so far in our firm. I think that due to the nature of our practice Nancy's future here is limited.
>
> I think Nancy tries hard and can handle relatively straight-forward matter with a degree of maturity and judgment, but when she gets into more complicated areas she lacks real analytical skill and just does what she is told in a mechanical way. She is not up to our minimal Wolf, Block standards.
>
> Nancy has avoided demonstrating ability in the area of [of legal analysis] because I believe she lacks it.... I would not want her in charge of a large, legally complex case, the traditional measure of a Wolf, Block partner.[23]

To the appellate panel, it was telling that in 1988, only a third of the partners submitting evaluations of Ezold recommended her for partner, and a third of them had mixed feelings. The only female litigation partner, Roberta Liebenberg, voted against Ezold's promotion.[24]

As the court of appeals also noted, one reason for the dispute over Ezold's eligibility for partnership was a dispute over what the standard should be. Some partners felt that ability to handle large complex cases

---

21. Id. at 1188.

22. 983 F. 2d at 528.

23. Id. at 517–18.

24. Id. at 520.

was not essential and that the firm had "enough business where we could fit everybody in usefully and productively."[25] However, other members of the Associates Committee rejected this view, and all but one voted against Ezold's admission to partnership.

The appellate court was also unpersuaded by other evidence of gender bias. Some comments fell into the category of "stray remarks," which courts in discrimination cases often discount as insufficiently probative of broader patterns. In the panel's view, Kurland's warning could be so viewed, since it occurred five years before the promotion vote and he had left the firm well before Ezold was rejected. Moreover, as the court emphasized, there was no direct evidence that gender-related comments by or about Ezold played a role in the partnership decision.[26] Several women testified at trial concerning the fairness of the firm's treatment toward them; no women testified on Ezold's behalf. With respect to the sexual harassment incident, the appellate court found no basis for concluding that Wolf, Block had treated the matter as "insignificant."[27] It was taken to the Associates Committee, the committee chair discussed the conduct with the offending lawyer, and a memo was placed in his file. Since the incident occurred after the committee already had determined that the associate was unlikely to be promoted to partnership, the Third Circuit panel declined to view the failure to impose stiffer sanctions as evidence of gender bias.[28]

In evaluating the record as a whole, the appellate court also stressed the limited role of federal courts in reviewing upper-level employment evaluations. Analogizing to cases involving academic tenure, the panel's decision noted: "we have cautioned courts on several occasions to avoid unnecessary intrusion into subjective promotion decisions...."[29] The firm "may have been wrong in its perception of Ezold's legal analytic ability, and if so, its decision would be unfair, but that is not for us to judge. Absent a showing that Wolf's articulated reason of lack of ability in legal analysis was used as tool to discriminate on the basis of sex, Ezold cannot prevail."[30] And, in the appellate court's view, no such showing had been made.

Following its success on the merits, Wolf, Block sought to recover the costs of trial and appeal, which are "allowed of course to the prevailing party unless the court otherwise so directs" under FRCP 54(d). Ezold agreed to pay the $12,810.25 ordered in appeal costs, but

---

25. Id.

26. Id. at 544–46.

27. Id. at 545.

28. Id.

29. Id. at 526.

30. Id. at 533.

contested the trial expenses of $24,822.84. Under prevailing law, a losing party can overcome the presumption favoring an award of costs on grounds that such an award would be unjust. Ezold claimed that it would be inequitable for her to subsidize the firm's expenses given the "disparity in financial resources between the parties, the difficult issues of significant public concern raised by her lawsuit, and Wolf, Block's efforts during the litigation to chill the rights of interested parties. . . ."[31] Wolf, Block responded that resource inequalities should not be a factor in assessing costs, and that only a showing of misconduct should justify denying compensation. The trial court rejected that claim and decided to split the costs between the parties. In reaching that decision, Judge Kelly reasoned that Ezold was not indigent and unable to pay the award, but also that she was then a solo practitioner of "comparatively modest means" who had already incurred substantial expenses and still owed almost $20,000 to her own attorneys for litigation costs. Moreover,

> in challenging the problem of discrimination at high professional levels, she raised an issue of public concern. It was a close case, concerning difficult legal issues regarding proof of discrimination, in which she prevailed in the district court. I am concerned that the fear of astronomical costs not become a deterrent against the assertion of legitimate disputes.[32]

The Participants' Perspectives

Interviews with the parties and their attorneys give a richer sense of what motivated the litigation, what prevented settlement, and what the consequences were to those most directly concerned. The litigants and lawyers on both sides described the reasons for the lawsuit in similar terms: what their opponent did was unjust. Nancy Ezold put it this way: "I went in on the partnership track. I was as good or better than many of the men whom the firm promoted. I felt the facts strongly supported me. What Wolf, Block did was wrong."[33] She also saw others being treated the same way and "wanted to do something to improve their situation."[34] Ezold's lawyer, Judith Vladeck, took the case on a contingent fee for similar reasons: "Lawyers have special obligations, and one of them is to treat people fairly. Employment decisions should be made on the merits. Nancy's wasn't."[35]

---

31.   Ezold v. Wolf, Block, Schorr and Solis–Cohen, 157 F.R.D. 13 (E.D. Pa. 1994).

32.   Id. at 17, 18 [citation omitted].

33.   Interview with Nancy Ezold (January 13, 2004).

34.   William C. Smith, Discrimination: Hirings, Firings, and Class Ceilings, Legal Intelligencer, March 18, 1998 (n.p.)(quoting Ezold).

35.   Interview with Judith Vladeck (January 15, 2004).

Wolf, Block attorneys also saw principles of fairness at stake. Robert Segal, who was managing partner during part of the time in question, put it bluntly: "We felt we were being smeared."[36] Roberta Liebenberg agreed. The partners "believed that they were right and were willing to fight for their principles. I admired that."[37] Counsel for Wolf, Block made the same assessment. According to Arlin Adams, "it was a matter of principle. Partners were being accused of discrimination who had spent much of their careers fighting against it."[38]

Underlying these conflicting views of principle were conflicting views of facts. Ezold felt that Wolf, Block's litigators had trouble with "strong intelligent women. They knew that they had to have at least one female partner. But that was enough." A large part of the problem was the assignment system. Ezold now represents women in sex discrimination cases with stories like her own. "They start out equal but don't get the same exposure and experience. They can't get assigned to the best cases and the most influential lawyers.... The discrimination may be unconscious. But the result is equally unfair."[39] Judith Vladeck offered a similar assessment. She felt that because Ezold was not from an elite law school, she had particular difficulty fitting in and establishing her abilities, given the firm's historic attitudes toward women: "Look at the numbers. This was a firm that for many years had no women partners, and the first one who finally made it was the daughter of a ... [prominent] partner." According to Vladeck and the women's groups that supported Ezold as amicus curiae, the mistake of both the partners and the Third Circuit panel was "to view each instance of sex bias in isolation" and to overvalue the one qualification on which the firm said it relied—analytic ability.[40] From the plaintiff's vantage point, "If you looked at the totality of the record, there was no difference in capabilities between Nancy and the male lawyers that the firm promoted."[41]

Wolf, Block partners saw it differently. According to Liebenberg, "Nancy just didn't meet the firm standard for legal analytical ability. This was a very demanding workplace. Wolf, Block had built its reputation as a legal powerhouse. For years, when no other major Philadelphia firm would hire Jewish lawyers, these partners had a monopoly on talent. So they were used to promoting only people who were really

---

36. Interview with Robert Segal (February 11, 2004).

37. Interview with Roberta Liebenberg (January 24, 2004).

38. Interview with Arlin Adams (January 22, 2004).

39. Ezold Interview, supra note 33.

40. Brief in Support of the Petitioner, Petition to the Supreme Court for Writ of Certiorari to the United States Court of Appeals for the Third Circuit, Ezold v. Wolf, Block, Schorr and Solis–Cohen, 1993, at 12.

41. Vladeck Interview, supra note 35.

smart." Liebenberg felt that she had been fairly treated, as had two other female litigators who testified for the firm at trial. As she pointed out, other male associates had been passed over for partnership based on lack of analytic ability despite favorable evaluations on other capabilities. And in the year Ezold was rejected, another female associate was promoted. Liebenberg attributed the underrepresentation of women partners in the litigation department to the nature of the work: "This was a tough place for any lawyer. And it was especially hard for women with families. There was a lot of traveling and unpredictable, late hours. The partners demanded a lot." Yet Liebenberg also felt that the firm had tried to accommodate women with family obligations. She had two small children during the time period in question and senior partners made an effort to assign her to cases that would not require as much overnight travel.[42]

Robert Segal had a similar view of the partnership decision. "Nancy just didn't have the intellectual capacity." If there was any fault on the part of the firm, "it was in hiring her in the first place. She didn't have the credentials." But "the litigation department was overwhelmed," and needed additional attorneys with trial experience.[43] Wolf, Block's trial counsel Mark Dichter offered a similar explanation. Ezold was "caught in the cross fire of an internal battle over the appropriate standard. Most members of the firm had better credentials, and many felt that they couldn't have a litigation partner who was unable to handle a major case or couldn't write a federal appellate brief." In Dichter's view, there was plenty of gender discrimination in law firms at the time, but Ezold's case wasn't an example of it: "This wasn't a situation of gender stereotypes or work/family conflicts. This was the right issue but the wrong plaintiff."[44] From Dichter's perspective, the case was not a close one. Although Ezold had many positive evaluations, they tended to come from partners who had worked with her and were easy graders. The litigators who did not have confidence in her abilities avoided having her on their team. It was true that she did not receive the best cases, but Dichter believed that the reason was ability, not gender. If there had been any unfairness in Wolf, Block's treatment of Ezold, it did not involve discrimination; it was the failure to resolve the firm's own internal dispute about standards and to provide a clear, consistent early warning about her poor partnership chances.[45]

Not only did the parties have sharply different views of the facts, they had equally different perceptions of the appropriateness of settle-

---

42. Liebenberg Interview, supra note 37.

43. Segal Interview, supra note 36.

44. Interview with Mark Dichter (January 30, 2004).

45. Id.

ment. To Ezold, it was "ironic that the partners criticized me for lack of analytic ability, when any lawyers in their right mind would have advised settlement."[46] Vladeck agreed. It would have been far cheaper for the firm to resolve than litigate the matter. At one point, an offer of one year's pay, about $75,000, was on the table. That was less than the cost of just one of the lawyers who worked on Wolf, Block's appeal.[47] And as noted below, the total price for the firm was considerable—not only in fees, expenses, and staff time, but also in reputation and acrimony. Given the projected cost of litigation, the refusal to settle struck both Ezold and her counsel as a reflection of partners' "arrogance," rather than rational decision making.[48]

But to those partners who made the decision, more was at stake than money. The firm's good name was on the line. In a press interview after the trial, Charles Kopp, the co-chair of Wolf, Block's executive committee, explained that settling the case "would leave the impression that maybe there was sex discrimination." That would have hurt the firm's recruiting efforts. In his judgment, the firm had no choice but to fight, and "I would do it again."[49] Trial counsel Mark Dichter similarly noted that rational employers frequently decide to defend themselves from accusations that they consider unjust, in order to protect their reputation and to deter frivolous suits. He recalled that to most Wolf, Block partners, "anything short of vindication in the courts would have been an admission. They got the vindication, and I think they would make the same decision again."[50] Yet at least one of the firm's leaders now has second thoughts, and press reports at the time indicated that others shared his reservations. Robert Segal is "not sure I would make the same judgment. The litigation was very expensive and very painful. This may have been a case that wasn't worth winning."[51]

The Price of Principle: Lawyers on Trial

One irony of adversarial processes is that cases where ethical principles are at stake often present the greatest risk of ethical lapses. Participants who believe that right and truth are on their side can sometimes lose sensitivity to what is on the other. *Ezold* was no exception.

---

46. Ezold Interview, supra note 33.

47. Vladeck Interview, supra note 35. As a tribute to Arlin Adams, the firm also made a $100,000 gift to his law school.

48. Ezold Interview, supra note 33; Vladeck Interview, supra note 35.

49. Feldman, supra note 1 (quoting Charles Kopp).

50. Dichter Interview, supra note 44.

51. Segal Interview, supra note 36.

To the plaintiff and her counsel, this was a textbook example of hardball litigation. Wolf, Block had substantial resources, expertise, and determination. In the view of Debra Raskin, Vladeck's co-counsel, the strategy was to "beat us down." The firm filed motions contesting everything, and "wouldn't even turn over Ezold's own work product without a fight."[52] No expense was spared, and Ezold ended up paying a substantial part of them, at law firm rates. For example, Wolf, Block charged 25 cents a page to copy documents, a service that a local business would have provided for a tenth of that amount.[53] Ezold estimated that her out-of-pocket litigation expenses were about $100,000 for her own case and $50,000 for her opponent's.[54] There were other costs as well, which some observers believed were needlessly inflated. In discrimination cases, plaintiffs are as much on trial as their adversaries, and while some humiliating details about their character and capabilities are to be expected, the treatment of Ezold struck many as exceptionally meanspirited. In one representative, widely quoted comment, Wolf, Block co-chair Kopp defended the firm's decision that Ezold lacked sufficient abilities to make up for her analytic deficiencies: "It's like the ugly girl. Everybody says she's got a great personality. It turns out [that Nancy] didn't even have a great personality."[55]

Another painful, although understandable, aspect of the litigation was that none of the women who had privately expressed support to Ezold were willing to testify on her behalf. But Vladeck did not press them to come forward, given the potential damage to their own careers. As she told a reporter at the time, "My preference is to avoid asking anyone to put their heads on the block."[56] In any event, it was not the lack of female witnesses that Ezold experienced as most hurtful, but Segal's vitriolic letter to the National Counsel of Jewish Women, which had rallied behind her. To Ezold, analogizing these groups to "kapos," Jewish guards at concentration camps, seemed unacceptable. Vladeck agreed: "It was the ugliest document I've ever seen."[57]

Lawyers for Wolf, Block felt that they, too, had been victims of "hardball" tactics.[58] According to Dichter, when Ezold left the firm, she took clients' files on which she had worked for use in the litigation, even

52. Interview with Debra Raskin (January 15, 2004).

53. Shannon Duffy, Wolf, Block Fight Over Costs; Letters Revealed, Legal Intelligencer, November 15, 1993 (n.p.). The rate was not atypical for law firms at the time. Shestack letter, supra note 4.

54. Ezold Interview, supra note 33; text accompanying supra note 31.

55. Feldman, supra note 1 (quoting Charles Kopp).

56. Id. (quoting Vladeck).

57. Vladeck Interview, supra note 35.

58. Liebenberg Interview, supra note 37.

though these belonged to Wolf, Block and included privileged information. The firm' initial resistance to turning over other Ezold files was attributable to concerns about confidentiality, and it ultimately agreed to provide redacted versions.[59] Many Wolf, Block lawyers also felt that their opponent was attempting to impose maximum humiliation and harm to reputation at the expense of innocent third parties. Dichter recalled that Vladeck had once characterized her trial strategy as "the white male turkey approach"; the objective was to highlight the flaws of men who had been promoted.[60]

The costs of this strategy became evident when, according to Dichter, Judge Kelly initially declined to redact these attorneys' names from documents introduced at trial because he felt that referring to them by code would be confusing. The costs were further compounded when he reportedly forgot an oral agreement not to identify the associates by name in his opinion.[61] As noted earlier, the version he initially released was unredacted, and reprinted in that form in a local law journal.

Of course, as defense counsel acknowledged, Ezold and her lawyers were not responsible for this identification of lawyers by name; indeed, they had agreed from the outset to redacted documents. But Vladeck did employ one tactic that struck some observers as needlessly humiliating. In cross-examining Roberta Liebenberg, the firm's only female litigation partner, Vladeck asked if Liebenberg was familiar with the term "Queen Bee." The phrase generally refers to those who enjoy their status as the only woman in a prominent position and who help to exclude other rivals. Liebenberg, who had never heard the term before, was deeply offended by the implication that she fit the description. "There was no basis for suggesting that I had been unsupportive of other women." To the contrary, Liebenberg recalled being more involved with women's issues in the community than Ezold.[62] There were, to be sure, limits on how much she had been able to do to assist all the younger women in the firm, particularly since she had small children and a highly demanding

---

59. Dichter Interview, supra note 44.

60. In response to this comment, Vladeck stated, "I have never in my long lifetime heard the expression attributed to me that my legal strategy was 'the white male turkey approach.' I never heard this phrase, don't know what it means, never said it, and, if that was my trial strategy, I would have stayed home." Personal e-mail communication from Judith Vladeck (February 26, 2004).

61. Dichter Interview, supra note 44. Vladeck recalled events differently than Dichter. In particular, she did not remember any defense request to code documents during discovery or trial, a request she would not have challenged. Personal e-mail communication from Vladeck, supra note 60.

62. Liebenberg Interview, supra note 37. Liebenberg later served as special advisor to the American Bar Association's Commission on Women in the Profession.

trial practice at the time. But it was difficult enough to be part of the defense in a sex discrimination case without having her own commitment to equal rights put in question.[63]

There were other costs for Wolf, Block lawyers, institutionally as well as individually. The litigation both revealed and exacerbated internal divisions within the firm. Disputes about whether to settle the case and what the partnership standards should be, together with negative comments about associates, all contributed to internal tension and to some lawyers' decisions to leave.[64] The firm's reputation also suffered in some circles, although how much, and for how long, is difficult to gauge. Some Wolf, Block leaders maintained that the firm had no difficulty in recruiting women, and some potential job candidates undoubtedly assumed that the firm would be on its best behavior in the aftermath of the litigation. However, other lawyers reported difficulties in convincing those who had followed the case in the press that the firm was a supportive environment for women.[65] Ezold recounted one incident that bears on the issue. Well after the case was resolved, she was speaking about the experience to a group of students at the University of Pennsylvania Law School. A member of the audience volunteered that she had recently interviewed at Wolf, Block, and had asked a partner whether "things were different for women at the firm following the litigation." The partner responded: "Yes, now we view every female applicant as a potential plaintiff." The student asked what Ezold would have said if she had been the applicant interviewing for a position: Ezold's response was: "I would have said, 'where's the door?' "[66]

Ezold's Legacy

Although the long-term significance of the *Ezold* ruling cannot yet be assessed, the litigation experience does suggest some broader lessons about the capacities and limitations of law in discrimination cases. The most obvious moral of the story is that current legal doctrine and procedures are a highly imperfect means of addressing workplace bias. As many *Ezold* participants and commentators have noted, the standard for proving discrimination is often out of touch with the practices it seeks to remedy. Much contemporary discrimination is not the product of intentional bias and pretextual justifications, but rather of uncon-

---

63. Id.

64. Dichter Interview, supra note 44; Segal Interview, supra note 36.

65. Interview with Jerome Shestack, January 6, 2004; Segal Interview, supra note 36. Jerome Shestack, who joined the firm after Ezold was denied partnership, and who was then running for President of the American Bar Association, frequently faced skepticism from women's groups about the firm's commitment to gender equality.

66. Ezold Interview, supra note 33.

scious cognitive patterns. As the American Bar Association's Commission on Women in the Profession explains:

> In virtually every society, gender is a fundamental aspect of human identity and gender stereotypes influence behavior at often unconscious levels. These stereotypes work against women's advancement in several respects, even among individuals and institutions fully committed to gender equality.
>
> First, and most fundamentally, the characteristics traditionally associated with women are at odds with many characteristics traditionally associated with professional success, such as assertiveness, competitiveness, and business judgment. Some lawyers and clients still assume that women lack sufficient aptitude for complex financial transactions or sufficient combativeness for major litigation. Particularly in high stakes matters, risk averse managers are often reluctant to gamble on female practitioners. Yet professional women also tend to be rated lower when they depart from traditional stereotypes and adopt "masculine," authoritative styles. Negative evaluations are particularly likely when the evaluators are men, or the role is one typically occupied by men. As a consequence, female lawyers often face a double standard and a double bind. They risk appearing too "soft" or too "strident," too aggressive or not aggressive enough. And what appears assertive in a man often appears abrasive in a woman.
>
> A related obstacle is that women often do not receive the same presumption of competence as their male counterparts. In large national surveys, between half and three-quarters of female attorneys believe that they are held to higher standards than their male counterparts or have to work harder for the same results. Only about a third of women are very satisfied with their opportunities for advancement.... Particularly where the number of women is small, their performance is subject to closer scrutiny and more demanding requirements, and their commitment open to greater question. The devaluation of women and the influence of gender stereotypes is especially likely in organizations that have few women in leadership positions.[67]

As other experts note, when such stereotypes adversely influence the quality of assignments that women receive and deprive them of opportunities to prove their abilities, the stereotypes will become self-perpetuating. Employers then "may apply discriminatory criteria to women and

---

67. American Bar Association Commission on Women in the Legal Profession, The Unfinished Agenda: A Report on the Status of Women in the Legal Profession (Report prepared by Deborah L. Rhode, 2001).

yet honestly believe that the employee's performance is sub-par."[68] And as long as those beliefs are not self-evidently implausible, the plaintiff cannot win, irrespective of prejudicial stereotypes.[69]

Victims of such stereotypes are, however, not entirely without remedies. Title VII of the Civil Rights Act gives workers an alternative means of establishing discrimination that does not require proof that their employer's justification is pretextual. As amended in 1991, the Act provides relief to plaintiffs who demonstrate that one of the prohibited classifications such as gender or race was a "motivating factor for any employment practice." But if an employer proves that it "would have taken the same action in the absence of the impermissible motivating factor," remedies are limited to declaratory relief, injunctive relief, and attorneys' fees. Financial damages, reinstatement, hiring, or promotion are not available.[70] Had Ezold tried her case under this "mixed motive" approach, it is unlikely that she would have fared better in the Third Circuit. The appellate panel could still have concluded that the evidence failed to show that gender, as opposed to analytic ability, was a motivating factor in the partnership decision, or could have concluded that even if it was, Wolf, Block partners would have made the same judgment. A ruling along the latter lines would have provided compensation for Ezold's lawyers, but not for her.

To those lawyers, as well as other experts on Title VII law, the impact of the Third Circuit's ruling was to make it extremely difficult for plaintiffs to establish discrimination in upper-level employment contexts. Debra Raskin put it bluntly: "If we could not win that case, then there are few cases that we will win."[71] Absent a "smoking gun," plaintiffs will rarely prevail.[72] And as other federal courts have recognized, such evidence has become increasingly difficult to come by: "Employers of even minimal sophistication will neither admit discriminatory ... [conduct] nor leave a paper trail demonstrating it."[73]

Without such unequivocal proof, the decisionmaker's own biases are likely to play an important role. Many observers believed that one reason for Ezold's success in the trial court was that the judge, an Irish Catholic graduate of Temple Law School, identified with her circumstances: "He probably couldn't have gotten in the door, at Wolf, Block" and may have

---

68. Katharine T. Bartlett, Angela P. Harris & Deborah L. Rhode, Gender and Law: Theory, Doctrine, Commentary, 202–03 (3d ed. 2002).

69. Id.

70. 42 U.S.C. Sections 2000e–2(m), 2000e–5(g)(2)(B) (1994).

71. Hank Grezlak, Bench, Bar Debates Ezold Impact: Discrimination Cases Difficult for Parties Involved, Legal Intelligencer, December 9, 1993, at 1 (quoting Raskin).

72. Brief for the Petitioner, supra note 40.

73. Riordan v. Kempiners, 831 F. 2d 690, 697 (7th Cir. 1987).

been especially sympathetic to claims that these criteria unjustly excluded talented lawyers with backgrounds like Ezold's and his own.[74] By
contrast, in the Third Circuit, the firm was among friends. Many judges
on that court had recused themselves because of ties to Wolf, Block, and
the willingness of Arlin Adams, a former colleague, to argue the appeal,
may have sent a message about what was at stake for the established
bar. Adams himself felt that he generally enjoyed no "special advantage"
when arguing before the Third Circuit. If anything, he believed that
panelists "leaned over backwards" to be fair, and "went out of their way
to put my feet to the fire."[75] But in this litigation, other observers saw it
differently. According to Ezold, this was a classic example of "the
brethren supporting the brethren."[76] Critics also questioned the appellate panel's decision to direct a verdict, rather than remand the case to
the court below. In effect, many commentators believed that the Third
Circuit did precisely what it had faulted the district judge for doing:
substituting its own view of the merits for that of the proper decision-
maker.

In any event, although there was considerable dispute about the
fairness of the trial and appellate courts' rulings, observers generally
agreed on one fundamental point: litigation of this type is extraordinarily expensive for all concerned. Given the difficulties of prevailing under
current standards, few professionals who believe that they are targets of
discrimination will be willing to incur the financial and psychological
costs of attempting to prove it. Even those who manage to win in court
may lose in life. They risk being branded as troublemakers and having
all of their personal deficiencies publicly aired; "[P]rofessional suicide is
a common description."[77] For defendants, the price of litigation is also
substantial, not only in financial terms, but also in the injuries to
reputation that often accompany trial proceedings.

Yet from a societal standpoint, these costs do have some countervailing benefits. The price for plaintiffs imposes a check on groundless
litigation. As Mark Dichter noted, many individuals who are denied
employment or promotions have a natural desire to believe that some
reason other than their own inadequacies is responsible.[78] Yet subjective
employment decisions can often be unfair without being discriminatory,
and in all but clear cases, it may be cost effective to encourage individuals to just get on with their lives.

So too, from potential defendants' vantage point, the costs of proceedings may encourage constructive preventive strategies. Shortly after

---

74. Feldman, supra note 1.

75. Adams Interview, supra note 38.

76. Ezold Interview, supra note 33.

77. Deborah L. Rhode, Speaking of Sex 162 (1997).

78. Dichter Interview, supra note 44.

the trial court's decision, the Chancellor of the Philadelphia Bar Association predicted: "Without question, the judge's opinion will be felt in every law firm in the country. Decision-makers will scrutinize themselves more carefully and ask if their decisions are really gender bias-free."[79] While this may have been somewhat of an overstatement, most commentators, and most participants in the *Ezold* litigation, felt that it had served as a useful wake up call to the profession.[80] Ezold herself reported that many women had told her that because of the case, their partnership chances had improved or they had gained leverage on diversity-related issues in their firms.[81] At Wolf, Block, some women up for promotion reportedly had gotten the benefit of the doubt in close cases, and lawyers of both sexes had benefited from improvements in the evaluation process.[82]

Yet some of these gains may have been double edged. Women lawyers who were perceived as beneficiaries of "special treatment" may have suffered some loss of credibility. Those at Wolf, Block were sometimes referred to as "Ezold partners." Revisions in evaluation processes undoubtedly meant that fewer candid reports were made.[83] More may also have been destroyed, leaving victims of bias with less opportunity to demonstrate it.[84] But in counting up these costs, the question is always, "compared to what?" One accomplished woman attorney who was repeatedly asked how she felt about getting a high level Justice Department appointment "because she was a woman," finally responded: "It's better than not getting [a] job because you are a woman."[85] So too, if lawyers are now more guarded in their performance assessments, that is not entirely a cause for regret. Making individuals conscious of their own gender stereotypes is a first step toward eliminating them. In the aftermath of cases like *Ezold*, more groups such as the ABA Commission on Women in the Profession began publishing materials on fair evaluation procedures, and more legal employers began to see the need for reform.[86]

---

79. Janet L. Fix, Sex Bias Verdict Shocks Law Firm: Victor Still Wants Partner Position, Chicago Tribune, January 7, 1991, at W6 (quoting Robert C. Heim).

80. Vladeck Interview, supra note 35; Raskin Interview, supra note 52; Dichter Interview, supra note 44; Adams Interview, supra note 38; Ezold Interview, supra note 33.

81. Ezold Interview, supra note 33.

82. Shestack Interview, supra note 64; Dichter Interview, supra note 44 (noting improvements for both sexes); Segal Interview, supra note 36.

83. Dichter Interview, supra note 44.

84. Vladeck Interview, supra note 35.

85. Rhode, supra note 77, at 69 (quoting Barbara Allen Babcock).

86. American Bar Association Commission on Women in the Profession, Fair Measure: Toward Effective Attorney Evaluation (1997).

In the final analysis, most participants in the Ezold litigation believed that it had been worth the price. Unlike the typical discrimination plaintiff, Ezold felt that the experience had been "extremely positive" in terms of her career. Despite the financial costs, and the difficulties of "getting her life on track" during prolonged legal proceedings, the media exposure had steered many clients with similar stories in her direction, and she had carved out a profitable speciality in employment discrimination.[87] Judith Vladeck, who had paid an even greater cost in unrecouped fees, was equally satisfied, although for different reasons. She would "do it again in a heartbeat," but not because of the professional advantages.[88] Her specialty had already been well established, and the *Ezold* case had no obvious payoff in client development. But it did advance her personal values and commitments. To her, the moral of the story is that lawyers who care about these issues, "just have to keep litigating them" until the profession truly changes and equal opportunity is not just an aspiration but an achievement.[89] Cases like *Ezold* are a way station towards a destination still to be reached.

Among Wolf, Block lawyers, feelings were more mixed. As noted earlier, some partners had second thoughts about whether the case should have been settled. But no one expressed doubts about the merits of the firm's position, and many were proud that it had been willing to fight for its principles and reputation. After the Third Circuit decision and the Supreme Court's denial of a writ of certiorari, Robert Segal told the press that this case was a "victory for justice, honor, character and integrity."[90] Paradoxically enough, Ezold and her lawyers felt the same.

---

87.   Ezold Interview, supra note 33.

88.   Vladeck Interview, supra note 35.

89.   Id.

90.   Shannon P. Duffy, Supreme Court Denies Ezold Appeal, Penn. L. J. Oct. 11, 1993, at 24 (quoting Segal).

*

9

In Re Arons: The Plight of the "Unrich" in Obtaining Legal Services

David C. Vladeck*

Introduction

Marilyn Arons is nobody's fool. Tall, with piercing blue eyes and a measured, powerful voice, she is an imposing presence in a courtroom. She is a riveting speaker. Her arguments are not simply lucid, they are forceful, well-reasoned, and almost always irresistible. She is in total command. It is no surprise that she wins most of her cases. And it is no surprise that for twenty-five years she has struck fear in the hearts of her adversaries—lawyers representing school boards in four different states. Her clients—disabled children and their families—revere her. More than any other advocate, she has shaped the law governing the educational rights of disabled children. What makes this story even more remarkable is that Marilyn Arons is not a lawyer.

In re Arons, however, is not only Marilyn Arons' story. It is also the story of the organized bar and its adherence to arcane rules forbidding non-lawyers from engaging in the unauthorized practice of law. These rules are not simply outdated. At times, *In re Arons* demonstrates, they are barriers to justice, denying millions of Americans access to the legal system.

The facts underlying *In re Arons* are straightforward. Marilyn Arons, although not a lawyer, is an expert in the educational and legal issues that define the rights of disabled children to a free public education. These rights are now guaranteed by federal statutes, includ-

* Associate Professor and Co–Director, Institute for Public Representation, Georgetown University Law Center. I would like to thank Marilyn Arons, who reviewed a draft to ensure that no client confidences were inadvertently revealed. The use of "Mrs." is a matter of personal preference for Mrs. Arons. I would also like to thank my long-time colleague, Alan Morrison, my predecessor as director of Public Citizen Litigation Group and now Senior Lecturer in Law at Stanford Law School, who also provided helpful comments based, in part, on his assistance in the *In re Arons* litigation.

ing the Individuals with Disabilities Education Act (IDEA),[1] which requires states that receive federal education funding to provide disabled children an appropriate public education. But educating disabled children is very expensive. Financially strapped school boards often cut corners, and disputes about what is an "appropriate" education frequently arise. To resolve these disputes, IDEA sets up an elaborate procedure that culminates in "due process" hearings held before state boards of education. At IDEA hearings involving significant issues, like the placement of the child in a private school, the school boards and the states may be represented by counsel; parents can rarely find or afford lawyers, however. Anticipating this disparity, IDEA says that parents may be "accompanied and advised" in these proceedings "by counsel and by individuals with special knowledge and training with respect to children with disabilities." Mrs. Arons is an individual with special knowledge and training, with a record of success in due process hearings in many jurisdictions.[2]

One morning in 1994, a group of Delaware parents literally appeared on Marilyn Arons' doorstep in Teaneck, New Jersey. They were searching for someone to help them to force their local school boards to provide for special needs of their children. The parents were unable to find any lawyer to help them, and they drove by the carload to New Jersey to plea for Mrs. Arons' help.[3] Unable to say no, Mrs. Arons began to provide assistance in due process hearings in Delaware, while continuing her work elsewhere. Over the course of four years, she helped dozens of Delaware families resolve their differences with school boards. But five cases went to hearing, with Mrs. Arons and Ruth Watson—an advocate Mrs. Arons had trained—winning substantial relief for their clients in each case. The Delaware parents were delighted; the school boards were not. A lawyer who represented school boards filed a complaint with Delaware's Office of Disciplinary Counsel (ODC, an arm of the Delaware Supreme Court), alleging that Mrs. Arons was engaged in the unauthorized practice of law (UPL). Other complaints followed. After

---

1. 20 U.S.C. § 1400 et seq.

2. Marilyn Arons's work on behalf of disabled children dates back to the early 1970s, when she persuaded her local school board to permit her neurologically impaired daughter to attend regular classes. This work led her to create the Parent Information Center of New Jersey, Inc., which advises parents with special needs children, publishes a newsletter, advises Congress and state legislatures on special education issues, and, at times, assists parents handling due process hearings. By the time *In re Arons* was filed, Mrs. Arons and a small group of advocates she trained had handled over 500 due process cases, mostly in New Jersey and neighboring states. See Richard B. Schmitt, Advocates Act as Lawyers, and States Cry "Objection!", Wall St. J., Jan. 14, 1999, at B1.

3. Debra Baker, Is This Woman a Threat to Lawyers?, ABA J., June 1999, at 55.

considerable deliberation, the ODC filed formal charges in 1996, thus firing the opening salvo in *In re Arons*.[4]

This chapter recounts the history of that litigation. It begins by asking why, in a nation with more lawyers per capita than any other, almost none of them will represent parents of disabled children in these kinds of cases. The story then turns to IDEA—a statute created at the height of the "rights revolution"—and that, at least on paper, guarantees parents every protection. In practice, however, IDEA is so intricate and process-laden that parents need help navigating its complexities. Then we will turn to a detailed account of the litigation in *In re Arons*, from its opening chapter before the Board on the Unauthorized Practice of Law, through proceedings before the Delaware Supreme Court, to our last-ditch effort to convince the United States Supreme Court to grant review.

In the interest of candor, this is not a dispassionate look at an important case, but is instead a personal account of a case that I handled and lost. While I try to be fair to the capable lawyers at the ODC who handled this case with the highest degree of professionalism, I make no pretense of objectivity. I remain convinced that, by enforcing its UPL rules against Marilyn Arons, the Delaware Bar has done immeasurable harm to disabled children and their families and achieved no countervailing public good. That is not justice.

I met Marilyn Arons in the mid–1980s, when she was already a renowned advocate for disabled children.[5] Her organization, the Parent Information Center, was the only group in the nation providing direct assistance to parents with disabled children who were challenging local

---

4. There were two respondents in addition to Mrs. Arons: Ruth Watson, who handled only one IDEA hearing in Delaware, and the Parent Information Center of New Jersey. Because Mrs. Arons was the focus of the Delaware charges, this chapter will treat her as the respondent.

5. At the time, I was a staff attorney at Public Citizen Litigation Group, a public interest firm founded by Ralph Nader and Alan Morrison. One might wonder why a public interest law firm would worry about cases involving the regulation of the legal profession. There are two reasons: First, the Litigation Group was founded, in part, to focus on consumer rights. Even in the early 1970s, access to affordable legal services was a serious problem for most Americans. Thus, one of the Litigation Group's goals was to use litigation to dismantle barriers to access to the legal system and to challenge the then-orthodox assumption that lawyers act in the public interest when they engage in self-regulation. The Litigation Group brought successful challenges to minimum fee schedules established by state bar associations that artificially raised the costs of legal services, and it attacked state restrictions on the advertising of professional services that stifled price competition and deprived consumers of important information about their legal rights. Representing Mrs. Arons was thus a logical step in this progression. The second reason is that no other institution or group of lawyers would bring these cases, which generally pitted the disenfranchised or impoverished against powerful state bar associations and state supreme courts, and held out little if any prospect of recovering attorneys' fees.

school boards. A trained educator, Mrs. Arons holds a Masters Degree in early childhood education from Bank Street College of Education, and has completed all the coursework for a doctorate in Neuroscience and Education from Columbia University's Teachers College. Earlier in her career, she had taught in New York City public junior high schools for over a decade. Our paths crossed because Mrs. Arons wanted to test the eligibility of non-lawyer advocates to recover attorneys' fees for work performed at IDEA hearings. I represented her in this failed effort.[6] So it was no surprise when I received a call from Mrs. Arons in August 1996 asking me to represent her in fighting the UPL charges filed by Delaware.

The Legal Profession

At this point, perhaps you are wondering why this issue arises at all. Why are parents of disabled children unable to find lawyers but are instead forced to use non-lawyers (if they can be found) to assist them? Don't we have enough lawyers? Answering this question requires consideration of four basic facts about the legal profession.

The first is the number of lawyers in the United States. According to most estimates, there are nearly one million lawyers in the United States.[7] The second fact is that a majority of lawyers in private practice in the United States now work in law firms that represent institutions, not people.[8] This marks a dramatic—even seismic—shift in the nature of legal work performed by lawyers. Three decades ago, only about one-quarter of the lawyers in private practice worked for corporate law firms.[9] This demographic shift has exacerbated a problem that has

---

   6. Arons v. New Jersey State Bd. of Educ., 842 F.2d 58 (3d Cir.), cert. denied, 488 U.S. 942 (1988). Mrs. Arons rendered her services free of charge, but wanted to establish her right to charge a fee—either to parents who could afford one, or to the school boards through IDEA's attorney fee provision. The court ruled that as a non-lawyer Mrs. Arons could not recover fees for her advocacy work in IDEA proceedings. Id. at 62. The Third Circuit's ruling was not a complete defeat, however. The court emphasized that Mrs. Arons was entitled to a fee for her expert assistance, just as any expert would be eligible for a fee under IDEA's fee-shifting provision, in cases where her client prevailed. Id. Thus, at least some of Mrs. Arons' work would be compensable.

   7. Del Jones, Lawyers, Wannabes on the Rise, USA Today, Dec. 26, 2003 at A3, (declaring that "[t]he number of lawyers in the USA exceeded 1 million for the first time in 2003"); available at http://keepmedia.com/Register.do?oliID=225 (last visited Sept. 20, 2004); see also Statistical Abstract of the United States, at 424 (U.S. Census Bureau 2000); see also http://www.census.gov/prod/99pubs/99statab/sec13.pdf (visited Oct. 2, 2000) (estimating 950,000 lawyers in the United States, taking into account judges and their law clerks).

   8. Galanter, "Old and in the Way:" The Coming Demographic Transformation of the Legal Profession and its Implication for the Provision of Legal Services, 1999 Wisc. L. Rev. 1081, 1088–90 (hereinafter "Old and in the Way").

   9. See, e.g., Nelson, The Futures of American Lawyers: A Demographic Profile of a Changing Profession in a Changing Society, 44 Case W. Res. L. Rev. 345 (1994); see also

existed for decades; namely, that for many Americans legal services are generally unavailable, not by reason of poverty (because most of these people are not poor) but simply because they are not sufficiently wealthy to afford the high cost of legal services. We'll call these people the "unrich." Indeed, many Americans cannot afford anything but the most routine legal services (e.g., the preparation of a will). The poor, unless they are among the lucky few who receive free legal services, are denied access to the legal system altogether.[10]

The third fact is sobering: According to the best estimates available, the number of lawyers in the United States who regularly represent poor people in civil litigation is about 6,000.[11] By any measure, that number is tiny, representing far less than one percent of the profession.

[handwritten margin note: 6,000 / 1 million]

Fact number four underscores the significance of fact number three: According to the Legal Services Corporation (LSC) and the American Bar Association (ABA), most Americans (60%–70%) cannot afford to have their legal needs addressed by lawyers. Take the poor first. The LSC estimates that fifty million Americans (out of about 280 million) live in households that are nominally eligible for free legal services.[12] The qualifier "nominally" is necessary, because the resources of the LSC and other providers of free or low-cost legal services have been spread so thin that these lawyers can take only a fraction of worthy cases brought to them by eligible clients.[13] Remember, these people are too poor to hire lawyers. As a result, the LSC estimates that between 80% and 90% of the legal needs of the poor go unmet.[14] The ABA has reached the same

---

Agenda for the 1990s, at 14. Nelson's statistics divide the profession on the basis of the size of law firms in which lawyers now practice. Although it may be wrong at the margins, my assumption, and the assumption of other commentators, is that most of the larger law firms, with fifty or more lawyers, principally represent institutional clients and not individuals.

10. The exception, of course, is for cases in which the plaintiff has some likelihood of recovering damages sufficient to allow for the payment of a lawyer's fee. In those circumstances, finding legal representation on a contingency fee basis is generally not an obstacle, especially since the Supreme Court dismantled the restrictions on advertising by lawyers. See, e.g., Bates v. State Bar of Arizona, 433 U.S. 350 (1977); Zauderer v. Office of Disciplinary Counsel, 471 U.S. 626 (1985).

11. "Old and in the Way", supra note 8, at 1003 n.55; see also David C. Vladeck, Hard Choices: Thoughts for New Lawyers, 10 Kan. J. of Law & Pub. Pol'y 351, 352 & n.7 (Spring 2001) (explaining why Professor Galanter's estimates may be too high).

12. Legal Services Corporation, Serving the Civil Legal Needs of Low–Income Americans: A Special Report to Congress, 12 (April 30, 2000) (hereinafter "Special Report").

13. Id., at 13 (pointing out that, as recently as 1993, legal service programs were turning away 50% of eligible persons because of resource limitations and observing that by 2000, the level had grown to 80%).

14. Id., at 12–13. See also Legal Services Corporation, Strategic Directions 2000–2005 at 1 (Jan. 2000) (estimating the same or even greater level of unmet needs).

conclusion.[15] To make matters worse, this epidemic of under-service is accelerating, along with the reduction of funding for legal services programs. And the private bar has not shouldered much of the burden; estimates suggest that fewer than 20% of lawyers in private practice accept any pro bono clients at all.[16]

What about the "unrich" or the middle class? Until now, we have looked at the inability of the bottom 20% of the economic ladder to have access to legal assistance. But the picture of the next 35% to 40%—the middle class—is not much brighter. According to the ABA, most of the legal needs of middle-income households go unmet as well.[17] And that should not be surprising. Assume that your parents are average Americans. They work hard. They make $60,000 between them. Because they are helping their children through school, they do not have a lot squirreled away in savings.

Suppose they encounter a serious legal problem. The house they purchased from a builder five years ago is falling apart and needs $30,000 in repairs. They believe that they have a strong breach of warranty claim against the builder. Can they afford to hire a lawyer to help them? Surely not on a fee-for-service basis. Even a modest hourly rate of $125 would likely strain their finances, and, if protracted litigation ensued, drain their savings. Unless they can find a lawyer willing to take their case for a contingency fee—which is hardly a certainty given the complexity of the case, the risks inherent in litigation, and the modest potential recovery—they might be out of luck in finding a lawyer to help them. But they have a chance.[18]

Now suppose that you, like millions of Americans, have a sibling with serious special education needs.[19] IDEA guarantees your sibling a free appropriate public education. But suppose the school board denies your sibling the educational opportunities that she needs to develop and progress. What then? Who will assist your parents in their battle with the school board? The reality is that they are unlikely to find legal

---

15. American Bar Association, Legal Needs and Civil Justice: Major Findings from the Comprehensive Legal Needs Study, at 23 (1994) (hereinafter "Legal Needs Study").

16. Lock, Increasing Access to Justice: Expanding the Role of Nonlawyers in the Delivery of Legal Services to Low–Income Coloradans, 72 U. Colo. L. Rev. 459, 465 (2001).

17. Legal Needs Study, supra note 15, at 23–25.

18. This example is based on several cases that arose in the suburbs surrounding Washington, D.C. In these cases, the plaintiffs succeeded in finding lawyers who managed to obtain significant relief for their clients and get paid. The point, of course, is that so long as there is real money on the table, a lawyer might be willing to take on a case. But once that possibility gets too remote, or the potential fee becomes too low to justify the work the case will entail, it will be difficult, if not impossible, to find counsel.

19. See Honig v. Doe, 484 U.S. 305, 309 (1988) (estimating that 8 million families have children with special educational needs).

counsel they can afford. Virtually no legal services organization provides assistance to parents in IDEA due process hearings because they place too great a strain on the organization's resources (and in this example your parents would be ineligible for legal services in any event, because their income far exceeds eligibility guidelines). To compound the problem, few lawyers want to handle IDEA cases. Not only is the prospect of a fee remote, but due process hearings are emotionally wrenching and involve complex issues about the child's mental and physical capabilities that are unfamiliar to most lawyers.[20] For these reasons the ABA found that there "appear to be few, if any, lawyers experienced and willing to handle" IDEA cases, even for a fee.[21] As a result, your parents may be forced into a Hobson's choice: represent themselves in a highly formal adversarial hearing against the school district, which is generally represented by counsel, or forfeit their right to challenge the school district's decision. As unfair as it may seem, their plight is not unusual.

IDEA

IDEA was enacted in response to Congress' longstanding concern that "more than half" of the 8 million children with disabilities in the United States "were simply 'warehoused' in special classes or were neglectfully shepherded through the system until they were old enough to drop out."[22] Congress wanted to ensure that all children with disabilities have access to a free appropriate public education tailored to their unique needs. IDEA also contains procedural safeguards that give parents and children with disabilities a number of "rights"—including the right (1) to have the school board prepare an "individualized educational plan" ("IEP") that sets goals for the child and evaluation procedures for determining whether the child is progressing at a proper rate; (2) to be provided notice whenever a school changes or refuses to change the IEP; (3) to present complaints about the IEP; and (4) when those complaints cannot be resolved informally, to have an impartial due process hearing.

At due process hearings held under IDEA, any party "shall be accorded" the "right to be accompanied and advised by counsel and by individuals with special knowledge or training with respect to the

---

20. IDEA does contain a fee-shifting provision that was added in 1986. See generally Moore v. District of Columbia, 907 F.2d 165 (D.C. Cir. 1990) (en banc). Following the addition of the fee-shifting provision, courts have held that disabled children and their parents are entitled to attorneys' fees for successfully contesting school board decisions at the administrative level and in court, although the standards for obtaining such an award are formidable, and fee awards are few. Id.

21. American Bar Association, Commission on Nonlawyer Practice, Nonlawyer Activity in Law–Related Situations, A Report with Recommendations (1995).

22. 20 U.S.C. § 1400(c)(2)(B); *Honig*, 484 U.S. at 309–312; see also Hendrick Hudson Dist. Bd. of Educ. v. Rowley, 458 U.S. 176, 179 (1982).

problems of children with disabilities."[23] In Delaware, due process hearings are formal, trial-like hearings before three-member panels appointed by the Department of Education. The panel consists of an attorney
(who is always the Chair), an educator, and a layperson. The parties are
parents, usually not represented by lawyers; the local school board,
which is always represented by counsel; and the Department, which is
represented by separate counsel whenever the parents are seeking substantial relief. Due process hearings often last several days. Although the
rules of evidence do not strictly apply, the Chair rules on legal issues, the
qualifications of experts, and objections to relevance, materiality, privilege and admissibility. After the hearing, the panel deliberates and issues
a written ruling that is generally prepared by the panel's lawyer-chair.[24]

Because IDEA due process hearings focus on the unique needs of
each disabled child, it is hard to generalize about the issues that arise in
these cases. But the transcripts bring to life the plight of the disabled
children and their families whose rights are at stake in these proceedings. It is one thing to talk in the abstract about the needs of disabled
children; it is quite another to hear their stories. They drive home the
fact that parents facing due process hearings are fighting for their
children's lives.

For example, at the time of his hearing, Philip Russ was a fifth
grader who was severely dyslexic and learning disabled. Classified as
"disabled" in kindergarten, Philip fell behind his grade level year in and
year out. By fifth grade, he was still reading at a late first-to middle-
second grade level, his written language skills were at a similar level,
and math was at approximately a middle-third grade level. Philip's
learning disability also had a devastating impact on his social and
emotional growth; he was teased and bullied in school and often struck
back, earning him a reputation as a "troublemaker." Philip's parents
were fighting for an enriched educational program to bring his reading
and math skills up to the point he could at least learn a vocation.[25] Or
consider the plight of Polly DeCrease, whose ten-year-old son Nick could
not read and was about to be thrown out of school for bringing a knife to
class and setting a fire in a bathroom. Nick had profound learning and
emotional disabilities, and his school had all but given up in trying to
meet his special educational needs. After his due process hearing, Delaware agreed to send him to a private school in Virginia that specialized

---

23.   20 U.S.C. § 1415(h)(1).

24.   Id. Parents who do not prevail in the administrative process have the right to
seek judicial review. 20 U.S.C. § 1415(i)(2)(A). Mrs. Arons did not claim a right to assist
parents in court proceedings.

25.   Transcript of Russ v. Cape Henlopen School District, at 24–25 (Nov. 27, 1995).

in helping children with Nick's disabilities, and he appears to be making tremendous progress.

Proceedings Before the Board on the Unauthorized Practice of Law

Round One—Delaware versus Mrs. Arons

On August 8, 1996, the ODC filed a petition with the Delaware Board on the Unauthorized Practice of Law asking for a declaration that Marilyn Arons had violated Delaware's UPL rules by representing families of children with disabilities in IDEA hearings. Although outraged at the charge, Mrs. Arons was not entirely surprised. In her view, the ODC was simply "carrying the water for the school boards, which were tired of losing," and thus enlisted the ODC in "an effort to preserve the status quo and save the school boards money, all at the expense of disabled children."[26]

Respondents face serious obstacles in UPL proceedings. Judges, who were all once practicing lawyers, have the power both to define what constitutes the practice of law and to limit the practice of law to lawyers only. To the extent that UPL has been defined, the definitions are expansive and indeterminate,[27] permitting state bar associations to aggressively pursue non-lawyers providing any sort of legal service at all. This means that many simple tasks that might easily be done by trained non-lawyers must be done by licensed lawyers, or not at all.

---

26. Telephone interview with Mrs. Arons on Oct. 1, 2004.

27. Consider one definition: "A person not admitted to practice as a lawyer may not engage in the unauthorized practice of law." Restatement of the Law Governing Lawyers (Third), § 4 (2000). The circularity of this definition is breathtaking, but not unusual. Some jurisdictions, like Delaware, have not codified restrictions on UPL but have instead developed them though the common law. For example, Delaware State Bar Ass'n v. Alexander, 386 A.2d 652 (Del. 1978), provides the following definition: "In general, one is deemed to be practicing law whenever he furnishes to another advice or service under circumstances which imply the possession and use of legal knowledge and skill. The practice of law includes all advice to clients, and all actions taken for them in matters connected with the law. Practice of law includes the giving of legal advice and counsel, and the preparation of legal instruments and contracts of which legal rights are secured. Where the rendering of services for another involves the use of legal knowledge or skill on his behalf—where legal advice is required and is availed of or rendered in connection with such services—these services necessarily constitute or include the practice of law." Id., at 661 (quotations and citations omitted).

As you can see, there is virtually no limit to this definition. A barber giving advice to a customer thinking about divorcing a spouse could easily be said to violate this rule, as could a real estate agent advising a client about the tax consequences of certain mortgage fees. Compounding the problem, because this definition is available only from case reports—and not in the state code—any non-lawyer would have a very difficult time learning Delaware's unauthorized practice rules. Nonetheless, the approach Delaware follows is not unusual. And, like most states, Delaware treats UPL violations harshly. Mr. Alexander was sentenced to five months in prison for violating an injunction barring him from engaging in unauthorized practice. Id.

The petition filed by Delaware posed two distinct problems. First, we were respondents (defendants) rather than plaintiffs, and we were in the wrong forum. From a test-case standpoint, we would have ideally sued Delaware first, and thus litigated the right of non-lawyers to assist parents in IDEA hearings in federal court, with Mrs. Arons as plaintiff. Why did the choice of forum matter? The advantages of forum choice are hard to overstate. For one thing, had we sued first, the litigation would take place when we chose, in the court we selected, before federal judges familiar with (and, in my experience, more sympathetic to) the kind of preemption arguments that would form the core of our case. For another, the litigation would focus on whether federal law authorizes non-lawyer representation in IDEA hearings, not whether Ms. Arons violated Delaware's UPL rules. Finally, in such a case Mrs. Arons would not be tarred with the label "law-breaker," a label that any litigant would prefer to avoid.

Unfortunately, it is difficult to bring a test case challenging a state law in federal court. There is only the briefest interval in which such an action may properly be filed. To challenge the constitutionality of a state law in federal court, a plaintiff must show that she faces a credible and imminent risk of having the state law enforced against her. Once state authorities begin an enforcement proceeding, federal courts are required to "abstain" or dismiss such actions until all state proceedings have been completed, absent the most unusual circumstances.[28]

Until the ODC filed its petition, however, Mrs. Arons did not anticipate that UPL charges might be filed in Delaware. In hindsight, there were two ominous signs. The first was that in August 1994, Mrs. Arons had received a letter from the ODC inquiring about her role in two then-pending due process hearings in Delaware.[29] Mrs. Arons promptly submitted a reply and heard nothing back from the ODC.[30] The other warning sign was that the lawyers representing the school boards routinely objected to Mrs. Arons's participation at the outset of each hearing. While no hearing panel disqualified her on UPL grounds, these complaints were forwarded to the ODC. Mrs. Arons' adversaries were

---

28. See, e.g., Middlesex County Ethics Comm. v. Garden State Bar Ass'n, 457 U.S. 423, 43637 (1982); Younger v. Harris, 401 U.S. 37 (1971). Adding to the complexity of the procedural tangle facing us, the ordinary rules governing abstention apply with greater force to bar matters, and it is clear that we were obligated to raise our constitutional defenses in the state proceeding or risk waiving them. See D.C. Court of Appeals v. Feldman, 460 U.S. 462 (1983); Rooker v. Fidelity Trust Co., 263 U.S. 413, 415, 416 (1923). Indeed, the "Rooker–Feldman doctrine" acts to keep cases challenging the activities of state bar associations out of federal court, which solidifies the power of states to regulate the practice of law without significant federal constitutional oversight.

29. Letter from David Curtis Glebe, Disciplinary Counsel, ODC, Supreme Court of the State of Delaware to Marilyn Arons (Aug. 10, 1994).

30. Letter from Marilyn Arons to David Curtis Glebe (Sept. 16, 1994).

also becoming increasingly antagonistic; by mid–1995 she routinely heard complaints that Delaware, which has no state sales tax, would have to impose an "Arons tax" to pay for expensive IDEA hearings and the costly relief Mrs. Arons was winning for her clients.[31]

Did these actions amount to a sufficient threat of a likely enforcement action to entitle us to federal court jurisdiction? Probably yes. The better course would have been to file a pre-emptive strike against the ODC in federal court, seeking a declaration that Mrs. Arons was entitled, as a matter of federal law, to assist parents in Delaware due process hearings. But the filing of the ODC petition foreclosed our ability to go to federal court. So the first bad news was that we were in a forum of our adversary's choosing playing defense, not offense.

The second problem was that, except for the allegation that Mrs. Arons charged a fee, the facts set forth in the petition were accurate. Mrs. Arons was, under Delaware's view of the law, providing legal representation in IDEA hearings, albeit free of charge. Our defense, therefore, would rest on the argument that federal law authorized her to "practice law" in IDEA hearings—an argument that amounted to asking a state court to resolve a conflict between federal and state law.

Round Two: Our Response

We had twenty days to file an answer to the petition. Drafting an answer was simple. I adhered to the rule for preparing answers that I teach civil procedure students—follow the motto attributed to the C.I.A: Admit Nothing, Deny Everything, Make Counter–Accusations. And that we did. We quarreled with every factual assertion we could plausibly dispute, we admitted what we had to, and we asserted a number of defenses.

The complication with filing the answer was not drafting it, but was instead, ironically, Delaware's UPL rules. I am not a member of the Delaware Bar and therefore needed local counsel. Finding local counsel is often a serious problem in non-fee-generating public interest cases. But this complication was a special hurdle in *In re Arons*, because the state's Supreme Court was both our adversary and final decision-maker. Few lawyers want to take on the court of last resort in their home state. I called every progressive lawyer in Delaware; then I called everyone else. None were willing to help out; everyone had what seemed to be a good excuse. Ultimately, Mrs. Arons had to file the answer pro se because we were unable to find a Delaware lawyer in time.[32]

---

31. Telephone interviews with Mrs. Arons on July 13 and Oct. 1, 2004.

32. It took over a year and countless hours to find a Delaware lawyer willing to lend a hand. Walter Speed Rowland, who had recently retired from his position in a corporate law department, agreed to help. I am extremely grateful for Walt Rowland's assistance and wise counsel in this case.

There was also a lurking UPL/ethics problem with my ghostwriting the answer to the petition. A number of courts have ruled that lawyers may not help pro se litigants draft pleadings and briefs without disclosing that fact to the court.[33] These decisions place public interest and legal services lawyers in a bind. There are untold occasions where a lawyer might have time to help a pro se litigant draft a brief or other legal document, but cannot handle the case in its entirety. Once a lawyer reveals his or her behind-the-scenes participation in a case, however, there is a real risk that the court may order the lawyer to assume responsibility for the case. Making matters worse, public interest lawyers often ghostwrite papers for filings in jurisdictions in which they are not admitted. A disclosure requirement might subject them to charges that *they* are engaging in the unauthorized practice of law. In *In re Arons,* we avoided this problem because Delaware has not adopted a disclosure requirement.

Once the answer was filed, we expected the ODC to move quickly to get the case ready for hearing. But, astonishingly, nothing happened. There were several possible explanations for the ODC's apparent complacency. One reason might be that satellite litigation was filed against the ODC in federal court by other parents of disabled children challenging Delaware's right to deny them non-lawyer representation.[34] That action, which was never seriously litigated, was dismissed by the parties in April 1997. Another reason might be that ODC assumed that simply filing the action would send Mrs. Arons scampering back to New Jersey. That assumption was wrong. Mrs. Arons took on new IDEA cases in Delaware, but, perhaps fortunately, these cases were settled. Nonetheless, for a year the case lay dormant.

Round Three: Full–Scale Hearing or Stipulation of Facts?

That changed in August 1997, when James S. Green, the head of the Delaware UPL Board, jump-started the case by holding a pre-hearing conference. Mr. Green wanted to get the case moving, and he began by asking if the parties had explored settlement. He then agreed to give the parties a brief opportunity to discuss settlement, but warned that if the settlement talks did not bear fruit, he would set a hearing date.

The ODC made a settlement offer in early October, but its "offer" was simply a demand that Mrs. Arons agree not to assist parents in IDEA hearings in the future. After discussions with Mrs. Arons, we responded with a letter setting forth our legal position in some detail.

---

33. See, e.g., Stewart v. Angelone, 186 F.R.D. 342, 344 (E.D. Va. 1999); Clarke v. United States, 955 F. Supp. 593, 597–98 (E.D. Va. 1997), vacated on other grounds, 162 F.3d 1156 (4th Cir. 1998); Johnson v. Board of Cty. Comm'rs, 868 F. Supp. 1226, 1231–32 (D. Colo. 1994).

34. DeCrease v. Brandywine School Dist., Civ. Action No. 94–483 (D. Del. 1994).

The letter stressed that the activities in which Mrs. Arons is "engaged are, in fact, authorized by both state and federal law, and thus your draft compliance agreement would in effect curtail, not clarify, Mrs. Arons' rights." The letter also pointed out that Delaware is "now the only state that places any barriers on non-lawyers assisting parents in IDEA due process hearings." The letter ended by asking that we try "to reach some sensible accommodation" that would permit Mrs. Arons to assist parents in due process hearings with some oversight by the ODC or another state authority.

In our view, this exchange of letters demonstrated that the parties were too far apart to consider settlement. As a result, we began to outline the case we would present at hearing. In a nutshell, our affirmative case would consist of a four-pronged attack: (1) testimony from Mrs. Arons about her background in education matters and her experience handling IDEA hearings; (2) testimony by her clients, who would say that they understood that Mrs. Arons is not a lawyer, that they had attempted but failed to find a lawyer to represent them, and that they could not have exercised their rights to a due process hearing in the absence of Mrs. Arons' assistance; (3) testimony by school board lawyers that they, not parents, had filed complaints with the ODC; and (4) testimony from an expert in education law that IDEA hearings focus on technical issues relating to the diagnosis and treatment of children with disabilities and thus non-lawyer experts are capable of handling IDEA cases.

At the same time, David Glebe, the Disciplinary Counsel, was considering another approach. He realized that there were at most trivial disagreements over the facts, while there was wholesale disagreement about the applicable law. Mr. Glebe then proposed that, in lieu of a hearing, we prepare a joint stipulation of facts, in which the ODC would concede virtually everything we intended to put into evidence.[35] The ODC understood that important principles were at stake. He wanted a resolution of the underlying legal issues, not to punish Mrs. Arons, but to have clarity on what he saw was a difficult legal question, and he thought that a lengthy and expensive hearing would serve neither party's purpose.

Mr. Glebe's proposal was intriguing. On the one hand, we would have much more control over a stipulated record than one developed at a hearing. Hearings never go quite as planned. Witnesses never say exactly what they intend to say or what their lawyers want them to say. Opposing lawyers ask inconvenient questions. Hearing officers do not always rule the way one thinks they should. And, in this case, many of

---

35. Letter from David Curtis Glebe to to David C. Vladeck, Public Citizen Litigation Group (Nov. 4, 1997).

the parents represented by Mrs. Arons were apprehensive about testifying.

On the other hand, a hearing held several advantages. Mrs. Arons could tell her story, in her own words, from her own perspective, in a voice we could not hope to capture on paper and could not embody in a stipulation. A hearing would also give the parents an opportunity to tell their stories, which were so poignant and compelling that anyone hearing them would be moved by their plight. And we thought that the publicity that would flow from a hearing would help convince the hearing panel and the public that our cause was just.

In the end, however, we decided to see whether the ODC would accept a stipulation that did, in fact, reflect the facts as we saw them. If so, then we would be willing to waive our right to a hearing. We made this decision for two reasons. First, we understood that the arguments favoring a hearing—chiefly, the dramatic impact of live testimony from the families caught up in IDEA cases and Mrs. Arons—were less powerful than they might otherwise be if the trier of fact (i.e., the UPL Board) was the final decision maker in the case. But it was not. The Delaware Supreme Court would ultimately resolve the case, and it would have before it only the cold transcript of the hearing. The second concern was practical; we were worried about the time and expense of a lengthy trial.

We therefore drafted a stipulation that pushed our case as far as we could, and represented the elements of the case we would have presented at hearing. To our relief, the Disciplinary Counsel agreed to the draft in substance. Apart from our legal argument, and the transcripts of the due process hearings, the stipulation formed the heart of our case.

Round Five: Briefing

The briefing in the case centered on two main issues: whether IDEA authorizes non-lawyer representation, and whether parents of disabled children have a constitutional right to be accompanied by non-lawyers in IDEA proceedings, especially where, as here, the state pays for the parents' adversaries to be represented by counsel.

The ODC's brief began by going straight for our Achilles' heel, boring into our argument that the "accompany and advise" language in IDEA authorized Mrs. Arons to represent parents in IDEA proceedings.[36] That language, said the ODC, fell short of an authorization to "represent" parties. When Congress intends to displace important state law protections (like the protection against UPL), it must do so expressly, the ODC argued, and the IDEA's language did not measure up to that

---

36. See Opening Memorandum of the Office of Disciplinary Counsel, submitted to the Board on the Unauthorized Practice of Law of the Supreme Court of the State of Delaware, April 16, 1999.

exacting standard. The ODC's position was also in keeping with the Third Circuit's reading of IDEA in *Arons v. New Jersey State Board of Education*. There, the court said that the "accompany and advise" language "does not authorize these specially qualified individuals to render legal services."[37] Although IDEA gives " 'any party to any hearing' the right to 'present evidence and confront, cross-examine and compel the attendance of witnesses,' those functions are not designated to be performed by lay advocates."[38]

The ODC brief ended with an explanation of the policy reasons supporting its position. ODC assumed for the sake of argument both that "every parent participating in a due process hearing can neither afford nor obtain the services of a Delaware attorney," and that Mrs. Arons is "fully qualified to act in a representational capacity during due process hearings." Nonetheless, creating an exception to Delaware's UPL rules, "without a system of lay advocate qualification and accountability would unnecessarily erode the primary purpose of regulating the practice of law: 'to protect the public against the drastic and far-reaching consequences of . . . inexpert legal advice.' "[39] Non-lawyers are not bound by the same ethical and fiduciary restraints imposed on lawyers. Nor are non-lawyers "accountable." They could "make factual misrepresentations to the panel with impunity," or withhold evidence, resulting in an unjust determination. "Unless a Delaware attorney participates, the public has no assurance of the quality of services provided and has no recourse should the lay representative's conduct, whether intentional or unintentional, prove detrimental to the interest of the disabled child."

We had our work cut out for us. Although the arguments were predictable, the brief was first-rate. But, as we saw the case, ODC had the policy argument backward: The public protection purpose of the UPL rules would be subverted, not advanced, by forcing parents in the most dire straits imaginable to face alone the school boards and the state, both represented by lawyers. For this reason, the introduction to our brief threw down the gauntlet. "This is not a run-of-the-mill UPL case. The charges against respondents were not brought by dissatisfied clients."[40] All of the activities that form the bases for these charges relate to services Mrs. Arons provided free of charge to parents involved in IDEA due process hearings. "There is no dispute that these parents were fully informed" that Mrs. Arons is not a lawyer. Nor is there any

---

37. 842 F.2d 58, 62 (3d Cir.), cert. denied, 488 U.S. 942 (1988).

38. Id.

39. ODC Opening Mem., supra note 36, at 14 (quoting Alexander, 386 A.2d at 661).

40. Memorandum of Respondents, In re Arons, UPL–4, 1996, submitted to the Board on the Unauthorized Practice of Law of the Supreme Court of the State of Delaware, May 21, 1999. (Rule 10.8.3) at 1.

dispute that, but for Mrs. Arons' assistance, "these parents would have foregone their statutory right to contest decisions by school boards because they were intimidated by the complexity of the due process hearings," and they lacked the education and experience to handle these hearings on their own. "[T]his proceeding," our brief continued, "is not brought to vindicate the interests of those parents [or] their disabled children." Rather, it was "initiated by the school boards" to "condemn these parents to face due process hearings without any assistance at all."

The brief then turned to our submission that IDEA guarantees parents the right to have non-lawyers represent them. The key to the case, we argued, was § 1415(h)(1) of IDEA, which gives parties "the right to be accompanied and advised" not only by counsel, but also by "individuals with special knowledge and training."[41] The Act draws no distinction between "counsel" and individuals "with special knowledge and training," treating the two exactly the same. We also pointed out that the U.S. Department of Education, the agency that administers IDEA, concluded as far back as 1981 that "lay advocates are permitted to represent parties at administrative hearings and appeals" under IDEA.[42] The Department's interpretation, we argued, was entitled to controlling deference.[43] The brief also took issue with ODC's reliance on the Third Circuit's ruling in *Arons*. The sole issue in *Arons* was whether a lay advocate authorized by state law to represent parents in IDEA hearings could collect attorneys' fees for work in IDEA hearings. The Third Circuit said no. But the question before the Board—whether federal law entitles parents to non-lawyer representation—was neither briefed nor argued in *Arons*, and the Third Circuit's discussion of the issue appeared only in dicta.

We next argued that the preemption doctrine, which holds that federal law displaces inconsistent state law addressing the same issue, required Delaware to permit lay representation in IDEA hearings. Our main case was *Sperry v. Florida Bar*,[44] which arose when the Florida Bar filed UPL charges against Mr. Sperry, a non-lawyer authorized to practice before the U.S. Patent Office, after he represented Florida patent clients for a fee. The U.S. Supreme Court held that Florida's UPL

---

41.   Id. at 8, quoting 20 U.S.C. § 1415 (h) (1).

42.   See Letter from Ted Sky, Acting General Counsel, U.S. Dep't of Education, to the Hon. Frank Brouillet, Superintendent of Public Instruction, State of Washington (Apr. 1, 1981).

43.   It is a basic principle of administrative law that "considerable weight should be accorded to an executive department's construction of a statutory scheme it is entrusted to administer," and a "court may not substitute its own construction of a statutory provision for a reasonable interpretation" made by an agency. Chevron, USA v. NRDC, 467 U.S. 837, 844 (1984).

44.   373 U.S. 379 (1963).

law could not be applied because it was incompatible with federal regulations governing practice before the Patent Office. Under *Sperry*, we maintained, Delaware could not enforce its UPL rules to interfere with Mrs. Arons' representation in IDEA proceedings, because that right was conferred by federal law.

The brief then turned to ODC's arguments about the perils posed by unlicensed and unaccountable lay advocates. As to competence, the brief noted that IDEA itself sets an exacting standard: to represent parents in due process hearings, non-lawyers must demonstrate "special knowledge or training with respect to the problems of disabilities." IDEA also answers ODC's concerns about accountability, because non-lawyers may appear at hearings only with the tribunal's permission. Thus, their appearance may be conditioned upon their willingness to undertake whatever reasonable obligations a state might impose, and some states require lay advocates to adhere to the rules of professional conduct that govern lawyers. Finally, we pointed out that non-lawyers routinely advocate on behalf of individuals in a broad array of proceedings—from social security, veterans benefits, and food stamps, to those involving domestic violence—without the dire consequences forecast by ODC.

The brief closed with our due process argument. We contended that decisions by the state affecting a child's right to basic educational opportunities must be made in accordance with due process. The ODC position—that parents have no right to non-lawyer assistance in hearings that pit them against well-represented and well-financed state agencies—if adopted, would violate due process by rendering IDEA hearings "unwholesomely unequal."[45]

The ODC filed a long brief in response, mostly repeating its prior arguments. But the brief urged the Board to discount the Department of Education's view, saying it was entitled to, at most, minimal weight because Congress had not given the Department authority to override state UPL laws. ODC also brushed aside our due process argument, contending that "there is no constitutional 'right to lay representation' in IDEA proceedings." And the brief defended ODC's position as a matter of public policy: "the public interest demands that parents in the State of Delaware who wish to obtain legal representation in IDEA due process hearings be afforded the kind of protection that is available only through the enforcement by the Delaware Supreme Court of the high

---

45. This phrase comes from Lassiter v. Department of Soc. Servs. of Durham Cty., 452 U.S. 18, 27 (1981), where the Court said: "If, as our adversary system presupposes, accurate and just results are more likely to be obtained through equal contests of opposed interests, the State's interest in the child's welfare may perhaps best be served by a hearing in which both the parent and the State ... are represented by counsel, without whom the contests of interest may become unwholesomely unequal." See also Mathews v. Eldridge, 424 U.S. 319, 335 (1976).

standards for the selection and conduct of members of the Delaware Bar."

Round Six: Argument Before the Board on the Unauthorized Practice of Law

At promptly 9:30 a.m. on June 23, 1999, Board Chairman Samuel A. Nolen called to order the hearing in *In re Arons*. Mr. Nolen, a Wilmington lawyer, had taken over as Chair of the Board, and sitting with him as co-panel members were John W. Paradee, another Wilmington lawyer, and Cherie Congo, a non-lawyer member, who was described in press accounts as "a funeral director in Wilmington."[46] The hearing was held in a small room in a state office building in Wilmington, which was jammed with parents of disabled children, reporters, and curious onlookers who had followed the case in the press. After introductions, Michael McGinniss, representing ODC, took the podium.

Mr. McGinniss quickly got to the heart of his argument. Mr. McGinniss wanted the Board to focus not on the activities of Mrs. Arons, but rather on the risk that a ruling in her favor would open the "floodgates" to non-lawyer representation in administrative hearings in Delaware. As Mr. McGinniss put it, his concern was that a "ruling by this Board that the practice of law at IDEA due process hearings by non-lawyers is authorized would be applicable to any future person who wished to represent parents and children at these hearings." It was therefore "essential for the Board to keep this big picture in mind when considering whether it is truly in the long-term interest for the State of Delaware for laypersons to perform traditional representational functions at these hearings."[47]

Mr. McGinniss then painstakingly went through each point of his argument, with few questions from the panel. His conclusion echoed his introductory remarks:

> The Board should be wary of establishing a precedent that could affect other state administrative proceedings in the State of Delaware. Other persons, without legal training, character and fitness screening or professional accountability, could argue that they should be permitted to engage in the practice of law, whether paid or unpaid, because there is an alleged interest at stake that is best protected by having some kind of legal representation, even if that representative is not a member of the Bar. In the absence of carefully delineated limitations pro-

---

46. Cohen, An IDEA Whose Time Has Come?: Proponents of Lay Advocacy Want Delaware to Allow Non–Lawyers to Represent Clients Under Individuals With Disabilities Education Act, Delaware Law Weekly, June 26, 1999, at 1.

47. Transcript of Proceedings in *In re Arons*, before the Board on the Unauthorized Practice of Law of the Supreme Court of Delaware, June 23, 1999, at 9–10.

hibiting the unauthorized practice of law, the public is simply inadequately protected from potential exploitation by less than scrupulous or unqualified individuals who may hold themselves out as lay advocates.

I then took the podium. I wanted the Board to focus on the problems parents with disabled children face, not the broad brush concerns that Mr. McGinniss had targeted in his argument. I began: "Let me start out by setting the stage, because much of what has been said this morning assumes a universe that simply does not exist. Congress enacted this statute fully aware of the fact that the men and women who find themselves confronted with the profoundly difficult dilemma of having a child with a serious disability and trying to confront a school district in order to get the best education possible for their child would not necessarily be able to hire" high-priced lawyers. "Congress was acutely aware of the fact that parents using IDEA come from all walks of life, and like most Americans, cannot afford legal services." This case, I argued, concerned only IDEA hearings, and thus Mr. McGinniss' "floodgates" arguments have nothing to do with this case. I asked the Board Members to "imagine having a child with a serious disability and trying to fight to ensure that your child got the educational opportunity that he or she deserved." Congress "was trying to empower parents who find themselves in this horribly difficult situation to have some lever of power," even if they could not afford counsel.

I then addressed each of our legal arguments, with little questioning from the Board. After fifteen minutes or so, Mr. Nolen asked whether the Department of Education had ever commented on the Third Circuit's *Arons* decision. I saw immediately what he was driving at. "I understand the dilemma you are faced with," I said. "You have dictum from the Third Circuit pulling you in one direction and you have a clear interpretation from the agency charged with administering the statute pointing in the other direction." The Department never addressed *Arons*, I said, because, until Delaware filed the UPL charges in this case, no state had ever questioned the propriety of the Department's position. All other states permit non-lawyer representation in IDEA hearings. But I said that, under governing law, the Board was "required to defer to the Department, unless and until there is a clear holding" to the contrary, and in *Arons* "there is no clear holding on that issue."

As I wound up my argument, I urged the Board to consider Mr. McGinniss' claim that a finding for ODC was necessary to protect the citizens of Delaware. "Protect them from whom?" I asked.

These are not people who have a choice to go out and hire a lawyer. It may be that in a perfect world, the world that Mr. McGinniss wants us to have tomorrow, they'd be able to find lawyers. But this statute has been on the books for over twenty years. They still cannot find lawyers. There still is no legal service available to them. So the notion that you would be serving their interests by depriving them of the only assistance they can find seems backwards to me. No other state in the country has done this. I urge that Delaware not be the first.

As I was sitting down, Mr. Nolen asked "is the remedy you seek one that should be available from us or one that should be legislative? Do you have a view on that?" This is a question I had considered, but had hoped would not be asked. After all, it would be an easy out for the Board, or the Delaware Supreme Court, to say that non-lawyers did not have a right to represent parents in IDEA hearings, but that the problem should be addressed by the legislature which could make rules to authorize and regulate non-lawyer representation. I wanted to win my case, not face a rule-making committee or the state legislature. I answered by urging the Board to "say that this is a matter of federal law and the Board should defer to the Department of Education." Rule-making or legislation would likely take years, and the delay would serve no purpose. If regulation of non-lawyers was needed, it could follow a Board ruling in our favor and be based on experience, not conjecture. After a brief rebuttal by Mr. McGinniss, the hearing concluded.

Although my clients were pleased with the argument,[48] I knew our chances of winning were slim. The Board's job was to enforce Delaware's UPL rules, not nullify them on the ground that federal law said otherwise. Had the Board been more active, had Mr. McGinniss been asked more probing questions, I might have been more optimistic. On the train back to Washington, I thought of ways to improve our chances of winning before the Delaware Supreme Court.

Round Seven: The Board Delivers A Knockout Punch

We had to wait only three months to hear from the Board. On September 24, 1999, the Board issued a unanimous decision adopting the ODC's position on all legal issues.[49] The Board rejected our argument that IDEA authorizes non-lawyer representation. The Board did not address whether application of the Delaware UPL rules would frustrate

---

48. Mrs. Arons said that the hearing "was extremely fair, absolutely impartial." Cohen, An IDEA Whose Time Has Come?: Proponents of Lay Advocacy Want Delaware to Allow Non–Lawyers to Represent Clients Under Individuals With Disabilities Education Act, Delaware Law Weekly, June 26, 1999, at 2. The same article claims that there was "even a little humor" during the hearing: "[a]t one point Vladeck characterized the argument from the Office of Disciplinary Counsel by saying, 'in New York we call it chutzpah.' Nolen asked what it would be called in Washington, and Vladeck quipped, 'A word I cannot utter.' " Id.

49. Findings and Recommended Disposition of the Board on the Unauthorized Practice of Law of the Supreme Court of the State of Delaware (Sept. 24, 1999).

federal law. Nor did it address our due process argument, other than to dismiss it in a footnote. The Board recommended that the Court direct Mrs. Arons to "cease the unauthorized practice of law" in Delaware, but no other sanction. The opinion was respectful of Mrs. Arons, noting that "[b]y all accounts, she is a vigorous and knowledgeable" advocate and acknowledged the plight of parents facing due process hearings without counsel. But, echoing Mr. Nolen's parting question, the Board said that the issue "must be addressed to the proper body with rule-making authority."

On to the Delaware Supreme Court—The U.S. Justice Department Joins the Case

As soon as I finished reading the Board's opinion, I made two telephone calls. I first called Mrs. Arons to give her the bad news, which she accepted with characteristic good grace. After a brief discussion, I had my instructions—take the case to the Delaware Supreme Court as soon as possible. Then, acting on an inspiration I had on my train ride, I called the Civil Rights Division of the U.S. Department of Justice. Having read countless IDEA cases, I knew that the government saw IDEA as an important civil rights statute and occasionally filed amicus briefs supporting disabled children and their families in significant cases. The Delaware Supreme Court might not take seriously the arguments for deference when we made them, but it would have to pay attention (or so I thought) if they were made by the United States government.

Fortunately, I was referred to two veteran Justice Department lawyers who were expert in IDEA. They had been following *In re Arons*, had already read the Board's ruling, and were troubled by Delaware's effort to deny non-lawyer participation in IDEA hearings. They explained that there were many bureaucratic hurdles to overcome in order to file a brief on our side—hurdles made even more formidable because ordinarily the Justice Department stays out of state courts. But they were guardedly optimistic that they could obtain approval, and on December 1, 1999, the United States filed a motion with the Delaware Supreme Court requesting leave to file a brief as amicus curiae in support of Mrs. Arons, which the Court quickly granted.

Briefing Before the Delaware Supreme Court

Meanwhile, I got to work on our brief. Having already written a detailed brief for the Board, the challenge was not what to say—we knew what we had to argue—but how to present those arguments in a way that might make them more appealing to the Delaware Supreme Court. We understood that the Board was constrained by Delaware law and would be unwilling to break new legal ground. But we hoped that the high court might take a hard look at both our statutory argument and due process arguments.

With respect to the statutory argument, however, we were concerned that, as a general matter, state courts are unreceptive to preemption arguments.[50] We therefore retooled our argument to focus less on preemption and more on statutory construction, contending that the Board's decision was "a textbook example of why courts should defer to expert agencies rather than setting sail on their own interpretative voyage." "[I]nterpreting section 1415(h)(1) to permit lay representation serves IDEA's overarching goal of giving parents a say in the educational opportunities available to their disabled child. On the other hand, adopting the Board's interpretation . . . would deal a body blow to the fair and effective enforcement of IDEA by placing due process hearings out of the reach of most parents." To pave the way for the Justice Department's brief, our brief pointed out the Department of Education is responsible for IDEA's implementation, and, for that reason, the U.S. Supreme Court had uniformly looked to and accepted the Department's construction of the Act.[51]

The brief also responded to the supervision point that had bothered the Board, which had invoked the generalized need to protect the public from unlicensed and unaccountable non-lawyers to justify its ruling. This concern, we argued, was misplaced because this case applied only to IDEA, but the Court, if it saw fit, could "impose measures to ensure that non-lawyer advocates in IDEA hearings are well qualified and meet the highest ethical standards."

As to due process, the brief spent more time explaining the constitutional status of the right to a public education and the role education plays in helping children become full participants in society. We reminded the Court that "the American people have always regarded education and [the] acquisition of knowledge as matters of supreme importance," and that the public school is "the most vital civil institution for the preservation of democracy." Because this case concerned access to a public education, we argued that the State "may not tilt the playing field decisively in its favor when adjudicating fundamental rights," and that Delaware was seeking to do precisely that by effectively denying parents assistance in due process hearings.

---

50. In my experience, federal judges are more likely than their state court counterparts to find state law preempted by federal law. That makes perfect sense if one sees state court judges as defenders of state law. While I have not attempted to prove this proposition empirically, consider one example: By the time the Court held in Cipollone v. Liggett Group, 505 U.S. 504 (1992), that the Federal Cigarette Labeling and Advertising Act did not preempt all state tort claims brought by smokers against tobacco companies, at least six federal circuit courts had ruled that the Act preempted all state tort claims. Id. at 509 & nn.2 & 3. No circuit court took a different view, although every state court to review the question had ruled that the Act did not preempt tort suits. Id.

51. See, e.g., Irving Ind. Sch. Dist. v. Tatro, 468 U.S. 883, 891–92 & n.9 (1984); Cedar Rapids Comm. Sch. Dist. v. Garret, *F.*, 526 U.S. 66, 74–75 n.6 (1999).

The brief for the United States began by declaring that the "assistance of informed lay persons for parents without counsel is critical" to the enforcement of IDEA.[52] "IDEA's language and structure unambiguously entitle" non-lawyers to represent parents. "Congress could not have intended to create a clearly wasteful, time-consuming, and imprecise process whereby the expert's questions and evidence are funneled through parents." The Board's ruling, the government said, "cannot stand" because it "unquestionably subverts" parents' rights to challenge educational decisions involving their children.

The ODC's brief was, for the most part, identical to the brief it had filed before the UPL Board. It did add emphasis to three points. First, with respect to the "accompany and advise" language, the ODC sharpened its argument to make clear that, in its view, the IDEA did not authorize either counsel or skilled non-lawyers to represent parties. As the ODC put it, "[c]ounsel have inherent and presumptive representational authority and training, while individuals with special knowledge or training" do not.[53] Second, the ODC dismissed the U.S. government's arguments as to IDEA's meaning as "serious[ly] flaw[ed]" and not "reasonable." And finally, the ODC claimed that our due process argument "grossly and unfairly exaggerated the risk" that children will be deprived of educational opportunities "unless the children and their parents are allowed to be represented by unaccountable, untrained lay advocates." The ODC brief ended with a plea for the Court to reaffirm that "all legal practitioners in Delaware must be accountable to this Court for their qualifications and their conduct."

We filed a short reply, chiding the ODC for arguing "that it is better equipped to interpret IDEA than the expert agency entrusted with the task of administering the Act by Congress," and urged the Court to defer to the "accumulated wisdom of the Department of Education."[54] We next pointed out that if ODC's interpretation of IDEA were correct, then the reference to "counsel" in § 1415(h)(1) would be meaningless, since it would add nothing to the lawyer's presumptive representational authority. And lastly, we defended our due process claim, noting that every child initially denied an educational opportunity by a school board whom Mrs. Arons represented obtained some relief, translating into an "error rate of 100%"—errors that would have been "unremedied without the assistance of Mrs. Arons."

52. Brief for the United States as Amicus Curiae Supporting Petitioners, No. 440 (Delaware Supreme Court, filed on Dec. 22, 1999), at 1–2.

53. Answering Brief of Appellee Office of Disciplinary Counsel, No. 440 (Delaware Supreme Court), at 3, 15; see also id. at 13–14.

54. Appellants' Reply Brief, No. 440 (Delaware Supreme Court), at 4.

We soon received an order from the Court scheduling oral argument for May 23, 2000, before the full five member Court, not the typical three member panels that hear most cases. At least, it seemed, the Court was taking the case seriously.

Argument

The first thing one notices about the Delaware Supreme Court is that, in contrast with the grandeur of many state courts of last resort that are housed in majestic, marble-clad buildings, its home is an unpretentious, small, colonial-style building that appears to date back a hundred years or more. It looks more like a county courthouse than the Supreme Court of a state that is the nation's corporate center. Once inside, one is struck by the intimacy of the courtroom. It is small but stately, decorated in somber gray and blue tones with plenty of highly polished hard wood. It is an intimate place to argue a case, with no more than a few feet separating counsel's podium from the justices.[55] At the time *In re Arons* was argued, the Court had the reputation of being conservative but fair-minded and scholarly.

Having lost below, I argued first. According to press accounts, I was "peppered with questions" from the moment I reached the podium.[56] The justices were well-prepared and "came out firing." Chief Justice E. Norman Veazey asked why IDEA entitles parents only to be "accompanied and advised" by special education experts instead of specifying that the parents may be "represented" by them. I began my answer by saying, "It beats me. If it did, we would not be here today." Justice Veazey's question permitted me to go directly to my argument that the text of IDEA, sensibly read, supported our position. On the other hand, the ODC's reading led to the absurd conclusion that a non-lawyer could coach parents throughout due process hearings so long as the parents did the talking. I was also able to explain why "[e]nforcement of state [UPL] law would frustrate federal objectives" in IDEA. Justice Randy Holland then asked what cases supported our interpretation of IDEA. I responded that there were none, because at no time in IDEA's nearly thirty-year history had any state interfered with the right of non-lawyers to assist parents in due process hearings.

Chief Justice Veazey then challenged my claim that lawyers were simply unavailable to help parents in IDEA cases. When I pointed to the stipulation between the parties that drove that point home, Chief Justice

---

55. See http://courts.delaware.gov/HowTo/courtproceedings/?oralargs.htm (visited on April 2, 2005).

56. Cohen, Preventing Overdue Process: Delaware Supreme Court Struggles with Issue of Allowing Lay Advocates to Help Parents Who Can't Hire Lawyers, Delaware Law Weekly, May 31, 2000, at 1 (hereinafter "Preventing Overdue Process"); see also Cohen, Nonlawyer Advocates Face Challenge, Nat'l L. J., June 12, 2000, at A5.

Veazey made it clear that he simply did not believe it. While I wanted to argue this point, I saw that my time was winding down, and I wanted to keep to my plan to spend my final few minutes focusing on what I thought was the evident unfairness of the ODC position. Here is what I said:

> There is no question that denying parents lay assistance—especially in Delaware, where the legal resources are inadequate to meet the needs of parents—will make the fight between the state and school boards on the one hand, and parents on the other, unwholesomely unequal. As we've just discussed, the disparity in resources could not be greater. The state and school boards can draw upon a wealth of public resources—school officials, principals, teachers, experts—to present their case effectively. Lawyers represent both the state and school boards. Why does the government send lawyers to these hearings? That is an important question to be considered. The government pays lawyers to handle these cases because it recognizes that the stakes are enormous—the cost of private placement and specialized care for disabled children can amount to hundreds of thousands of dollars annually.
>
> On the other side of the ledger are parents—just parents—fighting for their child's future. They are confronting one of the worst nightmares imaginable—trying to fend for a seriously disabled child in the face of what the parent perceives to be an unfeeling and unresponsive bureaucracy. These parents are often indigent; they are intimidated by the formality and complexity of the hearing process; and they are unrepresented by lawyers. The inequality of power and resources are profound. In these circumstances, unless parents are permitted some form of assistance, the statutory guarantee of an "impartial due process hearing" becomes an empty formality, promising justice but delivering nothing.[57]

Michael McGinniss argued for the ODC. As he had throughout, he focused on the state's "overriding interest in protecting parents from non-lawyers because there is no guarantee of professionalism and no

---

57. This quotation is not based on an argument transcript (apparently none was made) but on my argument notes, which appear above verbatim. I rarely script out any argument. I did so here, with what I hoped would be my closing remarks, because I wanted to make the point as emphatically as I could that rote application of Delaware's UPL rules here would be unjust. My intuition was that we could win the case only if the Court thought that the problem parents faced was truly grave and it could fashion an opinion that would be strictly limited to IDEA cases. My recollection, supported by those of colleagues at the argument, is that I was able to use my last few moments to make these points, although there is no guarantee that I followed the script word for word.

recourse for incompetent or unethical conduct."[58] He also stressed that the Delaware Supreme Court's right to regulate the practice of law in the state is a prerogative that should not be trumped by a federal statute like IDEA, which does not explicitly displace state UPL rules. Toward the end of his argument, he was asked by both Justice Joseph T. Walsh and Justice Carolyn Berger whether the Court should craft a rule that would allow specialized lay advocacy, but under terms and conditions set by the state. Mr. McGinniss responded: "The ODC has no objection in principle to the adoption of such a rule," although he cautioned that in "the interest of public policy, it would have to have very high standards."

I had a few minutes left for rebuttal, and both Justice Walsh and Justice Berger asked me to answer the question they had posed to Mr. McGinniss. I agreed "that something had to be done," not only to comply with federal law, but also to address the "intractable due process problems" that would exist were Delaware to bar lay representation. The case was then submitted.

As I left the courthouse, I was again struck with a sense that, despite our best efforts, the most we could hope for was an adverse ruling holding out the prospect of some kind of rule-making that might, in the future, provide my clients some measure of relief. After all, the questions from Chief Justice Veazey and Justice Holland reflected, I thought, a measure of skepticism about our legal arguments. And the questions from Justice Walsh and Justice Berger plainly proceeded from the premise that nothing in federal law compelled Delaware to permit non-lawyers represent parents in IDEA hearings. At most, Delaware might decide to allow them to do so, but only as a matter of grace. That, to me, was a disquieting sign.

More Bad News

It took the Supreme Court only six weeks to issue its opinion. Drawing heavily on the Board's recommendation, the Court ruled against us unanimously, with Justice Walsh writing for the Court.[59] On every issue, the Court agreed with the ODC and rejected our arguments. The presence of the Justice Department appeared to have no influence on the Court, which was just as dismissive of the government's argument as it was of ours. The Court found that "Congress knew how to authorize lay representation when it wished to do so," but did not do so in IDEA. The Court was even more skeptical of the due process argument—particularly the suggestion that IDEA hearings in Delaware were unfair. The opportunity for parents to present evidence, and examine witnesses, and the presence of impartial hearing officers guaranteed, in

---

58. Preventing Overdue Process, supra n.5b, at 1–2.

59. In re Arons, 756 A.2d 867 (Del. 2000).

the Court's view, adequate procedural protections, even when the parents lacked counsel. Nonetheless, the Court said that "[i]f it could be demonstrated that an unmet need exists and that the local bar could not adequately respond, this Court would consider the adoption of a rule allowing lay representation in a certain limited class of cases."

On to the U.S. Supreme Court

Although the Court's ruling was no surprise, it was still a blow to Mrs. Arons and the community she serves. The consensus was that the Court's invitation to consider rule-making if we could prove that "an unmet need exists" was a fig leaf to hide the fact that amounted to the Court turning a blind eye to a serious social problem. Mrs. Arons' was particularly bitter about this part of the Court's ruling. "The ODC effort to suggest that lawyers were available to help parents was nothing short of bad faith. All hell is breaking loose in Delaware, but there is no one to provide assistance. No one."[60] If the record here did not demonstrate an "unmet need," what would satisfy the Court? And how would we prove that parents who abandon hope and give up on IDEA have done so because assistance is unavailable? Set up some sort of registry for the disaffected and disenfranchised? My clients instructed me to go to the U.S. Supreme Court, even though our chances of obtaining review were slim.

We did have one potential ace up our sleeve, however. The United States had vigorously supported our position before the Delaware Supreme Court. I called the Justice Department lawyers who had worked on In re Arons to solicit their support, but they were noncommittal. Any decision about the government's participation at the Supreme Court level would be made by the Solicitor General, not the Civil Rights Division, and rarely did the Department support certiorari petitions. Nonetheless, they did not rule out the possibility that, were the Court to ask for the government's views, the Solicitor General would file a supportive brief.

A petition for certiorari is an unusual legal document. Its aim is not necessarily to persuade the Court that the petitioner's position is right, but instead that the issue is so important that it should be decided now. To do that, our petition was as hard-hitting as we could make it. The argument began: "Review by this Court is warranted because the decision below egregiously misreads a pivotal provision of IDEA—the provision that safeguards the right of parents to contest adverse school board decisions."[61] The flaw in the decision below, we argued, is that it

---

60. Telephone interview with Mrs. Arons (Oct. 1, 2004) (notes on file with the author).

61. Petition for a Writ of Certiorari in No. 00–509, Arons v. Office of Disciplinary Counsel, at 10 (filed October 2, 2000).

holds that "nothing in IDEA limits the ability of any state to enforce its UPL rules in a manner that forces parents to either handle IDEA due process hearings pro se or to forfeit their rights to a hearing altogether." The petition missed no opportunity to stress that the Department of Education strongly opposed the ODC's reading of IDEA, and suggested that "[s]hould the Court harbor any doubts about the Department's position in this case, we urge that the Court solicit the Department's views before acting on this Petition."

The ODC's brief in opposition was just what we had come to expect—it was comprehensive, unyielding, and crafted to appeal to Justices committed to preserving states' rights. According to the ODC, the case was all about "federalism," that is, "about respect for the constitutional role of the States as sovereign entities."[62] No incident of sovereignty is more important than "the regulation of the practice of professionals within their boundaries." Therefore, absent the most compelling evidence, the Court should not intrude on Delaware's power to regulate the professions within its own borders. The ODC opposition brief then went through its basic arguments on the statutory construction and due process issues, but, at every turn, the brief repeated the theme that federal displacement of state power here would be a serious and unwarranted intrusion on state authority.

We drafted a short response to try to blunt the force of the ODC's federalism argument. We noted that IDEA is "a federal statute of undeniable importance to the more than eight million American families with disabled children."[63] Although states are responsible for implementing and enforcing IDEA in the first instance, "the federal government has ultimate supervisory responsibility under the Act." Federal oversight serves "as a bulwark to ensure that parents do not get shortchanged by states and local school boards." The ruling below "turns that understanding upside down," and the "message sent to parents" is that "the federal government is no longer the guarantor of the procedural rights of parents and children under IDEA; rather, their fate is in the hands of state courts, which have less expertise in the interpretation and enforcement of federal laws, and little interest in the uniform administration of federal law." After filing this response, all we could do was wait.

On December 4, 2000, we finally got some good news. The Supreme Court entered an order inviting the Solicitor General to file a brief in the case. But our enthusiasm was short-lived. Eight days later, the Supreme Court, in its landmark ruling in *Bush v. Gore*,[64] essentially handed the

---

62. Respondent's Brief in Opposition, No. 00–509, at 4 (citations omitted).

63. Reply to Brief in Opposition, No. 00–509, at 6.

64. 531 U.S. 98; see also Bush v. Palm Beach County Canvassing Bd., 531 U.S. 70 (2000).

2000 presidential election to George W. Bush. This meant that the Solicitor General who would respond to the Court's invitation in *Arons* would be appointed by George W. Bush, not Al Gore. Republicans tend to be more sympathetic to states' rights arguments than Democrats, and former governors, like Bush, tend to be respectful of state prerogatives. Even though the Department of Education would want to defend its view that IDEA authorizes non-lawyer representation, the new Solicitor General would probably not want *In re Arons* to come before the Court.

As we feared, the Solicitor General's brief was not what we had hoped for. The first section was written as if the Solicitor General supported the Petition, arguing that, although the Delaware Supreme Court acknowledged that it "owed at least 'some level of deference to the Secretary of Education's interpretation of the Act,' " in fact, "the court neither deferred to the Secretary's interpretation, nor explained why that interpretation was not a 'permissible construction of the statute.' "[65] Indeed, the Delaware Supreme Court had "effectively 'substitute[d] its construction of a statutory provision for a reasonable interpretation made by the Secretary.' " But the remainder of the brief explained why the case "does not warrant this Court's review at the present time." The brief pointed out that there was no conflict on the issue and "the practical significance of this case is not yet clear." "Unless other States decide both to follow Delaware's lead as a matter of state law and to adopt its interpretation as a matter of federal law, the decision in this case will have little national significance." The ruling's significance might be further diminished because it was possible "that Delaware will, in the reasonably near term, either provide for the availability of free or low-cost legal assistance with IDEA hearings, or bring its law back into conformity with that of other States by adopting an appropriate express exception to its present legal practice rules." For these reasons, the government concluded that the petition should be denied.

Under the Supreme Court's rules, we had a right to reply, and we did so to make three points.[66] First, on the merits, there was complete accord between the petitioners and the United States. Second, although there was no judicial conflict warranting review, there was plainly an intolerable conflict between Delaware's position and that of the Department of Education. Permitting this conflict to go unresolved, we argued, only encouraged states to follow Delaware's lead. Third, the Solicitor General's " 'let's hope the sky doesn't fall in' approach" was not a sound reason to defer review. Other states were threatening to amend their rules to forbid lay representation in IDEA hearings, and Delaware had

---

65. Brief for the United States as Amicus Curiae, No. 00–509, at 12 (citations omitted).

66. Supplemental Brief of Petitioners in Response to the Submission of the United States as Amicus Curiae, No. 00–509, at 2–3.

taken no action in the year following its ruling in *In re Arons* to resolve the problem. We ended the brief by stressing that "[e]mpty promises are no substitute for enforceable rights."

Despite our efforts, on June 4, 2001, the Court issued a one-sentence order: "Petition for writ of certiorari to the Supreme Court of Delaware denied."[67] *In re Arons* was over.

Concluding Thoughts

In re Arons is a troubling case because the decision deals a body blow to the ability of parents with disabled children in Delaware to defend their children's right to an appropriate education. It seems unjust to condemn parents fighting for their child's future to have to go toe-to-toe, with no assistance, against school boards represented by well-financed, experienced counsel. But what is extraordinary about *In re Arons* is just how ordinary the result actually is. Time and again, people facing serious legal problems are denied access to justice because they cannot find an attorney to assist them. And all the while, the legal profession generally continues to insist that the lawyer's monopoly on providing legal services serves the public's interest.

In re Arons is, in some ways, the perfect storm that shows the crisis in the delivery of legal services in the United States, the organized bar's role in sowing the seeds of the crisis, and the bar's failure to take serious measures to resolve it. *In re Arons* arose because of the confluence of several phenomena that occur all too often. First, a massive need for legal assistance on the part of ordinary Americans—here, the need of eight million families with disabled children to have advocates to help fight for their children's right to an appropriate education. Second, the absence of any significant interest by lawyers in addressing that need because these cases are too much work for little or no money. Third, the failure of the Bar to respond to this need—other than to obstruct the provision of services by non-lawyers through the enforcement of UPL rules, even though these lay advocates make no pretense of being lawyers, receive no compensation, and do not compete with lawyers for clients. The silver lining in the otherwise dark cloud of *In re Arons* is that, at least as of now, the damage it wrought is limited to Delaware. Other states, fortunately, have not followed Delaware's lead.

The real tragedy of *In re Arons* is that it has done nothing to improve access to justice in Delaware. Instead, the litigation made insufferable what was once a barely tolerable situation. Today in Delaware neither lawyers nor non-lawyers represent parents at IDEA hearings.[68] Parents simply have no one to help them. Mrs. Arons says that

---

67. 532 U.S. 1065 (2001).

68. Telephone interviews with Marilyn Arons on July 13 and October 1, 2004.

she still regularly gets calls from Delaware parents, begging for her assistance. Hearings, which were a rarity even when Mrs. Arons helped out in Delaware, are today virtually non-existent, even though hundreds of families with disabled children have serious disagreements with their school boards each year. Nonetheless, the number of hearings held in Delaware is tiny—averaging just three a year from 1989 through 1996,[69] and that number has fallen since Mrs. Arons closed up shop in Delaware.[70] Although Mrs. Arons made an effort to assist a parent at a Delaware IDEA hearing by sitting with her and telling her what to do, as even ODC conceded was permissible, the outcry by the state and school board was so intense that Mrs. Arons decided not to return to Delaware and risk further UPL proceedings.[71] Meanwhile, the Delaware Supreme Court has taken no action to loosen the reins on non-lawyer practice in IDEA cases. No rule-making was ever commenced, and the Court recently rejected an application by an indigent parent, for whom English is a second language, to have non-lawyer assistance in an IDEA hearing challenging the expulsion of her disabled son from high school. The affidavits submitted by the parent and her lay adviser detail their exhaustive, yet unavailing, efforts to find any counsel, in Delaware or in nearby states, and they make clear that the parent is incapable of handling the hearing on her own.[72] In Mrs. Arons's view, this case is "just a nightmare, a complete catastrophe for the family. This child is seriously in need. No lawyer would ever take the case because it is too messy and too complicated." The parent's factual submissions were not contested by ODC.[73] Nonetheless, the Court denied her application in a

---

69. According to the Justice Department's brief to the Supreme Court as of 1999, there were over 16,000 disabled children in Delaware covered by IDEA. Br. at 15. Given that Mrs. Arons and Ms. Watson handled five hearings from 1994 through 1996, it appears that they handled the majority of Delaware due process hearings during that time-frame. Id.

70. Telephone interviews with Marilyn Arons on July 13 and October 1, 2004.

71. Mrs. Arons has since left the Parent Information Center to found the Melody Arons Center, named after Mrs. Arons' daughter who was tragically murdered in 1997, just when the litigation in *In re Arons* began in earnest. Mrs. Arons has decided to spend her time focusing on advocacy issues for infants with disabilities, which is the mission of the Melody Arons Center. See http://www.melodyaronscenter.org/index.html (last visited on April2, 2005). Mrs. Arons continues to trains non-lawyer advocates.

72. See Affidavit of Barbara Machette, executed on June 1, 2004; Affidavit of Barbara L. Hayes, executed on June 1, 2004.

73. Letter from Michael S. McGinniss, Disciplinary Counsel, to Assistant Clerk, Supreme Court of Delaware, regarding In the Matter of a Motion for a Preliminary Injunction (June 8, 2004). Mr. McGinniss' letter states that the ODC "does not have sufficient information to agree with or deny the facts alleged by the petitioners in the[ir] affidavits," but that their petition should nonetheless be dismissed because the Supreme Court of Delaware lacked power to order the relief they requested. Id., at 2.

brief order.[74]

IDEA promises disabled children an appropriate education and parents the right to contest decisions by school boards that adversely affect their child. But as *In re Arons* demonstrated, most families will not exercise their rights to a due process hearing without assistance. Thus, at least in Delaware, *In re Arons* goes a long way to rendering the promises made in IDEA a dead letter.[75]

---

74. In the Matter of the Petition of Barbara Machette and Barbara Hayes for an Extraordinary Writ, 852 A.2d 908 (Del. 2004).

75. Efforts were made to overrule *In re Arons* legislatively. IDEA was up for reauthorization in 108th Congress (2004–05), and the House bill contained a provision explicitly authorizing non-lawyers to represent parents and disabled children in IDEA hearings. There was no counterpart provision in the Senate bill. See H.R. 1350, 108th Cong., 1st Sess. (2004); S. 1248, 108th Cong., 1st Sess. (2004). In conference, the Senate Bill prevailed and so *In re Arons* remains the governing law in Delaware.

10

Greed on Trial

Alex Beam

The question before the jurors was not whether legal fees amounting to $7,700 an hour were "unreasonable." It was whether the lawyer-plaintiffs should get $1.3 billion more.

My favorite moment during last winter's $1.3 billion Massachusetts tobacco fee trial came near the end, when Ronald Kehoe, an avuncular, white-haired assistant attorney general, was questioning the state's star witness, Thomas Sobol. Sobol was describing how his former law firm, Brown Rudnick Berlack & Israels, prepared in 1995 to sue Big Tobacco on behalf of the Commonwealth.

Sobol testified that to reduce its risk on what looked like a long-shot lawsuit, Brown Rudnick hired a bunch of cheapo "contract" lawyers, at $25 to $35 an hour, and also cut back on its pro bono commitment, redirecting $1 million worth of work to the anti-tobacco litigation:

KEHOE: Was the tobacco litigation seen by the firm as a form of pro bono activity in part?

ROBERT POPEO [Brown Rudnick's attorney, jumping out of his chair]: Objection, your Honor.

JUDGE ALLAN VAN GESTEL: Sustained.

Did Brown Rudnick view the anti-tobacco lawsuit, which would later pay out the largest legal fee in the Commonwealth's history, as pro bono work? I asked Sobol that question over hot chocolate at Johnny's Luncheonette, in Newton, Massachusetts. Both on and off the stand the forty-six-year-old Sobol cuts a bold figure, closely resembling Bruce Springsteen before the Boss started showing his age. For want of a better term, Sobol—not unlike Jan Schlichtmann, the Boston lawyer who litigated the toxic-waste case made famous in the book and movie *A Civil Action*—has star quality. In one of several tendrils linking the two cases, which were tried in the same downtown courtroom, Schlichtmann and Sobol were briefly colleagues, before quarreling over the—yes—fees in a high-profile class-action suit, unrelated to tobacco.

Sobol told me that some of his Brown Rudnick colleagues did view the tobacco project as pro bono work. "It wasn't considered 'real lawyering,' " he said, "because we were suing corporate America, not defending corporate America. And we weren't making any money on a day-to-day basis." He added, "But this was a fee transaction. We weren't rendering services for free."

No, not exactly. Brown Rudnick and four other firms representing Massachusetts had secured a 25% contingency fee in the tobacco litigation. And that litigation paid off hugely. In 1998 a master settlement agreement (MSA) between forty-six states and Big Tobacco awarded Massachusetts $8.3 billion over twenty-five years, in purported Medicaid losses resulting from smoking. The tobacco companies also agreed to pay the states' legal fees, in many cases relying on an arbitration panel to decide how much each legal team deserved. As the lead law firm for the Commonwealth, Brown Rudnick hit the jackpot. Having invested about $10 million in time and expenses, it won $178 million from the panel, which awarded Massachusetts, of all the states covered by the MSA, the highest legal fees—$775 million in all. In court the state noted that Brown Rudnick's chief of litigation, Frederick Pritzker (also the chairman of its ethics committee), had siphoned off $14 million for seventy hours of work: a rate of $200,000 per hour. Sobol, the lead lawyer, received $13 million. On paper each Brown Rudnick partner stood to make an average of $140,000 a year from this case alone.

But the big numbers equaled only 9.3% of the $8.3 billion award. Brown Rudnick asked the state for a compromise between the 9.3% and the promised 25% fee. Attorney General Thomas Reilly refused to pay a penny more than the arbitration award. Now Brown Rudnick and the four other firms were back in court, asking for the full 25%: $1.3 billion more in fees. Brown Rudnick and the others were actually making the tobacco companies look good.

The events that landed the lawyers in Judge van Gestel's cavernous Art Deco courtroom had not exactly heaped honor on either side. Lawyers for every state in the Union had collected unheard-of fees from the lawsuits that led up to the MSA; Big Tobacco had signed the agreement which reimbursed the forty-six states for $206 billion worth of smoking-related medical costs, in exchange for protection from further litigation by the states. In Florida, one of four states that settled outside the MSA process, lawyers had also negotiated a 25% contingency fee; that fee equaled $2.8 billion, a sum that "simply shocks the conscience of this court," one Florida judge observed. A year after Florida settled, arbitrators awarded its eleven law firms an even larger fee: $3.4 billion— or an average of $300 million each.

The MSA fee arbitration resulted in the doling out of checks on a generous if unscientific basis. The first states to sue won a bonus for getting the ball rolling; the Massachusetts lawyers' $775 million (which amounted to an average of more than $7,700 an hour) reflected the state's role as one of the key participants. In other states lawyers lifted their fingers to the wind of public opinion and eventually settled for the arbitration awards, which were by any reasonable standard gargantuan. (Lawyers in Texas ended up accepting "only" $3.3 billion. They had asked for $25 billion—more than the state's settlement amount—but soon came around. The former Texas attorney general is in jail for trying to defraud the tobacco fund; but that, as they say, is another story.) Brown Rudnick and a co-plaintiff, the San Francisco partnership of Lieff Cabraser, Heimann & Bernstein, decided to sue for their full fees.

While the lawyers were grubbing, the state was hardly covering itself in glory. Scott Harshbarger, who as the Massachusetts attorney general signed the contingency fee deal in 1995, ran for governor three years later. His opponent, the incumbent Paul Cellucci, made the "obscene" tobacco fees a campaign issue—as did Governor George W. Bush in Texas. In the heat of the campaign Harshbarger pulled Massachusetts out of the increasingly controversial MSA negotiations. He lost the election anyway, and the state joined the agreement. This allowed Cellucci and his Republican successors to feast on the multimillion dollar settlement revenues.

By 2000 the word was out across the country that many states were squandering the vast sums raining down on them from the MSA. In theory the money was earmarked for medical care, or for anti-smoking education targeted especially at young people. In practice most legislatures used it for budget balancing or more exotic purposes. In Los Angeles some of the money was designated for improving wheelchair access on sidewalks; and then-mayor Richard Riordan proposed using some to settle abuse claims filed against the Los Angeles Police Department. In Massachusetts the governor and the legislature pillaged the tobacco awards in short order to balance the state budget.

Perversely, the tobacco money proved to be addictive. In 2003 the attorneys general of thirty-three states sided with Philip Morris against an Illinois court that wanted the company to post a $12 billion bond after it lost a huge class action case. Philip Morris loudly proclaimed that posting the bond would bankrupt it, thus threatening its MSA payments to the states. The litigating lions saved the shorn tobacco lamb; at the behest of the states, the court reduced the bond to a more manageable $6.8 billion.

During the course of *Brown Rudnick, et al. v. The Commonwealth of Massachusetts*, in a sidebar conversation with Robert Popeo and the Commonwealth's lead attorney, Dean Richlin, the sixty-eight-year-old Judge van Gestel, an old-fashioned lawyer who referred to the law in wistful tones as a "learned profession," expressed shock at the states' plumping for Big Tobacco:

> VAN GESTEL: That's, in my view, a very sad event, in that the states have to keep the evil empire, as it's been called, afloat.
>
> RICHLIN: Exactly so.
>
> VAN GESTEL: The next thing you know, the states will be having Joe Camel as the logo. I mean, I only meant that partly facetiously . . . To me, it's an outrage.

The humorist Dave Barry had great sport with the tobacco litigation, noting, "[The states] are distributing the money as follows: (1) Legal fees; (2) Money for attorneys; (3) A whole bunch of new programs that have absolutely nothing to do with helping smokers stop smoking; and (4) Payments to law firms. Of course, not all the anti-tobacco settlement is being spent this way. A lot of it also goes to lawyers."

SKIRMISHES

To sue the Commonwealth, Brown Rudnick hired the Boston firm Mintz Levin Cohn Ferris Glovsky & Popeo, perhaps best known for its partner Robert Popeo. A compact bantam of a man, the ferocious Popeo, who is sixty-five, once garnered a few moments of national fame by halting on camera a *60 Minutes* interview with his sulfurous client John Silber, then the president of Boston University. Popeo likes high-profile clients (he recently represented Suzy Wetlaufer, the inamorata of General Electric's retired chief executive Jack Welch, when she was leaving her job as editor of the *Harvard Business Review*), and he is quite comfortable in a courtroom. The youngest of six children from an Italian immigrant East Boston family, he comes by his flat vowels honestly. His hard-earned affluence notwithstanding, Popeo put on a credible still-a-man-of-the-people act for the jury and did his best to jolly up the judge.

At sidebar conferences Popeo and Richlin looked like Mutt and Jeff, with the tall string bean Richlin towering over his adversary. One might have expected the assistant attorneys general—Richlin and his boyish forty-two-year-old deputy, David Kerrigan, the head of the Commonwealth's Trial Division—to be outmaneuvered by their private-sector opponents. But the lawyering was well matched. At first glance the balding, dark-haired Richlin looks like an undertaker; he proved to be a smooth operator in court, however. His boss and former law partner, Attorney General Thomas Reilly, had entrusted Richlin with delicate work before: Richling was chosen to monitor the sale of the Boston Red Sox and the investigation of sexual abuse by Roman Catholic clerics. I had heard Richlin called "Tom Reilly's brain"—a backhanded compliment that falls wide of the mark. Reilly showed plenty of brains by giving his hot potato cases to Richlin.

Both sides wanted a jury trial, because deep down neither fully trusted its case in the hands of van Gestel, a veteran litigator and a business-law specialist. "The judge is just another lawyer—we had to get the public involved," Richlin told me during the trial. Popeo had a gut feeling that van Gestel didn't like the plaintiffs' case, and said so to his face. "His feelings were clear from the outset," Popeo told me after the trial was over. "Look, I've known him for forty years, and I think he's a terrific judge, but the law is an industry now, not a 'learned profession.' When you start asserting that lawyers aren't entitled to their contractual rights, you're saying you want to put a cap on lawyers earnings. He should not have done that."

Both sides retained jury consultants, who convened focus groups similar to those assembled by television networks and advertisers. The mock jurors heard the lawyers' proposed "clopenings"—abbreviated versions of possible opening and closing arguments—and pushed buttons when they heard an argument they liked. "The state's obligation was a hot issue," Popeo told me. "Potential jurors wanted the state to keep its word." But he had a problem. His clients had already been paid more than most jurors could hope to earn in several lifetimes. "You were never going to convince anybody that $775 million wasn't enough," he said. "We had all the equities, they had all the emotions."

Across town, Brown Rudnick's case looked pretty strong to the state's attorneys, who had holed up in a small war room in an adjunct office overlooking North Station. They, too, commissioned focus groups, and polls as well. "We learned that 'a deal is a deal' is a very compelling argument for most people," Richlin recalls. "We had to break through that cognitive resistance. And worse yet, as lawyers for the state, we were representing ourselves. We had a huge credibility problem." The polling showed that inveighing against "greedy lawyers" would prove counterproductive over the course of a long trial. Richlin had included a reference to the Brown Rudnick partners' $140,000–a-year take in a draft of his closing argument, but he took it out. "That wasn't going to win the case for us," he told me. "There were better ways to communicate the issue."

Ultimately, Richlin & Co. decided to educate the jury on the doctrine of "reasonableness," which means what it says: lawyers' fees should be reasonable. The problem was that 25% had seemed quite reasonable in 1995, when the state contracted to pay it, and when winning the case against Big Tobacco seemed a remote possibility. After all, many contingency fees are 33% or higher. Only after the lawyers scored their $775 million windfall could the case be made that they were not entitled to more. Kingman Brewster was once asked what he had learned during his years as a professor at Harvard Law School, and he shot back, "That every proposition is arguable." Whether the doctrine of reasonableness could be applied both at the time the contract was signed and at the time of payout provided for many hours of soporific debate in van Gestel's courtroom.

One wintry day during the trial, I struggled to match strides with the much taller Richlin as he walked quickly from the courtroom up Beacon Hill to the attorney general's office. He decided to make his case simple for me: "What we're saying, in essence, is 'It's too much money.'"

It is no accident, as the ever dwindling corps of Marxists like to say, that Brown Rudnick filed its claim against the state two days after Christmas of 2001. "LAW FIRM ASKS COURT FOR MORE TOBACCO MONEY," *The Boston Globe* reported demurely.

Although the trial would not start until November 3, 2003, much of the serious combat took place over the preceding twelve months. Some of the pretrial maneuvering seemed trivial. For instance, the state persuaded the judge to prevent Popeo from mentioning Boston's $14.7 billion "Big Dig," a downtown highway and tunnel construction project, in court. While arguing for a summary judgment, Popeo had pointed out that even in the face of mounting cost overruns, the state wasn't reneging on its payments to the highway contractors. So why single out the tobacco lawyers? "The only thing [the anti-tobacco team] did wrong was succeed," Popeo argued—"a pretty good line," Richlin later admitted.

Van Gestel threw the Big Dig out of his courtroom and also granted Popeo's request to keep certain inflammatory phrases out of evidence. The formal-sounding "Plaintiffs' Motion to Preclude the Commonwealth From Introducing Any Evidence Regarding Private Counsel's Post–Contractual State of Mind on Reasonableness of the Fee" forbade Richlin from including any lawyers' statements that they considered the demands "patently unethical," "f-ing absurd" or that the demands made them "look like a pig." These were in fact statements from Thomas Sobol and Frederick Pritzker that had cropped up in depositions. The same motion was also meant to exclude one of Pritzker's many inane observations: that the Brown Rudnick partners' $140,000 annual payoff was "not enough for anyone to retire on." Pritzker decided to repeat it on the witness stand anyway.

Each side fielded motions to knock out potential opposing witnesses. Richlin rejected two academics who were prepared to testify for the plaintiffs on the "risk paradigm"; they would have argued that Brown Rudnick's eighteenfold return on its $10 million investment in the tobacco litigation might have been duplicated in the venture-capital market. He may have done Popeo a favor, by shortening the plaintiffs' four-and-a-half-week presentation. "It seemed to me that the plaintiffs' lawyers' strategy was to be very thorough and tedious," the juror Craig Stevens, a mechanical engineer at the General Electric aircraft factory in Lynn, Massachusetts, told me. "It would take three, four, five days for a witness to tell his story, and then another witness told the same story all over again."

Popeo returned the favor by initially including Richlin on his witness list. As the No. 2 man in Reilly's office, Richlin could testify about his boss's decision not to pay Brown Rudnick any more than the arbitrators gave them. (Reilly could testify too, of course.) "As a tactic, it would be useful for them to put me on the stand and attack my credibility," Richlin told me. If it was a trick intended to get inside Richlin's head, it worked. Richlin offered to withdraw from the case entirely, but two weeks before the trial began van Gestel granted a motion that kept him off the stand.

Richlin had a trick up his own sleeve. Only Brown Rudnick and Lieff Cabraser had filed suit for the extra fees; the three other law firms that had worked for the Commonwealth demurred. Invoking a provision of Massachusetts law, Richlin forced the three other firms to join Brown Rudnick and Lieff Cabraser at trial. Throwing these firms into the case accomplished two goals for the defense. First, instead of two firms, which would have sued for $564 million, there were now five firms suing for $1.3 billion; Richlin wanted the jury to hear the biggest numbers possible. Second, it was at the very least an annoyance to the lead plaintiffs to sit at the same courtroom table with co-plaintiffs who, if asked, would be happy to say that they opposed the case. "I never would have brought this lawsuit," said Joe Rice, a partner in Motley Rice, of Mount Pleasant, South Carolina. "We begged Brown Rudnick not to file the case." The original plaintiffs "went batshit," one state lawyer told me. A full month after the trial was over, Popeo could not contain his scorn for the "free riders" who had contributed not a penny to the plaintiffs' multimillion-dollar effort: "They don't want to look like 'greedy lawyers,' but they want all the benefits of the case. We did all their work for them."

The three firms' official line throughout the trial was that they had not decided whether they would take their share of any Brown Rudnick winnings. The sole partner willing to discuss this subject with me, however, indicated that he had no reservations about sharing the money

I asked Richlin why he didn't put Rice, one of the architects of the master settlement agreement, on the stand and have him trash Brown Rudnick's case. For one thing, Richlin answered, just because Rice opposed the lawsuit didn't necessarily mean that he thought the 25% fee was unreasonable. And anyway, he said, "I had Tom Sobol."

In any complex litigation both sides have "bad facts" their lawyers need to avoid. In addition to its questionable use of tobacco settlement money, the state had signed the contingency fee deal not once but twice. Moreover, Harshbarger's office had, in 1998, defended the fee agreement to skeptical state officials, who had toyed with the idea of slashing the lawyers' cut to one percent.

As for the plaintiffs' bad facts, Brown Rudnick and Lieff Cabraser had both represented other states in the tobacco settlement for contingency fees lower than 25%. That was inconvenient. Another problem was that they had originally asked the arbitration panel for fees payable for twenty five years. But because the tobacco companies had negotiated an annual cap on payments of legal fees to the states, Massachusetts's lawyers might not receive their full share of the payment in twenty five years. So now Brown Rudnick was asking that the fees be paid in perpetuity. That demand seemed excessive to Francisca Evans, a juror who left the trial shortly before its completion for economic reasons: her employer, a large mutual fund company, refused to keep her on the payroll, and she couldn't provide for her six-month-old baby and young daughter on the court's $50 per diem. "I had a problem with the lawyers' getting paid forever," she told me, "knowing that my family is surviving on fifty dollars."

Van Gestel, who indulged in occasional sardonic asides out of the jurors' hearing, confessed that he, too, found the fees at stake very large indeed. At one point he said to the lawyers, "Just for your own benefit, I get interested in this case from time to time, and I did the calculations last night, and I find that Mr. Pritzker's share is such that in thirty five minutes he will make what the Commonwealth pays me for a year. That's an interesting number."

But the ultimate bad fact for the plaintiffs was the presence of Thomas Sobol, the One Just Man in the eyes of the state's lawyers. Popeo called Sobol a "bitter, disgruntled partner, not from one law firm, but two law firms"—he had briefly worked at Lieff Cabraser after leaving Brown Rudnick. Sobol was the dream witness for the state. He had led all the private attorneys in the Massachusetts case, yet after the $775 million arbitration award—and he fared quite well in the division of the spoils—he had parted company with Brown Rudnick on the fee issue. His first significant disagreement with the firm came over allocation of its $178 million. Sobol had been hoping to use a portion of the money to endow public interest work by the firm. Ultimately, that didn't happen. Worse yet, to his shock, Brown Rudnick awarded no bonuses to the associates, contract lawyers, and paralegals who had been part of his team and had been paid as little as $10 per hour. The firm suggested that because Sobol left Brown Rudnick less than two years after the settlement award, he wasn't entitled to his full $13 million share of the tobacco swag. A contested $3 million went to charity, and in May of 2000 Sobol signed a separation letter that would later become a cause célèbre in the courtroom, mainly for the state's futile efforts to have the letter's restrictive provisions introduced into evidence. Brown Rudnick agreed that Sobol did not have to speak on behalf of any claims the firm might file against Massachusetts. For his part, Sobol would "not publicly oppose, disagree with, or advocate against [Brown Rudnick's] position."

A year and a half later, Sobol read in the newspaper that Brown Rudnick and Lieff Cabraser were suing the state for the extra fees. One way or another, he was going to have to testify. In 2002, alone among the many lawyers named in the case, Sobol hired his own lawyer and filed an answer to his former firms' lawsuit. Buried at the end of a twenty-four page document was Sobol's request that the court determine if the Brown Rudnick claim violated a rule of professional conduct that "bars a lawyer from charging or collecting a clearly excessive fee."

Lawyers are paid a great deal of money to read, say, 269 dull paragraphs. Sobol's request appeared in paragraph 268. Suddenly Sobol was showing up on everyone's radar. "He files a response that he didn't have to file, saying the fees may be unreasonable," Richlin said, explaining how the document caught his attention. "And he has his own lawyer. If he's so aligned with them, why does he need his own lawyer?"

Bells went off at Mintz Levin, too. Popeo summoned Sobol's lawyer and reminded him of the nondisparagement clause in the May 2000 letter—Sobol was putting his share of any additional tobacco proceeds at risk. Sobol responded that he wouldn't volunteer information, and that he couldn't be punished for telling the truth under oath. He was deposed for nine days, surrounded by lawyers constantly asserting privileges and filing objections.

Here was the real problem looming for Brown Rudnick: in the bloodless world of corporate law, Sobol was an unabashed crusader who exuded passion for his adopted causes. He hated the tobacco companies ("a true believer," one fellow lawyer called him, half admiringly), and he could communicate his loathing. Of all the witnesses I heard on the stand, only Sobol spoke heatedly about suing Big Tobacco. "The tobacco industry is as close to evil as you can get," he said. Sobol had no objection at all to collecting more money—so long as it came out of Big Tobacco's pocket. "When there is less smoking, there is less human misery," he testified. But he opposed taking the extra money from his former client—the state.

Richlin and his colleagues were confident that 90% of Sobol's deposition testimony would make it into the trial. "His answers were a treasure trove," Richlin said.

THE BATTLE IS JOINED

Trials are boring, and long trials are excruciatingly boring. Most days van Gestel's vast courtroom was empty save for the lawyers, the jury, the judge, and we happy few, the handful of interested onlookers. After a while I felt like a passenger on a cruise ship, perhaps headed for someplace interesting, but becalmed week after week in a windless (not exactly) Sargasso of mindchoking legal seaweed. There were a few brief moments around Christmastime when I could have told you what a "Lodestar cross-check" is (don't ask), or the proper role of a "19(a) defendant" (the three extra law firms were 19(a) defendants) in a Massachusetts courtroom.

My fellow passengers proved to be friendly, if cautious. A neighbor of mine, Betsy Burnett, was arguing the plaintiffs' case alongside her better-known partner, Popeo. She and I chatted occasionally, though for understandable reasons she was mostly in what a friend of hers called "lawyer mode" for the lengthy trial. The media services engineer, Ian McWilliams, whose firm had wired the courtroom for jazzy, oversize screens on which the plaintiffs would display their exhibits, was also amiable, although he had been instructed not to talk to me. So had most everyone else. Case in point: Betsy has full, juror-head-turning blonde hair, and I wanted to identify its shade precisely. I asked a young lawyer for the Commonwealth what shade it was. She thought for a moment and answered, "Ash blonde. But that's off the record."

Frederick Pritzker, as Brown Rudnick's chief of litigation, showed up almost every day. For better or worse he had become the public face of the plaintiffs. He was amenable to chatting, although not to being quoted. The tightly wound litigator, once a tenacious upper-level squash player at the Harvard Club, turned out to be a comparatively impoverished Boston Pritzker, only tangentially related to the Chicago real estate barons. Perhaps he needed another $8 million to remain competitive with his Windy City cousins.

When I first shook his hand, I remarked that he was the most reviled man in Boston, which evoked a knowing smile. Obviously intelligent, and a valued mentor to Sobol, Pritzker had evinced an almost uncanny ability to say silly things in public—he was the rare lawyer to fall victim to excessive candor syndrome. In his pretrial depositions he had made an unfortunate allusion to not looking like a "pig" in pursuing additional fees. " 'Pig' is probably the wrong and improper word that I used," Pritzker said the moment it escaped his lips. But it was too late. "PIGS AT THE TROUGH," read the inevitable headline of *The Boston Globe* widely read "Downtown" column, which quoted from the leaked deposition.

In an interview with another *Globe* reporter, Pritzker made his observation that his partners' $178 million take was "not something that anybody can retire on." Van Gestel, as noted, had agreed to keep the remark out of the courtroom, but on the witness stand Pritzker blabbered on about how he had been misquoted and how he had been proved right: not one of his partners had retired since the tobacco award.

In court Richlin read out yet another embarrassing Pritzkerism from the deposition: when contemplating the tobacco suit, Pritzker had said, "I had dollar signs in my eyes, even back at that early stage. And I know that they were large dollar signs."

Pro bono work indeed!

The first week of the plaintiffs' case (which I missed) was taken up by Harshbarger's testimony. This was a smart opening démarche, because the earnest Harshbarger, the former president of Common Cause, is well regarded in Massachusetts. As the man who had approved the 25% contingency fee, he had nothing but praise for the law firms' excellent work, and his presence posed a special challenge for Richlin, who, as a top state official, could not overaggressively cross-examine his boss's Democratic predecessor.

I happened into court when the partners of Lieff Cabraser were furiously explaining away a bad fact—their secret negotiations with the Liggett tobacco company, which took place just as Massachusetts was signing the contingency fee agreement. The state wanted to prove that if Harshbarger had known of Liggett's willingness to settle the states' medical claims, he might have negotiated a lower fee.

The following day I savored the testimony of the plaintiffs' first expert witness, introduced as Lawrence Fox, of the University of Pennsylvania Law School. (Later in the trial one of Fox's colleagues uncharitably noted that Fox was an adjunct faculty member, and not strictly speaking a professor.) Fox sported a bow tie and addressed the jury in a booming, self-assured voice. He turned out to be what every expert witness is—a trained seal—only more so. Fox went so far as to say the 25% fee might be deemed too low, perhaps something like 33, 35, or 40% might have been more appropriate.

In one of many lengthy digressions, Fox waxed eloquent about the possible fee structure of the royalties for *Gone With the Wind*, prompting a rare intervention from the courtly judge. "This is not Hollywood here," van Gestel said. "We are not dealing with Hollywood cases, and we are not dealing with copyright cases ... I think Hollywood is a stretch from here."

Hearing this, Popeo jumped to his feet and called for a sidebar:

POPEO: I am concerned that your statements reflect a view that the jury will pick up on. I know your views of this case, and you are entitled to them. It may not be Hollywood, but these are lawyers and that is not at all—

VAN GESTEL: I appreciate your comment. I take it very seriously, and I apologize if I have done so.

I just think that Mr. Fox is one who kind of tends to ramble on, in my view, somewhat wildly. I have known Mr. Fox for many years. I hold him in very high regard. He knows a lot about ethical things. We need to keep this case tied to this kind of case, and he is happy to go on and on. He would lecture for an hour if we let him. It isn't so much your questions. It's that the witness takes them as an opportunity to demonstrate how profound he is in the subject and—

POPEO: Experts sometimes do that.

They do. The plaintiffs' final expert witness was another legal megaphone—a tall, strapping law professor named Charles Silver, of the University of Texas. The co-director of the university's Center on Lawyers, Civil Justice, and the Media, Silver boasted of having advocated on behalf of the private lawyers in Texas who angled (unsuccessfully) for the $25 billion tobacco award. Silver was a card-carrying, University of Chicago-trained free-market guy: the price is what the market will bear, end of story. "I only know one tune," Silver told Richlin during cross-examination. The line worked quite effectively in Richlin's closing argument.

As with Fox, van Gestel expressed reservations about the supremely self-confident Silver, although the judge carefully kept his remarks away from the jury. Betsy Burnett wanted Silver to talk about "hindsight bias"—the notion that the lawyers' fees looked excessive only when viewed with the benefit of hindsight. Richlin objected, on the grounds that Silver's training was in law and political science, not psychology. Again at sidebar the lawyers were treated to a dose of van Gestel's skepticism:

VAN GESTEL: You know, obviously Professor Silver is a very bright man, and he's been to very good schools . . . I don't know that that gives him the qualifications to talk about some psychological effect . . .

BURNETT: I just want to make sure the record reflects it's not pop psychology. Some fellow won the Nobel Prize for talking about it . . .

VAN GESTEL: He's not a psychiatrist. He's not a psychologist. He never practiced in those professions, and he's now going to give what sounds to me like a—tell the jury . . . "Well, you have to understand, because I'm very smart about this and I've read a lot about it and 1 went to a good school and I read what some people who have won Nobel Prizes have said, and, therefore, you have to rule or discount what Scott Harshbarger said because—"

Silver influenced the course of the trial, although not in the way he intended. As part of his testimony he showed a slide of contingency-fee awards from a list that appeared in a trade publication called *Class Action Reports*; it was designed to show that what the plaintiffs asked was not unreasonable. Under cross examination he admitted that his choice had been selective. He had not shown the jury the complete list. The omitted awards were well below 25%—some as low as 2.2 or 3.4%. Richlin put all the awards up on the jumbo screen, and the jurors remembered them. "That was very powerful," the jury forewoman, Jo–Ann Schwartzman, recalled to me. When the jury eventually decided to award the lawyers an extra 1.2%, for a total of 10.5%, she said, they used the *Class Action Reports* numbers to backstop their decision.

Schwartzman added that Silver's freebooting commitment to market capitalism rubbed her the wrong way: "I was concerned that Silver said the only way to motivate lawyers was to dangle more money in front of them. He was clear that that would be their sole motivation. That was heartbreaking." Later in our conversation she said, "Who wants to live in a world with that kind of do-or-die attitude, where there's no allowance for change, for humanity, or for reasonableness?" I asked if she was referring to Charles Silver's world. "Yes." she said. "The law is the rules, but justice is the spirit. The rules say we have only an hour for lunch"—our lunch meeting had extended well past the hour—"but we don't want to live in that world."

ENDGAME

The plaintiffs' case dragged on, but van Gestel was adamant that the trial not run past Friday, December 19. Two of the fourteen jurors had already quit the case: Francisca Evans and a woman who couldn't arrange child care during school snow days. The trial could not reconvene in the new year, because two more jurors would be leaving, one to return to school, and another for a month-long non-refundable trip to Africa. Popeo had painted Richlin into a corner. The state's lawyers had about a week and a half to present their case, and they had to ask the jurors to sit for extra sessions in the afternoons, risking their wrath.

In retrospect (this must be hindsight bias at work), everything went fine. Richlin's experts were no more or less convincing than Popeo's; they were merely paid less—$250 rather than $500 per hour. Richlin expected Sobol to be his star witness, and Sobol did not disappoint him. He was convincing on the stand, and he introduced all kinds of facts that proved to be significant. He said that he and Pritzker had thought a $1 billion award from the MSA would be a "home run"; the state eventually received more than eight times that. He confirmed that the $25-to-$35-an-hour contract lawyers racked up at least a fifth of the billable hours in the case—a fact the jury remembered. Furthermore, he repeated on the stand his deposition testimony that an additional $1.3 billion fee would be "patently unethical"—a quotation the jury was never supposed to hear, at least not from the lawyers.

Sobol also dropped an unexpected bombshell, testifying that Robert Lieff, of Lieff Cabraser, had told him the extra fees weren't worth suing over. "Mr. Lieff told me . . . that he did not think it would be in the best interest of the firm to have to sue the Commonwealth," Sobol said. "Mr. Lieff said our lawsuit did not make this money, that he found it offensive for the two law firms to take full credit for those funds, and that it had been Joe Rice in connection with the master settlement agreement who had been negotiating for the industry, and that Brown Rudnick and Lieff Cabraser had gotten a free ride." Lieff flew in from San Francisco the next day to rebut Sobol, affording Richlin some effective rhetoric for his closing argument: "Mr. Lieff has testified consistent with his claim for millions, tens of millions, hundreds of millions of dollars to himself. Tom Sobol testified in a way that, if you accept it, you will bring him zero. Who are you going to believe?"

Popeo needed to tarnish Sobol in cross-examination, but he chose a curious tack. Wasn't it true, he asked, that Sobol entertained hopes of becoming a judge, and that supporting the Brown Rudnick fee claim might hurt his chances? Sobol answered yes. But his chances of becoming a judge with such powerful law firms aligned against him suddenly seemed very remote indeed.

At Johnny's Luncheonette I asked Sobol if he still hoped to become a judge. "That's not in my thoughts at this stage," he admitted. "I am concentrating on being a public interest lawyer." He may be alone among public-interest lawyers in receiving about $100,000 every year from the tobacco companies—his share of the MSA settlement. Accompanying each check is a "reservation of rights" letter signed by Brown Rudnick's chief financial officer, Barry Berman. Translated into English, the letter says, "Don't get too comfortable, pal; we may still sue you for testifying against us at that trial."

After Sobol's testimony, the trial wrapped up quickly. In his closing statement Popeo repeated the essential mantras of his case: "A deal is a deal, a promise is a promise, and a contract is a contract." He compared the state's not paying its legal fees to the Lottery Commission's not paying off a winning ticket—an unfortunate analogy that implied his lucky clients had hit a winning number. He railed against the state's "shameless intellectual dishonesty," and likened Richlin and his team of young lawyers to the attorneys for Big Tobacco, which angered them. By comparison, Richlin seemed almost Lincolnesque, appealing to the better angels on the jurors' shoulders. "You have an important job," he declaimed, "and we who represent the Commonwealth have total faith and confidence that you will discharge your responsibilities." Van Gestel's carefully worded instructions were typical of his style. He reiterated his view that the law is "first and foremost a learned profession," evidence to the contrary notwithstanding. He expatiated on the doctrine of reasonableness in a manner favorable to the state (his instructions had been the subject of endless wrangling among the lawyers): "If there is a disagreement about the reasonableness of the fee, every client, including the Commonwealth, is entitled to a determination of reasonableness."

I have served on a jury, and in my experience nothing is more powerful than a Friday deadline. Not surprisingly, this jury announced its verdict before lunch on a Friday. A reasonable fee, it concluded, would be 10.5%. The cap on annual payments by the tobacco firms virtually ensured that the lawyers would never receive their full fee. Frederick Pritzker's grandchildren would have to go out and earn a living, just as their grandfather had.

It must have been a good decision, because both sides claimed victory, and neither party appealed the verdict. Brown Rudnick and Mintz Levin contended that they had won another $100 million in fees. "I don't have many cases with verdicts of $100 million," Popeo crowed. "If that's not a victory, you have great expectations." But Richlin's boss, Tom Reilly, pointed out that the extra money would probably never reach the lawyers, because the payment stream would be halted in 2025, before the full fee had been paid. "The state of Massachusetts doesn't owe a dime to the law firms," Reilly said. "They got what they deserved."

If Reilly runs for higher office, he may lose twelve potential votes—those of the jurors. When she read the quotation in the newspaper, JoAnn Schwartzman told me, "It all hurt. We had a very difficult job, and we weren't trying to make a political statement. We weren't trying to reward or punish anyone."

I've said the trial was boring, and it was. But it was the kind of ennui that commercial airline pilots describe—boredom punctuated by rare moments of intense concentration. During Silver's lengthy testimony Richlin introduced an excerpt from one of Silver's articles that spoke of the "war . . . waged for control of the civil justice system":

> RICHLIN: Sir, did you feel then that a war was being waged for control of the civil justice system?

SILVER: I felt then that the war was waged, and I know today that the war continues to be waged. It's being fought in this courtroom in front of this jury.

RICHLIN: You feel that what we are doing here is part of the war for the civil justice system, sir?

SILVER: Absolutely. I think you would have to be blind not to recognize the political overtones in this lawsuit.

I caught up with Silver on his cell phone while he was grading exams at a Starbucks in Austin. ("Mind-numbing agony," he confessed.) What, exactly, had he and Richlin been talking about? "Well, you have the trial lawyers on one side, and the insurance companies, the tobacco companies, and the other product defendants on the other side," he said. Richlin agreed, and was even willing to fill in some details of Silver's vision: trial lawyers are generous financial supporters of the Democratic Party, and their opponents in industry, as a rule, support Republicans.

Not for nothing did Joe Rice, a veteran of the asbestos and tobacco wars, donate to the campaign of the Democratic Senator John Edwards, himself an accomplished plaintiffs' lawyer. Likewise, Rice also opposed the recent failed effort by Senate Republicans to confiscate all legal fees collected after June 1, 2002, by plaintiffs' and class action lawyers. Officially proposed as the Intermediate Sanctions Compensatory Revenue Adjustment Act, it was nicknamed the "one-yacht-per-lawyer bill." Rice called the bill "the greatest attack on civil rights that's occurred in this century outside of racial [issues], obviously," according to *The American Lawyer* magazine.

The war never ends, this line of theorizing goes. Yesterday the lawyers bankrupted the silicone breast implant and asbestos industries. Today they have targeted cigarette and handgun manufacturers. Tomorrow, as everyone knows, they will take on the nefarious merchants of trans fat: McDonald's, Frito–Lay, and Taco Bell.

The Richlin–Silver exchange made for great theater, and ever since I have been wondering: Did I sit in a courtroom off and on for six weeks watching lawyers battle for the heart and soul of our civil justice system? Was the case, as Popeo explained to me afterward, a unique test of the separation of powers, of the sanctity of the contract—indeed, of the integrity of the state? Or was I simply watching some of the best litigators on the East Coast wrangle over astronomical sums of money— sums that few of us laypeople could even understand?

I think I know the answer.

Biographies of *Legal Ethics Stories* Contributors

A native of Washington, D.C., **Alex Beam** graduated from Yale College in 1975. He worked for the House Select Committee on Intelligence, and also as an English–Russian interpreter for the U.S. Information Agency in Russia. He began his career in journalism as a researcher at Newsweek magazine in 1977. From there he moved to Business Week as a correspondent in Los Angeles, and then as bureau chief in Moscow and Boston.

In 1986, Beam joined the Boston Globe as a business reporter. A year later he started writing a thrice-weekly column that combined gossip, humor and purported insight into the world of New England business. The column won several awards, including a Best of Boston citation and the John Hancock Award for Excellence in Financial Journalism. Beam is now a columnist for the Globe's Living/Arts page. During the 1996–1997 academic year, he was a John S. Knight Journalism Fellow at Stanford University.

In addition to his journalistic work, Beam is also the author of two novels about Russia, "Fellow Travelers" (1987) and "The Americans Are Coming!" (1991), both published by St. Martin's Press. The fictional president of the United States in "The Americans Are Coming!" is Arnold Schwarzenegger. His non-fiction book about McLean Hospital, "Gracefully Insane," was published in January, 2002. It won a Massachusetts Book Award and was named a New York Times Notable Book for 2002.

Beam lives in Newton, Massachusetts with his wife and three sons.

Roger C. Cramton Except for about five years of government service as a law clerk, head of a independent federal agency and assistant attorney general, U.S. Department of Justice, Cramton has served as a law professor since 1957 (University of Chicago; University of Michigan; and Cornell since 1973). His principal field of scholarship since 1980 has been the law and ethics of lawyering. A former dean of the Cornell Law School, Cramton served as the initial chairman of the Legal Services

Corporation and has subsequently served on two national commissions concerned with the federal courts and their judges. In his capacity as a member of the Council of the American Law Institute, he was an active participant in the deliberations that produced the Restatement of the Law Governing Lawyers. Cramton lives with his wife, Harriet, in Ithaca, New York and enjoys frequent contacts with his four children, eleven grandchildren and six great grandchildren.

Stephen Gillers has been professor of law at New York University School of Law since 1978 and served as Vice Dean from 1999–2004. He holds the Emily Kempin chair. He does most of his research and writing on the law governing lawyers and the regulation of the legal profession. His courses include Regulation of Lawyers, Evidence, and Law and Literature (which he teaches with Graduate School Dean Catharine Stimpson). Professor Gillers has written widely on legal and judicial ethics, including in law reviews and the legal and popular press. He has taught legal ethics as a visitor at other law schools and has spoken on lawyer regulatory issues at federal and state judicial conferences, ABA conventions, state and local bar meetings nationwide, before Congress, at law firms and corporate law departments, and in law school lectureships.

Professor Gillers is the author of **Regulation of Lawyers: Problems of Law and Ethics**, a widely used law school casebook now in its seventh edition. He and Professor Roy Simon edit **Regulation of Lawyers: Statutes and Standards**, an annotated volume of rules governing American lawyers and judges which has been published annually since 1989. Following a clerkship with Chief Judge Gus J. Solomon in Federal District Court in Portland, Oregon, in 1968–69, Professor Gillers practiced law in New York City before joining the NYU faculty. He is currently Chair (and since 2002 has been a member) of the American Bar Association's Joint Committee on Lawyer Regulation. He is often quoted on lawyer regulatory issues in the legal and national press.

Leslie Griffin holds the Larry & Joanne Doherty Chair in Legal Ethics at the University of Houston Law Center, where she teaches professional responsibility, constitutional law and torts. She has written about whistleblowers in *Watch Out for Whistleblowers*, 33:1 Journal of Law, Medicine & Ethics 160 (Spring 2005) and *Whistleblowing in the Business World,* in Enron: Corporate Fiascos and Legal Implications 209–36 (N. Rapoport & B. Dharan, eds., Foundation Press, 2004), and about professional responsibility in *What Do Clients Want? 6dA Clients' Theory of Professionalism*, 52 Emory Law Journal 1087 (2003) and *The Prudent Prosecutor,* 14 <?xml:namespace prefix = st1 ns = "urn:schemas-microsoft-com:office:smarttags" />Georgetown Journal of Legal Ethics 259 (2001). She was formerly Assistant Counsel in the Department of Justice's Office of Professional Responsibility.

<?xml:namespace prefix = o ns = "urn:schemas-microsoft-com:office:office" />

Professor Griffin thanks Yvonne Ho, David Chang and Michelle Wu for their expert research assistance, and Anita Bernstein and Ken Rosen for comments on the manuscript.

David Luban is the Frederick Haas Professor of Law and Philosophy at Georgetown University Law Center. Among his publications are *Lawyers and Justice: An Ethical Study*; the textbook *Legal Ethics* (with Deborah L. Rhode); the edited collections *The Ethics of Lawyers* and *The Good Lawyer*; and the forthcoming *Ethics, Justice, and Lawyers*.

Michael Mello, Professor of Law at Vermont Law School, teaches capital punishment, legal ethics, constitutional criminal procedure, and criminal law. He has published five books on capital punishment, including *The Wrong Man: A True Story of Innocence on Death Row*, and *Deathwork: Defending the Condemned*. Mello worked as a Florida capital appellate public defender from 1983 to 1987.

Milton C. Regan, Jr. is Professor of Law at Georgetown University Law Center, where he teaches courses on legal ethics, the legal profession, and ethical issues in corporate representation. He is the author of *Eat What You Kill: The Fall of a Wall Street Lawyer* (University of Michigan Press 2004), and co-author with Jeffrey Bauman of the forthcoming casebook *Legal Ethics and Corporate Practice* (Thomson 2005). He also is the author of several articles on ethics and the legal profession, such as *Teaching Enron*, forthcoming in a 2005 Fordham Law Review Symposium on Ethics in Corporate Representation; *Ethics, Law Firms, and Legal Education*, 55 Maine L. Rev. 363 (2003); *Corporate Norms and Contemporary Law Firm Practice*, 70 Geo. Wash. L. Rev. 1701 (2002); *Taking Law Firms Seriously*, 16 Geo. J. Legal Ethics 155 (2002); and *Law Firms, Competition Penalties, and the Values of Professionalism*, 13 Geo. J. Legal Ethics 1 (1999).

Deborah L. Rhode is the Ernest W. McFarland Professor of Law and Director of the Stanford Center on Ethics. She is the former Director of the Keck Center on Legal Ethics and the Legal Profession at Stanford University School of Law; the former chair of the American Bar Association's Commission on Women in the Profession and the former president of the Association of American Law Schools. She also served as senior counsel to the Minority members of the Judiciary Committee, the United States House of Representatives, on presidential impeachment issues. She has received the American Bar Foundation's W. M. Keck Foundation Award for Distinguished Scholarship on Legal Ethics and Professional Responsibility, and the American Bar Association's Pro Bono Publico Award for her work on expanding public service opportunities in law schools. Professor Rhode graduated Phi Beta Kappa and summa cum laude from Yale College and received her legal training from Yale Law School. After clerking for Supreme Court Justice Thurgood Marshall, she joined the Stanford faculty. She is a former director of Stanford's Institute for Research on Women and Gender and writes primarily in the area of legal ethics and gender discrimination. She is the author or co-author of fifteen books and over 100 articles. Her recent legal ethics publications include *Pro Bono in Principle and in Practice* (Stanford University Press, 2005) (ed. with Charles J. Ogletree, Jr.); *Access to Justice* (Oxford University Press, 2004); *Legal Ethics* (Foundation Press, 4th ed. 2004) (with David Luban); and *Professional Responsibility and Regulation* (with Geoffrey Hazard, Jr., Foundation Press 2002).

Tanina Rostain is Professor and Co–Director of the Center for Professional Values and Practice at New York Law School. She received her B.A. from Swarthmore College and her J.D. from Yale Law School, where she served as an Articles Editor on the Yale Law Journal. After clerking, she worked in private practice and then joined the clinical faculty at the University of Connecticut School of Law. Prior to joining New York Law School in 1998, she was a Keck Fellow for Professional Ethics and Culture at Yale Law School. Her publications include *Professional Power: Lawyers and the Constitution of Professional Identity* in the Blackwell Companion to Law and Society (A. Sarat ed. 2004); *Educating Homo Economicus: Cautionary Notes o the New Behavior al Law and Economics Movement*, 34 Law & Soc'y Rev. 973 (2000); and *Ethics Lost: Limitations of Current Approaches to Lawyer Regulation*, 71 S. Cal. L. Rev. 1273 (1998). Her current work focuses on the roles of tax lawyers and accountants in the tax shelter controversy.

David C. Vladeck is the Director of the Institute for Public Representation and Associate Professor of Law at Georgetown University Law Center. He teaches courses in civil procedure, first amendment litigation and federal courts, and co-directs the Institute for Public Representation, a clinical law program at the Law Center handling a broad array of civil rights, civil liberties, first amendment, and open government litigation. Prior to joining the Georgetown faculty in 2002, Professor Vladeck spent over 25 years with Public Citizen Litigation Group, serving as its Director from 1992 to 2002. He has handled a wide range of complex litigation, including first amendment, health and safety, civil rights, class actions, preemption and open government cases. He has argued several cases before the United States Supreme Court, and over 50 cases before the federal courts of appeal and state courts of last resort. Professor Vladeck also testifies before Congress, advises Members of Congress on legal matters, and writes on administrative law, first amendment, legal ethics and access to justice issues. He serves as a Scholar with the Center for Progressive Reform and on the boards of various non-profit organizations. He has also served on the Council of the Administrative Law and Regulatory Practice Section of the American Bar Association and as a Public Member of the Administrative Conference of the United States. Professor Vladeck received his undergraduate degree from New York University, his law degree from Columbia University School of Law, and an LL.M. degree from Georgetown University Law Center. Professor Vladeck would like to thank Marilyn Arons, who reviewed drafts to ensure that no client confidences were inadvertently revealed and that her views were accurately portrayed, and Alan B. Morrison, Senior Lecturer in Law at Stanford Law School, who provided helpful comments based on his experience litigating unauthorized practice of law cases.

David B. Wilkins is the Kirkland & Ellis Professor of Law and the Director of both the Program on the Legal Profession and the Center on Lawyers and the Professional Services Industry at Harvard Law School. He is also a Visiting Senior Research Fellow of the American Bar Foundation and a Faculty Associate of the Harvard University Center in Ethics and the Professions. Since joining the Harvard faculty in 1986, Professor Wilkins has written extensively on the legal profession, with an emphasis on the experiences of black lawyers in corporate law firms. He is the author of *The Black Bar: The Legacy of Brown v. Board of Education and the Future of Race and the American Legal Profession* (forthcoming, Oxford University Press), *Problems in Professional Responsibility for a Changing Profession*, (Carolina Press 4th ed. 2002) (along with Andrew Kaufman), and more than 40 articles on legal ethics, law firms, and the legal profession in books, law reviews, and in the legal and popular press.

†